Roxana Marin

The Role of Local Political Elites in East
Central Europe

To the memory of my grandmother, Ştefana,
and my grandfather, Toader

Roxana Marin

The Role of Local Political Elites in East Central Europe

A Descriptive Inquiry into Local Leadership in
Six Transitional Democracies of the Region

Budrich Academic Press
Opladen • Berlin • Toronto 2021

A CIP catalogue record for this book is available from
Die Deutsche Bibliothek (The German Library)

© 2021 by Budrich Academic Press GmbH, Opladen, Berlin & Toronto
www.budrich.eu

ISBN   978-3-96665-031-1
eISBN   978-3-96665-973-4
DOI   10.3224/96665031

All annexes are available for free download on the publisher's website:
https://doi.org/10.3224/96665031A

Die Deutsche Bibliothek – CIP-Einheitsaufnahme
Ein Titeldatensatz für die Publikation ist bei Der Deutschen Bibliothek erhältlich.

Budrich Academic Press
Stauffenbergstr. 7. D-51379 Leverkusen Opladen, Germany
www. budrich-academic-press.de
86 Delma Drive. Toronto, ON M8W 4P6 Canada

Jacket illustration by Bettina Lehfeldt, Kleinmachnow, Germany –
         www.lehfeldtgraphic.de
Technical editing by Anja Borkam, Jena, Germany – kontakt@lektorat-borkam.de

Table of Contents

Acknowledgement

I would like to express my gratitude to Prof. Radu Carp, PhD, for his support and pertinent observations throughout the three years of the PhD programme. I would like to extend my gratitude to the accompanying committee which supervised my work, Prof. Dragoş Petrescu, PhD, Senior Lecturer Alexandra Iancu, PhD, and Prof. Laurenţiu Ştefan, PhD. I would like to especially present my deepest appreciation, for his constant guidance in the preparation of this book, to Prof. Laurenţiu Ştefan, from whom I embraced the passion for the study of political elites, who significantly inspired my desire for doing research in political science, and who constantly contributed to my work ever since I started inquiring into the membership of the Local Council of my birth town, in December 2011. Moreover, during the research workshop "Building an Effective Research Design in the Social Sciences" he initiated and coordinated during October 2014 and January 2015, his pieces of advice contributed decisively to my book, along with the precious observations of other colleagues in the workshop, among whom I mention Irina Ionescu, PhD.

During June 2014 and September 2015, I was given the opportunity of a scholarship through the Sectoral Operational Programme Human Resources Development (SOP HRD), under the contract no. SOP HRD/159/1.5/S/133675, at the Romanian Academy, Iaşi branch. During this period, I worked within the research group "A guverna / a fi guvernat. Ipostaze ale raportului dintre stat şi cetăţean" ["*To govern / to be governed. Hypostases of the report between the state and the citizen*"]. Firstly, the scholarship provided me the possibility to reach a larger audience with my research topic, as it financially supported and encouraged the publication in international scientific reviews and the presentation in international conferences of the main findings of the field work. Secondly, it facilitated the discussion of parts of my book with colleagues in the PhD programme and with more experienced researchers. I would like to thank them and to the two tutors of the research group, Associate Prof. Ruxandra Ivan, PhD, and Researcher Vasile Pleşca, for their constant support and help throughout the scholarship.

During March 2015, I was given the opportunity of a one-month CEEPUS study trip at the University of Wien. There, within the research group of the Institute for Social Ethics at the Faculty of Catholic Theology, the productive observations received from another research field significantly improved my preliminary findings and gave a new perspective on the research, from a new prism. I thank Prof. Ingeborg Gabriel, to Yaroslav Gerbut, PhD, and to Christoph Tröbinger, MA. Secondly, the study trip to Wien represented a terrific time for improving my bibliographical notes, the Library of the University in Wien being in itself quite impressive. I thank to Prof. Radu Carp, PhD, for selecting me as a beneficiary of a CEEPUS scholarship.

I also like to thank those members of the Political Science Department of the University of Bucharest who constantly supported me and who gave me the first impulses to engage on this path: Prof. Mihai Chioveanu, PhD, Senior Lecturer Silvia Marton, PhD, Prof. Cristina Petrescu, PhD. Their example of guidance and support for a student at the very beginning of his / her work is particularly illustrative.

I would like to thank the several translators who consistently helped me with the translation of the questionnaire and with other subsequent translations of other pieces employed in the empirical research: Ilona Kovács (University of Pécs), Dariusz Piwonski, Agata Nowak, and many others. My gratitude goes especially to Associate Prof. Katarzyna Kobielska, of the University of Wrocław, who helped extensively with the gathering and translation of data for the Polish case and who suggested the case of Oleśnica in the first place. These translators provided me with the immense opportunity to learn more about the local and national particularities of the towns and states discussed below first hand.

I have greatly benefited from talks and debates with colleagues about the topics covered in this book. Hence, I thank the anonymous reviewers of my articles submitted for publication and to countless participants in the conference panels in which I have presented my work. These debates and reviews occasioned my ability to seriously update and rework parts of my study. I thank Dragoş Dragoman, PhD, for his suggestion to and support in publishing with Budrich Academic Press, throughout my teaching time at the "Lucian Blaga" University of Sibiu.

I am terribly indebted to my family for moral and financial support and patience throughout my eight years spent in the University. Special thanks go to my sister, Emanuela, who proved an immense patience during this time.

This PhD thesis has been awarded the "Best PhD Thesis" of the University of Bucharest, and the "Best PhD Thesis in Social Sciences", in December 2016, by the Senate of the University of Bucharest. The author received a grant of 16.500 lei (approximately 3,500 euro).

Parts or chapters of this book have been published as:

- Review for „Heinrich Best, John Higley (eds.), *Democratic Elitism: New Theoretical and Comparative Perspectives*, Brill, Leiden, 2010", in *Studia Politica. Romanian Political Science Review*, vol. XII, no. 1, March 2012, pp. 108-117 (ISSN 1582-4551).
- Review for „Conor O'Dwyer, *Runaway State-Building: Patronage Politics and Democratic Development*, The Johns Hopkins University Press, Baltimore (Maryland), 2006", in *Studia Politica. Romanian Political Science Review*, vol. XII, no. 1, March 2012, pp. 122-127 (ISSN 1582-4551).
- Review for „Fredrik Engelstad, Trygve Gulbrandsen (eds.), *Comparative Studies of Social and Political Elites*, Elsevier Science, Oxford (UK) & Amsterdam (The Netherlands), 2007 ("Comparative Social Research",

vol. 23), 267 pp.", in *Studia Politica. Romanian Political Science Review*, vol. XII, no. 2, August 2012, pp. 344-357 (ISSN 1582-4551).

- "Democratic Elitism at the Local Level and Local Governance in East-Central Europe. A Comparative Assessment on the Elites of Tecuci (Romania), Česká Lípa (the Czech Republic) and Oleśnica (Poland)", in Stelian Scăunaş, Vasile Tabără şi Eugen Străuţiu (eds.). *Political Science, International Relations and Security Studies. International Conference Proceedings, the VIIth Edition, Sibiu, 24-26 May 2013*, Department of International Relations, Political Science and Security Studies (Faculty of Social Sciences and Humanities, "Lucian Blaga" University of Sibiu), Sibiu, 2013, pp. 29-56 (ISSN: 2343-7774).
- Review for "Jan Abbink, Tijo Salverda (eds.), The Anthropology of Elites: Power, Culture, and the Complexities of Distinction', Palgrave Macmillan, New York & Basingstoke (UK), 2013, in Studia Politica. Romanian Political Science Review, vol. XIII, no. 3, October 2013, pp. 565-578 (ISSN 1582-4551).
- "Incomplete Modernization and State Socialism in East-Central Europe. A Framework of Analysis of Post-Communist Local Political Elites", in Daniel Dumitran, and Valer Moga (eds.). *Economy and Society in Central and Eastern Europe: Territory, Population, Consumption. Papers of the International Conference Held in Alba Iulia, April 25th-27th, 2013*, LIT Verlag, Wien (Austria), Zürich (Switzerland) & Berlin & Münster (Germany), 2013, pp. 363-379 (ISBN: 978-3-643-90445-4).
- "Decentralization in East-Central Europe and its effects on the outlook of local political elite", in Vasile Alcaz et al. (eds.), Conferinţa Ştiinţifică Internaţională a doctoranzilor. Tendinţe contemporane ale dezvoltării ştiinţei: Viziuni ale tinerilor cercetători, 10 Martie 2014. Teze, Academia de Ştiinţe a Moldovei & Artpoligraf, Chişinău, 2014, p. 130 (ISBN 978-9975-4257-2-8).
- "Dynamics of decentralization in East-Central Europe. Definition, taxonomy, applications", in Nicolaie Georgescu and Mircea Cosma (eds.), *Papers of the Sibiu Alma Mater University Conference, Eight Edition, 27-29 March 2014, Sibiu*, Volume 1, Editura *Alma Mater*, Sibiu, 2014, pp. 122-129 (ISSN 2067 – 1423).
- "Profilul elitei politice locale în Europa Central-Estică. Aplicaţie pe membrii consiliilor municipale din Tecuci, Česká Lípa şi Oleśnica", in Cristina Manolache, Anamaria Elena Gheorghe, Roxana Marin (eds.), *Tineri Cercetători: Abordări Multidisciplinare. Revistă studenţească în domeniul ştiinţelor sociale*, Vol. I, No. 1, Aprilie 2014, pp. 34-55 (ISSN 2344-6455).
- „Descentralizarea în Europa central-estică: conceptualizare şi operaţionalizare. Definiţie, taxonomie, aplicaţii", în Cristina Manolache şi Anamaria Elena Gheroghe (eds.). *Sesiunea naţională de comunicări ştiinţifice în domeniul ştiinţelor sociale* Tineri cercetători: Abordări multidisciplinare. *Culegere de abstracte*, Şcoala Doctorală de Ştiinţă Politică

9

(Univrsitatea din Bucureşti), 13 decembrie 2014 (ediţia a II-a), pp. 44-45 (ISSN 2344-6455).

- "The Dynamics of Decentralization in East-Central Europe. Application on Four Municipal Councils" in *Journal of Law and Social Sciences*, Year I, No. 1 (February 2014), pp. 153-173 (ed.: the International Association of Law and Related Sciences – IALRS) (ISSN 2392-6112; ISSN-L 2392-6112)

- "Local Leadership in East-Central Europe: Socio-Demographical Profiles and Value Attainment in Four Towns" / „Leadership local în Europa Centrală şi de Est: profile socio-demografice şi forme ale împlinirii valorice în patru oraşe", in *Philologica Jassyensia*, Year X, No. 1 (19) (Winter 2014) (Special Issue: Proceedings of the International Conference *Perspectives in the Humanities and Social Sciences: Hinting at Interdisciplinarity*, 1st ed., Iaşi, May 23-24, 2014), pp. 715-726 (ISSN 1841-5377, ISSN online 2247-8353, ISSN-L 1841-5377)

- "Value Attainment, Orientations, and Quality-Based Profile of the Local Political Elites in East-Central Europe. Evidence from Four Towns", in *Symposion. Theoretical and Applied Inquiries in Philosophy and Social Sciences*, Vol. 2, No. 1 (January 2015), pp. 95-123 (EISSN 2392-6260; ISSN-L 1584-174X)

- "La construction du profile de l'élite politique locale en l'Éurope Centrale et Orientale", in Iulian Boldea (coord.), Identities in Metamorphosis. Literature, Discourse and Multicultural Dialogue. Studies on Literature, Discourse and Multicultural Dialogue. Proceedings of the International Conference Literature, Discourse and Multicultural Dialogue. Political Sciences, Sociology, International Relations Section, Vol. 2, Arhipelag XXI Press, Târgu-Mureş, 2014, pp. 154-169 (ISBN: 978-606-93691-9-7)

- "Patterns of Recruitment at the Local Level in East-Central Europe", in The Alpha Institute for Multicultural Studies (ed.), Iulian Boldea (coord.), *Communication, Context, Interdisciplinarity: Studies and Articles. Proceedings of the International Conference Communication, Context, Interdisciplinarity, 3rd edition. Section: Political Sciences and International Relations*, Vol. 3, "Petru Maior" University Press, Târgu-Mureş, 2014, pp. 344-356 (ISSN 2069-3389)

- "Instances of decentralization in East-Central Europe: operationalization, taxonomy and applications on local political elites' outlook", in *Romanian Journal of Political Science*, Vol. 14, No. 2 (Winter 2014) (Thematical Issue: "*Peace Building and Development*"), pp. 99-125 (ISSN 1582-456X)

- "The Local Political Elites in East-Central Europe: Between the Legacy of the Past and the Decentralization of the Present", in Jădăneanţ, Alexandru, Claudia Turşie, Ciprian Niţu, and Claudiu Mesaroş (eds.), *Procedia – Social and Behavioral Sciences Vol. 183 – Proceedings of the International Symposium on 'Ideologies, Values and Political Behaviors in*

Central and Eastern Europe', 12th ed., 6 December 2013, Timişoara, Elsevier B.V., Amsterdam (the Netherlands), 2015, pp. 30-39 (ISSN: 1877-0428)

- "Value Attainment in Local Political Leadership. Evidence from Four Towns of East-Central Europe", in Jădăneanț, Alexandru, Claudia Turşie, Ciprian Nițu, and Claudiu Mesaroş (eds.), *Procedia – Social and Behavioral Sciences Vol. 183 – Proceedings of the International Symposium on 'Ideologies, Values and Political Behaviors in Central and Eastern Europe', 12th ed., 6 December 2013, Timişoara*, Elsevier B.V., Amsterdam (the Netherlands), 2015, pp. 30-39 (ISSN: 1877-0428)
- "Rețelele de putere, contactele şi interacțiunile elitelor politice locale din Europa central-răsăriteană", în Ruxandra Ivan şi Vasile Pleşca (coord.), Academia Română, Filiala Iaşi (prin IDSRC – doc postdoc POSDRU/ 159/1.5/S/133675) (ed.), *A guverna / a fi guvernat. Ipostaze ale raportului dintre stat şi cetăţean*, PRO Universitaria, Bucureşti, 2015, pp. 189-218 (ISBN: 978-606-26-0343-4)
- "Types of Local Government Systems and Types of Local Political Elites: An Application on ECE", in Cristina Manolache and Anamaria Elena Gheroghe (eds.). *International Interdisciplinary Doctoral Conference (IIDC 2015). Book of Abstracts*, Romanian Association of Young Scholars (RAYS), September 25th-26th, 2015 (1st edition), pp. 121-122 (ISSN 2457-7944)
- "The Impact of Socio-Demographical Profile and of Passive Representativeness of Local Political Elites on the Construction of a Typology of Local Political Elites of ECE", in Liviu-Adrian Măgurianu and Simona-Roxana Ulman (ed.), *Proceedings of the International Conference 'Humanities and Social Sciences Today. Classical and Contemporary Issues' (Iaşi, 2015). Social and Political Theory*, PRO Universitaria, Bucureşti, 2015, pp. 177-198 (ISBN: 978-606-26-0415-8)
- "Accounting for moral superiority of elites. Political elites caught between normative and descriptive approaches", in Proceedings of the International Conference 'European Union's History, Culture and Citizenship', 8th edition, Piteşti, 8th – 9th May 2015, C.H. Beck Publishing House, Bucharest, 2015, pp. 799-822 (ISSN 2360-395X, ISSN-L 2360-1841)
- "The Profile of Local Political Elite and Strategy Prioritisation at the Local Level in ECE Countries. Case Studies: Tecuci (Romania), Česká Lípa (the Czech Republic), Oleśnica (Poland), and Gyula (Hungary)", in *Federal Governance*, Vol. 12, No. 1 (June 2015), pp. 60-88 (ISSN 1923-6158)
- "Power networks, contacts, and interactions of local political elites in East-Central Europe", in Iulian Boldea (coord.), Globalization and National Identity. Studies on the Strategies of Intercultural Dialogue: Sociology, Political Sciences, and International Relations, Vol. 3, Arhipelag XXI Press, Târgu-Mureş, 2016, pp. 386-402 (ISBN: 978-606-8624-03-7)

Abstract

The present book is concerned with the issue of local leadership in the countries of East-Central Europe. Concretely, it is an attempt to examine, in a comparative fashion, the profile and the role of the local political elites in six transitional democracies of the region, Romania, the Czech Republic, Poland, Hungary, Slovakia, and Bulgaria, and the elites' further impact on the evolution of the local communities in the developing region of former Sovietized Europe. This research project constitutes actually the continuation of the analysis undertaken in the preparation of the Masters' final thesis, as it develops on the research elaborated in the period December 2010 – May 2012 for the Municipal Councils in Tecuci (Romania) and Česká Lípa (the Czech Republic). In the period October 2012 – February 2013, the analysis on the local political elites in East-Central Europe has been continued for Poland, with the focus on the case of the city of Oleśnica. In the period October 2013 – January 2016, the field work has been completed with three similar towns in Hungary, Slovakia, and Bulgaria. Consequently, the emphasis is put on the small-to-medium-sized communities, those municipalities of around 30,000 – 40,000 inhabitants in the said region, largely similar in regard to economic activities and developmental strategies (an economy based on food industry, commerce activities and investments in infrastructure). Therefore, for further exploring the *problématique*, the book proposes, as focal case studies, six small towns in these six countries, quite similar in terms of demographics (roughly 40,000 inhabitants) and developmental strategies (*i.e.* an economy based on the alimentary industry and on commerce activities, etc.): Tecuci (Galaţi county / *judeţ*, Romania), Česká Lípa (Liberec region / *kraj*, Czech Republic), Oleśnica (Lower Silesia voivodeship / *województwo*, Poland), Gyula (Békés county / *megye*, Hungary), Targovishte (Targovishte province / *oblast*, Bulgaria), Levice (Nitria region / *kraj*, Slovak Republic).

The proposed inquiry employs mainly the positional method in identifying and analyzing the local political elites, by operationalizing the phrase "local political elites" through the following definition: The local political elite is that group comprising those individuals in legislative and executive positions within the local leading, decision-making structure. Therefore, the empirical part of the present research uses as its samples the members of the Local (Municipal) Councils in Tecuci, Česká Lípa, Oleśnica, Gyula, Targovishte, and Levice (the compositions of the six decisional forums in the period 2011-2015, for some modifications did happen from the composition of the Councils, as they were constituted after the local elections of 2008 and 2012). For Tecuci, the Local Council includes nineteen persons, for Česká Lípa, the Municipal Council is formed of twenty-five members, for Oleśnica, the Municipal Council comprises twenty-one members, for Gyula, the Municipal Council counts fourteen members, for Targovishte, the Local Council encompasses thirty-three members, for Levice, the Municipal Council numbers twenty-four members, with various political affiliations, with very different occupations, of different ages, enjoying different degrees of popular support and prestige, but of largely similar social *status* and with resembling social backgrounds and political trajectories.

The main argument put forward by this study is that, similarly to the national level, at the local level, the responsibility of the ruling elite is major in the governance of the community, since the regional and local development in the six countries is dependent on the efficient administration of funds, which is presently exclusively the prerogative of the political elite. Viciously caught in a perennial transition to democracy – at different stages and various levels of democratic consolidation and economic development – the six countries of East-Central Europe discussed here (*i.e.* Romania, the Czech Republic, Poland, Hungary, Slovakia and Bulgaria) depend heavily on their elites more than ever in their pursuit of democracy. The national political elites of each of these countries – either governing or oppositional – became central in the communist breakdown and the inauguration of democratic transition in the late 1980s and the beginning of the 1990s. Equally, either central or local, these elites can fasten or ease the overall political and socio-economical development of their countries. It is this researcher's firm conviction that an account on the characterization of these groups at the local level – through the means of analyzing Municipal Councils – can provide an insight into the actual development, the opportunities and the future evolution – generally on short term, the period of a mandate – of the communities they govern. Therefore, the social background and the characteristics of the local elites tell something about their personal and political interests and aims. The main contention put forward by the intended study on local leadership is that the social background and an inquiry into the values, interactions, and beliefs of the local elite are particularly telling and instrumental for the elite's priorities, its personal and political interests and aims, for its behavior as leaders of their communities.

Since the scope of the research bears a rather descriptive, explanatory nature, the first section of the book introduces a theoretical basis in understanding the role of the Municipal Councils on local politics and development, by generally presenting the main functions and the workings of these forums in the countries under observation here (Romania, the Czech Republic, Poland, Hungary, the Slovak Republic, and Bulgaria, respectively); a separate discussion on the local budget is inserted. The next six sections are dedicated to the six cases selected and follow the inquiries into: (1) the social biography of the members of the six Municipal Councils under scrutiny; (2) patterns of recruitment of these local elites and the importance of the local branches of the main parties; (3) interactions of the members of the Local Councils with other groups and institutions (and the subsequent power networks and formal and informal linkages); (4) values and principles embraced by the local political elites in the six analyzed cases; (5) priorities of the local political elites in the six selected Municipal Councils, and (6) representativeness of the Local (Municipal) Councils in the six towns, in the context in which the Municipal Council is, after all, an instance of legislative representative government (with a special emphasis on passive representation). The structure of the study is largely the result of the observations drawn from an empirical endeavor conducted among the members of the six Councils in the period December 2010-August 2015, in the preparation of the MA and PhD theses.

Introduction. Theoretical assessments on political elites

"If we know how the participants [to the political game] got there, where they came from, by what pathways, what ideas, skills and contacts they acquired or discarded along the way, then we will have a better understanding of political events. [...] [K]nowing their abilities, sensitivities, aims and credentials, we are better able to anticipate what they say and do, and to evaluate elites, institutions and systems performance." Dwaine Marvick (1968: 273-282)

When engaging in an argumentation, rarely does an issue present itself which cannot be best illustrated by one of Aesop's fables. Abiding by this principle, the contemporary understanding of the concept of elites, as rendered in the writings of many scholars, receives a fair portrayal within such a tale where reason and guile are left to have their moment. The fable entitled "The Fox and the Lion" proceeds with its moral as follows:

"When first the Fox saw the Lion he was terribly frightened, and ran away and hid himself in the wood. Next time however he came near the King of Beasts, he stopped at a safe distance and watched him pass by. The third time they came near one another, the Fox went straight up to the Lion and passed the time of day with him, asking him how his family were, and when he should have the pleasure of seeing him again; then turning his tail, he parted from the Lion without much ceremony." (Aesop, as cited in Gibbs 2002: 216).

Expressed in fuller form, this fable offers a brief account of the first instance from which the concept of elites departed as well of its last and present condition. Owing to its close ties to other concepts beset in the field of political science, the concept of elite rose and counted its gains once with political science, remaining largely true to itself. As such, it is advisable to set about this short journey which oversees the implications that the concept of elites bore across time, with a general definition provided by one of the elitists and summarized here by S. J. Eldersveld:

"In all regularly constituted societies [...], the ruling class or rather those who hold and exercise the public power, will be always a minority and below them we find a numerous class of persons who do never, in any real sense, participate in government but merely submit to it. These may be called the ruled class." (Eldersveld 1989: xv)

As phrased above, all early elite theorists consent that it is particular to each and every at least moderately complex societies that power and privilege are set aside for those few ones addressed as elites. It is they who accrue the greater part of that which has been laid for grabs. This fact stems from the early days of humanity, when the wretched ways of a yet debased social and political order distinguished between master and slave. In order to salvage his life, the weaker opponent of those days of yore, admitted to his limits revealed to him by his thereafter master. He then wept and begged for his life, bowed and began praising his master, as accustomed to all subjects in front of the triumphant, the powerful and the grand heirs. Rejoicing in their victory, those distinguished by birth and riches thrived upon those of infinite lesser breeding and earthly possessions. In the words of Sidney Hook, "all political rule is a process [...] by which a minority gratifies its own interests [...] the masses who have fought, bled, and starved are made the goat" (Hook 1939: 562-563).

In this initial landscape, Ancient philosophers made the first attempts in accounting for the immanent division of power, influence, privilege and morals. Books III and VI of the *Nicomachean Ethics* contain the Aristotelian perspective in regard to the normative approach on the political elite. Aristotle constructs here the cornerstone of the normative direction in the definition of the "political elite", in which this group of powerful, influential "few" represents the ones possessing a series of special, distinguished qualities. Among these qualities, *"arete"* of the *dianoia* [thought] becomes of paramount importance for the ones in leadership, for the potentates in the *agora*. Indeed, these patricians, these potentates are (or should be) the bearers of *"arete"*, of mere virtue, of some form of intellectual excellence. Aristotelian "virtue" tends of overlap with the Platonian "virtue", in the sense that *"arete"* would always constitute a faculty, a capability of the soul, not of the mind. Paradoxically, *"arete"* is the halfway, the median between virtue and vice, the *"aurea mediocritas"*; therefore, the leading ones, in Aristotelian *imaginarium*, should have the capability of finding a middle ground between virtue and vice, hence excelling in moderation, in *equilibrium*. The measure in which the elite is able to reach *"eudaimonia"* ["happiness"] is an aspect not discussed by the Greek philosopher, though one might hypothesize that, since *"eudaimonia"* is defined as the "activity of soul in accordance with *arete*, or [...] in accordance with the best and most complete *arete"* (Aristotle, Bartlett, & Collins 2011), the leading few might be prone to acquire *eudaimonia*. In a nutshell, it appears sure for Aristotle that the political elite is to possess moral and intellectual prominence, is to consist of men of distinguishable virtue.

However, precisely because the slave alone has performed for ages the real work, thus renouncing his immediate delight, it grew in him the ability to open the world (Sloterdijk 2000/2002: 41). The skills which he acquired meanwhile his master indulged in the outcomes of foreign labour and abandoned himself to the working hands of others, paved the road of the subject's emancipation from the stale authority of unjustified rule. Removed of that "certain material, intellectual, or even moral superiority" (Mosca 1939: 35) over those they govern, as the latter grew in intellect and skill, the ruler ceased to be so, and the ruled knew of a different destiny. As a consequence of the Enlightenment, this concept of leadership was deprived of part of its content, namely blind faith in the ruler's arbitrary decisions. Among many, Napoleon was one to remark upon the new political reality and the opportunities it offered: "the idea of

16

equality, from which I could expect nothing other than rise, had for me something seductive" (Von Falkenhausen 1941: 104). From heretofore, it is precisely this equal ground from which men of greater ambitions and higher expectations rose above, and that rising distance is the measure of their power and the sign of them being an elite.

This newly found equality is the reason why men began preoccupying themselves with their *status* among the rest and voicing indignation at the superiority of others. The elitists wrote of the conscious, cohesive and conspiring groups, Mosca's "political class" and Michels' "oligarchs", with deference and compliance. Mosca stressed the advantage of numbers in out-organizing and out-witting the larger masses, Pareto rooted the unrestricted social mobility as the prerequisite for the rise of those most adept at using force and persuasion, and gifted with inherited wealth and family connections. Michels postulated that through and through and without omission, elites will surface all large organizations, as a necessity of the inner workings of any functioning body of people. Together they grounded the thought that elites are incessantly placing themselves above the majority and that "democracies are divided into the wielders of power and those who are subject to it and have little power of their own" (Etzioni-Halevy 1997: 44). Within this framework, the concept of elite was tantamount to a detractor of democracy, and consequently of the better virtues of others. In agreement with the elitists, Weber supports the view that even in a democracy the *demos* itself never governs. Nevertheless, Weber and Mosca ascribe certain merits to democracy for counterbalancing the leverage of the bureaucracy, a second peril to the autonomy of the *demos*. However, the fact remains that, according to the elitists,

> "political rule involves organization and all organization no matter how democratic its mythology, sooner or later comes under the effective control of a minority elite; the history of societies, despite the succession of different political forms, is in substance nothing but the succession of different political elites; democracy is a political form that conceals both the conflicts of interest between the governing elite and the governed and the fact that these conflicts are always undemocratically resolved in favour of the former." (Hook 2008: 240)

Skepticism about the contingencies of ethics among the political elite imbued even the Weberian readings that conceive politics founded on the "principle of small numbers" and imagined, in turn, the "leader democracy" (Roth & Wittich 1978/1920: 41-71, 1111-1155, 1414, 1459-1460). Pareto, few years before him, did not imagine: he rather described a "demagogic plutocracy" (as opposed to "military plutocracy"), as a dangerous compromise between elites and democratic ideals, in which the former retain prevalence over the later through "deception, demagogy and bribing" (thus, everything but moral stances!), giving only the appearance of democracy to the masses (Finer and Mirfin 1978/1902: 142). In effect, political elites are "persons at or near the top of the 'pyramid of power'" (Putnam 1976: 14), "persons with the 'organized capacity to make *real and continuing political trouble without being promptly re-pressed'"* (Higley and Burton 2006: 7 [italics added]).

Defenders of democracy took offence at the slight odds which this most lauded regime was offered. Liberty and equality were brought to the fore, as universal suffrage was deemed the foundation of all sound government for it ensured that the general will shall be expressed and popular sovereignty will be entrusted to its chosen representatives. However, the rationale that elites, thus dignified under the name of representatives, are decided by the will of the people is somewhat inexact. In this respect the argument is forced into the direction of representation and the accompanying "mandate-independence controversy", which has become an ordinary and familiar subject of discussion. The controversy resides in deciding whether the representative is to do what his constituents urge him to do or what he thinks best.

The beginning and the first half of the 20th century advanced the shift, not only towards an "over-consciousness" of the power gap between elites and the masses, but, paradoxically enough, the acknowledgement of the fact that political elites were, as an intrinsic rule, deprived of any moral prominence over the led masses, they actually eluded any moral stance of excellence and prevalence[1]. Therefore, probably, the veritable transmutation within the *academia* in respect to the moral overview on the political elites and the fashion of defining this group through the lances of ethic excellence and intellectual preeminence is to be found at the beginning of the last century, with the triptych of Italian "elitists" Vilfredo Pareto, Gaetano Mosca and Robert Michels. Paradoxically, though the newly-emerging perspective on the moral dimension of the constitution of the elite is – especially to the latter two – descriptive *par excellence*, daringly honest in the field of sociological research – though quite feeble in the sphere of empirical inquiry –, the exegetes, the observers, the critics hurried to express innumerable rejoinders, labelling – more or less justifiably – the descriptive approach to elites as inseparably intertwined with the prematurely and dangerously rising fascist-corporatist movement in politically infant Italy. Yet, the three prominent sociologists were observers *tout court*. The realities within the group of power- and influence-holders had irrefutably changed since Aristotle and, in addition, the realities of the polity *per se* and its expectations from the leading ones suffered transformable mutations. These modifications in the people's, citizens' expectations had to be voiced out in the very fashion in which the relationship between the political elite and morality was to be constructed. The descriptive line of thinking about elites has been courageously and vigorously continued and embraced in the 1950s, with the publication of C. Wright Mills's *Power Elite* (1956), a painful radiography of

---

1   It might be argued that the premises for this grim, coldhearted perspective on political elites are to be found on the Italian soil once more, with the Machiavellian depiction of the Prince, the philosophical cornerstone of modern politics. See Machiavelli, Skinner and Price (eds.) 1998/1505.

the American potentates at the middle of the century. Definitely and evidently enough, what conspicuously lacks from these descriptions is the moral dimension of the political leadership, which became diluted under the weight of sociological considerations regarding the corruptible nature and the mundane qualities of the political elite. Fair enough, attempts to rejuvenate elitism as moral and intellectual prominence have been unceasable from Machiavelli and his *virtu* onwards, particularly in the 19th century.

Suffice it to say that democracy eludes the overbearing power of elites solely within the first instance of representation where representatives heed their constituents' wants and interests with deference and devotion. With all honesty of purpose, each representative championing the interest of his district, even against the interest of other districts, ensures that democracy prevails by disallowing for any faction that may form itself. Where interests are multiple and diverse it is "less probable that a majority will have a common motive to invade the rights of other citizens; or if such a common motive exists, it will be more difficult for all who feel it to discover their own strength and to act in unison" (Madison 2003/1787: 45).

The other side of the argument is led by Edmund Burke whose address to the people of Bristol makes the most compelling argument. To Burke, the representative remains as with the Federalists a spokesman for the interest of the district, with the slight difference that "he owes his constituents a devotion to their interests, rather than to their opinion" (Pitkin 1967: 144). His case is argued most eloquently in the ensuing passage:

> "Parliament is not a congress of ambassadors from different and hostile interests, which interests each must maintain, as an agent and advocate, against other agents and advocates; but Parliament is a deliberative assembly of one nation, with one interest, that of the whole-where not local prejudices ought to guide but the general good, resulting from the general reason of the whole. You choose a member, indeed; but when you have chosen him he is not a member of Bristol, but he is a member of Parliament."[2]

Fair enough, at this end of the argument, elitism is somehow rejuvenated, as the mandate of the representative is thus relieved of a strict accountability to the grievances and demands of his constituents. The political elites retreat within the Parliament under the panache of more qualitative representation, and govern from this enclosed, higher ground, in an Enlightened fashion, those whom they can barely distinguish from the distance. If democracy is to rely upon the responsiveness of the elected to their electors, given the previous *scenario*, the decisions of the government may tend to reflect the wants of the

---

2   The famous address of Edmund Burke to the electors of Bristol (Speech to the Electors of Bristol, 1774), in Browne 1993: 67-82. The mandate of the representative, of the political leader, is thus relieved of a strict accountability to the grievances and demands of his constituents, pointing out the superior qualities of the leading few once more.

governors, more so than those of the governed and popular sovereignty may be abandoned by the wayside, only to be picked up again upon securing a subsequent mandate.

As the debate lingered on, the concept of elite was again revisited, once with Schumpeter's minimal, procedural, instrumentalist concept of democracy (Schumpeter 1942). Democracy was defined as a limited political regime in which power is achieved through competitive elections. To his mind, due to the development of mass democracy, popular sovereignty as depicted in all classical works became inadequate. "A new understanding of democracy was needed, putting the emphasis on the aggregation of preferences, taking place through political parties for which people would have the capacity to vote at regular intervals" (Mouffe 2000: 1). Schumpeter impresses upon his readers the banished thought of the elitists; modern times disavow notions like "common good" and "general will" which they replace with pluralism of interests because only self-interest is held to move and stir any individual who is engrossed only with his own pursuits. Drawing on the elitists' appraisal, individuals are not motivated to act by the moral belief that they should pursue the interest of the whole and consent to the general will, but by more narrow preferences and interests. These preferences are to be voiced and heeded by political parties in their struggle for gaining the votes. Schumpeter manages to rebalance the gains in favor of the descriptive, "a-moral" (one might be inclined to label it) perspective, by eloquently pleading for an elite that seems rather selfish in nature, manipulative towards its voters, displaying no moral, superior stance in reference to the masses.

Therefore, the concept of political elite has arrived at the admission that within representative democracy, each elite is to be confirmed by popular vote. However, the conditions under which the vote of the people is expressed, pose some objections to democracy itself. Firstly, as stated above, "there can be no guarantee that these decisions as well as the discretionary powers they entail will be carried out in the same spirit as that in which they were authorized" (Hook 2008: 242). This is mainly the case of the Burkean elite who think of themselves as being unbound to the views of their constituents and who take pride in following only their conscience and principles. Therefore, what the representative thinks is of paramount importance. However, the followers of the mandate theory are not to be exempt of weariness towards their devotion. Secondly, "we can never be sure that consent is freely given, that is not in bondage to ignorance, rhetoric, or passion" (Hook 2008: 115). Democracy frequently receives such blows, as the speech of a gifted demagogue can override the better judgment of people. Similarly, passions may cloud their mind, just as indecision and disregard may mislead their vote. Lastly, and in close connection to the previous two factors, the vote of the people is usually guided by the political parties' selection of candidates. The electorate is limited in expressing its preference by the initial, prevailing preference of the party. Nonpartisan municipalities necessarily fall outside this category. Thus, it may be concluded that popular legitimization appears to be less of a democratic safeguard when facing the pervasive influence of elites. In order to safeguard the many led, a revitalization of the Aristotelian virtue should have taken place in contemporaneity.

A great number of scholars accuse a rampant crisis of legitimacy affecting Western democracies. This crisis is closely connected to the manner in which political elites are easily legitimized by popular vote following the recommendation of political parties. Therefore, a short comment on the influence that political parties possess within the process of legitimizing political elites is needed. Needless to say that if each voter were to vote for the candidate whom he saw fit to be his governor, then we would most likely be faced with a wide scattering of votes. Therefore, it was found necessary to coordinate and organize the votes of the people because, if left untutored, they would never come to an agreement on a given candidate. "If his vote is to have any efficacy at all, therefore, each voter is forced to limit his choice to a very narrow field, in other words to a choice among the two or three persons who have some chance of succeeding; and the only ones who have any chance of succeeding are those whose candidacies are championed by groups, by committees, by organized minorities" (Etzioni-Halevy 1997: 56). This prerequisite for an efficient, working election restrains the liberty of choice of the voters to a number of eligible candidates endorsed by different kinds of organizations among which political parties.

A candidacy endorsement is not without previous reflection and deliberation. In order for a political party to nominate a candidate for an upcoming election, the soundness of the candidate is brought to bear. The ritual of candidate selection is "the predominantly extralegal process by which a political party decides which of the persons legally eligible to hold an elective public office will be designated on the ballot and in election communications as its recommended and supported candidate or list of candidates" (Butler, Penniman, and Ranney 1981: 75). There are various aspects attached to candidate selection and many issues to consider before putting forth a nomination. Important to bear in mind is the fact that parties enjoy a degree of centralization, meaning that they have party agencies present at the national, regional and local levels. Candidates are usually elected by local party agencies, under supervision by the national or regional agencies. Just as frequent, candidates are selected by national agencies at the suggestion of regional and local agencies. The process of selection can therefore be top-bottom, and just as easily bottom-top. There is however such a thing called "placement" known for stirring resentment among local selectors, when the national leaders take the liberty of suggesting the nomination of candidates whom they support against the preference of local agencies. Instead, the national and regional agencies have the power to refuse their support to a locally selected candidate and even deny him the use of the party's label, if they disagree with the nomination of the respective candidate. However, any veto practice may render the party divisive and therefore, the national leaders "rely instead upon the local selectors' discretion to avoid choosing candidates that would have to be vetoed".

Another thing to consider during the selection is how many candidates will be enlisted and in what constituencies. This allocation *calculus* will ensure that a balanced number of candidates will be put forth in each constituency, because "too many will spread the party's votes so thin that all its candidates will lose and too few will waste the party's votes and keep it from electing as many candidates as its voting strength permits" (Butler, Penniman, and Ranney 1981: 83). However, being included in the list of nominations does not secure a mandate to any candidate. The number of seats won by the party during the election is distributed according to the list, starting with those at the top and ending with those placed at the bottom, until the number of seats is exhausted. Chances are that only the upper part of the list will assume incumbency, while the rest, though victorious, cannot share in the seats. Hence, "positions on party lists are almost as important as their presence on them" (Butler, Penniman, and Ranney 1981: 84).

Hence, on the background of increasing accusations regarding a rampant crisis of ethics and morality (deontologically understood) affecting the political leadership, the recent, largely empirically scholarly, emerged in order to reconcile somehow the dispute between those voicing the downfall of morals among politicians (that is, professionalized political elite) and thusly asking for moral and intellectual prominence and virtuous qualities, and those boldly pointing out that, with the virtually unrestricted access of individuals in politics, the moral and intellectual quality of elites became inherently decadent. Based on vast and almost exhaustive quantitative research on political elites (conducted especially in Western, highly developed, democracies), this "neo-descriptive" direction is set up to measure the impact of values – either moral, political, social, etc. – on shaping the existing tableau of the "leading few". Moreover, this approach tends to consider aspects that were previously neglected (e.g. commenting on the influence that political parties as "selectorates" or "gate-keepers" possess within the process of recruiting, selecting and legitimizing political elites, considering the importance of preference aggregation in shaping the form of the elites). As such, the overbearing presence of parties and their intricate system of selection and appointments expand to the very outskirts of the political society in which they dwell. Political elites are daily recruited and groomed so to occupy their higher political standing once with the coming of elections. Very little is left to odds, much is thought ahead. The tightly woven system of nominations is solid proof of the capacity of the leading minority to organize itself better than the heavy and robust masses. Political elites spare no effort or wit in achieving incumbency. Popular sovereignty is professed as both political parties and elites are clothed in skins of humility and reserve towards the word of the people. "The vast machinery of party politics convey to most citizens the belief that minorities finally chosen to govern have been selected by procedures which permit an acceptable measure of popular control" (Prewitt 1970: 110). Upon sober reflection, everyone will be made sensible to their inconsequence within the process of determining the candidates whom they will later entrust with the right to present the person of them all. Democracy is given the backseat in politics because men regularly consent to authorize all the actions and judgments of one man or an assembly of men at the biased advice of political parties.

In these sentiments and in fully descriptive vein, political elites go to the extent of fully organizing themselves in order to secure a popular mandate which they obtain in violation of popular sovereignty. Michels was among the first to argue openly that any "system of leadership is incompatible with the most essential postulates of democracy" (Michels 1962: 364). The inconsistency of leadership with democratic values is owed to the idea and the content of leadership itself. When closely examined, the skills, talents and other qualities embodied by our leaders discriminate against the average citizen, less gifted with those attributes and who is refused the opportunity of being the governor and not the governed.

All researchers who ventured in the field of political elites agree that:

"Legislators are far from being an average assortment of ordinary men. Almost everywhere legislators are better educated, possess higher-status occupations and have more privileged backgrounds than the people they represent." (Loewnberg, Patterson, and Jewell 1985: 18)

Aspirants to political leadership find their chances have improved considerably if they are possessed with private wealth, sufficiently large to fund their electoral campaigns in entrepreneurial political systems, or simply to secure them a higher education. This rationale applies to candidates from both parts of the ideological spectrum, and it remains as true for conservatives as for socialists. The reason is rarely snobbery because these people "are more likely to speak and write well, they are more likely to look healthy and well dressed" and "to work in occupations with flexible hours" (Butler, Penniman, and Ranney 1981: 102) leaving them sufficient time for leadership duties. As a rule, when this above-average socioeconomic and educational status is attributed to a member of the male sex, this man will embody the general definition of an eligible candidate. The most disadvantaged aspirants to national or even local leadership are by far women. Statistics show that 41 percent of the women who served in the American Congress before 1979 were given the seat vacated by their recently deceased husbands. Therefore, "lawmaking remains essentially a man's game" (Loewnberg, Patterson, and Jewell 1985: 21).

The nature of the profession that the candidate is practicing is of equal importance, lawyers and people with verbal jobs, alongside businessmen being the most frequent incumbents of all legislatures. These elites are more apt for legislative roles owing to the skills which they acquired in their instruction and experience, not quite to their moral outlook. Also, these professions may be thought to encourage an interest in political activity.

As can be deduced from previous comments, being member of a party is a valued asset and almost a vital one outside nonpartisan municipalities. Equally valuable is having occupied the same position for which one is running once more. Incumbents are preferred to non-incumbents because of their experience. These political elites are familiar to the electorate, to the party, to the campaign funders and "they already wear the mantle of the elected public official" (Butler, Penniman, and Ranney 1981: 98). Being guided by the lights of experience and having the weight of precedence to justify its measures, the leadership of an incumbent is favoured by the majority of electorates. Similarly, another attribute of political elites is their local connections, which make them known and trusted throughout their constituency. Unlike an outsider, a local is "more likely to have contributed work and money to the local party and thus to have earned its candidacy" (Butler, Penniman, and Ranney 1981: 100). It is worth mentioning that affiliations either to an interest group, say labour union, religious laymen's league, farmer organization, or to a certain faction of the party to which the political elite is member, emphasize his *status* and make him a true commodity for his party, but it might cast a shadow of morality in the front of the electorate, as well.

Together, all assets listed above render the candidate for political leadership more commendable than his peers who may lack them, but may cherish ethical positions instead. With these differences in mind, if one is to conclude if democratic principles and ethics – as commonly defined as incontestable human attributes – are at work in present-day societies, inductive reasoning seems to have fallen down to a certain extent. Indeed, one may reason that "elites don't believe in democracy. They pretend to be interested in the public and engage in deceptive patterns of behaviour in appealing for public support. Hence, they assume a passive public, and they are not really accountable, responsive, nor egalitarian" (Eldersveld 1989: xv-xvi).

Generally, in the field of political elite studies, two intellectual and research directions are customarily distinguished: (1) the normative theories on elites, and (2) the descriptive elite approach. Chronologically, the normative approaches precede the descriptive ones, for they are inclined to identify elites on the basis of their excellence (or "*arete*"), furthermore, on their moral stance or virtue. Pareto, the pioneering name in the descriptive tradition in studying elites, is actually in between the two approaches: the elite was formed either by those who are the best in their field of activity – namely, politics –, who excel in the realm in which they work or by those who are more or less circumstantially, but always temporarily, ephemerally in top decision-making positions in the hierarchy of power, those being in possession of "residues" of "combinations" or "persistence of aggregates" (Finer 1966/1916). The descriptive manner was, starting from Pareto and the Italian "elitists" Mosca and Michels at the beginning of the 20th century, happily and exhaustively embraced by the contemporary scholarly, but most prolific oeuvres written in this fashion appeared in the context of a new "elitist" wave of studies, overwhelmingly empirical ones, at the end of the century: Higley's numerous books (most important, those co-authored with Dogan (1998), Pakulski and Wesolowski (1998) and Lengyel (2000)), Mattei Dogan's *Elite Configurations at the Apex of Power* (2003), Etzioni-Halevy's *Classes and Elites in Democracy and Democratization* (1997), Hoffman-Lange's compelling study on elites in FRG (1987: 27-47), Scott's *The Sociology of Elites* (1990) and the countless studies conducted by Eyal, Szelényi and Townsley, separately or in co-authorship (*Making Capitalism Without Capitalists: The New Ruling Elites in Eastern Europe*, 1998) on "transformative" and "revolutionary" elites in East-Central Europe. These largely empirical inquiries appear in the special context of a decade after the communist breakdown and, consequently, treat extensively the process of elite transformation in transitional societies, in the new democracies. Their contribution to the overall scholarly production in the field of elite research is irrefutable, since the focus, the interest of research shifts from the Western democracies to the mutations in East-Central Europe, opening new paths of scientific endeavor for a region constantly in development. In this climate, C. Wright-Mills's *Power Elite* (1956) appears as an enclave for the descriptive tradition in Western developed democracies in the middle of the 20th century. In the center of the normative "preoccupations" remains the issue of the "quality of elites", i.e. excellence, which is somehow intrinsic, inherent in the very definition of "elites"; the moment in which the "quality of elites" becomes problematic is the transition between normative and descriptive approaches, when the collocation "the quality of elites" starts to pose serious problems of definition and operationalization: what is, in effect, this "quality"? Is it a moral one, denoting an elite that is ethnically superior, acting for the supreme "good" and being in itself of special "fabric", axiologically righteous and virtuous? Is it a professional, technocratic one, linking the *status* of "political elite" to a certain degree of efficiency, performance, proper decision-making, good governance? Eventually, is it the representation constructed by a group of individuals able to seize and retain political power, a public image in the face of the masses in order to consolidate power? In his attempt to answer this series of pressing preliminary questions, György Lengyel quoted his compatriot and forerunner István Bibó, when discussing "quality of elites" as degree of "social sensitivity", defined as both "*caritas*" and "a wide sense of culture-creating, needs-refining sensibility" (Bibo 2004/1942, as cited in Lengyel 2007: 6). To this, Lengyel adds predictability, accountability, replaceability – but only if one inquires on elites as a fully-fledged, comprehensive, unified, largely homogeneous group. If analysed as heterogeneous, fragmented, well-differentiated, easily distinguishable islands of political power forming an all-encompassing group under the banner of "political elites", the three features mentioned above might tell too little or close to nothing about the "quality of elites", about what makes a political elite actually an "elite". For the author of this study on local political elites, what seems of paramount importance in the definition of "political elites" in contemporaneity particularly in East-Central Europe are the capacity to negotiate, to alternate between conflict and consent, the willingness to compromise, the inclination to political and social dialogue, the ability to cooperate for the benefit of the community or for the "general good" and problem-solving capabilities. Providing for "the people", insuring sustainable well-being for the population and social justice for the masses are seen to be inscribed in the series of tricky preconditions a group in leading position should fulfil in order to become a "political elite"; the trickiness of these prerequisites lies in the fact that they borrow significantly from the normative stance and in the impossibility of comprehensively operationalizing and measuring the degree and fashion in which these conditions are fulfilled. This type of preconditions lacks instrumentality in the empirical study of elites. Eventually, although traditionally it has been distinguished between normative and descriptive perspectives on the definition and the problematic interpretation of the group of political elites – with the former retaining a significant emphasis on the moral dimension of the "leading few", while the later vigorously refuting it – the recent empirical efforts showed a certain degree of reconciliation between the two main trajectories, juxtaposing and combining the ethical model of political elites, with additional, supplementary model of thinking about elites (technocratic, political, pragmatic, gender).

Famously, Tom Bottomore aptly details on the infant steps of the word "*élite*" on the soil of social sciences: "The word '*élite*' was used in the seventeenth century to describe commodities of particular excellence [...]. In the English language the earliest known use of 'élite', according to the *Oxford English Dictionary*, is in 1823, at which time it was already applied to social groups. But the term did not become widely used in social and political writing until late in the nineteenth century in Europe, or until the 1930s in Britain and America, when it was diffused through the sociological theories of elites" (Bottomore 1964: 3), consecrated by the "neo-Machiavellians" or the classical Italian "elitists". Eventually, in contemporaneity, the elite studies favored a "functionalist theory of stratification"[3], according to which present-day "knowledge society" and its constant developments and subtleties present some complexities manageable only by a certain type of elite: the "meritocracy" model of power, presently fashionable in the literature consecrated to elites introduces the reader with a political elite who is highly skilled and experimented in public administration and government business, who is recruited based on some performance parameters out of a narrower and narrower pool of candidates, who

---

3   The phrase defining a new line in the elite theory is customarily associated with Davis and Moore 1945: 242-249.

is "talented" or benefits from a certain likeable or favorable "cultural capital"[4], but who becomes, consequently, more and more alienated with "the mass", the citizenry, widening the gap between the rulers and the ruled. In a literature review of social and political elites, from "neo-Machiavellians" to the contemporary debate, Patrick Akard differentiates between the conception of "functional elites" (specific to a certain area, institution, context, or activity, what Keller coins as "strategic elites" (Keller 1963)) and "political (ruling) elites", exerting "societal-level power" (Akard 2000: 2623); the latter are the focus of this endeavor.

Surely, the selection of "the chosen" (from the French "*élire*") is the prerogative of either "God, nature, or public esteem" (Girvetz 1967: 30). The "elitist paradigm", the elite theory, has developed considerably after the empiric studies and the theoretical recalibrations conducted under the guidance of Higley, Burton, and Best, among other Western sociologists and political scientists. The efforts of the Italian "elitists" have been surpassed, for, as Field and Higley rightly put it, "to advance elitist hypotheses today it is not enough merely to argue, as Pareto, Mosca and Michels could, that elites always or usually exist and that they are probably of decisive importance. In addition to this, it is now necessary to refute the widely held assumption that values such as equality, liberty and freedom are universal and objective. Probably only by making this refutation can contemporary thought be brought to see the importance and the propriety of elitist assumptions." (Field and Higley 1980: 3) Hence, the "elitist paradigm" is presently much more than the *problématique* of "[h]ow to govern oneself, how to be governed, how to govern others, by whom the people will accept being governed, how to become the best possible governor" (Foucault 1991/1978: 87).

The very incontestable reality that power has ceased to be regarded as unified, monolithic, unilateral, is being highlighted by American psychologist William A. Gamson, who differentiates between "authorities" (i.e. those who can make binding decisions in a particular social system", the rulers, the political elite), and the "potential partisans" (i.e. "those who are affected by the outcome of a particular decision in some significant way", the ruled). This is not to say that the power system is a static one, for "power" is to be analyzed symmetrically, bilateral: (a) "power" as "authorities acting on potential partisans (social control)", "targets of influence" and "agents of control", and (b) "power" as "potential partisans acting on authorities (influence)", or "agents of influence" or "targets of control", whose influence is exerted under the form of either "constraint" (i.e. "the exercise of influence by threat of deprivation") or "inducement" (i.e. the exercise of influence by "the promise of indulgence" (Lasswell and Kaplan 1950: 97, as cited in Gamson 1968)). Subsequently, one

---

4   One should not overlook the very fact that "talent", "cultural appreciation", "prestige" are part of the very difficulty in operationalizing and measuring the rise of the "new (i.e. meritocratic) elite".

can easily remark that power is exerted on both sides, on that of the ruler and on that of the ruled, although preeminence of the former is acknowledged. For a pluralist as Dahl, the "ruling elite" is "a controlling group less than a majority in size that is not a pure artifact of democratic rules. It is a minority of individuals whose preferences regularly prevail in cases of differences in preference on key political issues. […] [T]he composition of the ruling elite must be more or less definitely specified." (Dahl 1958: 464) Following Dahl, in a historical-political account on "power" seen as a "dispositional concept", Steven Lukes equates a "ruling elite" with a group of individuals verifying the three "tests": (a) "[t]he hypothetical ruling elite is a well-defined group"; (2) "[t]here is a fair sample of cases involving key political decisions in which the preferences of the hypothetical ruling elite run counter to those of any other likely group that might be suggested"; (3) "[i]n such cases, the preferences of the elite regularly prevail" (Lukes 1974; Lukes cites extensively from Dahl 1958: 466). Once with the integration and pluralism of power, elite manifestations embrace different features, facets, and forms. Famously, Mannheim differentiates between: (1) the "organizing and directing elites" (i.e. those groups of individuals in power managing concrete aspects of leadership, immediate goals and programmes), and (2) the "more diffuse and informally organized elites" (Mannheim 1940/1935) (i.e. those groups of individuals in power managing more abstract matters of leadership, such as spiritual, cultural, artistic, or moral problems). But one of the most profoundly constructed classifications of elites belongs to Suzanne Keller, who differentiates among four types of elites, based on the four "functional problems which every society must resolve": (1) "goal attainment" (i.e. "the setting and realization of collective goals"), (2) "adaptation" (i.e. "the use and development of effective means of achieving these goals"), (3) "integration" (i.e. "the maintenance of appropriate moral consensus and social cohesion within the system"), and (4) "pattern maintenance and tension management" (i.e. "the morale of the system's units – individuals, groups, and organizations" (Keller 1968: 27)). Keller's resulting four types of "strategic elites" are: (1) "elites of goal attainment" (or the current, existing political elite); (2) "elites of adaptation" (the economic, military, scientific, diplomatic elites); (3) "elites of integration" (elites exerting moral authority, from priests, philosophers, spiritual leaders, to educators, teachers, and first families); and (4) "pattern-maintenance elites" (elite charged with "keep[ing] the society knit together emotionally and psychologically", from celebrities, artists, writers, actors, pop stars, to top figures in sports and recreation and entertainment) (Keller 1968: 27 [addition mine]). This web of functions is generally applicable for industrialized societies, in which the four types of "strategic elites" operate more and more independently of each other. The very formation of what Keller coins "strategic elites" is a historical process, during which firstly the "ruling caste", then the "aristocracy", afterwards the "ruling class" succeed each other in different ages of government. Eventually, "strategic elites" come to denote, in Keller's vocabulary, "those elites which claim or are assigned responsibilities for and influence over their society as a whole, in contrast with segmental elites, which have major responsibilities in subdomains of the society" (Keller 1968: 26), consequently having "the largest, most comprehensive scope and impact" upon society.

Indeed, the preservation of the ruling class and its very self-identification are dependent upon the moderation of the pressures exerted from *populous*, from the popular masses. Hence, Frank Bonilla aptly contends that "[a]t issue here is a fundamental feature of self-image among elites and a keystone of any ideology or theory of political development. As a result of the consolidation of elite power in countries where democracy has survived longest, such groups have come to be widely regarded as the most genuinely dynamic and innovative force and as the guarantors of continuity in national systems. In this view the vital functions of *the gifted, the expert,* and *the entrepreneurially able* require that they be shielded from mass pressures." (Bonilla 1970: 256 [italics added]) Canonically, one can discern from here the paradoxical position of elites in democracy, with regard to the scrutiny of the citizenry. Quite clearly, in opposition to any pluralist-tailored assertion, "elites comprise fairly closed units, and [...] inequalities in the distribution of power (the resources that facilitate the exercise of power) tend to be cumulative, meaning that resourceful agents are better equipped to increase their power and their resources for exercising power than those who are deprived of resources." (Dyrberg 1997: 43)[5] This is the typical, canonical presumption of the reproduction of power, consonantal to Lasswell's "agglutination" model of political elites, detailed below.

With this knowledge in mind we will now turn our attention to the small constituencies of Tecuci, Česká Lípa, Oleśnica, Gyula, Targovishte, and Levice, as we will attempt to restate by means of example all which was said above. This unerring test of all arguments will shed further light upon the broad issue of political elites by looking into the ways and manners in which the local leaderships of Tecuci, Česká Lípa, Oleśnica, Gyula, Targovishte, and Levice are made manifest and the implications it entails.

The intention to study local political elites through the prism of Local and Municipal Councils is motivated by the general study of patterns of government at the level of small-to-medium-sized communities and by the inquiry in the role played and the features displayed by the elites of these type of communities, with a special emphasis on the transitional space of East-Central Europe. Particularly in the context of a marked tendency towards increased devolution and decentralization, the local political elites acquire a specifically important set of new prerogatives.

---

5   Studying historical conceptualizations of power, Dyrberg emphasizes Foucault's "nominalistic and presuppositionless conceptualization of power that is both epistemologically and ontologically coterminous with power as 'the ability to make a difference'." (p. 116)

Brief Literature Review of the Territory
of Local Leadership

"Power" is an "ability"[6]; as holders of power, the political elite bears the ability to decide over the community. If the *ouvres* of the "Italian elitists" were equally empirical to the ones undertaken in the 1970s, when the elite studies reached a climax, only with the latter, political elites were employed as a means to identify the specific characteristics of national political institutions; this new line of analysis has been labeled "the second generation of empirical studies" (Czudnowski 1983: 243-255), with a special significance for the study of local representative bodies, for instance.

The literature dedicated to the study of local political elites is impressively reduced: the bulk of this literature derives from the broad study of political elites and consequently dates from the 1970s, once with the climax reached by the elitist empirical studies. In this respect, the most frequently quoted, the renowned *oeuvre* pertains to Robert Dahl who constructed its poliarchic model on the study of the municipality of New Haven. Among the most prominent studies on the slippery and feeble soil of local political elites, the mentionable titles are the pioneering works authored by Robert Staughton and Helen Merrell Lynd, *Middletown* (1929) and *Middletown in Transition* (1937)[7], undertaken in Muncie (Indiana). Despite the anthropological overload of their volumes, it is important to bear in mind that the two American scholars were among the first to endeavor in such an inductively-driven urban inquiry, and the first to consider the impact of economic changes and development strategies on various segments of the town's population, including the leading *strata* of the community, on these segments' values and behaviors. Lynds' work is equally significant for it paves the way for Dahl's future observations, stressing on the relevance of power – even in the very confined, narrow space of a small town – and on the place of economic notables in Muncie, the "businessmen", on their conspicuous influence upon the political leadership of the town and on the entire activity and life of the urban community. From the prism of these conclusions, when discussing the "Middletown Studies", Nelson Polsby (1963: 14) labels them as "Marxist" (for they contend that property among the means of production provides for absolute power within a municipality) and the

---

6   "Power" as "ability", as external to the "subject", as "influence" and "decision-making", is a standard reference in behaviourist studies. See, for prominently, Ball 1975: 211-222.
7   Even though predominantly anthropological, the so-called "Middletown Studies" are indeed groundbreaking for the study of the local political elites, as well, as they are the first empirical undertakings to consider the importance of local leadership on the developmental strategies of a town.

representatives of the "stratification theory" in elitist studies, for they ultimately reach the conclusion that the local elite is the one that possess political power – usually springing from other form of power exerted at the local level, e.g. economical –, as an instrument for governing the community in accordance to its own vernacular interests. Illustrative for the cases selected here (particularly for the Romanian case), although they stress on the "net separation" between the economical institutions and the political ones, even at the local level, the Lynds do acknowledge the immanent interdependence between the two institutions and leadership, since "those that dominate from an economic standpoint the community exert their control on the political problems, as well, only to avoid the too accentuated increase in taxation or a too strong involvement in their own affairs [by the political leadership].Otherwise, they are totally disinterested in the political life." (Lynd and Lynd 1937: 129) This assessment might appear yet too hazardous, taking into consideration the frequency and the intensity of interactions and network formation between the political and the economic elites; a series of tentative evaluations somehow antagonizing with Lynds' conclusion are drawn from the present study, but, while the American study is focused on Muncie in the 1920s and 1930s, the present study is extremely contingent on Tecuci, Česká Lípa, Oleśnica, Gyula, Targovishte, and Levice in 2010-2015, making hence opposite views and results virtually irreconcilable for the simple fact that the two studies are circumscribed to particular instances, settings and time frames, with no pretence to exhaustive generalizations. As a matter of fact, the Lynds' studies on "Middletown" and their feeble conclusions in respect to the connections between economic and political elite at the local level (dominantly in urban areas) opened the way for similar, more mature and more meaningful empirical endeavors oriented towards the analysis of the said connections and of their impact on the developmental strategies and the general profile of the urban communities; notable in this sense is William Lloyd Warner's study on "Yankee City" (Newburyport, Massachusetts)[8], the hypothetical urban center dominated by entrepreneurs, businessmen, freelancers and liberal professionals, who managed to forge a sort of "class consciousness" and who virtually ousted any

---

8   William Lloyd Warner's study on "Yankee City" includes five volumes: Warner, W. L. & Lunt, P. S. (1941). The Social Life of a Modern Community. Yankee City Series, Vol. I. New Haven, Conn.: Yale University Press; Warner, W. L. & Lunt, P. S. (1942). The Status System of a Modern Community. Yankee City Series, Vol. II. New Haven, Conn.: Yale University Press; Warner, W. L. & Strole, L. (1945). The Social Systems of American Ethnic Groups. Yankee City Series, Vol. III. New Haven, Conn.: Yale University Press; Warner, W. L. & Low, J. O. (1947). The Social System of a Modern Factory. Yankee City Series, Vol. IV. New Haven, Conn.: Yale University Press; Warner, W. L. (1959). The Living and the Dead: A Study in the Symbolic Life of Americans. Yankee City Series, Vol. V. New Haven, Conn.: Yale University Press. See also the abridgement of the series, under the title Warner, W. L. (1963). Yankee City. New Haven, Conn.: Yale University Press.

trace of autonomy from the political institutions. Surely, such a stance is too vehement and radical, since it implies the blunt reality that, at the local level, the economic elite is the one that ultimately governs in town. Notwithstanding his categorical positions, Warner and his work on "Yankee City" are to be kept in mind when endeavoring in the thin and narrow field of local political leadership at least from two perspectives: firstly, his observations are heavily utilized and partly confirmed – albeit in a nuanced form – by the present research, which point to the pertinence and contemporaneity thereof; secondly, he employs a singular method, that of an "index of evaluated participation" (i.e. the construction of a scale comprising the expertise's evaluation of the "prestige" enjoyed by key-individuals within the community, and their placing on the social hierarchy), quite similar to Hunter's method (presented below and further utilized, as well, in this study), which stresses and manages somehow to operationalize the concept of elite "prestige"[9]. Soon after Warner's "Yankee City" studies had known scholarly recognition, Floyd Hunter advanced a resembling work, conducted in "Regional City" (different researches in Atlanta, Georgia) among the members of the local upper class. Hunter's findings are strikingly similar to Warner's: as in "Yankee City", in "Regional City", "the businessmen are the leaders of the community [...], as they actually are in any town. The wealth, the social prestige and the political machinery are functional to the wielding of power by these leaders." (Hunter 1953: 81; see also Hunter, Schaffer, and Sheps 1956) In confronting dilemmas of "prestige" and "reputation" of local notables, Hunter contends that "their visual influence [and virtual recognition] is transformed into power". Yet again, the study is diverged towards the economic portions of the ruling class, while the local political elite is completely overshadowed by the magnitude of the reputation the businessmen possess. The emphasis on the predominance and preeminence of the economic elite on local decision-making and on its "caste" behavior are furthered in Delbert Miller's inquiry into "Pacific City", although this time the scholar minds about the political decision-makers, as well, mentioning their role as mere "counterbalance" for the interests of local big business (Miller 1985: 9-15, esp. 13-15). If C. Wright Mills is central for the "positional method", Warner and Hunter are exemplary for the "reputational method", Robert Dahl's *Poliarchy* and *Who Governs?* (1961) are the referential works for the "decisional method"[10]: the research in New Haven (Connecticut) revealed that those who hold the political power are essentially that quite exclusive group of

---

9   Actually, Warner's scale and Hunter's method of accounting for elite "prestige" lie at the fundament of the "reputational method".

10 Ivor Crewe identifies three "research traditions" in the study of power: the "reputational" tradition (whose object of study are the "images of power"), the "structural" tradition (called here "positional", whose object of study are the "positions of power"), and the "decisional" tradition (whose object of study are the "agencies of power"). See: Crewe 1974: 9-54.

individuals who take a decision, i.e. who initiates a proposition and who subsequently validates or opposes it. Definitely, the scope of Dahl's study is laudable, as his primary intention was to provide a rejoinder to both Marxist and elitist interpretations on local politics and to somehow "rehabilitate" the traditional image and model of the American democracy – even at the local level – as veritably democratic and integral, hence refuting Mills's, Warner's and Hunter's "invitations" to perceiving national and local elites as some sort of complotistic and clandestine caste. Dahl's elites are factionalist, fragmentary, placed in a continuous fight for the control over society (similar to the struggle between "lions" and "foxes" in Pareto's accounts); it is their meeting and their subsequent negotiations in the decision-making process that actually matters in describing elites. Surely, these factional leaders and groups do agree on the very basis of the "rules of the democratic game" and on the accountability of the citizens, making "poliarchy" probably the best "approximation" of democracy. On the other hand, the observations drawn from the small town of New Haven conclude: the central position of the Mayor, who participates to decision-making in all spheres of competence; the extreme specialization of the elite group; the absence of economic elites in the process of decision-making at the local level (with the partial exception of decisions taken in the sphere of urban development), etc. Notwithstanding the importance of and the central role played by these works in the general scholarly evolution of the local elite studies, quite unfortunately, few of them concentrated their attention and interest in the composition of the Municipal Council as legislative centers of power at the local level, particularly within small-to-medium sized communities. In opposition to Hunter's "ruling-elite" model, to Mills' "power-elite", to the "stratification model" advanced, for the local level, by Lynds, W. Lloyd Warner, to the "mass-society" theory put forward by Mills, Vidich and Bensman, and Warner and Lowe, are all to be the expected targets of theoretical – but, most importantly – empirical attack by the "pluralist" theories, whose *spiritus rector* is Robert Dahl, and whose major achievements are linked to such notions as "decentralized power structures, fragmented causation, [and] complex systems" (McFarland 1969: 32). But, the pluralist "drive" is, in itself, particularly heterogeneous. Andrew McFarland identifies two "major chains of reasoning" (McFarland 1969: 32-33) in the pluralist vain: (a) the "community-power" studies (e.g. Dahl, Nelson Polsby, Aaron Wildavsky), studies that are characterized by a virulent and unmediated attack on the then widely embraced and canonical "power-elite" theory; and (b) the "group-process" theory (e.g. A.F. Bentley, David Truman), a milder attack on "oversimplification" and "insufficient empiricism" (Bentley 1908).

Apart from the canonical Western studies on local political elites, from Lynds' to Warner's, one should not overlook the empirical efforts, started in the first years of democratic transition in East-Central Europe and in other countries of the "developing world". One of the most important ones has been undertaken by "The Democracy and Local Governance Research Program", resulting in two extended and systematic studies including national reports on the local political leaders' perceptions on internal globalization of their localities, on democratization dynamics, and on the general evolution of the localities (Jacob, Ostrowski, and Teune 1993; Jacob, Linder, Nabholz, and Hierli 1999).

The two major scholarly pieces that majorly influenced the present study are Samuel Eldersveld's *Political Elites in Modern Societies* (1989) and Virgil Stoica's *Cine conduce Iaşul?* (2004). The former constitutes a series of three lectures sprung out of the empirical inquiries conducted in the late 1970s in Ann Arbor (Michigan) among the political activists of the town. The latter is a remarkably compelling and extremely close to exhaustiveness study of the local elite in Iaşi (Romania) after 1989; the research is focused on the mayors succeeding in the leadership of the city, on the municipality's functionaries and on the members of the Local Council, without actually (or always) discriminating among these three clusters.

The population of this research was constituted by the local political elites in ECE middle-sized towns (i.e. with a population ranging from 25,000 inhabitants to 250,000 inhabitants). Broadly, the present study will focus on seven main topics: (1) the Local (Municipal) Council as a group of local political elites and as an instance of political power at the local level (general presentation and main functions); (2) the social biography of the members of the six Local (Municipal) Councils under scrutiny; (3) patterns of recruitment of these local elites and the importance of the local branches of the main parties; (4) interactions of the members of the Local (Municipal) Councils with other groups and institutions (and the subsequent power networks and formal and informal linkages); (5) values and principles embraced by the local political elites in the six analyzed cases; (6) priorities of the local political elites in the six selected Local (Municipal) Councils, and (7) representativeness of the Local (Municipal) Councils in the six towns, in the context in which the Local Council (Municipal) is an instance of legislative representative government. In order to account for the various differences and discrepancies and the equally challenging similarities among the six cases, the present endeavor favors two main tentative explanatory trajectories, namely (1) the present level of decentralization specific to each of the countries whose municipalities are the case-studies here, and (2) the "legacy of the *ancien régime*", peculiar to the six countries of the former Sovietized Europe; two separate sections are dedicated to the development of these two independent variables. A final section proposes and develops on a typology of local political elites, which distinguishes among (1) "predominantly elitistic" local elites, (2) "democratic elitist" local elites, and (3) "predominantly democratic" local elites, in the attempt to systematize and generalize the observations drawn from the six cases, and to add theoretical substance to the topic of local political leadership. A concluding section is summarizing and closes the present endeavor.

Brief Digression on the National Elites in East-Central Europe: Elites Effectuating Change

"It is difficult for the elites to discern exactly what society wants [...], society itself finds it difficult to define its interests [...], the political elite does not receive from society strong and specific signals about what is expected of it. This gives the political elite considerable freedom to choose the precise path of reform and to determine how the 'general will' ought to be translated into detailed measures. The decisions of the political elite are characterized, then, by a high level of social indeterminism." (Wesołowski 1992: 77-100)

Within the transitional process towards democracy, a central role of paramount importance is played by the elites. A special discussion should be reserved to the literature within the realm of transitology, since the six Municipal Councils under scrutiny are functioning in towns of countries of former Sovietized Europe, experiencing state socialism for almost half-a-century. Consequently – and as the "legacy of the *ancien régime*" is intensely and extensively employed as an explanatory route –, the book utilizes pieces of transitology developing on the theories concerning the "new elite" of East-Central Europe following the communist breakdown and the "elite circulation" vs. "elite reproduction" paradigm, famously elaborated in the *oeuvres* of Szelényis, Eyal, Hankiss, Szalai, Lengyel, Pakulski, Seleny, etc. Moreover, the former communist dictatorships, irrespective of their variant, were organized as "elitist" societies, with an elite structure that is "typically more centralized in the fused party, military [or rather police], and state-administrative bodies, power [being] more concentrated at the executive apex, and elite selection [being] more clientelist." (Dogan 1989) According to Konrád and Szelényi's intelligent analysis during the last decade of state socialism in Hungary, three are the conditions that markedly define the "communist" society and state, from an elite and counter-elite prism: (1) "the state has a monopoly in the economy"; (2) "social structure of [the] society is marked by a hierarchy, in which political loyalty and educational credentials determine the individual's *status*"; and (3) both the society and the state are "under the rule of a Party that identifies itself as Marxist-Leninist" (Konrad and Szelényi 1991: 339). For the analysis to follow, Konrád and Szelényi's most significant observations are those regarding the *embourgeoisment* of the establishment intellectuals and of the incipient middle-class (Konrad and Szelenyi 1991: 345-346), formed, in East-Central Europe, especially after the Kádárist "*gulyáskommunizmus*"; the social standing and positioning of these categories are telling for the manner in which future elites will identify their family background and their first instances of political socialization. Therefore, a discussion on the profile of ECE political elites, generally, appears imperiously necessary at this point.

36

This chapter is a short digression into the tentative examination of the process of elite transformation in the six countries of East-Central Europe experiencing regime change in 1989. More particularly, this introductory inquiry is instrumental for the study of local political elites in East-Central Europe, for it partly explains the profile of the main artisans of power at the local level in East-Central Europe, by analyzing their social background, their political inclinations and the values embraced. Considerations on the transitional paths undertaken by the ECE countries, in respect to the elites triggering regime change, will be further drawn. The main argument put forward is that, along with the nature of the regime, the cultural traits and the specific internal and external conjuncture, the profile and the role of both the governing and, most significantly, the alternative elites put a definitive imprint on the transitional paths and the major priorities of each of the East-Central European countries. The circulation and the reproduction of elites in Central and Eastern Europe after 1989 become instrumental in this respect. The pertinent questions regarding post-communist leadership and elite recruitment following the regime change have been already addressed by a range of prominent scholars of the region: "[W]hat happened to socialist elites with the transition to postcommunism? Who were the people who held command positions under socialism, and how were these people affected by the post-communist transformation? If there was a change in the composition of Eastern European elites, what happened to the old cadres and where did the new elites come from?" Furthermore, in their inquiry of 1995 on elite transformation in post-communist Europe, Iván Szelényi and Szonja Szelényi distinguish between two, somehow opposing, theories: (1) the "elite reproduction theory", and (2) the "elite circulation theory" (Szelényi and Szelényi 1995: 615-638). The elite reproduction theory argues that the *annus mirabilis* 1989 failed to put a revolutionary imprint on the composition of political elites. Since the revolutions in East-Central Europe bore a non-violent character – in two cases (Poland and Hungary), negotiated "roundtable talks", in other three (East Germany, Czechoslovakia and Bulgaria), non-negotiated, still non-violent revolutions, the only violent exception being Romania –, a complete overthrow of the *nomenklatura* was virtually impossible. Hence, the former *nomenklatura*, though fragmented and repudiated, preserved some of its positions and perpetuated themselves in power, in the newly formed structures. On the other hand, the elite circulation theory postulates that the revolutions did manage to trigger a restructuring in the composition of elites, by installing new principles and rules for the recruitment of such elites. In Poland, for instance, the newly-formed leadership denounced the "elite reproduction theory", by claiming that top members of the former *nomenklatura* were allowed to become proprietors and were enjoying other similar benefits. This situation was envisaged as early as 1989, that is from the very beginning, by the Hungarian scholar Elemér Hankiss (1990) who convincingly argued that the "old elite", as opposed to the former party rank-and-file, would soon reconfigure itself into the "new grande bourgeoisie" as soon as the market economy is installed; therefore, while it might not remain the political elite, the former leadership will switch to become the new economic elite. The same conclusion seems to have been reached by Polish political scientist Jadwiga Staniszkis, in his *The Dynamics of Breakthrough in Eastern Europe*, by suggesting that members of the former first echelons of power would tend to employ their political power to acquire private wealth (Staniszkis 1991). Resembling concerns were raised in all the six former communist countries, concerns linked to both the superficiality of the revolution and its limited transformations and to what may be conducted as a "witch-hunt" within the leadership strata of these transitional states. In addition, it resulted that the processes of privatization and formation of free market economy would benefit, again, the former Communist political elite.

In the dynamics of elite change and communist breakdown followed by the initiation of democratic transition, three possibilities are identified by Higley and Pakulski: (a) "increasingly unchecked and violent power struggles between elites, with regimes oscillating between democratic and authoritarian forms"; (2) "restrained elite competitions in accordance with democratic game rules and tacit accommodations, with regimes gradually becoming stable democracies"; and (3) "takeovers by ultra-nationalist elites through *coups* or plebiscitary victories, with regimes becoming state-corporatist in form and *quasi*-fascist in operation" (Higley and Pakulski 1995: 415-435).

During the first years of democratic transition, it seemed that the economic and political reforms gravitated around a vicious circle that led to the same, initial point: the position and the role played by the former leadership in the newly-established democracies. Renowned scholar of political elites John Higley defines elites as exceptionally "small groups of persons who occupy strategic positions in powerful institutions, organizations, and movements and who therefore play a disproportionate and often decisive role in revolutions." (Higley 1998: 153; see also, for further analysis, Higley 2009) In this respect, the importance of the "counterelites" (i.e. those elites opposing and alternative the governing or the ruling elites) is central to any discussion on regime change in East-Central Europe at the end of the 1980s and the beginning of the 1990s. Much more detailed studies on leadership in East-Central Europe have shown that, in those countries in which regime criticism was to some extent allowed – the "national accommodative" dictatorships of Poland and Hungary – a separate elite gradually formed in opposition to the "old *nomenklatura*": the so-called "new elite", or "the new class" (Bozóki 2001; see also Bozóki 2007) or "the new technocracy" (Szalai 1994: 61-114) a younger, highly educated (specialized in the technocratic sense) group of individuals, envisioning radical socio-political and economic transformation as the only viable solution for the regime survival and proving itself willing to negotiate with the opposition groups: "bureaucrats", "technocrats", "engineers", "managers", "critical, counter-cultural, adversary culture intellectuals" (Martin and Szelényi 1988: 645-667)[11], etc. Surely, the rise of new elites produces implacably the marginalization of other groups and factions: "The less-privileged groups that are negatively affected become hostile and resentful toward the newly developing elites [...], may react to the change brought by [such] development[s] with indifference and eventually stop participating in the community." (Dogan 1989: 226) This group was one of the essential parts, the "regime softliners", in the "roundtable" talks of 1989, in the four player-game of the "pacted revolution", conceptualized by Juan Linz and Alfred Stepan (1996: 356). Of course, as the largest part of the scholarly warns, the "sofliners" appropriated, in its own benefit, privileged positions among the economic elite, transferring the political power in the hands of the communist opposition, reserving for itself the possibility to exert pressure on the new, democratic political leadership. Elsewhere, in the "patrimonial" or "modernizing-nationalizing" dictatorships of Romania and Bulgaria[12], the "elite reproduction" hypothesis verifies in a rather exhaustive fashion. The scholarly has already reached a consensus that the "palace *coup d'état*" in Bulgaria and the much-contested Romanian revolution failed in promoting in leadership positions a new, anti-communist elite, but they rather replace – more or less violently – the old, top echelons with the second-ranked party personnel, rhetorically reformist, but conservative in practice and policies, the initiators of rather "neo-communist" regimes as instances of transitional democracies. Generally, as Iván Szelényi concludes, in a study for *Theory and Society* review, the only aspects that changed in leadership following the movements of 1989 were "the principles by which they [i.e. the elites] legitimate their authority, power, and privilege". In specific cases, as it is shown, this book tends to disagree with the above-mentioned assertion. While it is true that genuine circulation of elite failed to produce in "patrimonial" communist dictatorships[13], replacements in leadership and in political elite composition did happen at least partially in the "welfare" dictatorships of East Germany and Czechoslovakia and, to a greater extent in the "national-accommodative" state socialisms[14].

---

11 Martin and Szelényi reclaim a constant ambiguity, among scholars, with respect to the central concepts in the "new class theory".

12 The phrase "modernizing-nationalizing" communist dictatorships, in reference to the Romanian and the Bulgarian cases, is used by Petrescu 2010: 48 and 404.

13 As a matter of fact, the transitological study of Irina Culic on political elites concludes that the former nomenklatura has reproduced itself, but a limited circulation allowed the rise of a technocracy (favored by the second-ranked of the former regime). See: Culic 2002: esp. 60-78.

14 The distinction between "national-accommodative" (Poland and Hungary), "bureaucratic-authoritarian" (GDR and Czechoslovakia) and "patrimonial" (Romania and Bulgaria) communist dictatorship is conceptualized in Kitschelt, Mansfeldova, Markowski, and Tóka 1999: 39-40. "Welfare" communist dictatorship (for GDR and Czecho-

Hence, (1) in the two countries experiencing revolutionary change towards democracy through negotiated, non-violent "roundtable" talks, i.e. Poland and Hungary, the entire communist elite was downwardly mobile on the political ladder, being replaced by the members of the anti-communist or reform opposition groups; (2) in the three countries facing the step towards democratic transition through the means of a non-negotiated, though non-violent revolution, i.e. East Germany, Czechoslovakia and Bulgaria (despite the great differences in the "paths" and "tasks" of each of these three cases of transition), partial replacement did occur, with significant parts of the former leadership being downwardly mobile, while democratic alternative groups and some reformer neo-communist groups meeting an upwardly mobility on the political hierarchy of the newly-established democracies. (3) Finally, the special case of Romania, that went through a violent, therefore non-negotiated revolution, is puzzling for the scholarly, in the sense that, until 1996, only the allegedly reformist – often coined as "neo-communist" – group of second-ranked party members, formed around Ion Iliescu, actually experienced an upwardly mobility in leadership. During the first years of the troubling Romanian transition, this group systematically limited all opposition and the forms of civil society still in its infancy, sometimes even violently.

Reproduction is often substituted by "persistence", a term employed by John Higley, Judith Kullberg and Jan Pakulski, in their "The Persistence of Postcommunist Elites" (Higley, Kullberg, and Pakulski 1996: 133-147). What the three authors describe a regime change that takes place peacefully with the complicity of the old elites, who "opted for adaptation, instead of struggle; they survived the collapse of communist regimes and adapted themselves to new conditions." Within the landscape of transitology, a similar theoretical construct is carried on by Anna Seleny, when the scholar refers to the dynamics of compromise and confrontation in Poland and Hungary and "old political rationalities" in the "new democracies"; the argument pleads for a "significant" elite circulation in the two countries, but, in spite of it, those "old political rationalities", influenced by (1) "the nature of core conflicts between communist political elites and society" and by (2) "the patterns of political accommodation", seem to be the rule in East-Central Europe (Seleny 1999: 484-519). Hence, persistence in Higley and Pakulski's framework becomes in Seleny's hypothesis "old political rationalities", present and pregnant in the postcommunist era and rooted in the mechanisms of "pretransition conceptual frames and informal political settlements". Nonetheless, classical threefold differentiation of communist regimes / democratic transitions / levels of democratization is simplified by Seleny in the form of the dichotomous distinction between the group of "stable and essentially consolidated democratic systems" (Poland, Hungary, the Czech Republic) and the "highly problematic camp" (Slovakia,

---

slovakia) is the alternative term for "bureaucratic-authoritarian" dictatorship, employed by Jarausch 1999: 59-60.

Bulgaria, Romania, but also Russia, the countries of former Yugoslavia and Albania), characterized "feudalization of the polity", "extremes of corruption", "fervid ethno-nationalism", and "demagogic populism". Discussing the first group, Seleny describes two models of elite circulation during transition and successful democratization: Poland – the "confrontational-pluralist" country – , and Hungary – the "compromise-corporatist" paradigm. "Confrontational-pluralist" Poland is a democracy with "high levels of political mobilization, contentious party competition around several overlapping, deep ethical-ideological cleavages, relatively low levels of elite consensus, and a moralistic political discourse" (Seleny 1999: 488); a major influence in this "moralistic" content of the Polish elite rhetoric is exerted by the Catholic dogma. At the opposite pole, the Hungarian model of "compromise-corporatist" democracy proposes "low levels of political mobilization, relatively high levels of elite consensus and bargaining, and a generally 'economistic' or pragmatic political discourse" (Seleny 1999: 488). Undoubtedly, the nature of values, principles, priorities of the national elite played a decisive role in shaping the pathway to democratic consolidation and socio-economic development to be followed by the two countries. Though both successful democratic experiments, Seleny emphasizes, Poland and Hungary represent, to some extent, divergent models of arranging elite relations and social conflict on democratic pillars. Even so, one can easily argue the fact that Poland, despite its "confrontational" facet, enjoyed, in the crucial moment of 1989, the elite consensus managed after the inaugural Roundtable Talks. Even though the Polish politics seem today some sort of a battlefield, with irreconcilable divergences, unresolved conflicts and insurmountable cleavages, with clearly established political camps unavailable for coalition and collaboration, describing Sartori's "polarized pluralism" (Sartori 1966: 137-176), the Polish elites proved capable of compromise particularly in moments that went beyond normal politics, during episodes of intended radical change and sometimes gradually, in a piecemeal fashion (exemplifying, in this sense, is former dissident and major intellectual Adam Michnik's *rapprochement* with General Jaruzelski, "the communist in uniform" of the last decade of Polish state socialism). On the long run, however, at the societal level, the confrontational characteristic remained a constant in Poland, for, permanently during the communist regime and afterwards, open protests (strikes, demonstrations, etc.) against the leadership put a marked imprint on the relations between the state and the society. It might be true: the Hungarian society and political scene appear more consensual. Besides the conspicuousness of consensus displayed during the Roundtable Talks, the Hungarian political elite seemed to be inclined to compromise with the population and to avoid any open confrontation. Elites in Hungary, prior and after 1989, proved willing to reach a consensus with the society, especially after the lessons taught by the Revolution of 1956; the Kádárist "tacit compact" is instrumental in this sense. Post-communist elites perpetuated this practice and encouraged low popular

41

mobilization, particularly because politics is perceived as an occupation reserved to elites and any "popular" involvement might prove to be explosive.

Renowned scholars of political elites, John Higley and György Lengyel, discuss the issue of elite circulation vs. reproduction, by identifying and connecting four distinct types of elite configuration in East-Central Europe with four corresponding types of elite circulation. Therefore, (1) a "consensual elite" is the one characterizing "classic circulation" (i.e. "wide and deep in its scope, but gradual and peaceful in its mode"), (2) a "fragmented elite" is the feature of "reproduction circulation" (i.e. "narrow and shallow in scope, gradual and peaceful in mode"); (3) an "ideocratic elite" accompanies "replacement circulation" (i.e. "wide and deep in scope, sudden and enforced in mode"), and (4) a "divided elite" is the agent of "quasi-replacement circulation" (i.e. "narrow and shallow in scope, sudden and enforced in mode") (Higley and Lengyel, 2000: 1-21, esp. 4-7). Somewhat opposing Higley and his complicated framework, Frane Adam and Matevž Tomšič – two scholars discussing in particular the Slovenian case – redefine Szelényis' elite circulation-reproduction theory, by distinguishing between what they coined almost poetically "catalysts of social innovation" and "rent-seekers" (Adam and Tomšič 2000: 138-160)[15].

As Aviezer Tucker, following Holmes, puts it, "decommunization is a struggle between elites" (Holmes 1994: 33-36), i.e. "new non-Communist politicians and unsuccessful dissidents against the *nomenklatura*, the reformed Communist political parties, the government bureaucracy, the police, the military, the secret police, the judiciary, and the managers of the economy." (Tucker 2006: 192) Despite the "dark" and rather pessimistic perspective Tucker advances in calling the Eastern and Central European dissidents "unsuccessful", there is, in his simplified picture of the "struggle between elites" in the eve of democratic transition, a quite pertinent observation: the new, non- / anti-Communist centers of power had to face with a never-ending Pleiade of alternative centers of power, decision-making and influence, constantly attempting at curtailing the democratic trajectory, particularly for preserving their positions and benefits from the *status quo ante*. In the vacuum of power created in the days of 1989, the non-Communist elite enjoyed the feeble legitimacy provided by its democratic message, which reached the masses with its ideals of liberty, free market economy, rule of law. In some cases, after few years, in the second electoral test, the democratic leadership of the transitional countries proved unable to retain power and was fatally defeated by the neo- and reformist Communists, who consecrated a virtual *interregnum* in the chronology of democracy, a *hiatus* in the path towards fully-fledged democracy. A second issue revolving around the discussion on the difficulties of the new leading elite bears a popular nuance: the political revolutions of 1989, the

---

15 The discussion is continued in Adam and Tomšič 2002: 435-454.

regime change in East-Central Europe triggered rather uncontrollable popular expectations which the non-Communist leaders at the debut of transition were unable to manage and fulfill. The citizens' disillusionment and disdain with the new democratic power structure came predictably and abruptly, and it resulted in the electoral return to power of the Communist-oriented groups. (Nonetheless, they too proved economically and socially inefficient.)[16]

It is Tucker again, in his discussion of political actors as independent variables in the process of transitional justice after 1989, that distinguishes among four types of "democratically elected representatives" in the new context of an infant democracy, i.e. four types of political elites in East Central Europe: (1) the "non-Communists" (either former dissidents, opponents of the regime, or those living in-between, in the so-called "gray zone", i.e. mainly professionals who entered politics after 1989 and who had previously neither collaborated with nor resisted to or opposed the regime, but rather survived making those small necessary compromises); (2) the "former communists" (a necessary and inevitable "evil" in the first years of transition, when they were able to retain power, in the absence of viable alternative elites, generally until the first free elections); (3) the "reformed communists" (portrayed as "Western-style left-wing" politicians, rather socialists or social-democrats, on the model consecrated in the highly developed democracies), and (4) the "old communists" (a quite peculiar specie, since it managed quite cleverly, by successfully preserving their monopolies on the former "fiefdoms" and by being actively involved in corrupt moves within the privatization process after 1989, to prosper economically) (Tucker 2006: 182-183). The "old communists" are central to the present discussion, for they were unique in reconverting themselves as an elite: they were the political elite in the *ancien régime*, they are the economical elite in the *nouveau régime*. Moreover, for the purpose of being spared of any manifestation of transitional justice upon them – which, nevertheless, they have constantly hampered so far –, they acknowledge their allegiance to an unbreakably unified group whose main principle was internal solidarity and which preserved its monolithism as the sole, *sine qua non* condition to survive unchanged and intangibly as an elite in the strange and unpredictable waters of transition. In the context of a still confused and fragmented democratic leadership during the first decade of transition, the reformed communists managed

---

16   Indeed, the notion of "decommunization" is inextricably linked to the role, actions, evolution, nature of post-communist elites. Furthermore, following Gonzalez Enriquez, one can distinguish among three species of "decommunization" in Central and Eastern Europe, analogous to the type of political elites dominating in each case: (1) "the failed de-communization", in Poland and Hungary; (2) "the symbolic de-communisation", in Slovakia, Bulgaria and Romania, and (3) "the significant de-communisation", in Czechoslovakia, the Czech Republic and Albania. As a rule, elites used the term "decommunization" as a "fig leaf", ostensibly, i.e. as a smoke screen in the face of the electorate, while the elites generally followed the lines of the reproduction theory. See Gonzalez Enriquez 1998: 277-295.

to gather the popular vote, usually in the second free elections after 1989: examples are to be found in the Polish parliamentary elections of 1993 and in the Hungarian elections of May 1994. Therefore, for East-Central Europe, Pierre Bourdieu's thesis of the convertibility of political capital into economic capital (Bordeau 1986: 241-258) is, to a great extent, clearly verifiable. Its limitations refer more specifically to the Hungarian case, where, as Szalai discriminates, the "new political elite" (i.e. former dissidents, representatives of the "gray zone", anti-communists, etc.) turned its cultural (to some degree, moral) capital into political one. The "old elite" (the Party leaders prior to 1956), enjoying exclusively a political capital, experienced a definitive fall after the Hungarian Revolution, its Stalinist practices becoming soon anachronistic; with the economic restrictions of state socialism, they were unable to convert their political capital into an economic one, and after 1989, their importance as political actors was completely and irrecoverably lost. The opposite situation is to be found in the case of what Szalai coins as the "new technocracy" (Szalai 1999: 3-12), i.e. the Communist leadership following the events of 1956, who developed initially as an elite enjoying economic (and, to some extent, cultural) capital; after acquiring political capital, their position became untouchable, even with the Roundtable Talks of 1989 inaugurating democratic transition: this event marked only the "new technocracy" of 1956 losing its political capital, but, being increasingly united and bearing a high adaptability to change, it managed to preserved beautifully its economic capital, transfiguring itself into the "new economic elite" of the newly-emerging democracy.

Attila Agh (1996: 46-49) differentiates five typologies of transitional politicians; some of the profiles briefly described above might be included in one of these categories. The politicians of morality (or "of morals" or the "revolutionary aristocracy", how they came to be labeled in the Czech Republic) are a quite rare type in post-communist politics. This very exclusive group is formed out of those political figures who constituted the dissidence and the opposition towards state socialism (e.g. Adam Michnik, Václav Havel). Generally, public figures, powerful engaged writers or good rhetoricians, they had suffered serious abuses during the communist regime and their legitimation after 1989 was a "moral" one. However, due to their permanent tendency to "moralize" politics and to maintain the same "closed, secretive and improvised political style" practiced in the years of clandestinity and opposition, due to their unwillingness to compromise in the political game, due to their pretence of practicing a sophisticated type of "post-modern politics", they proved unable to transform themselves into professional politicians in a democracy still in its infancy and they were gradually marginalized by disappointed electorates. When discussing the history of this particular type of "intellectual politicians", G. M. Tamás observes that "people in the modern age have come to the conclusion that, in spite of everything, intellectuals might be responsible after all" (Tamás 1990: 248). Therefore, the idea of morality is immediately associated with that of "responsibility", and, moreover, to that of "political re-sponsibility"; no wonder, then, that the citizenry existing the communist dic-tatorships put their hopes and expectations in this particular type of seemingly "responsible" politician, and the higher the disappointment and disenchant-ment when faced with these politicians' inability to address salient problems while in government, during transition. Most of the "moralist" politicians of the first years of transition to democracy in ECE were part of a critical mass of intellectuals who, nevertheless, had a cardinal drawback, as quite aptly ob-served by Karabel: "[T]he fundamental problem with the moralist tradition ex-emplified by Havel is that it treats intellectuals not as they actually are, but as they should be, [hence providing] an idealized *normative* form of reference for thinking about intellectuals, rather than an empirically grounded *analytical* one." (Karabel 1996: 205 [italics in original]) This moralist-normative stance of post-1989 intellectuals-turned-politicians immediately resulted in a flagrant lack of pragmatic strategies for dealing with a handful of seemingly inescapa-ble situations posed by the democratic transition. The second category, the "politicians of historical vision" is, again, a very exclusive, narrow group: as Agh describes them, politicians of "historical vision" (e.g. József Antall) are those "who arrived on the political scene just before the transfer of power, without real oppositional legitimacy, but who also, because of their grasp of the historical nature of that turning-point, served to link post-communism with the period preceding communist rule", acting exactly like a buffer zone be-tween leadership and opposition, "with a determined historical vision of re-storing the historical continuity of the nation and re-creating the past in the coming future" (Karabel 1996: 205). If the "politicians of morals" "moralize" politics, the "politicians of historical vision" "historicize politics and politicize history". Here the compromise, even unprincipled, is no problem; what is in-deed problematic is their arrogant lack of political professionalism, their na-tionalistic, holistic approach of politics that eventually transformed them into the vehicles of "elite continuity" in transition. Both the politicians "of morals" and those "of historical vision" are seen as "negative products" of the defunct regime, though paradoxically being in explicit or implicit opposition towards it. The "bulk" of the post-communist political elite is to be found in the third category, that of the "politicians of coincidence", generally office-seekers, with no innovatory perspective regarding reforms to be implemented during the democratic transition. If the first three types pose significant difficulties in identification and definition, the fourth category, the old *nomenklatura*, char-acterizes an easily-distinguishable group, with marked features of monolithism and strong group solidarity, in a nutshell, the actors of elite reproduction. It becomes even harder to differentiate between the old cadres and Agh's fifth category, the "emerging professional political elite". What is peculiar to this last elite group is a generational, age gap, that the members of this "new" elite tend to emphasize, as a mark of specificity and differentiation. Although their family background is blurry, their youth allows them a departure and a cold-hearted posture towards the defunct regime to which they do not belong in either dissident or collaborationist form. Expectedly, the emerging professional political elite is vehement regarding the necessity of transitional justice, though it acknowledges as well the usefulness and convenience of the tendency to negotiate and bargain. Generally, the careers of the members of this fifth group start immediately after the communist demise and their professionalization comes with a routinization of electoral tests and democratic norms and procedures. The "emerging professional political elite" is the agent of elite circulation in East-Central European developing democracies. As will be concluded below, it eventually appears that the elite groups forming the Municipal Councils in the six case-studies may be included in Agh's last type, being on their way to professionalized politics, though not completely and exhaustively deprived of the pressing communist "legacy" or by retrograde viewpoints.

It is one of the pioneers of the elite theory, Gaetano Mosca, to postulate that "large-scale societal change produces a need for new capacities in managing the state." (Mosca 1939: 65-69) No surprise, then, that one might expect that circulation, rather than reproduction of elites to be the norm in post-1989 East-Central Europe. It has been compellingly argued by an impressive series of scholars that the reverse is valid in fact. Therefore, the schematic distinction proposed by the book – among the strength and the completion of the circulation of elites process after 1989 and the extent of actual change each of the six countries of East-Central Europe has experienced – is based on Valerie Bunce's assertion that "those post-communist countries which initially excluded their former leaders from political power have shown the most progress in economic and political reform." (Bunce 1998: 187-211) Steven Fish stresses the same idea, by arguing that the ascendant evolution of the political and socio-economic reforms is directly dependent on the actual replacement of the political elite as consequence to the first free elections organized immediately after the communist breakdown (Fish 1998: 31-78). Hence, Fish refutes the scenario in which the recently "freed" population of East-Central Europe would vote for a species of communist leadership once again, deliberately. But one should take into consideration the ideological flexibility, the pragmatic ambivalence, the extraordinary capacity of adapting to the new economic and political realities – that the former *nomenklatura* is able to display; moreover, at least in the Bulgarian and Romanian instances, it was the *nomenklatura* – generally the second-ranked echelons of the Party leadership – that became the artisan of change. A second aspect concerning the limitations of the elite replacement process in post-communist Europe points to the expertise and – what Rivera coins as – "institutional memory" (Werning Rivera 2000: 415), that constitute the appanage of the former leadership. The democratic opposition has been and remained a largely idealistic (or, at best, skeptical, in the Hungarian case) and this attitude put an imprint on the fashion in which politics

46

was perceived and conducted. In Hungary, the manner in which the new democratic, formerly dissident, elite envisaged change and reform cost it the victory in elections, while in Romania and Bulgaria, only after several years, the accession to power was possible for the democratic opposition, due primarily to the sense of solidarity and unity of the neo- / reformist communists, on the one hand, and to an inability of the democratic reformers to organize themselves into solid political formations and to conduct a coherent political agenda, on the other hand. Thusly, lacking internal cohesion, confronted with interminable and exhausting inner quarrels and bearing a rather idealistic, devoid of pragmatism, of tone, the democratic opposition – composed primarily of the former dissident groups and the reemerged "historical", interwar parties – experienced significant and sometimes insurmountable difficulties in acquiring power after 1989.

A third concluding aspect refers to the very meaning of the concept of "elite reproduction" and the actual extent this phrase embraces. Debate has been focused on what "reproduction of elites" after 1989 should refer to, and the alternatives arousing out of these definitional debates gravitated around: (1) reproduction means the physical continuity of individuals in leadership positions, or rather (2) reproduction means the continuity of "the aggregate social characteristics of the elite stratum" (Lane 1997: 861), i.e. the persistence of the value system and the ranking system of priorities of the successor elites, as the two are inherited from the defunct regime. The present study employs the first hypothesis, though in an in-depth account on the evolution and the profile of transitional elites, one should consider especially the value system embraced by the rising young leadership. It is particularly in this area – of formation of value system embraced by the new political elite – that Sharon Rivera develops her studies. Her model of analysis, i.e. the linear "*continuum* of association" (with the former regime), is to a significant degree instrumental in assessing the manner in which the members of the new leadership (if such a case exists) constructed their identities as leaders (governing principles, values, priorities, identifications to particular societal aspects or social group, etc.). "Association" does not mean collaboration with the regime, but rather any form whatsoever of interaction, of societal connection with the state, encapsulating a countless number of possible individual attitudes towards the regime, from blind subordination and complete acceptance to full rejection and public fight against it. She even differentiates, on the *continuum*, two *in extremis* types of activities, (a) "the regime-challenging" (i.e. dissident activity), and (b) "the regime-supporting" (i.e. part of the government *nomenklatura* and, finally, member of the party *nomenklatura*) activities; in between these extremes, closer or more distant to one of it, various forms of "association" can be identified: reading *samizdat*, listening to foreign radios, party membership, part of the nonpolitical *nomenklatura*, member in a party committee, conducting party education, etc. (Werning Rivera 2000: 417) According to the degree in which the "association" with the communist regime climbed on the ladder-type *contin-uum*, the internalization by the individual (existing or would-be member of the political elite) of a political culture suitable to state socialism, with the attached principles and values, is more liable to produce. After the communist break-down, getting rid of such an "elite political culture"[17] becomes more and more difficult, if not impossible. Changing value systems and priority ranking will not happen overnight, as may be the case with regime changes. Hence, follow-ing this reasoning, at the level of elite characteristics of value and culture (not to be confounded with education!), a reproduction of elites is to some extent inescapable during the first decade of transition, even in spite of a physical circulation of elites.

A fourth final aspect to be considered in this discussion about post-com-munist elites take into account the re-emergence of the interwar, "old", "his-torical" parties and the formation of new parties after 1989 (including here the redesign of the communist parties in the countries of East-Central Europe, gen-erally re-titled into "socialist" or "workers'" parties). It goes without saying that the so-called "historical" parties of the post-communist era are by no means the same to those of the interwar, pre-communist era, though bearing the same denomination. Firstly, these organizations were banned during the communist dictatorship and their subsequent clandestine activities were re-duced; their leaders activated in exile and their members were either arrested, imprisoned or degraded during the Stalinist period of maximum terror, while after 1965, they were repudiated or simply let go to their former political alle-giance. How, then, did part of the pre-communist elite managed to resurface after 1989? For one, the elder generations and the leading figures of the re-emerged "historical" parties returned from exile after the communist downfall; nevertheless, their success in re-imposing themselves as elites is debatable, with huge and interesting variations from country to country. In Romania, for instance, former exiled party leaders were popularly perceived as "outsiders" and their legitimacy as elites – denied.

More importantly, while pre-communist figures might be repudiated through popular vote, due to the period of communist exile, the "career politi-cians", often born during the last instances of communist rule and emerging victorious out of the restless and unpredictable times of transition are to be confirmed through the same popular support. The profiles presented above,

---

17 The phrase "elite political culture", as distinguishable from a "community political cul-ture" ["a set of informal adaptative (behavioral and attitudinal) postures that emerge in response to the historical relationships between regime and community"] and a "regime political culture" ["a set of informal adaptative (behavioral and attitudinal) postures that emerge in response to the institutional definition of social, economic, and political life"], is to be found in Jowitt 1992: 51-52 and 54-56. "Elite political culture" is "a set of informal adaptative (behavioral and attitudinal) postures that emerge as response to and consequence of a given elite's identity-forming experiences."

though far from describing great political figures with spotless pasts, continued to inspire trust and familiarity in the eyes of the masses. In addition, prior political experience is much appreciated at the beginning of a period of uncertain outcomes. For the populations of East-Central Europe, elite circulation may as well be limited since skilled, charismatic or dedicated politicians inherited from the defunct regime can perfectly adjust to the realities of democratic transitions. Despite the countless dangers of reproduction, from the perpetuation of communist-styled practices, values and priorities to the "fossilization" of important institutions, elite circulation remains a contingent phenomenon in East-Central Europe, in the first decade after 1989, a process popularly underappreciated. Part of the scholarly on post-communist elites, among them Best, Hausmann and Schmitt, discusses the case of "career politicians": "Between sclerosis and an anemic state of elite reproduction, there is a middle way of *elite adaption*, ensuring a constant but limited influx of fresh elite members [...]. Elite turnover in representative democracies is expected to follow the middle way. [...] After an interruption of the normal course of elite reproduction and renewal, this equilibrium should reemerge within a limited time." (Best, Hausmann, and Schmitt 2000: 184 [italics mine]) In this respect, probably much more significant than the perpetuation in democracy of communist career politicians is the professionalization of a new political elite during the initial decades of transition. (The fashion in which this "new elite" is to emerge, apart from the lines of the former dissidence, is still quite problematic. Circulation is virtually impossible when a too "smaller proportion of the population had been able to accumulate [during state socialism] political skills, resources, and experience in the opposition movement (i.e. political capital) that could facilitate ongoing involvement in politics [...] in the new democracy." (Shabad and Slomczynski 2002: 337))

In a nutshell, party politics in East-Central Europe cannot be analyzed through the eyes of traditional, consecrated, Western models. This is conspicuous, for instance, in the case of James Toole's attempt (Toole 2007: 541-566) to employ Rokkan and Lipset's model of the emergence of party politics in the West (Lipset and Rokkan 1967: 1-64), which seems contingent and its findings are limited. The series of interconnected cleavages lying at the basis on party formation and development in the Western Europe during centuries of social and political transformations can only partially and incompletely explain the mechanisms of party formation and re-appearance in Central and East European countries after 1989; its *lacunae* are evident, mainly because in the interwar period, only Czechoslovakia managed to develop some sort of a "consistently democratic regime" (Toole 2007: 545, n. 7) with a significant degree of party competition, hence being the exception among the six countries analyzed here, which were constantly haunted by different forms of authoritarianisms and totalitarianism. Secondly, the legacy of almost half-a-century of state socialism proved to be extremely profound and marked implacably the post-communist institutions (see, in this sense, Jowitt 1992). More likely seems the conjecture that in only viable cleavage in aggregating interests through political organizations in post-1989 East-Central Europe was the cleavage between the communists (be their reformer, old or neo-communists) and anti-communists (regularly, democratic reformers organized in fronts or forums, comprising a mixture or an assembly of political doctrines and orientations, but sharing the same agenda, whose main point was the anti-communist message, the implementation of democracy, the observance of individual liberties and free market economy). Though using the Western methodological device in analyzing East-Central European realities, John T. Ishiyama endeavors in a quite perceptive study on the communist successor parties (i.e. "those parties which were formerly the governing party in the communist regime and which inherited the preponderance of the former ruling parties' resources and personnel" (Ishiyama 1999: 88)): the Social Democracy of the Republic of Poland Party, the Hungarian Socialist Party, the Communist Party of Bohemia and Moravia, the Slovak Party of the Democratic Left, the Bulgarian Socialist Party, the Party of Social Democracy of Romania, the Communist Party of the Russian Federation (and its counterparts within the former USSR, the Communist Party of Ukraine, the Estonian Democratic Labor Party, the Lithuanian Democratic Labor Party). These were the parties out of which a significant part of the new political elite was recruited. But their place on today's political scene of East-Central European countries is quite different. As a rule, the dynamics and the mechanisms of regime change dictated the subsequent role that the successor parties will play in the new democratic, developing systems. The first instance is represented by those transitions in which a gradually reformed communist party, conscious of its regime's political and economic capabilities and limitations, of popular pressure and of the external context, decided to organize negotiations with the opposition groups for inaugurating systemic transformations and reformist endeavors. After the regime change became a reality, it seemed natural that the party with which negotiations on an equal footing were made possible – though deprived of its retrograde "hardliners" – will became a major player on the political scene. Hence, circulation was made possible in Poland (an initial former dissident leadership, followed by the socialist victory in 1993, which, in turn, led to the reassertion of the center-right in 1997) and Hungary (with the former communist opposition losing power in 1994, in favor of the reformed communists who hold power until 1998, when a rightist democratic coalition won the elections). To some extent, the Slovak Party of the Democratic Left might follow closely the Polish and Hungarian counterparts in its ability to maintain some key positions in the governing *apparatus*, through the Czechoslovak case of regime change does not resemble the two national situations presented above. This fact is shown more conspicuously when considering the role of the successor party in the Czech Republic: the Communist Party of Bohemia and Moravia is virtually nonexistent on the national political scene and this might be particularly due to the auspices of the regime change here. After 1968, the Communist Party in Czechoslovakia suffered a clear involution and any attempt towards internal reform was hampered following the "Prague Spring". In 1989, thanks to external "snowball effect" and to internal popular and dissident pressure, the Czechoslovak *nomenklatura* gave power willingly, without previous negotiation. Soon, it was rapidly repudiated by the rightist democratic and centre-left groups, and, unless part of it was able to transform the political capital into economic resources, it became completely obsolete to Czech politics. On the other hand, one should not forget about the collaborators of the regime and the party rank-and-file who, in spite of lustration measures, managed to penetrate the wall of public officialdom and to accede to a governmental position.

Finally, in evaluating the degree of elite circulation or reproduction in East-Central Europe through the portraits and profiles of post-communist leaders, another aspect should be taken into consideration: the role of what Szelényi calls "the counter-elite" (Szelényi and Szelényi 1995: 619-620). There is a line of argumentation that points to the connection between the strength of the "counter elite" and the actual extent of elite circulation. The counter-elite is indeed of paramount importance, for it provides alternatives to the existing leadership and is a basis for circulation of cadres in a bureaucracy. Moreover, it is again Szelényi who argues that the instability, the unpredictability, the fluctuations that characterize a democratizing regime and society are prone to inhibit new courageous attempt to engage into politics of those coming from outside the circles of power of the defunct regime (Szelényi and Szelényi 1995: 620). Hence, regime instability after 1989 is likely to act as inhibitor to the appearance and development of a "counter-elite" and thusly to the circulation of elites. One should distinguish between the "new elite" of the *ancien régime*, composed of educated, skilled, reformist individuals – i.e. the "new technocracy" –, who were often co-opted by the regime or simply remained in the "gray zone"[18], and the veritable "counter-elite", formed largely from the dissidents and opponents, a proactive group, but comprising intellectuals of the "gray zone", as well. Despite its ambivalence and its unclear, uncertain character, the "gray zone" proved to be a fertile soil for the emergence of counter-elite, especially in those "bureaucratic-authoritarian" dictatorships in which the dissidence was sharply repressed. The "counter-elite" might be labeled as the practitioner of Konrád's "anti-politics", described by a vivid contestation stance towards the regime. As shown above, the ability of the "counter-elite" to penetrate the walls of monolithic power or the veil protecting the inner

---

18 The "gray zone" is a label used, more recently, by Tucker (2006: 182), defining "mostly professionals who neither collaborated nor resisted [with and to the communist regime] but survived while making necessary compromises on the lower echelons of the totalitarian hierarchy."

circles of communist power is contingent and more often than not its accession to power is quite problematic.

This ability of the "counter-elite" – transformed after 1989 into the "new elite" – to limit the influence of the communist forces in the wake of democracy depends largely on the relationship between the anti-communist elite and the former *nomenklatura*. This relationship is perfectly mirrored in the type of regime change each of the six countries of East-Central Europe experienced. Where the communist breakdown was rather a regime implosion, with the communist leadership obligated to renounce power in a context of unfavorable internal and external factors, the new anti-communist leadership purged the remains of the former administrative personnel; in exchange, the leadership of the *ancien régime* was fast and skilled enough to transfer political capital into economic resources, becoming the "new economic elite". Where the regime change embraced the features of a negotiation, the communist leadership, with its softliner, moderate, reformist faction, retained its political capital, accepting at the same time the new rules of the game (e.g. free and fair elections, party competition, democratic legitimacy, rule of the law, etc.) and, hence, making possible the victory of the democratic opposition in a multi-party system; the new elite saw the communist reformers as another rival party and the elite circulation underwent a natural process, in a democratic context.

What Wesołowski describes in the quotation from the beginning of this chapter is, indeed, independent of the mechanisms behind the recruitment of the political elite after 1989. Social indeterminism is a syndrome the countries of former Sovietized Europe confront with irrespective of them having experienced circulation or reproduction of elites during the restless years of democratic transition. What the Polish scholar notices is rather a bilateral autism, in which the aggregation of interests and, then, their channeling towards the ruling elite is considerably problematic. Though it might seem so, elite circulation is hardly an indicator to the extent to which democratic values and procedures are internalized in the new democracies. On the other hand, the chances for elite circulation or reproduction cannot be contextual, accidental: as already seen, the scholarly on transitology discusses the two phenomena as being either results of popular will (generated, in turn, by elite response to social-economic demands) or side-effects of a certain type of regime change, or marks of specific political cultures. Iván's and Szonja Szelényi's inaugural study on the topic represents a basis for further inquiry, since its results are preliminary and the evolution of the countries under scrutiny has shown, since the end of the said study, new trajectories.

Under all circumstances, nevertheless, one should take into consideration that, after all, political elites are "mortal gods, they can never feel safe in their position nor have they full control over their succession" (Best 2007: 23), their *status* as elites is "fluctuating and time-limited" (Best 2007: 23). The Paretian lesson of the struggle between "lions" and "foxes" teaches that circulation will eventually happen. What remains under question is the magnitude that the perpetuation of old styles of leadership will display.

In addition, it is quite difficult to assess the magnitude of elite reproduction, understood in a broader sense as the perpetuation of the moral and value legacy of the former regime. Hence, the actual extent of reproduction of communist elites after 1989 is virtually impossible to evaluate. Moreover, while it might be simpler to label as "elite reproduction" instances in which former holders of power are installed in key ministerial positions in post-1989 governments, it is definitely harder to argue the same "reproduction" in the case of the representatives of the "gray zone" and petty party members that, after the communist breakdown, succeeded in imposing themselves in leading positions. Since reproduction embraces the facet of political-turned-economic leadership and of exercising power, pressure and influence through new mechanisms and stances, the picture becomes increasingly complicated and beyond the limitations and scope of this book. On the other hand, the same biographies demonstrate that part of the former *nomenklatura* has in itself suffered tremendous mutations and value transformations that allowed its persistence on the post-communist political scene: a group that embraced the new democratic rules of the "game", partly the values and principles of individual liberty, and that attempted reforms aimed at consolidating the free market economical structure. Exactly this reformist group shows that the *nomenklatura* was not that unified and monolithic as it was initially presumed and that, indeed, its capacity of self-adjustment and adapting to new circumstances permitted their alleged "perpetuation", in fact a limited persistence, in which both the regime and its former elites experienced profound, though gradual and slow, change.

Although not necessarily and immediately connected with the outlook and dynamics of the decision-making at the local level in contemporaneity, the form the transition to democracy embraced in each of the six countries of East-Central Europe – i.e. the extent to which the communist breakdown and the regime change actually generated a more or less synchronized change in the ruling elite, or, contrarily, favored the persistence of the former political leadership – determined, largely indirectly, the elite political culture at the local level, some segments of the profile of the local leaders in the towns of the six countries discussed here, and, eventually, the fashion in which the decision-making proceeds.

Methodology: the Scope, the Questions, the Sampling and the Sampling Methods

"I cannot recall hearing about 'elites' in my college courses in political science, back in the thirties; and while I would not want to say, without further study, that the term was never used before 1935 or so in the American literature on politics, I am quite sure that it would have been rarely used. This is not to say that the *phenomena* to which the term refers were not investigated. But if one goes, for instance, to the writings of Water Lippmann, the American political theorist who perhaps more than any other was sensitive to the differentiation between elite and mass, and to the problematic this differentiation creates for democracy, one does not encounter the term. Harold Lasswell's use of the elite concept in his early writings was, therefore, quite novel. [...] [This means] the chronic curse of discontinuity in social studies' [scientific development]." (Eulau 1976: 8 [additions mine])

The scope of the present research project bears a descriptive, exploratory nature. Consequently, it does not essay at stating from the beginning a working hypothesis to prove or to verify during a deductive endeavor, but it is rather founded on an inductive, observatory process – an inquiry into a range of aspects worth pointing out when dealing with the study of political elites, such as their representativeness, the general patterns of recruiting them, their interactions with others groups or institutions, their values, perceptions, orientations, political priorities, etc. Subsequently, in the chapters below, various remarks are drawn, which would constitute, at least, a fragile basis for further inquiries and research. In order to pursue such objectives, the present research project uses, as a research method, the case study, with the focus on the local elites in six small-to-medium-sized municipalities, located in Romania, the Czech Republic, Poland, Hungary, Bulgaria, and the Slovak Republic: Tecuci (Galați county / *județ*), Česká Lípa (Liberec region / *kraj*), Oleśnica (Lower Silesia voivodeship / *województwo*, Poland), Gyula (Békés county / *megye*, Hungary), Targovishte (Targovishte province / *oblast*, Bulgaria), and Levice (Nitria region / *kraj*, Slovak Republic). The case selection is based on the logic of "the most similar design systems", for the six towns are quite similar in terms of demographics (roughly 35,000 inhabitants) and developmental strategies (i.e. an economy based on food industry and on commerce activities, with an important linkage with the surrounding rural area). By using a case study approach, no generalizations will be made on the entire local elite of the county / region. Based on the method employed and on the chosen sample, the main questions of this research project are the following:

- Which are the main patterns in the evolution of the local administration of the six towns and, particularly, in the evolution of the Local / Municipal Councils of these municipalities?

- Which are the principal socio-demographical features the local political elites of Tecuci, Česká Lípa, Oleśnica, Gyula, Levice, and Targovishte display?
- How are the members of the local political elite, in each of the six cases, politically recruited?
- To what other groups and institutions the local political elites in Tecuci, Česká Lípa, Oleśnica, Gyula, Levice, and Targovishte interact most frequently? Which is the structure of these networks of power, of interactions and contacts, in each particular instance?
- Which are the values, the perceptions, the orientations, embraced by the members of the local political elites in Tecuci, Česká Lípa, Oleśnica, Gyula, Levice, and Targoviste, respectively? Which are their attitudes towards certain key aspects concerning democracy, decentralization and autonomy, state intervention in economy, and cultural-geographical self-identification?
- What are the main political priorities of the members of the local political elite of Tecuci, Česká Lípa, Oleśnica, Gyula, Levice, and Targoviste? How does each of the six groups assess the importance of some problems their towns presently confront with? Do they enjoy living in their towns?
- How representative is each of the six Local / Municipal Councils for the entire population of their towns, especially in terms of socio-demographic characteristics?

Considering the answers to the above-mentioned interrogations, does each of the six selected leading groups display a certain degree of "elite consciousness" and how is this distinctiveness constructed? What are the traits of each group's "elite political culture" and how could their mere existence be explained?

To the initial questions above, a series of other secondary questions are added during the research process whose tentative, partial, preliminary answers will be attempted in the chapters below.

This research book uses mainly the positional method in identifying and analysing the local political elites, by operationalizing the phrase "local political elites" through the following definition: The local political elite is that group of comprising those individuals in legislative and executive positions within the local leading, decision-making structure. Moreover, the "positional" approach on identifying and analysing elites is useful in distinguishing among different types of authorities and "soft" leaderships within the community: "The key distinction between political office holders [i.e. "those people at the top of cities' and towns' formal political structures"] and other types of political leadership (challengers, interest group and social movement leaders) is that the first group has influence over public resources and hence has accountability and power relations with all the citizens within the area." (Greasley and Stoker 2009: 126) The renowned definition and description of the concept of "elite" by American scholars Harold Lasswell, Daniel Lerner, and C. Easton Rothwell sheds some light on what exactly needs to be studied and analyzed when dealing with this group: "What is lacking is a term to cover both the leadership and the *strata* of society from which leaders usually come. [...] *The concept of the elite is classificatory and descriptive, designating the holders of high positions in a given society.* There are as many elites as there are values. Besides an *elite of power* (the political elite) there are *elites of wealth, respect,* and *knowledge.*" (Lasswell, Lerner, and Easton Rothwell 1952: 6-7) The preference for the positional analysis, in the detriment of the reputational and decisional methods, is justified through what C. Wright-Mills convincingly argued: "If we took the one hundred most powerful men in America, the one hundred wealthiest, and the one hundred most celebrated away from the institutional positions they now occupy, away from their resources of men and women and money, away from the media of mass communication that are now focused upon them – then they would be powerless and poor and uncelebrated, anonymous. [...] To be celebrated, to be wealthy, to have power requires access to major institutions, for the institutional positions men occupy determine in large pat their chances to have and to hold these valued experiences." (Wright-Mills 1969/1956: 10-11) However, parts of the study occasionally combine the positional method with the reputational one, for, in some cases, the attribute of "member of the local elite" is determined less by the position in the Local / Municipal Council, but rather by the prestige and the reputation the person enjoys within the community. Actually, one of the specificity of the local political elite in the small towns of Tecuci and Targovishte, for instance, is particularly the fact that formal (positional) hierarchical structure is similar – i.e. contains approximately the same names on largely the same layers – to the informal (reputational) hierarchy.[19] The situation is dissimilar to Česká Lípa, Levice, and Oleśnica, although here the political elite partly overlaps on the cultural elite. This fact is somehow commonplace for small communities, where local / municipal councilors enjoy both the political-economic or political-cultural, and popular recognition within the municipality.

"Local councils can be different from one another, too, reflecting the differences of local people, local places and local politics." (Armstrong 2000: 24)[20] This was precisely the initial framework on which this study developed, in spite of the fact it put forward a "most-similar design system" research rationale: experiencing the largely similar historical trajectories, the six cases selected for the region of East-Central Europe can only be meaningfully analyzed in clusters, for their societal backgrounds prior to the installation of state socialism and their developmental trajectories following the communist

---

19   At the time of the study, prominent local councilors such as Vasile Dănăilă, Costică Florea or Petru Papuc were part of both the leading political and economic groups of Tecuci.

20   Discussing the same topic, in the context of British Labour Party's attempts to "go local" (i.e. bringing decision-making closer to the citizens), at the end of the 1990s and throughout the 2000s, see, also, Ashworth, Copus, and Coulson, 2004: 459-466.

breakdown are essentially different. The "positional" definition, identification, and analysis in the elite studies implies that "local elites" are "persons who, through their organizational positions, are able to affect local politics in a much more regular and substantial way than are ordinary citizens." (Burton, Gunther, and Higley 1992: 8) In the same vein, Anders Uhlin defines "local political elites" as "all elected members of the local parliament" (Uhlin 2006: 152, n. 9), as different from the "local administrative elite" (mainly, civil servants in key position within the municipality), and "local economic elite" (the local entrepreneurship and the managers of firms whose activity is locally based).

The present research on local political elites employs as its populations the members of the Local / Municipal Councils in Tecuci, Česká Lípa, Oleśnica, Gyula, Targovishte, and Levice, as they are in 2011-2015 (for some modifications did happen from the composition of the Councils, as they were constituted after the local elections of 2008 / 2010 and 2012, firstly given the very different timing of the local elections of the six countries, secondly given the changes in the membership of the Councils during their four-year mandate, and thirdly given the chronology of the research itself, which has been started in December 2011, with the case of Tecuci). For Tecuci, the Local Council includes nineteen persons; for Česká Lípa, the Municipal Council comprises twenty-five persons; for Oleśnica, the Municipal Council contains twenty-one persons; for Gyula, the Municipal Council includes fourteen persons; for Levice, the Municipal Council comprises twenty-four persons; and for Targovishte, the Local Council counts thirty three persons, in all instances, people with various political affiliations, with very different occupations, of different ages, enjoying different degrees of popular support and prestige, but of largely similar social *status* and, more often than not, of resembling social backgrounds and political trajectories. Indeed, "the most important principle for selecting municipalities and cases [becomes] the need to maximize the ability to learn [...] from the cases" (van Hulst 2008: 64) included in the research; taking into consideration that this research aims only partially and tentatively to a generalization, the main objective being that of constructing and describing elite profiles in small-to-medium-sized towns of East-Central Europe, it is, consequently, the cardinal scope of this empirical endeavor to contribute to the knowledge and "learning" on the topic, in the elite theory research field.

As in all cases of the research, the continuation of the study presupposed the administration of a standard written questionnaire to the members of the Local / Municipal Councils in the six towns. All approachable members of the six Councils were administered the questionnaire. The composition of the standard questionnaire remained unchanged throughout the entire period of the research (with the exception of some *sine qua non* modifications, resulting from the different realities of the six cases). This questionnaire includes sixteen questions, with two being open-ended questions and the other fourteen being closed ones. The scope of the first three closed questions is to identify patterns of recruitment. The variables which constitute the possible answers for questions no. 1 and no. 2 were used previously by S. Eldersveld, in *Political Elites in Modern Societies* (1989: 33). The next four closed questions are designed to emphasize the political priorities of the Local Council, while the eighth question concerns the contacts and the networks of interactions between the members of the Local Council and other groups and institutions. Closed-ended questions no. 9, no. 10, no. 11, no. 12, no. 13, have, as main objective, the identification of the values, perceptions, attitudes embraced by the local political elite, by pointing to: its orientations towards citizen participation, change, political conflict, economic equality (in a nutshell, the perceptions on the various features of a democratic construct); its perceptions towards state intervention in economy and to local autonomy and decentralization; its perceptions on the direction in which the town is heading; its inclinations towards localism or centralism and their cultural-geographical identification. The following question, the fourteenth one, is an open-ended question; it triggers to the political priorities of the members of the local political elite, in their capacity as members of the Local Council, i.e. the identification of the major problem the town currently confronts with. The fifteenth question is a closed one and it deals with political priorities as well, by asking the degree of personal satisfaction of being an inhabitant of Tecuci, Česká Lípa, Oleśnica, Gyula, Levice, and Targoviste, respectively. Finally, the sixteenth, open question tries, based on the answers received, to sketch the bases of social representation of the local political elite, by asking for five qualities and characteristics a local councilor should possess.[21] The questionnaire was chosen as the main method of collecting *data*, along with a theoretical framework provided by bibliographical references, for three main reasons: the time dedicated to its filling is of 5 to 10 minutes, which would make the collection of *data* easier and accessible (whereas an unstructured interview of one hour with each of the local councilors under scrutiny would have been largely impracticable and nearly impossible due to the busy schedule of the representatives, but, most importantly, due to the distance and language barriers such a methodological empirical approach would eventually presuppose); the *data* thusly collected can be easily codified and measured. In practice, given the experience accumulated in the surveys, the actual manner in which the questionnaire was filled in (i.e. the time and place) had surely diverged from case to case. Initially, the questionnaire was meant to be filled in by the respondents at their working place[22],

---

21 An English translation of the administered questionnaire is in the Appendix.
22 For instance, for the case of Tecuci, initially, the filling in of the questionnaire has been envisaged for the extraordinary meeting of the Local Council of 23rd of December 2010. Nevertheless, in practice, the distribution of questionnaires followed the scenario:
   • the questionnaires were given to the civil servants working for the Permanent Working Bureau of the Local Council, along with an application form asking for

approval; the questionnaires were included in the working folder of each local councilor for the ordinary meeting of the Local Council of 14th of December 2010;
- at the extraordinary meeting of 23rd of December 2010, the questionnaires were supposed to be handed over to the student-researcher, who received only 2 of them;
- it was established that the rest of the questionnaires will be delivered to the Secretariat of the Mayor, from where the student-researcher will recuperate them: only one questionnaire was thusly received;
- five other questionnaires were filled in by the local councilors at their working place (notary office, school, lawyer's office, etc.) at the beginning of January (in the presence of the student-researcher);
- as a reminder, 11 other questionnaires were sent through postal mail at local councilors' home/ work address (on the 28th of December); three were sent back;
- also as a reminder, those local councilors who did not return the questionnaires (five in the last phase) were called by the student-researcher (at home, office or working place, using the list of phone numbers provided by the Public Relations Department of the Town-Hall) and asked about a convenient place for delivering the questionnaire; other three questionnaires were thusly recuperated;
- three questionnaires were returned during the weekly sessions of the five Committees, on Tuesdays and Wednesdays;
- two local councilors refused to filled in the questionnaire.

For the Czech case, the approach of the respondents proceeded in a similar manner, though some modifications were necessary since there is a significant space limitation in addressing the Municipal Council by the student-researcher. As expected, face-to-face interviewing was not an option in gathering the data, nor was the presence of the student in the ordinary or extraordinary sessions of the Council or during the session of specialized committees, or, by the same token, the application of the questionnaire at each councilor's workplace. The interaction between the student-researcher and the members of the Municipal Council in Česká Lípa was made possible exclusively via e-mail or through phone. The list with the contacts of the Czech councilors was available on the website of the municipality and some other contact pieces of information were obtained with the mediation of the mayor of Česká Lípa. The same questionnaire was applied, with some conjunctural modifications, to the Municipal Council in Česká Lípa. A model of the intended questionnaire, accompanied by a cover letter explaining the usage of thusly gathered data, were firstly sent to the Mayor and to the Secretariat of the Town hall; only after a third e-mail, a positive answer was received for the further development of the empirical endeavor, though, nonetheless, collaboration concerning the dissemination of the questionnaire towards the local councilors was limited. The written questionnaire was distributed to all twenty-five members, after the positive reply of the Mayor; during this initial phase, only 3 of the questionnaires were filled in and returned to the student. Another problem aroused at this stage: since the questionnaire was formulated in English, the language barrier could not be overcome and another six of the respondents replied negatively, with the motivation of not knowing the language. During a second phase, the questionnaire was resent, this time translated in Czech; another two questionnaires were returned. A third stage in the administration of the questionnaire made recourse to phone calls to the local councilors of Česká Lípa, based on the list made available by the Secretariat of the Town Hall; as a result of the phone calls, 13 other questionnaire were sent, filled in, to the student, while one was filled in over the phone. Also as a reminder, for those local councilors who did not return the questionnaire (six in this last stage), letters including the questionnaire were during the ordinary and extraordinary meetings of the Local / Municipal Councils; the manner of approaching the respondents has largely been time motivated. Nevertheless, practically, the distribution and the filling in of questionnaires followed the scenario: at the working place of the respondents (notary offices, schools, NGOs' headquarters, schools and universities, lawyer's offices, SMEs' offices, etc.), during the ordinary and extraordinary meetings of the Councils, during the weekly sessions of the Council's Committees, through intermediaries (e.g. normally and most frequently, the civil servants working for the Permanent Working Bureau of the Local / Municipal Council, the Secretariat of the Mayor, the Public Relations Department / Compartment of the Town-Hall, etc.), *via* postal mail at the local councilors' home or work address, *via* phone, and especially *via* e-mail, etc.

Beside the questionnaire, the assessments and remarks presented in this book were also based on direct observations during the meetings of the Local / Municipal Councils selected here (both ordinary and extraordinary meetings) and in their specialized Committees, on the documents' analysis (minutes of the Local / Municipal Council's meetings, announcements, decisions, the parties' statutes, etc.). The empirical research was planned to constitute the initial phase of the research and was designed to follow the sequence: (1) the identification of the members of the Municipal / Local Councils, from a formal standpoint, and (2) the gathering of *data* concerning each of the local / municipal representatives and the brief description of their social and economic *status* (including pieces of information concerning age, place of birth, gender, occupation, professional *status*, educational level, income, etc.); this initial step – consisting actually of the socio-demographical biographies of the members of each of the selected Municipal Councils – has also consisted in the analysis of the local councilors' interests and wealth declarations (in those circumstances in which the state legislation provides for the mandatory character of such documents, e.g. Romania, Bulgaria, Poland). The main source of these *data* was generally the websites of the Municipalities of Tecuci, Česká Lípa, Oleśnica, Gyula, Levice, and Targovishte, which proved instrumental and were extensively employed in the initial phase (www.primariatecuci.ro, http://www.mucl.

---

sent via postal mail at their home or work-place address; three of these letters received a reply and were sent back to the student, in a completed form. Finally, three local councilors declined filling in the questionnaire. Space and linguistic barriers considerably hampered the gathering of the data and transformed the process of collecting empirical, quantitative material into a prolonged one, from July 2011 to March 2012. As in the case of the Local Council of Tecuci, the questionnaire was not the exclusive method of collecting data. The assessments, observations and evaluations presented in the case of the Municipal Council of Česká Lípa are founded also on the document analysis of the minutes of the Municipal Council's meetings, on various announcements, resolutions taken during the Council's meetings, even on the limited reading of the statutes of the parties represented in the Council of Česká Lípa (despite flagrant language contingencies).

cz/, www.olesnica.pl, www.gyula.hu, www.targovishte.bg, www.levice.sk), while the rest of the characteristics presented in the tables and inquired into (i.e. religion, father's occupation, relatives involved into politics, matrimonial *status*) were gathered through the administration of the questionnaire. The observations resulted from the reputational analysis were mainly based on a procedure previously employed by Floyd Hunter: hence, journalists at the main local newspapers and websites, local elites in other domains (culture, education; e.g. the Director of the Cultural Foyer, the Presidents of the Permanent Bureaus of the Local Party Organizations, the editors-in-chief of newspapers and radio stations, local prominent members of CSOs, etc.[23]), and the leaders of the principal local party organizations were asked to write down three names of members of the local political elite – in accordance to their subjectivity and mere perception –, they delivered to the student-researcher the sheets of paper with the three names who, from a reputational stance, would be or would qualify as members of the local political elite. The names thusly provided were compared to the present composition of the Municipal / Local Councils, for assessing the extent to which the positional method of analyzing elites coincides and overlaps with the reputational one. Finally, for the *data* concerning the populations of Tecuci, Česká Lípa, Oleśnica, Gyula, Levice and Targovishte, employed in the study of the representativeness of the local political elites, the following *data* bases were publicly available and were consequently used: for Tecuci, the one of the County Direction of Statistics Galați [*"Direcția Județeană de Statistică Galați"*], of the National Institute of Statistics [*"Institutul Național de Statistică"*] and of the 2002 Census; for Česká Lípa, the one of the 2011 Census of the Czech Statistical Office [*"Český Statistický Úřad"*]; for Oleśnica, the one of the 2011 Census, conducted by the Central Statistical Office [*"Główny Urząd Statystyczny"*]; for Gyula, the one of the 2011 Census, conducted by the Hungarian Central Statistical Office [*"Központi Statisztikai Hivatal"*]; for Levice, the one of the 2011 Census of the Statistical Office of the Slovak Republic [*"Štatistický úrad Slovenskej republiky"*]; for Targovishte, the results of the 2011 Census, conducted by the National Statistical Institute of Bulgaria [*"Natsionalen Statisticheski Institut"*].

The fashion of approaching each of the six Councils circumscribed to the path followed in the previous cases: the same individual file was composed for

---

23 For instance, for the case of Tecuci, the persons scrutized through Hunter's reputational method of identifying elites were: the Director of the Cultural Foyer, the Presidents of the Permanent Bureaus of the Local Organization of PD-L, PSD, PNL and the Green Party, the editors-in-chief of "Favor", "tecuci.eu" and "Semnal T". The same procedure was employed in the case of Oleśnica. For the cases of Česká Lípa, Levice, Gyula, and Targovishte, Hunter's procedure was not used per se, as in the Romanian case, simply due to language limitations. The reputational method, complementary to the dominant, positional one, was facilitated through the analysis of the media coverage each of the councilors enjoyed, i.e. by a quantitative, counting procedure of keeping record of the media appearances of each councilor.

each local / municipal councilor, containing age, place of birth, gender, occupation, educational level, income, level of acquaintance or prestige within his / her community, local media coverage of the councilor's activities within both the political and the business life, etc. In the absence of the legal obligation of the representatives to publicly display some corresponding declarations to the Romanian, Bulgarian and Polish "interest" and "wealth declarations", putting together short biographies of each municipal councilor of Česká Lípa, Gyula, and Levice proved to be problematic.

The Local (Municipal) Council: General Presentation

a) Theoretical overview on local government systems

Jens Hesse identifies two main phases in the development towards increased devolution, and decentralization, in the region of East-Central Europe, following the *anuus mirabilis* 1989: (a) the "first radical phase of *administrative transformation*", directed towards the reduction of state centralism, and (b) the phase of "*administrative modernization*", during which "institutions and processes will be more gradually adapted to fit the functional needs" (Hesse 1993: 218 [italics added]) of citizenry. Hesse refines this sequence of events and processes afterwards: (a) "the initial phase of *transformation*", with the following traits: "the emergence of multi-party systems; regular elections at the national, regional, local levels; the overhaul of public sector institutions [...]; the formulation and partial implementation of what often were radical economic reform programmes; [...] [and] heated constitutional debates", but with quite problematic results (e.g. "volatile voting patterns, unstable coalitions and unresolved power struggles between different governmental institutions", inconclusive constitutional debates, incomplete privatization programmes, and short-lived "institutional arrangements and rearrangements"); (b) the "process of *consolidation*" (in which "increased political stability allowed for a more systematic approach to *de-étatization*, privatization and marketization"); (c) the "third phase of *modernization*" (with other mixed results: notoriously difficult "reorganization of the machinery of central government" and an equally problematic "functional and territorial demarcation of competencies"; "a widespread problem of discontinuity in personnel, resulting on the one hand from the increased attractiveness of private sector employment, and on the other from the practice of incoming governments of replacing large functions of the administrative leadership"); (d) "a fourth and party overlapping phase [...] of *adaptation*" both to the Western standard ("the state of the art of public sector performance" (Hesse 1997: 122-124 [italics added])[24]) and to the pressures during the EU pre-accession and accession processes of the countries of the region. The ECE countries' reply under the form of "adaptation" to the EU pressures is developed by Emil Kirchner, under the form of three main types of external influences on regional and local governance of the countries of the region: (a) "direct attempts by the EU to secure greater political democratization", (b) "the link between the *acquis communautaire* and decentralization", and (c) "the impact of EU Structural Fund programmes on local infrastructure, regional imbalances, ethnic conflicts and cross-border cooperation" (Kirchner

---

24   See, for an elaborated study on this contribution, Hesse 1995.

1999: 209 [italics in original]. Although an important variable – especially in respect to what the local leaders can actually do at the local level in terms of infrastructural and economic development[25], and to community empowerment, generally –, such external (i.e. international), exogenous variable and its impact upon the outlook of the local political elites in the small-to-medium-sized towns of East-Central Europe are beyond the scope of this study.

Renowned scholar of local developments in the region of ECE, Tamás Harváth isolates three principal "routes of development of institutional transition at the local level in this part of Europe": (1) two "coherent models": (1.a.) the Polish route (in which local elections were held prior to the general ones, according to former, non-democratic regulations, and only after the general elections, legitimate legislation on local elections was established), and (1.b.) the "professional-technical" (Davey 1995: 57-75)[26] route, Hungary-specific one (in which legislative changes, especially in the financial sphere, were taken prior to the communist breakdown, whereas the democratically-elected national legislative established the political and electoral regulations governing the local level, immediately after the initiation of transition, so that the first post-1989 local elections were seen a democratic); and (2) one "gradual model", quite typical for the region, having been adopted by almost all former communist states, with the exception of Poland and Hungary (in which the changes were actually effectuated under political pressures, following the steps: the "transfer of authority without altering elected council bodies", impeding former communist local leaders to access top positions in the new local administration; the "elimination or restriction of former executive committees", in order to reinstate the predominance of the legitimate, popularly elected Municipal Council in local decision-making; the "abolition of the competence of the upper level of territorial government", with the purpose of eliminating the preeminence of the county or the regional level in local decision-making, and hence transferring the autonomous governance to the local level; and the "transfer of property to local government, mainly state property companies" (Horváth 2000: 38-39), with the objective of ensuring the fiscal capacity and the financial independence of the local communities.

It may be the case that, due to the importance given to the (almost artificial) creation and construction of regions in ECE countries, as a prerequisite for the preparation of EU membership (see, in this respect, Illner 1997: 23-

---

25 The importance of this variable has been mentioned during interviews conducted with the municipal councilors in Oleśnica in 2012, especially in what concerns the local decision-making and the citizen's expectations.

26 See, also, for two other countries of the region and under scrutiny here, Davey 1995, in Coulson (ed.) 1995: 41-56.

45)[27], the significance of the local level, of the tier placed the closest to the citizen, has significantly decreased for both the logic of leadership and the scholarly interest in elite studies. Nonetheless, the local government maintains its role of paramount significance in democratization in East-Central Europe. In the study of American city councils, Leach et al. isolate four cardinal tasks for local elites, relevant irrespective of the peculiarities of the governed town or city: (a) "maintaining political support"; (b) "developing policy direction"; (c) "representing and defending the authority's goals in negotiation with other bodies", and (d) "ensuring task accomplishment" (Leach, Hartley, Lowndes, Wilson, and Downes 2005). Among other, secondary, tasks for the local political elites, Leach et al. mention: "trying to engage the public, institutional development or managing community conflict".

Within the East-Central European political and administrative systems, Local or Municipal Councils are generally designed as legislative *fora* at the local level, created with the purpose of bridging the gap between the elite group or local political potentates and the masses, as the Municipal Council is constituted through popular, direct vote of the citizens of a given constituency. The Council is "a deliberative body whose members are elected and whose legislative decisions are influenced by political considerations for which [the said] is politically accountable to the electorate. [...] [It] is a legislative assembly that is legally instituted through its elected members to govern the municipality as an organ of state and legal entity, and that exercises its legislative and executive authority in collaboration with the local community." (van der Walt 2007: 68 [additions mine]) A municipal council has the obligation of developing a framework of delegation of executive powers, initially vested in it, to the executive instance *par excellence* at the local level, i.e. the mayor, for the purpose of maximizing the administrative, operational and organizational efficiency and effectiveness. Surely, a limited set of attributions are exclusive to, reserved for the Council (e.g. the adoption of its own regulations and by-laws; the approval of the budget, of taxes and tariffs, the acquisition of loans; etc.); the Council's decision-making process is based on the reports and recommendations issued by the Mayor. Conversely, the Mayor and other executive instances working under the Mayor's supervision are obligated to report on the fashion in which the Council's decisions are executed and on the mentioned bodies' decisional repercussions.

While trying to account for the diversity in the development of Russian towns, Ledyaev and Chirikova distinguish among different "urban regimes": (1) "development regimes" (aimed at providing for the local business); (2) "maintenance regimes" (aimed at routine service delivery and low taxation, with fewer benefits for the inhabitants); (3) "middle-class progressive regimes"

---

27 On the topic of EU impact on the drive towards decentralization, but, most importantly, regionalization in ECE countries, with a special focus on Romania, see Dobre 2011: 685-714.

(aimed at solving problems such as environment protection, heritage preservation, affordable housing etc.); (4) "lower-class opportunity expansion regimes" (aimed at solving the issues of the lower class). These "urban regimes" tend to draft the prioritization strategy at the local level.

In order to adequately analyze the role and the importance of Municipal Councils in the decision-making process at the local level and to determine the "elite" character of the members of these Councils, it appears advisable to pause for a brief digression on the typology of local government systems. Such typologies have been utilized by the literature for the purpose of explaining differences in "recruitment patterns, professionalization, the position of mayors in local and multi-level governance arrangements (or horizontal and vertical policy networks), the interpretation (or notion) of democracy, problem definition as well as attitudes and opinions towards decentralization or centralization and reforms ('modernization') of the public sector ('new public management')." (Heinelt and Hlepas 2006: 21) Although the present research attempt does not consider primarily the impact of local government system on the above-mentioned aspects featured by the local political elite, all these aspects are, indeed, scrutinized by the present endeavor. This is particularly the reason why a short inquiry into the taxonomical diversity of local government systems is perceived as necessary at this point. Hence, the scholarly literature has constructed such categorizations following two main dimensions: (1) the "vertical power relations" (i.e. the nature and the outlook of the relations established between the local authorities and the regional and central ones), and (2) the "horizontal power relations" (i.e. the character and the outlook of the interactions entertained internally, at the local level, by the Municipal Council with the mayor and with other executive instances of the municipality). The first dimension, that of vertical, external, trans-local relations, yields the distinctions among: (1.a) a "dual" (i.e. in which the central government bodies function side by side with the municipal authorities, but enjoy different attributions and deal with separate areas of competence), a "fused" (i.e. in which the only bodies operating at the local level are the municipal ones, but their competencies are enlarged, being provided for by the central and regional governmental authorities), and a "mixed" local government system (i.e. in which the concomitant functioning of both local and central authorities at the local level provides for an overlapping of competences) (Bennett 1989; Bennett 1993: 28-47)[28]; (1.b) a "Northern" (i.e. in which the strong decentralization of functions towards the local authorities is the rule and the municipal bodies enjoy a wide range of attributions, leading to a consequent remarkably high level of legal discretion from their part within their communities, with the local leaders

---

28 The main rejoinder to Bennett's typology lies in the fact that its static character fails to capture the hybridized forms resulting from territorial (multi-layered amalgamations) and functional (devolution, decentralization, etc.) reforms. See, in this sense, Kersting and Vetter 2003.

having extremely poor access to the central government, due to the simple reason they concentrate their interest almost exclusively to the municipalities they represent), and a "Southern" local government system (i.e. in which the municipalities possess few attributions, competences and prerogatives and a subsequent low degree of discretion, while local politicians enjoy a high degree of access to the regional and central levels of government, representing "politically weak communes", in which the dysfunctional bureaucracies and the feebleness of impersonal interactions pave the way for clientelistic and patronage-styled relations) (Page and Goldsmith 1987; John 2001)[29]; (1.c) the "clientelistic / patronage model" (i.e. in which the main concern of the local leadership is that of "support" among the local leaders themselves and between the local instances and the regional / central ones, in exchange for benefits for some exclusive, selected circle), the "economic-development model" (i.e. in which the primary concern of the local leadership is that of "partnership" wither with the central government or with the private sector, in order to further economic growth in its community), and the "welfare-state model" (i.e. in which the main concern of the local leadership is that of "(social) empathy" and "social sensitivity", for providing welfare services through redistributive practices and *calculi* for their community) (a forth model is the "market-enabling model", in which the three above-mentioned models are combined; furthermore, Heinelt and Hlepas equates this forth model to what they coin as "the Central East Europe type", hence observing the limitations of this typology in respect to the region of East-Central Europe (Heinelt and Hlepas 2006: 27)) (Goldsmith 1992: 393-410); (1.d) the "Anglo" type (e.g. England, Ireland, etc.), the "Franco / Napoleonic" type (e.g. France, Greece, Italy, Portugal, Spain, Belgium, etc.; the most structured and comprehensive local governmental system), the "North-Middle European type" (e.g. Germany, Austria, Denmark, Sweden, Netherlands, Switzerland, etc.), and the "Central-East European type" (e.g. Poland, Hungary, Czech Republic, Slovakia, Romania, Bulgaria, with quite recent radical forms of decentralization, etc.) (Hesse and Sharpe 1991: 603-621). Underpinning on the second dimension, the internal, horizontal one, yields the following classifications: (2.a) the "dualistic" (i.e. in which the tasks and functions are separated between the legislative and the executive instances: "the elected council is recognized as the prime decision-making body of local government, but the head / chief executive of the local administration is seen as possessing some 'executive' decision-making powers of his / her own that are

---

29   Allegedly, the Northern-Southern divide has a historical inheritance which can be traced back to the Napoleonic rule, a political arrangement aimed at the abolishment of local strongholds and to centralism and which led to the movement of local notables and patrons to the central administration in order to be able to further their localized interests. The reserve is valid for the Northern Europe, with the 18th and the 19th centuries' local elites carrying out national politics, and with powerful decentralizing traditions in territorial administration.

not derived from the local council" (Wollmann 2004: 151; see also Wollmann 2004: 639-665)), and the "monistic" local government system (i.e. in which legislative and executive tasks and functions are locally merged in one institutional instance: "the elected local council is regarded as the sole supreme decision-making body, while the local administration, including its head / chief executive, acts under the instruction and scrutiny of the council without any autonomous 'executive' decision-making power of its own" (Wollmann 2004: 151)[30]; (2.b) the "majoritarian" (i.e. in which the local decision-making process is dominated by the Municipal Council, in the detriment of the Mayor, who is obliged to implement the decisions thusly taken), and the "consociational" local government system (i.e. in which the local decision-making process takes the form of a negotiation, a bargaining and a compromise between the main decision-maker, the Council, and the Mayor, who will operate the resultants of this negotiated decisional undertaking); (2.c) the "assembly government" (i.e. the combination of "monism" with "consociationalism": "where executive power is in the hands of a proportionally composed committee of the council"); the "parliamentarism" (i.e. the combination of "monism" with "majoritarianism": "[where] a collective executive, appointed by the council [is] not using proportional techniques but some variation on the majority principle"); the "presidentialism" (i.e. the combination of "dualism" with "majoritarianism": "[where] a separately elected mayor appoint[s] his / her own cabinet of deputies without consideration of the party-political composition of the council"), and the "semi-presidentialism" (i.e. the combination of "dualism" with "consociationalism", with majoritarian traces, as well: "[where] the mayor is surrounded by a council-appointed collective executive") (Back 2005: 82-83 [additions mine]); (2.d) "the strong mayor form" (i.e. "the elected mayor controls the majority of the city council and is legally and in actuality in full charge of all executive functions"), "the committee-leader form" (i.e. "one person is clearly 'the political leader' of the municipality – with or without the title of mayor; [h]e may or may not control the council. Executive

---

30 Furthermore, Wollmann refines the dichotomous typology, by introducing three additional distinctions: (a) the extent to which the role of the mayor is actually exercising (or not) the executive function; (b) the exercise of the executive function by the mayor alone or together with a collective or collegiate body, and (c) the electoral formula employed for the election of the mayor (pp. 151-152). Though the place and role played by the executive instance, i.e. by the Mayor, at the local level is beyond the scope of this book, it should not be overlooked that the two selected cases are dissimilar in terms of Mayor's election: in the case of Tecuci, the Mayor is popularly elected, appearing as the counterpart, in the decision-making process, of the Local Council, whereas, in the case of Česká Lípa, the Mayor is elected by the Municipal Council itself, from among its members, the Czech case being actually one of the fewest cases of appointed Mayor in Europe, where a drive towards more democratic procedures in the construction of the executive function at the local level has been in place, more prominently starting from the 1990s.

powers are shared. The political leader may have responsibility for some executive functions, but others will rest with collegiate bodies [e.g. standing committees composed of elected officials], and with the CEO"), "the collective form" (i.e. "the decision center is one collegiate body, the executive committee that is responsible for all executive functions; [t]he executive committee consists of locally elected [officials] and the mayor, who presides"), and "the council-manager form" (i.e. "all executive functions are in the hands of a professional administrative – the city manager – who is appointed by the [municipal] council, which has general authority over policy, but is restricted from involvement in administrative matters. *The council is the main decision-maker.*") (Mouritzen and Svara 2002: 50-56, esp. 55-56 [italics mine; additions mine])[31]; (2.e) the "executive mayor" (i.e. in which mayors are both "formally the heads of municipal administrations which hold the responsibility for a broad *spectrum* of public provisions" and "in full charge of their administrations"), the "political mayor" (i.e. in which mayors are both strong, "lead[ing] a municipal administration that is responsible for a relatively limited scope of 'state' functions", and "clearly the political representative (and agent) for the local community"), the "ceremonial mayor" (i.e. in which mayors "exercise a mainly ceremonial function / role, while there is no elected local leader at the head of the municipality and the municipal administration is directed by a professional manager"), and the "collegial leader" local government system (i.e. in which mayors / elected local leaders of the municipality without bearing the official title of "Mayor" "are required to cooperate collegially with other powerful actors or bodies") (Heinelt and Hlepas 2006: 36-37).

---

31 The typology starts from the hypothesis that "[t]he structural features of municipal government in any specific country reflect a balance or compromise among [...] three organizing principles: layman rule, political leadership, and professionalism." (1) "Layman rule" signifies that "citizens elected for political office should be involved effectively and intensively in the making of decisions". (2) "Political leadership" is the keynotion in Mouritzen's and Svara's scheme, implicating the situation of "politicians [officials] promoting value choices and feeding energy and passion into policy systems". (3) "Professionalism" describes the hypostasis of "professionals respond[ing] to and seek[ing] to address needs", exactly as "politicians respond to demands". Mouritzen and Svara conclude that "political leadership is the starting point for the development of a typology of government forms [at the local level]. The key issue is how political power is obtained, maintained, exercised and shared. [...] Political power is a function of the degree of control a political actor – a person or a collective body – has in two arenas. First, to what extent is the city council controlled by one or more political actors? The second arena is the executive, and the question is to what extent is control over the executive in the hands of one or more political actors. Formal structure is important to answering these questions, but so are informal institutional rules and norms." [italics added; additions mine] Not surprisingly, the two scholars consider – though breviloquently and hardly in a structured, comprehensive fashion – the impact of informal, patron-client-styled interactions and relations between the members comprising the local political elite.

Firstly, this book inquired into the pieces of legislation, for the six respective countries, regulating the form and the substance of decentralization and administrative organization: Law No. 215/2001 on Local Public Administration (for Romania); the 1990-1994 legislative series – Constitutional Act No. 294/1990 Col.; Act of the Czech National Council No. 367/1990 Col. on Municipalities, amended as 410/1992; Act of the Czech National Council No. 425/1990 Col. on District Offices, the Regulation of the Sphere of Their Activities; amendments to Acts of the Czech National Council No. 266/1991, No. 542/1991, Act No. 21/1992, Act No. 403/1992, Act No. 152/1994 and Act No. 254/1994 – (for the Czech Republic); Law of March 8, 1998 on Local Self-government, (for Poland); the Law on Local Self-government No. LXV of 1990 and the Cardinal Act on Local Government No. CLXXXIX of 21st of December 2011 (for Hungary); Slovak National Council Act No. 346 of 1990 on Local Government Elections, Slovak National Council Act 369/1990 on Municipalities, Law No. 221/1996 on the territorial and administrative subdivisions of the Slovak Republic, Slovak National Council Act No. 222 of 1996 on the organization of the local state administration (for the Slovak Republic); and the Local Self-Government and Local Administration Act of 1991, the Municipal Budgets Act of 1998, and the Local Taxes and Fees Act of 1997 (for Bulgaria). From the study of the pieces of legislation for the six states under scrutiny, the following types of systems of local government are highlighted:

(1) For the municipality of Tecuci (Romania): from the standpoint of the vertical relations, a system of local government that is "mixed", "Southern"-styled (hybrid, in fact, as the local elite is paradoxically largely isolated), with the dominance of "the clientelistic / patronage model", based on "support", completed by "the market-enabling model" (for it exists a imbrications between the political elite and the economic one), of "Central-East European type"; from the standpoint of the horizontal relations, a system of local government that is accentuated "dualist" (for both the Council and the Mayor are popularly elected) and "consociational", out of which resulting a model of "semi-presidentialism" type.

(2) For the municipality of Česká Lípa (the Czech Republic): from the standpoint of the vertical relations, a system of local government that is "fused", "Northern"-styled, with the preponderance of "the economic-development model", founded on "partnership", alongside "the market-enabling model" (with a pragmatic-technocratic approach), of "Central-East European type"; from the standpoint of the horizontal relations, a system of local government that is moderate-to-weak "dualist" (for the popularly elected Council appoints the Mayor, who is hence responsible towards the council) and "majoritarian" (with the Council's dominance in decision-making), out of which appearing a model of hybrid "presidentialism" type, with "parliamentarism" tendencies (for the appointed Mayor elects his executive committee by himself).

(3) For the municipality of Oleśnica (Poland): from the standpoint of the vertical relations, a system of local government that is "dual", "Northern"-styled, with the prevalence of "the welfare state model", sustained on "social empathy (sensitivity)", and juxtaposed to "the market-enabling model" (with a special emphasis on local investments), of "Central-East European type"; from the standpoint of the horizontal relations, a system of local government that is accentuated "dualist" (for both the Council and the Mayor are popularly elected) and "consociational", the combination of which cumulatively determining a model of "semi-presidentialism" type.

(4) For the municipality of Gyula (Hungary): from the standpoint of the vertical relations, a system of local government that is "dual", hybrid "Southern"-styled (with a local elite who is paradoxically largely isolated), with the dominance of "the economic-development model", based on "partnership", completed by "the market-enabling model" (with a pragmatic and a technocratic perspective), of "Central-East European type"; from the standpoint of the horizontal relations, a system of local government that is accentuated "dualist" (for both the Council and the Mayor are popularly elected) and "consociational", out of which resulting a model of "semi-presidentialism" type.

(5) For the municipality of Targovishte (Bulgaria), from the standpoint of the vertical relations, a system of local government that is "mixed", "Southern"-styled (hybrid, in fact, as the local elite is paradoxically largely isolated), with the dominance of "the clientelistic / patronage model", based on "support", completed by "the market-enabling model" (for it exists a imbrications between the political elite and the economic one), of "Central-East European type"; from the standpoint of the horizontal relations, a system of local government that is accentuated "dualist" (for both the Council and the Mayor are popularly elected) and "consociational", out of which resulting a model of "semi-presidentialism" type.

(6) For the municipality of Levice (the Slovak Republic), from the standpoint of the vertical relations, a system of local government that is "fused", "Southern"-styled (hybrid, with the local elite relatively isolated), with the predominance of "the economic-development model", underpinned on "partnership", coupled by "the market-enabling model" (for it combines with a pragmatic-technocratic perspective on local matters), of "Central-East European type"; from the standpoint of the horizontal relations, a system of local government that is accentuated "dualist" (for both the Council and the Mayor are popularly elected) and "consociational", out of which resulting a model of "semi-presidentialism" type.

According to Bennett, the "new democracies" of East-Central Europe – hence Romania, the Czech Republic, Poland, Hungary, the Slovak Republic, and Bulgaria –, are confined to a "fused local government system". Quite clearly, the scholarly propensity is to classify the six selected cases as instances of the "Southern local government system", but this mechanical assertion is not completely adequate, since the present study shows the general lack of inter-actions of the local political elite to the central level of government, an obser-vation that might hint to the contingencies of the Southern-Northern dichoto-mous categorization and to the "in-between", intermediate nature of the local government systems in the six selected case-studies (or, probably, for the re-gion of East-Central Europe at large). At a horizontal consideration of the local government systems of the six selected cases, all the six cases studied here are epitomes of dualist local systems – even though, dualism is expressed in dif-ferent degrees for all the six instances, with a more accentuated dualism in the case of Tecuci, Gyula, Oleśnica, primarily due to the fashion in which the Mayor is elected and to the legal position of the Local Council in the institu-tional framework of the municipality –, and of consociational local decisional arrangements – again, in different degrees. Following Bäck's fourfold classi-fication, the municipalities of Tecuci and Targovishte fall rather in the category of "presidentialism", whereas the municipality of Česká Lípa constitutes a classical example of "parliamentarism", with a "consociationalist" touch, as the executive committee assisting and sharing the responsibility of implement-ing the Council's decisions with the Mayor is formed as to reflect the propor-tionality of seats among the winning parties from the Municipal Council. The municipalities of Oleśnica and Gyula belong rather to a "semi-presidental" logic, with two equally strong, popularly elected Council and mayor. Finally, the municipality of Levice is, to a large extent, an exemplification of "parlia-mentalism", weaker than the case of Česká Lípa, for the popularly-elected mayor is surrounded by an advisory committee, with executive responsibilities, whose composition is established by the Municipal Council. Ultimately, be-yond and irrespective of the legal *codex* regulating the functioning of the two main instances of power at the local level and establishing the character of the power relations between them, the local authorities display a propensity to rely on a "socially determined and locally embedded *logic of appropriateness*", coupled with a "pragmatically driven political *logic of consequentiality*"[32], that is, on the actual, effective *nuclei* of power at the local level (including here even economic and cultural local notabilities, and their recognition by the local political leadership) and with the acknowledgement of the subsequent locally determined and maintained, perpetuated patterns of policy-making and net-works of power and elite interactions.

In one of the earliest analyses of local reforms and decentralization in East-Central Europe, Baldersheim puts forward a fourfold typology of local gov-ernment systems, underpinned on two dichotomous variables: (a) the "territo-rial consolidation" of the local government system (for a certain country), and (b) the "functional consolidation" of the local government system (of a given country); each variable takes two characteristics, either "fragmented" or

---

32 The terminology belongs to March and Olsen 1989 [italics added].

"consolidated". Based on the typology, Baldersheim estimates that the Czech and the Hungarian local government systems are "functionally consolidated and territorially fragmented" (Baldersheim, Blaas, Horváth, and Illner 1996: 30) examples. Additionally, Baldersheim perceives the Czech local government system as being the closest to the typical Northern local system (Baldersheim, Blaas, Horváth, and Illner 1996: 40), among the states of the former communist world, with distinctively "administrative-integrated types of subnational government" (Baldersheim, Blaas, Horváth, and Illner 1996: 41).

In addition, Page and Goldsmith propose a twofold categorization of local government systems and government traditions at the local level: (1) the "integrated" systems of local government (i.e. in which local administrative units or municipalities are thusly adjusted so as to correspond to an *a priori* established optimal size for the efficient provision of services and for a manageable administrative load; e.g. the Anglo-Saxon and Northern Scandinavian local systems), and (2) the "nonintegrated" systems of local government (Page and Goldsmith 1987) (i.e. in which local administrative units or municipalities have no correspondence to a planned framework of service provision, small units bearing their own administrative *apparatus* and elected officials, and ensuring basic public service with the help of central or integrative institutions; e.g. the French and most of Mediterranean local government systems). For the region of former "Sovietized Europe", Poland resembles the better the "integrated" system of local government (i.e. where less than 5% of the municipalities have less than 100,000 inhabitants), whereas the Czech Republic, Slovakia, Hungary, Romania, and Bulgaria correspond to a "nonintegrated" system of local government (where, according to Page and Goldsmith (1987), more than 20% of municipalities have less than 100,000 inhabitants).

Employing Maurithzen and Svara's typology[33], Polish analysts Agnieszka Pawlowska and Katarzyna Radzik (2007: 40-52)[34] differentiate among three types of local leadership; their taxonomy is utilized for a comprehensive inquiry into the transformations characteristic to the Polish local self-government, but it can be easily instrumentalized for the entire region of East-Central Europe. Three models of local leadership are distinguishable: (a) "technocratic" (i.e. focused on service delivery, rather than the political aspect; decision-making is consensual and pragmatic; a "dynamic stabilization" form of leadership, of general rules, allowing for a considerable degree of independence in institution building; transformation in local leadership is dominantly determined by endogenous triggers; e.g. Northern countries), (b) "bureaucratic" (i.e. featuring high level of institutionalization of leadership, with a focus on political aspects, due primarily to a mayor enjoying broad party support and being entrusted with a wide range of executive attributions; having a quite conservative institutional settlement, this model of local leadership can only permit exogenous factors of transformation; e.g. Southern countries), and (c) "transformative" (i.e. marked by a low degree of institutionalization of leadership, by an even significance of service delivery and political representation for the mayor; transformations in local leadership are uneven, while disparities in change may arise mainly from citizens' disenchantment and pressure, not from functioning legal and institutional order; e.g. UK, Ireland).

---

33 Probably one of the most comprehensive typologies of models of local leadership, the four "ideal types of governmental form", belongs to Paul E. Maurithzen and James H. Svara: (1) "the strong-mayor form" (i.e. in which the popularly elected mayor exercises control over the council, drafting, proposing, and overseeing the implementation of policy lines at the local level, leading the municipal professional apparatus, discretionarily hiring and firing civil servants, including the chief executive or the city manager, if such position exists in the organizational framework of the town; the dominant principle is the "political leadership" one); (2) "the committee-leader form" (i.e. in which the mayor is "the political leader" of the town, without actually controlling the council, while the executive functions are divided among the mayor, the council – through standing committees –, and the city manager, if existent; all three principles are equally operating in this case); (3) "the collective form" (i.e. in which the executive prerogatives are locally exercised in a collegiate fashion, under the form of a committee or commission formed by local councilors and the mayor; the prevailing principle is the "layman" principle); (4) "the council-manager form" (i.e. in which a professional administrator, chief executive, or city manager conducts the executive attribution of the municipality, being appointed by the local council, under criteria of proficiency, efficacy, efficiency, and high qualification, whereas the mayor – who is elected by the councilors from among themselves – exerts only ceremonial attributions; the guiding principle here is professionalism).

34 When constructing their typology, the two Polish scholars employ three criteria: (a) "institutional and legal conditions of local leadership", (b) "raison d'être of local governance" (i.e. either service delivery or community representation), and (c) "adaptability of local structures to governance arrangements".

Clarence N. Stone develops a compelling model of urban leadership, a model with an extensive applicability for the American politics, but with a clearly limited one for the case of East-Central European states. Nevertheless, this model of local leadership might be telling for the formation and the construction of fellowship-*qua*-purpose, i.e. the gathering of populace around a set of specific locally relevant (long-term) objectives. Stone distinguishes among different styles of local personal leadership, based on the "scope of policy impact" (either "minimal", "redistributive", or "reallocative"), the impact on followers or citizens (ranging from insignificant, little, to significant), and the extent of the leader's policy orientation on institution building process (placed on the "none – some (within government / among citizens) – extensive (within government / among citizens)" *continuum*) (Stone 1995: 96-116, esp. 107-110). Employing these variables and its indicators, different styles of local leadership are discerned, although the focus is reserved for the "strong" mayoral type, in which the mayor is popularly elected and is often associated to the so-called "ward politician". This particular type can be partly extended for the cases of the local councilors in Tecuci and Targovishte, for a series of observations is worth bearing in mind: (1) as opposed to a typical "community" leader, a "ward" politician is dominantly and primarily interested in forming a stable group of followers, initially through a political organization meant to ensure electoral success and a constant political support afterwards (particularly, within a Local Council characterized by weak party discipline, by inexistent ideological affiliations, and by back-staged alliances); (2) the scope of "ward politician" is to preserve his / her group of supporters for the future candidacy for an office at the national level (usually, an MP position), a move which is, to a large extent, predictable, as the politician is unable or unwilling to advance long-term developmental strategies at the local or community level, and to coalesce citizen participation and involvement around a given objective of local significance (what Stone called "institutionaliz[ing] community involvement in governance" (Stone 1995: 110)); (3) instead, this type of local political elite is concerned with cultivating and entertaining close and closed interactions with specific groups (especially, party-related and business-related groups), whose members are thusly "institutionally well-connected"; (4) finally, since local elections are generally candidate-centered, this type of local politician is quite visible, present, especially in small towns, where he / she is perceived as a provider (hence, conserving and perpetuating, according to Stone, a logic of the inhabitant (or of "the ruled") as a "consumer", not as a "citizen").

Inspired by the American urban case, Frederickson et al. differentiate between two types of cities: (1) "political cities" arranged on a "mayor-council legal platform", with the following traits: "a directly elected mayor, the separation of powers between the mayor and the city council, district elections for the council, and no professional chief administrative officer"; a rather "presidential form of [local] government"; (2) "administrative cities" arranged on a "council-manager" legal platform, bearing the following characteristics: "councils elected at large, a symbolic mayor selected from the council, and unity of power. The administrative city is operated by a city manager, chosen on the basis of merit, at the head of a merit-based civil service system all reporting to the manager" (Frederickson, Johnson, and Wood 2004: 30-31); the manager is usually appointed by the Council; a rather "parliamentary form of [local] government" (Frederickson, Johnson, and Wood 2004: 100). The assertion the three American scholars advance is that the two types of local urban government suffered major changes such as they become particularly resembling; as a consequence, two other types are proposed: (3) the "conciliated city" (i.e. "a complex mix of the primary principles and logic of political and administrative cities" (Frederickson, Johnson, and Wood 2004: 107)[35], with: a separately and popularly-elected mayor, serving full time and with a staff, with no position in the Council, but able to veto its decisions; a city manager with extended executive power, but whose mandate can be terminated by a joint mayor-Council decision, and whose activity is reported to both the Council and the mayor); and (4) the "adapted city" (i.e. a local government arrangement in which the mayor is directly elected, while the Council is likely to be elected in a mixed form – by district and at large –, the city manager is likely to exist, but he/she can equally be absent in this arrangement; being a full-time position, with a staffing and remuneration, the mayor is not part of the Council, although he / she can has the power to veto the Council's decisions, while the Council itself may work either full-time or part-time, having or lacking a specialized staff). The six cases subscribe to a classical "political city", for, except for the Czech case of Česká Lípa – which partially corresponds to a "parliamentary" form of local government, with a mayor appointed by the Council and an administrative-executive committee / board, replacing the typical "city manager" –, the Local/Municipal Councils of Tecuci, Oleśnica, Levice, Gyula, and Targovishte work, at least theoretically, on a "sepration-of-powers", "mayor-Council" legal logic, having no "city administrator" position incorporated in the organization framework of the municipality, as the mayor represents the principal executive office (with the partial exception of the "advisory (executive) committees" functioning in the Slovak case).

"Traditional democracy placed city council, the local representative assembly, in juxtaposition with and in opposition to the properly elected 'higher administrative officials of the city,' which blunted any hope of dramatic initiatives while protecting individual options." (Marcus 2001: 43, quoting Pennsylvania's political scientist Leo S. Rowe's contributions on city government, at the end of the 19th century) In discussing the concept of "local governance", Denters and Rose find "polycentricism" at the core of the notion, namely "a

---

35 See, also, the schematic presentation of the five types of local government systems in urban America, at p. 108.

constellation", "a multitude of relatively autonomous" (Denters and Rose 2005: 1-11) actors or units (including central and local political elites, NGOs, corporate organizations, private entrepreneurship, concerned citizenry, etc.) working together in decision-making at the level of municipality. Two main perspectives plead in favor of local governance: (1) the "democratic perspective", according to which the locality is undoubtedly considered the most accessible power level for citizen participation, which thusly encounters the most varied possibilities of active involvement in the community business, for, in addition, the local level presupposes more easily comprehensible and more immediate aspects of governance; and (2) the "managerialist" or "functional perspective" (Denters 2011: 315), according to which local government is perceived as the most effective and efficient form of public policing and service delivery, because local elites have a more clear, accurate, down-to-earth, grassroots knowledge and standpoint on the specific conditions and needs of the locality, and can properly decide on local matters. Nevertheless, in the region of East-Central Europe, the pace to local governance and decentralization has been particularly slower, while the complexity of these processes has been diffused. Only sporadically, "local politicians in at least some of the CEE countries (Poland, Hungary, the Czech Republic) have been attracted by the idea of the shift from traditional government to the wider concept of governance, and by management styles identified often with the New Public Management" (Swianiewicz 2005: 123). Though clearly fashionable, the trend of the NPM has not reached extensively into Eastern and Central European countries, although reliable studies in this respect lack. However, in the three above-mentioned states, a concern for managerial forms of local leadership or, at least, an inclination towards more pragmatic approaches towards local administration and decision-making can be observed even for the cases under scrutiny here. Hence, although purely managerial forms of local governance may be absent in ECE countries – with the partial exception of the Polish case, extremely influenced by the neighboring German local development, and of the Czech case –, the trend towards NPM, whose boom in the Western administrations is dated in the 1980s, may anachronically extend to this region.

b)   Local Councils in Romania

Within the Romanian political, legal, and administrative systems, the Local Councils are designed as deliberative organisms, meant to collaborate with the

Mayor, the executive-administrative institution at the local level[36]. The members of the Local Council are popularly elected, through a proportional representation formula, on lists. The prefects of the counties are the ones to establish the number of local councilors for each city, municipality and commune, according to the population of these administrative units (but with a minimum number of eleven and a maximum one of thirty-five). According to the Law 215/2001 on Local Public Administration, the Local Councils fulfill the following functions and prerogatives: the approval and modification of its own organic regulations and of the organic regulations (statutes, bylaws) of the various departments and organisms of the local administrations; the approval of the formulation and the execution of the local budget and the authorization of other budget-related issues (local expenses, use of budgetary reserves, credit transfers, loans, closing accounts, etc.); the appointment of the Vice-Mayor(s); the establishment of the creation of autonomous bodies of the local administration, at the proposal of the Mayor, and the establishment of their organization and stuff (scales and sub-scales of civil servants); the approval of various studies, project, projections and strategies on socio-economic development and improvement; the establishment of local taxes and duties for limited periods of time (usually yearly); the determination of forms of managing services and the resolution to create self-managing public business entities / municipal entities and mercantile (trading) companies of local interest, and the approval of their corresponding organic regulations and their bylaws of foundations; the administration of the public and the private domains and of the public business entities / municipal companies (furthermore, the appointment and dismissal of the administrative boards of such companies / entities with integral state capital; the reviewing of quarterly or yearly reports of those state representatives sitting on the boards of local mercantile companies); the resolution on the concession of public services to trading entities / companies; the insurance of the functioning of the administration's community services, such as local transport, housing and unemployment assistance services, etc., of the municipal networks of service delivery, of the institutions addressing education, healthcare, culture, sport and youth; the implementation of public works and improvements; the implementation of social security and social assistance programs; the approval for the foundation of institutions of and economic agents of local interest; the establishment of local charity organizations; the insurance of maintaining public order and of providing public safety and security; the insurance of observing the fundamental rights and liberties of the citizens, inhabitants of the town (commune, village); the insurance of free trade and fair competition and the stimulation and promotion of free individual initiative in economy; the organization of markets, cattle markets, parks, fairs and other ways of entertainment;

---

36 A quite comprehensive summary on the legislative framework of the local administrative system in Romania, up to the reform of 2001, is to be found in Coman, Crai, Rădulescu, and Stănciulescu 2001: 351-416.

the creation of recreational facilities and centers; the insurance of the provision of opportunities for cultural, scientific, artistic, sporting and other activities alike; conferring of the title of honorary citizen (or "The Citizen of the Town") on Romanians or foreign citizens of special merit; the preservation of historical and architectural edifices and monuments, natural parks and natural reservations; the protection of the environment; the collaboration and cooperation with other local authorities (local councils, local administrations) and with local, national or foreign economic agents, in order to advance and pursue common interests; the exercise of other attributions, competences and prerogatives established by law.

Generally, the Local Councils meet regularly once a month, in ordinary sessions. The dates for the ordinary sessions are decided by the Mayor. The sessions of the Local Council are public. The Local Councils meet also in extraordinary sessions and emergency sessions. The former are those gatherings of the local councilors that are convened whenever necessary, after the explicit request of the mayor or after the request of at least one-third of the local councilors. The issues discussed in each meeting, i.e. the setting agenda, are announced to the inhabitants through the edict board of the Town Hall. The decisions in the Local Council are adopted either by simple majority or by absolute majority of votes of the members present in the session; the decisions taken through a majority of two-thirds of the votes are those referring to: the local budget, the establishment of local taxes and other fiscal duties, the administration of the public domain, the cooperation and collaboration with other local authorities or with local, national or foreign economic agents, the organization, development and improvement of the town (commune, village). The Local Council itself decides the manner of voting: secret or open vote. (Usually, decisions concerning aspects linked to private individuals are adopted by secret vote.) The mandate of a member of the Local Council is of four years.

The Local Councils are working in specialized Committees, constituted according to the needs of the community; the number and the specialization of these Committees are not regulated by law. The composition of each Committee and the structure on certain specialized Committees of the Local Council are permanent, unchanged during the mandate of the Council. The Committees initial the resolutions' projects, they initiate inquiries, they decide on different issues raised and submitted by the Council for approval.

c) Municipal Councils in the Czech Republic

Within the Czech political system and administrative scheme, the Municipal Councils ("*Zastupitelstvo města*") are envisaged as deliberative, representative institutional entities, collaborating closely with the Mayor, the executive institution at the local level, together with the Municipal Board. Self-government in the Czech Republic functions on the basis of the Law no. 367 regarding Municipalities, adopted in September 1990: the principal constitutionally-defined administrative units are the municipalities (*"obce"*), but, following an amendment in 2000, the local tier has been supplemented by a regional one, with fourteen regions (*"kraje"*). The Law on Municipalities no. 128 of 2000 determines the institutional framework of self-government: the Municipal Council (*"zastupitelsvo"*), the legislative *forum*, is the expression of autonomy in decision-making of the community. Following an Austro-Hungarian administrative tradition, "the functions of municipalities are divided into independent functions assigned to municipalities by laws (*samostatné působnosti*) and functions delegated by the state administration to municipalities (*přenesené působnosti*). Both sets of functions are exercised jointly by the municipalities" (Brusis 2010: 34), in a dualism between state administration (*"státní správa"*) and self-administration (*"sámospráva"*). The concept of "local autonomy" is closely linked to that of "decentralization": "The concept of autonomy arose from notions of political separateness in local government, its adherents arguing that because local government is closest to its citizens, it is in the best position to represent their interests. This 'grass roots' notion of democracy demands an autonomy and freedom from interference by higher tiers of government. An examination of the bureaucratic and financial dimensions of central-local relations, however, shows real limits of local autonomy. In matters of finance, for example, fiscal dependence is a characteristic common to all countries, and [...] the trend is towards increasing levels of dependence." (Caulfield and Larsen 2002: 12)

Due primarily to the severeness of the communist regime following the "Prague Spring" of 1968, debates on the administrative-territorial centralism of Czechoslovakia – in spite of the lands' incipient interwar traditions of local relative independence – were taken outside the decision-making area, despite being carried in the *academia*[37]. The discussion on decentralization started, exactly like all throughout the region, only after 1989, with the process of transition to democracy. As in all the six countries scrutinized here, three main features dominated the territorial-administrative and leadership logic prior to 1989: the principles of "democratic centralism", that of "homogeneous state authority", and that of "dual subordination" (Illner 1991: 23-24) (central authorities had the prerogative of even suspending a Local Council). The principal characteristics of the former communist regime, as identified by Illner, refer to that: "1. it was undemocratic", "2. it was centralist – any authentic territorial self-government was excluded", "3. territorial government lacked economic and financial foundation", "4. public administration and self-government were amalgamated into a single system based on the ideology of

---

37 See, in this respect, the efforts of scholar Michal Illner, particularly, for the present discussion, Illner and Jungmann 1988.

'democratic centralism'", "5. horizontal integration within and among administrative areas was weak, a sectorial perspective was far the most important" (Illner 1991: 23-25).

Hence, the Czech Republic presents a series of peculiarities in terms of regional and local administration. Firstly, levels of decentralization constitute a central preoccupation. Secondly, while local councilors are popularly elected, the Mayor is elected by and responsible to the Council. The members of the Municipal Councils are extremely diverse in the case of the Czech Republic; the Municipal Council itself is a remarkably heterogeneous organism. It gathers individuals, representatives of different legitimacy, diversely selected and, subsequently, exhibiting various allegiances and political loyalties.

The Municipal Council in Česká Lípa meets regularly one time each month, usually during the last week, with the exception of February, July and September, when there are no ordinary meetings of the Council; in October, two ordinary meetings are customary (one during the second week, the other in the last week). According to the existing legislation, the Municipal Council must hold a session at least once every three months; if the Council fails to meet at least once within a period of six months, the head of the District Office can initiate a proposal of disbandment to the Parliament. The sessions of the Municipal Council are, of course, public. As in the Romanian case, extraordinary and emergency sessions of the Municipal Council can take place in legally mentioned circumstances. The setting agenda is available for the citizens of the town through the edict board of the Town Hall, but also *via* the website of the Municipality. The members of the Municipal Council can jointly decide to opt for secret vote in adopting local decisions, but generally, the vote in the Czech Municipal Councils is open. The mandate of a member of the Municipal Council is four years. As in the case of Romanian Local Councils, the Czech Municipal Councils are normally working in specialized Committees; their constitution is in accordance with the needs and demands of the community and the date for weekly sessions of each Committee is decided jointly by the members of each Committee, with the approval of the Council. Nevertheless, the formation of three Committees is compulsory by law: the Financial and the Audit (Control) Committees and, for the communities comprising more than 10% non-Czech nationals, the Committee for Ethnic Minorities (this is not the case with Česká Lípa). The structure of the Committees is permanent for the duration of a four-year mandate, though other specialized Committees can be established by the Council, for meeting special, temporary needs within the community.

d)   Municipal Councils in Poland

Within the Polish legislative system, the Municipal Councils are designed as local legislative *fora*. Until the local reform of 1998, the Municipal Councils' main attributions and responsibilities were the approval of the local budget and the appointment of the Mayor of the Municipality[38]; after the reform, only the former remained an exclusive attribution of the Council, the Mayor becoming a popularly elected instance (see, for this change, Regulski 2003: esp. 165-178). At the local level, the Polish institutional arrangement translated the parliamentarian model of democracy: the legislative body, i.e. the Municipal Council, was the only entity that was popularly elected, while the Mayor ("*burmistrz*" or "*sołtys*"), i.e. the executive instance, was elected and appointed by the Council, being the indirect emanation of the popular vote. The Municipality Self-Government Act, adopted on the 8th of March 1998 by the Polish *Sejm*, sets the institutional and organizational framework at the local level. According to the Self-Government Act of 1998, the Municipal Council adopts resolutions within an extended range of spheres of competences by ordinary, qualified majority of votes in the presence of at least half of the statutory composition thereof, in open vote (unless otherwise provided for in a separate legislation). The Council meets in ordinary and extraordinary sessions, which are disclosed to the public, openness of the proceedings of the authorities of the Polish municipalities being particularly guaranteed and protected. The mandate of a member of the Municipal Council is four years, with the possibility of reelection; the number of mandates a local councilor can win is unbounded by any legislation. Art. 18 of the Self-Government Act details in respect to the exclusive competences of the Municipal Council: (1) the adoption of the municipality charter; (2) the determination of remuneration levels for the Mayor, deciding also on the main lines of his work and the adoption of reports from his activities; (3) the appointment and dismissal of the Municipal Treasurer, i.e. the chief accountant of the municipal budget, and of the Municipal Secretary, at the motion of the Mayor; (4) the adoption of resolutions on the municipal budget, the examination of reports resulting from the execution of the budget and the adoption of resolutions concerning a vote of approval for the budget execution; (5) the adoption of resolutions on the conditions and directions of the spatial development of the municipality and on the local zoning plans; (6) the adoption of resolutions on economic programs; (7) the determination of the scope of activity of auxiliary entities, the rules of handing over to them municipal assets for use, and the rules of handing over budgetary resources for the performance and execution of tasks by these entities; (8) the adoption of resolutions on taxes and charges, within the framework of the limits set forth in

---

38   For a brief, but comprehensive, summary on the legislative development of Polish local administration, prior to the reform of 1998, see Cielecka and Gibson 1995: 23-40.

separate legislation; (9) the adoption of resolutions concerning the management of the municipal assets and exceeding the scope of the ordinary management, pertaining to: (9.a) the determination of the rules of purchase, transfer and encumbering of land property, and of the lease or rental thereof for periods longer than three years (if not otherwise provided for in specific legislation); prior to the determination of such rules, the Mayor may perform such actions exclusively with the consent of the Municipality Council; (9.b) the issuance of bonds and determination of the rules of transfer, purchase and repurchase thereof by the Mayor; (9.c) the contracting long-term loans and credits; (9.d) the determination of the *maximum* amount of short-term loans and credits contracting by the Mayor in the course of the fiscal year; (9.e) obligations with respect to investments and renovation projects, the value of which exceeds the limit set annually by the Municipal Council; (9.f) the creation and joining, dissolution and leaving companies and cooperatives; (9.g) the determination of the rules for contributing, withdrawing and transferring shares by the Mayor; (9.h) the creation, the liquidation and restructuring of enterprises, plants and other municipality's organizational units, and the allocation of assets to such entities; (9.i) the determination of the *maximum* amount of loans and guarantees granted by the Mayor in the course of the fiscal year; (10) the determination of the *maximum* amount of obligations which the Mayor may contract acting as a sole person; (11) the adoption of resolutions concerning cooperation with other municipality/ies and allocation of adequate assets for that purpose; (11.a) the adoption of resolutions concerning cooperation with local and regional communities of other countries and joining international associations of local and regional communities; (12) the adoption of resolutions concerning: coat of arms of the municipality, names of streets and public squares, the erection of monuments; (13) the granting honorary citizenship of the municipality; (14) the adoption of resolutions regarding the rules governing scholarships to pupils and students, and (15) the adoption of decisions on other matters reserved by separate legislation for the competences of the Municipal Council. In a nutshell, the Municipal Council in the Polish local institutional framework is responsible for controlling the activities of the Mayor, of the municipality's organizational units and auxiliary entities. The Polish Municipal Council works in committees, either permanent (standing) or temporary; each committee is thusly organized as to respond to the pressing issues within the municipality, with the exception of the Audit Committee, which is compulsory in the institutional framework of the town and in the working manner of the Council. Generally, the Audit Committee issues opinions on the execution of the municipal budget, and makes motions to the Municipal Council concerning a vote of approval for the execution of the budget by the Mayor. The committees are subordinate to the Council, to which they advance plans of work and activity reports. Even though, each committee has a standing membership, other councilors may attend the meetings of the committees, may speak and put forward motions during the committee's sessions, but may not vote; a local councilor can vote only within the committee whose standing member he / she is.

The Self-Government Act establishes, as well, the magnitude of the Municipal Councils in accordance with the population (Art. 17); consequently, a municipality comprising 20,000 inhabitants is to be represented by a Municipal Council comprising 15 individuals; the Council includes 21 members for a town with a population of up to 50,000 inhabitants; 23 for municipalities with a population not exceeding 100,000; 25 local councilors for a municipality counting up to 200,000 inhabitants, and an additional three for every additional number of 100,000 inhabitants (however, not more than forty-five councilors altogether in the legislative body of the community). As a consequence of this regulation, the Municipal Council of Oleśnica, a municipality of 30,000 inhabitants, is formed of 21 members of different social and economic *status*, of different educational and family background, of various ages, but largely homogeneous in terms of gender, religious affiliation and political experience.

Interestingly enough, the Self-Government Act sets forth a sketch of the municipal councilor's portrait: Art. 23 reads as follows: "The councilor is obliged to pursue the best interest of the local self-government community of the municipality. The councilor is in permanent contact with inhabitants and their organizations, and, in particular, accepts postulates reported by inhabitants of the municipality and submits them to the authorities of the municipality for decision. However, the councilor is not bound by the instructions of the electors." In the said article, one can grasp a rather Burkean conception on representation at the local level, as the local councilor is freed from any "mandate"-like form of exercising his function in the benefit of the community; nevertheless, the member of the Municipal Council, having been directly elected, should appeal to his / her constituency in the same direct fashion, establishing and maintaining constant, permanent relations with the citizens of community for which (s)he is part of the political elite. This understanding of representation, as expressed in Art. 23 of the Polish Self-Government Act, coincides with the results obtained from the administration of the questionnaire on the members of the Municipal Council in Oleśnica, since the group forming the local political elite is an isolated one, connected primarily to parts of its constituency (neighbors, local reform groups, friends, supporters, etc.); the scale of proximity proves meaningful *data* with respect to the fashion in which the local councilor sees himself / herself within the community and the manner in which he / she perceives his / her position within the municipality. Due to the fact that most municipal councilors are non-affiliated, being elected rather extramurally, they may nonetheless form "clubs of councilors", i.e. a substitute for party affiliation, more informal, answering to some sort of a coalition of perspectives and beliefs concerning the priorities at the local level, but regulated by the Municipality Charter, as becoming somehow the replacement for party affiliation. As in the Romanian case, the Polish legislation forbids the municipal councilor from: (1) entering into an employment relationship with the office of the Municipality in which (s)he has obtained a mandate; (2) performing the function of a head / deputy head of a Municipality's organizational unit; (3) participating in the vote within the Municipal Council or in one of the Council's committees if such a vote concerns his / her legal interest. Among the principal incompatibilities to the position of a member in the Municipal Council, the Polish legislation enumerates: (1) the mandate of a member of the national Parliament (deputy); (2) the position of *voivode* or *vice-voivode* (i.e. the representative of the national Cabinet at the regional level, at the level of the "*voivodeship*"), and (3) the membership in a body of another unit of the local self-government.

The Municipal Council elects – by secret vote, by an absolute majority of votes, in the presence of at least half of the statutory composition of the Council –, from among its members, the chairperson and his deputies (one to three), but the tasks of the chairman and of his vices consist solely of organizing the work of the Council during ordinary sessions and of chairing its meetings. Customarily, the absence of the chairperson and his deputies will entail the presiding of the session by the most senior local councilor. The chairman can be revoked through a motion of at least one fourth of the statutory composition of the Council; equally, the chairperson can resign its position. Normally, he will convene the Council if necessary, but not less frequently than once per quarter, and he will forward the session agenda to his / her colleagues in the Council, who may, by an absolute majority of the statutory composition, amend it. The convocation of the Municipal Council in extraordinary session is the result of the motion of the Mayor or of at least one fourth of the Council's statutory composition.

The Local Government Reform of 1998 in Poland resulted in the formation of three "tiers of territorial government"[39]: around 2,500 municipalities ("*gminy*"), 308 counties ("*powiats*", plus other 65 cities bearing a county status) and 16 regions ("*województwa*"). It is significant to mention that "[o]n both a municipal and a county level, self government is the only form of public administration. On a regional level, there is a dual structure, on the one hand, elected self-government, and on the other, a governor (*wojewoda*) nominated by the Prime Minister [...]." (Swianiewocz and Herbst 2002: 224) "*Selectwo*" are generally larger, more populous villages (approximately 40,000 out of a total of 58,000 Polish rural settlement units).

---

39 The present brief account is based on the Polish Act on Local Government of 15th of March 1998 and Swianiewocz and Herbst 2002: 219-325.

e) Bodies of Representatives in Hungary

Gabor Soós differentiates two "waves of change", or "types of change", in the evolution of the Hungarian local administration: (1) the "single largest and most important change in the history of Hungarian local administration" in the 1990s, when "the communist system was abolished at the local level and the principle of democratic centralism was replaced with the values of decentralization, local democracy and autonomy"; and (2) the second phase of changes happening "after the inception of the new local government system" (Soós 2010: 108), aiming at full institutionalization of the local administration. Article 20 of the Hungarian Constitution of 1949, and the Act on Local Self-Government of 1990 (allowing for a limited, contained, "relative autonomy of local governments"[40]), followed by the Act No. CLXXXIX of 2011 on Local Government in Hungary (customarily referred to as "*Mötv*"), refer to the local level of the Hungarian administrative organization[41]. In effect, the territory of Hungary is divided into nineteen counties ("*megyék*") and 3,177 municipalities ("*települések*", out of which twenty-three cities of "county *status*" or "*megyei jogú városok*"). Each such municipality has a deliberative assembly ("*képviselő-testület*"), popularly elected every five years, while the executive matters of the community are conducted by the Mayor ("*polgármester*") and his office ("*Polgármesteri hivatal*"), elected by the citizens for a five-year term[42]. The regional tier of the administration is the "county" (the equivalent of "*județ*" in Romania, or of "*kraj*" in the Czech and Slovak Republics); the citizenry of the county elects, for a five-year mandate and under a proportional representation *formula*, the members of the County Assembly ("*megyei közgyűlés*", the deliberative body at the regional level). Whereas the Body of Representatives constitutes the legislative body at the local level, the Mayor and the "Chief Executive" are the executive instances. The *formula* of dual or bicephalous local executive in Hungary is similar – though, simpler – to the one in Slovakia: the Mayor is responsible with the implementation of the Local Council's decisions, whilst the Chief Executive (sometimes called "notary", "*jegyző*") is responsible with the leadership of the local bureaucratic *apparatus*. The Mayor represents the political facet of local government (being directly elected by the citizens), whereas the Chief Executive represents the bureaucratic facet of local government, a mark of professionalism, skillfulness, proficiency, and

---

40 A detailed analysis of the conditions of adopting the Act on Local Self-Government of 1990 in Hungary is to be found in Pál Kovács 1999: 53-76.
41 For a short and comprehensive account on the legislative evolution of Hungarian local administration, up to 1995, see Davey 1995: 57-75.
42 A more detailed presentation of the local administrative system and its constitutional and legal foundations in Hungary is to be found in: Dezső, Bodnár, and Somody 2010: 39-42 and 43-44; and Bodnár and Dezső 2010: 219-259.

permanence in local public administration (being appointed by the Local Council for an undetermined period). The responsibilities of local authorities are clearly determined for each type of municipality (either "commune" or "city"); they are not area-determined, but are rather separated into "obligatory" (further separated into "first category" and "second category" of local responsibilities) and "optional" responsibilities, in accordance with the provisions of the Act on Local Government of 1990[43]. According to the Local Government Law of 2011, the Local Council in the Hungarian local government system ("*képviselő-testület*", literally translated as "body of representatives")[44] "has the right to manage independently so-called 'local public affairs'. Its decisions in this area may be reviewed only by a court on grounds of legality. The representative body exercises the ownership rights over local government property; it manages – within the limits of the law – its own revenues, and imposes local taxes. It determines the annual budget of the municipality, and may decide whether to take out credit and loans (although such decisions have been controlled by central government since 2011). The council decides on the organizational structure of the municipality (e.g. whether it maintains a separate mayor's office or not). The body may establish local government institutions, and may associate with other local authorities. It may issue local decrees, which cannot be in conflict with higher-ranking legal norms." (Szente 2013: 158-159) Law No. CLXXXIX on Local Government lists, under the Article 13, paragraph (1), the "mandatory tasks" to be performed by every Body of Representatives / Local Council: (a) performing settlement development, settlement planning; (b) performing settlement operations (development of public cemeteries and maintenance of public lightning care, providing chimney sweeping services, local roads and accessories and street furniture, for the design and maintenance of public parks and other public areas, providing parking for vehicles); (c) oversight of the public areas and the public institutions owned by the local government; (d) providing basic healthcare services for the promotion of healthy lifestyles; (e) ensuring environmental health (sanitation, ensuring the purity of the urban environment, through insect and rodent control);

---

43 E.g. of "first category" responsibilities of local authorities in small-to-medium-sized towns are: drinking water purification, healthcare and welfare benefits, public lightning. "Second category" responsibilities at the level of this type of communities are determined through special laws, and only when the municipality owns the necessary financial means to carry such responsibilities. "Optional" responsibilities are determined through Local Council's decisions or through local referendum. These responsibilities are equally dependent on the financial capacities of the municipality. Such e.g. are: employment incentives, support for scientific research, artistic and sport activities, public safety, etc. See, in this respect, Dobos 2014, 18 pp.

44 In reference to the local representative authority in the Hungarian local government system, the collocation "Body of Representative" (as more accurately translating the equivalent in Hungarian) will be employed all throughout this book, meaning Local/ Municipal Council.

(f) providing pre-school care; (g) supporting and providing cultural services, in particular through the public library service, the movie theater, supporting local arts performing organizations, protecting the local cultural heritage, and supporting the cultural activities of the local community; (h) providing social services, child welfare services and benefits; (i) managing local housing and space planning, through housing care and rehabilitation, as well as providing homelessness prevention for at least ten homeless persons on the territory of its constituency; (j) ensuring local environmental and nature protection, water management, and water damage control; (k) ensuring defense of its constituency, civil protection, disaster management, and local employment; (l) establishing local taxation, together with economic and organizational tasks related to tourism; (m) ensuring sales opportunities (including the possibility of selling during weekend) for local small and primary producers, in accordance with the products specifically defined by law; (n) ensuring and promoting sports and youth activities at the local level; (o) managing local ethnic affairs; (p) contributing to public safety by ensuring local settlement; (r) ensuring local public transport; (s) ensuring waste management at the local level; (t) ensuring or providing heating for the houses of the municipality; (u) being responsible of other public utility services, under the provisions of the local government. In addition to the "mandatory responsibilities", set up by the Law of 2011, the Body of Representatives of Gyula has decided upon other "voluntary responsibilities", comprised in the article 4 of the Organizational and Operational Regulations No. 2 of 2013: (a) financing tourism jobs and tourism development overall; (b) deciding on twinning the town with other municipalities and on the development of other international relations; (c) actively supporting Gyula and its surroundings in the "Multipurpose Small Region Association"; (d) operating the school bus; (e) operating the municipal guest houses and other forms of local accommodation; (f) ensuring or providing junior soccer, handball, and swimming lessons for the community; (g) operating local museums and theaters; (h) supporting the local media; (i) providing support for Church-run boarding schools of the constituency; (j) providing social assistance, under municipal regulations; (k) creating and protecting local jobs; (l) maintaining operations of public educational institutions functioning at the local level; (m) organizing agricultural production, sale, dissemination, training, on the local markets; (n) supporting locally the deconcentrated bodies of the national authorities; (o) performing any other task undertaken by the Body of Representatives, in accordance to the provisions, regulations, or decisions of the Body of Representatives itself.

Generally, Hungary, although experiencing one of the earliest transitions to democracy, was one of the slow countries in the region to develop meaningful local autonomy and decentralization. Hungarian political scientists Gábor Soós and László Kákai discuss the case, from two main positions: "The local democratization yielded a mixed outcome. On the one hand, local governments were able to successfully replace the old system of communist councils, and became the basis of the functioning system of public administration and legal autonomy. However, the subnational system now has to overcome four challenges, all of which have roots in the various aspects of democratization: the democratic deficit; the highly fragmented local government system with a high cost of local administration and services; the lack of consensus on the powerful meso-governmental level; and the weakness of the societal autonomies." (Soós and Kákai 2011: 528-551) As already presented, then, the democratic deficits (in the form of either weak citizen participation or high levels of corruption locally) and the financial-budgetary deficiencies (in the form of the inability of the municipalities to raise budgets independently) are the constant problems of the local level in East-Central Europe, replicated in the case of Hungary, as well.

f)   Municipal Councils in the Slovak Republic

From the very birth of the Slovak Republic, on the 1st of January 1993, through constitutional provisions, the (re)establishment of "self-governing municipalities with a high level of independence" (Nemec, Bercik, and Kuklis 2000: 302) has become a *desideratum*. In the initial phase of democratization and decentralization, the rule was indeed "independence", resulting in the formation of thirty-eight districts within a relatively small territory, which, in turn, generated "atomization and fragmentation", leaving parts of the county relatively alienated from one another. As in the Romanian case, the post-communist territorial-administrative construction of Slovakia envisaged an operational "regional" level, particularly important for the yet-to-come European accession. Article 64 of the Slovak Constitution establishes the primacy of the "region" ("*samosprávne kraje*") in the local administrative system: "Territorial self-administration shall be composed of a municipality and *a higher territorial unit* [i.e. the region]." (The Constitution of the Slovak Republic, Art. 64 [italics and additions mine]) After a democratic backlash, the local administrative reforms were initiated in 1996, leading, by the end of 1998, to the present administrative framework of the country.

Law No. 221 of 1996 regarding the territorial and administrative subdivision of the Slovak Republic constitutes the basis for the functioning of the bodies of local autonomy: the Municipal Council ("*mestské zastupitel'stvo*") and the mayor ("*primátor mesta*"). The Municipal Councils in the administrative landscape of the Slovak Republic are local deliberative bodies aimed at increased autonomy and independence toward the central authorities. The gradual reform of the local public administration in Slovakia culminated during 2001: in July, the Act on Regional Self-Government Units has been adopted –

hence, inaugurating a system of local autonomy and management focus on the regional level as the most important tier –, while in September, the "Act on Transfer of some of the Competencies from the National State Administration to the Municipalities and Regional Self-Governmental Units" has been approved by the Parliament. Finally, in October, the adoption of the so-called "Municipal Establishment" led to beginning of the process of fiscal and financial decentralization (or, more accurately, regionalization)[45]. Following this process, stretching from 1996 to the end of 2001, three administrative units were established: the region (*"kraj"* – similar to the Czech region), the district (*"okres"*, seventy-nine, with no significant attributions, but rather of statistical importance), and the municipality (2891 in number, 38 of them bearing a special status, *"mesto"*). Two main components compose the local public administrative system in the Slovak Republic: (a) the regional and municipal self-government, and (b) the regional and district state administration. State or central administration is represented in the territory by eight regional and seventy-eight district offices (deconcentration), whereas local authorities *per se* are: the eight regional self-governments (VUC) and 2,871 municipal self-governments (decentralization). Whereas interconnection exists between the district offices and their respective regional office, regional and municipal self-governments are in a relation of independence to one another, coupled by cooperation in specifically designated areas (e.g. the maintenance of regional roads, the organization of universities, etc.). The Slovak local administrative system is conducive to produce a quite "integrated" political elite, independent from the central power, coherent in local decision-making. In practice, this construction – that should generate a high degree of responsiveness to the community needs, and a synonymity of values between the citizens and the local leaders – fails to provide any mechanism for "upwards accountability", and is thusly prone to abuses. Ludmila Malikova explains: "It is within the competence of state administration to oversee the work of self-governmental bodies *only in certain areas where the latter carry out tasks delegated by the state*"[46].

---

45 For a comprehensive account on the regional and local reform of the Slovak public administration, see the works authored recently by Ludmila Malikova: Malíková and Staroňová 2001: 268-294; Malíková and Buček 1997: 194-215; Surazska, Buček, Malíková, and Daněk 1997: 437-462. See, also, Verheijen and Rebrenovic 1999, and Nemec and Berčík 1999/1998: 184-212.

46 Two examples of such delegation of competences (in which the regional and district offices are rendered futile) are education and infrastructural constructions; in these two spheres, local authorities are customarily checked by the state authorities, through regional and district offices, in the manner in which the attributions are fulfilled. Not the same distribution of power dominates other fields (e.g. environmental matters), in which the state representatives in the territory (i.e. the regional and district offices) retain the upper hand in decision-making. See, for the specific distribution of powers among the regional, municipal, and national levels in the Slovak public administration, Nemec, Bercik, and Kuklis 2000: 318-330.

According to the Law No. 346 of 1990, on Local Government Elections, the Municipal Council[47] is composed of individuals directly elected by the inhabitants, for a mandate of four years, on a single majority voting (quite uncommon for local elections in the region of East-Central Europe). The mayor is directly elected, as well, for a four-year mandate. The Municipal Council bears extensive prerogatives, particularly in the case of *"mesto"* (namely, towns of special status, as is the case of Levice): (a) determines the main lines and the principles of management of the town, together with the disposal of municipal property, approving the most important tasks related to these assets and the management control thereof; (b) approves the city budget and its changes and modifications, exerting control over the spending, approving the account of the city, authorizing the issuance of municipal bonds, approving contracts concluded following art. 20, paragraph (1) of Act no. 369 of 1990, concerning the Organization of Municipalities, deciding on borrowings and loans and on the acceptance of debt guarantee obligations; (c) approves the zoning plan or the development concept for different areas of city life; (d) decides on the establishment or abolition of local taxes, and decides on the imposition of local taxes of special regulation; (e) identifies the requirements of local taxes and of public benefits, deciding on borrowing and lending; (f) calls for local *referendum* on the most salient and important issues of city life and city development, and convenes assemblies of citizens for public consultations on policy directions; (g) votes city regulations; (h) approves agreements of international cooperation and the city's membership in international associations; (i) determines the mayor's salary, under a special regulation; (j) appoints the auditor or the chief inspector of the city, determines the scope of the position of chief inspector (auditor), decides on the salary of this position, votes his dismissal; (k) approves the city statute, the rules of procedure, its own regulation, the remuneration of Mayor's and deputy Mayor's advisory boards and executive committees; (l) establishes, dissolves, and controls the budgets and allowances of local organizations under its supervision, decides the appointment and dismissal of the directors (heads) of these organizations (at the Mayor's proposal); (m) approves the pooling of resources and urban activities, in respect to the participation of the city in associations, regional communities, or in the establishment of a common regional interest fund; (n) establishes and dissolves those institutions necessary for the borough, determining the content and scope of their work; (o) confers honorary citizenship of the town (of Levice), municipal awards and other prizes of the city; (p) establishes the coat of arms, the flag, and the seal of the city; (r) appoints and dismisses the chief of the municipal police, at the Mayor's proposal; (s) decides on setting up special committees in urban areas, defining their responsibilities and attributions, their structure, and their relation to the Municipality; (t) decides on the naming

---

47   Throughout the corpus of this book, the phrase "Municipal Council" will be employed for what, in Slovak legislation, would be literally translated as "self-government".

of streets, squares, and other public spaces; (u) decides on other important matters in other spheres of activity, as prescribed by the Law on Municipalities, the Statute of the town, or other special regulations and provisions. The Municipal Council in Slovakia meets regularly, at least once every three months, though usually once a month. The Council meets in ordinary meeting, the sessions being convened and chaired by the Mayor. The sessions are public, a notice of the Council's meeting, together with the draft agenda of the discussions, being displayed on the official board of the city at least three days before the meeting. Secret sessions are only possible in cases in which the issues discussed are matters specifically protected by special laws. Extraordinary sessions of the Council are organized with the support of at least one third of its members and are being convened within 15 days after the Mayor receives a request in this respect. The adoption of a local decision requires an absolute majority of the councilors present in session; the voting of the local budget must gather three-fifths of all the members of the Municipal Council.

g)   Local Councils in Bulgaria

The drive towards the transformation of local administration in Bulgaria started in 1991, with the adoption of the Local Self-Government and Local Administration Act. Steps towards decentralization were initiated in 1995, when the Act on Administrative and Territorial Structure of the Republic of Bulgaria was adopted.[48] The law of 1995 sets up the legal framework in which self-government is to function in Bulgaria, underpinned by a series of governing principles: "territorial neighborhood", "subsidiarity", "succession and territorial stability" of the administrative structure, "democratic choice" in decision-making, and, finally (and, probably, the most important aspect) the "compliance between the size of the administrative units and their competencies and resources" (Stoilova 2008: 1). The Municipal Property Act of 1996 opened the way for municipalities to autonomously acquire, dispose, and manage the public assets, while the Municipal Budgets Act of 1998 laid down the procedure of organizing, drafting, and adopting a local budget, on a basis of an adjacent legislation – i.e. the Local Taxes and Fees Act, adopted one year earlier, in 1997, a law which will be subsequently developed in the Municipal Debt Act of 2005, establishing the procedure and the contingences of the local debt service.

Administratively, the Bulgarian territory is governed through three tiers: centrally, regionally, through 6 "planning regions" and 28 districts, and locally,

---

48   A brief historic detour on the evolution of local administrative reform in Bulgaria is to
       be found in Stoilova 2008.

through municipality ("*obshtina*"), as the main administrative unit (a number of 264 municipalities divide the territory of Bulgaria). While the "planning regions" were designed as a compliance to the European Charter on Local Self-Government, and, consequently, constitute only statistical units, having no administrative or fiscal prerogatives (similar to the "development regions" in Romania), the provinces ("*oblast*"; assimilated to the "counties" in Romania) are the expression of the state's deconcentrated organization: without being financially autonomous and without actually providing independently any public service, the provinces are designed to oversee the compliance of local decisions with the national law, and the fashion in which the state policy is implemented locally, and to encourage cooperation among territorially closed municipalities in larger projects. The municipality, the main unit of local autonomy, governs itself independently in budgetary and decision-making aspects. According to the Local Elections Act of 1995, the local authorities, the Municipal Council and the Mayor, are both popularly elected, for a four-year mandate. The Municipal Council in Bulgaria is elected on a proportional representation *formula*, while the Mayor is elected after a two-round, majority voting system. The National Association of Municipalities in the Republic of Bulgaria (NAMRB, "*Национално сдружение на общините в Република България*") plays an important role, particularly in the relation of municipalities with the central authorities and in the initiation of cooperation between municipalities on large-scale projects.

The legislative *forum* at the local level in Bulgaria is constituted by the Municipal Council ("*общински съвет*"), "the body of the local self-government" (Law on the Local Government and the Local Administration, Chapter III: "Municipal Council", Art. 18, paragraph (1))[49]. Article 21 of the Law on Local Government and Local Administration of the Bulgarian state, adopted on September 6, 1991, enumerates the general attributions of the Municipal Council: "(a) creates permanent and temporary commissions [i.e. committees, as referred in this book], and elects their members; (b) determines the structure of the municipal administration and the resources for the remuneration of the staff, from the municipal budget; (c) elects and discharges its chairman; (d) elects and discharges the deputy-mayors, upon a proposal of the mayor, and – in towns with district divisions – the district mayors; (e) determines the amount of the remuneration for the mayor, within the framework of the normative provisions in effect; (f) approves the annual budget of the municipality, implements the control over thereof, and approves the report about its fulfillment; (g) determines the amount of the local taxes and fees within the legal limits, provided by law; (h) approves decisions about acquiring, managing, and disposal of municipal assets, and determines the concrete attributions and compe-

---

49 Law on the Local Government and the Local Administration, Chapter III: "Municipal Council", Art. 18, paragraph (1), at http://unpan1.un.org/intradoc/groups/public/documents/untc/unpan016312.pdf, last accessed: 15.02.2016.

tences of the mayor (and of the district mayoralties), in this respect; (i) approves decisions for the creation, transformation, and termination of commercial companies [employing] municipal assets, and determines its representatives in [the board of these companies]; (j) approves decisions for use of bank credits, for conceding of interest-free loans, and for issuing of bonds, under conditions and by order determined by law; (k) approves decision about creating and approval of development plans, and their changes for the territory of the municipality, or parts of it, under the conditions and by the order of the Law for the spatial planning; (l) approves strategies, prognoses, programmes, and plans for development of the municipality; (m) determines requirements for the activity of the individuals and of the corporate bodies on the territory of the municipality, which ensue from the ecological, the historical, the social, and from the other peculiarities of the settlements, as well as from the *status* of the engineering and the social infrastructure; (n) approves decision for establishing and terminating of municipal foundations, and for the management of granted property; (o) approves decisions for participation of the municipality in associations of local authorities in the country and abroad, and determines its representatives in [such associations]; (p) creates districts and mayoralties, under conditions and order determined by law; (r) makes proposals for administrative-territorial changes referring to the territory and the boundaries of the municipality; (s) approves decisions for naming and renaming of streets, squares, parks, engineering facilities, *villa* zones, resorts and resort localities, and other sites of municipal significance; (t) discusses and approves decisions, upon proposals of mayors of districts and mayoralties, on issues of its competence; (u) approves decisions for conducting of *referenda* and general meetings of the population, on issues of its competence; (v) approves the symbols and the seal of the municipality; (w) honors with honorary citizenship Bulgarians and foreign citizens." (Law on the Local Government and the Local Administration, Chapter III: "Municipal Council", Art. 21, paragraph (1) [additions mine]) Following adoption, each document of the Municipal Council should be sent to the Regional Governor, within seven days, for check regarding the compliance to the national legislation. The Municipal Council must be convened at least six times per year; the sessions of the Council are valid, if more than half of all the councilors are present. The Council's decisions are taken by a majority of more than half of the councilors present, in open ballot; decisions regarding the local budget should be taken by a majority of more than half of all councilors (Law on the Local Government and the Local Administration, Chapter III: "Municipal Council", Art. 27). The Council's sessions are public, unless differently decided by the Council itself. (Art. 28) Interestingly enough, the councilors have the right to request corrections and additions to the Council's decisions, within seven days after the date of the session, but these corrections and additions will be, nevertheless, discussed during the next session of the Council (Art. 29). Another interesting point in the regulation of the Bulgarian Municipal Council is the fact that, as opposed to the Permanent Office of the Local Council in Romania, the Municipal Council in Bulgaria does not have a permanent staff (Art. 29a), other than the temporary support received from the executive *apparatus* of the municipality. In the Bulgarian legislation, the municipal councilor terminates his / her mandate ahead of term in the case of: legal incapacity, of him being sentenced to imprisonment for a premeditated crime (with the sentence having come into effect), of resignation handed to the Council, of him being elected Mayor or vice-mayor, or being appointed in a position in the municipal administration, of a continued incapacity or a habitual dereliction of his / her duties for more than six months, by a resolution of the Council made with the majority of more than half of all councilors, and of death. ((Law on the Local Government and the Local Administration, Chapter IV: "Municipal Councilor", Art. 30, paragraph (3)) Member of standing or temporary committees of the Council, the municipal councilor can address queries to the mayor, which can be answered, orally or in writing, during the next session of the Council (Art. 33, paragraph (1), point 4). The councilor should be in permanent touch with and should inform his / her constituency all throughout his / her mandate. It is forbidden for a municipal councilor to participate in decision-making in connection to his / her personal interest (or the interests of his close relatives, in direct or collateral lineage) (Art. 37). Specifically, the Municipal Council of Targovishte meets every last Thursday of the month. The sessions are convened and presided by one Chairman (elected during the first session following the local elections, through secret ballot), helped by two vice-chairmen.

The main functions of the Local / Municipal Council: Organizational Chart and Budget in Tecuci, Česká Lípa, Oleśnica, Gyula, Targovishte, and Levice. The Committees of the Local / Municipal Council

a) Organizational chart of the local administration of the municipality

Because one of the main attributions of the Local / Municipal Council is the approval of the organizational chart of the public administration of the town, Annexes no. 9 displays, in a schematic manner, the organization of the local authority in Tecuci and Česká Lípa, respectively. Being a rather small town, Tecuci is governed by a limited bureaucratic apparatus, of 132 people, specialized in various domains: town architecture, investments, infrastructure and public acquisitions; budget, accountancy and local taxes; agricultural register; human resources; traffic safety; waste capitalization, etc. This organization, with its particular components and departments, mirrors "the priorities of public policies of the town, in accordance with the budgetary and human resources" (Stoica 2003: 86) the town disposes of. The structure of the local authority is a pyramid-like one, stratified on six layers, with a dominance of vertical relationships, with the subordination and centralization of attributions being a particular feature. The horizontal relationships are specific to inter-Component and inter-Service cooperation and, at the top, between the Mayor and the Local Council and between the Vice-Mayor and the Secretary of the Local Council. The various specialized bureaus and departments are centralized around the Mayor. According to the organizational chart, the Mayor operates directly seven institutions (the Mayor's Cabinet, the Vice-Mayor, the Chief-Architect, Technical Direction, Economic Direction, the Component for Human Resources and for the Distribution of Public Functions, the Component for Public Internal Audit) and indirectly fourteen others (the Service for Monitoring Public Services, the Service for Investments in Infrastructure and Public Acquisitions, the Service for Budget and Accountancy, the Service for Local Taxes, the Informational and Data Bureau, the Component for Discipline in Urbanism, the Component for the Authorizations of Constructions, the Component for Owners' Associations, the Component for Emergency Situations, the Component for European Integration, the Administrative Component, the Component for Traffic Safety, the Component for Waste Capitalization, the Component for Forced Execution).

On the other hand, the Local Council entertains horizontal relations with the Mayor and vertical relations with the Secretary of the Town Hall. Directly, the Local Council of Tecuci coordinates the activity of the Permanent Working Apparatus of the Local Council, a department which is subordinated, at the same time, to the Secretary. Indirectly, through the Secretary, the Local Council of Tecuci is leading the Service for Local Public Administration and three Components: the one for Tutelary Authority, the one for Public Relations and the Legal Department. Indirectly as well, through the Service for Local Public Administration, the Local Council coordinates the activity of the Component for Agricultural Register.

The organization scheme of the public administration of Česká Lípa bears a series of both similarities and discrepancies in comparison to the organization of the local authority in Tecuci. Firstly, both are small town, therefore, are employing the service of a quite contingent officialdom. At the Town Hall of Česká Lípa, there are 191 employees, out of which 181 are public officials, functionaries, with the rest of 10 being laborers and auxiliary personnel (referred to as "SUPM", an acronym of their job description in Czech). The bureaucratic work is divided among many departments and divisions: there are 9 Departments (e.g. for Investments, for Human Resources, for Environment, for Criminal acts, for Transport, for Social Affairs and Health, for Taxes, for Development, for Budget, etc.) and 12 Divisions (for Vehicles, for Registration, for Personal Documents, for Sales and Leasing, for Roads and Infrastructure), working within 26 Sections (Government, Press, Internal Control, Administration, Registration, Control, Roads and Authorization of Driving, etc.). The Sections are directly subordinated to the Mayor and responsible to the Municipal Council; the relationships between them can be both horizontal and vertical. Divisions work under the supervision of the Secretariat and of the Council; among them, the Divisions entertain exclusively horizontal relations, of collaboration and cooperation, though each of them delivers a different public service. The Departments coordinate the activities of both Sections and Divisions, while they are independent of each other, their relations being only horizontal. There is, nevertheless, a vertical relation between the Secretariat of the Municipality and the Municipal Council and the Departments.

b)   The Committees of the Local / Municipal Council

The evolution and the eventual modifications regarding the object of interest for the Committees of the Local Council in Tecuci are largely indistinguishable. The perpetuation of the same specialized Committees within the Council during six electoral cycles (i.e. 6 mandates) would indicate a similar perpetuation of the same issues the town confronts with, of the same demands and necessities the inhabitants have. The Local Council of Tecuci works in five specialized Committees: Committee No. 1, for studies, socio-economical prognoses, for budget-finances and for the administration of the public and the private domains of the municipality; Committee No. 2, for urban organization and development, for the achievement of public works, for environmental protection and for the conservation of historical and architectural monuments; Committee No. 3, for scientific activities, education, healthcare, culture and social protection; Committee No. 4, for public services and commerce; Committee No. 5, for local public administration, for juridical issues, for the observance of public order and for the observance and promotion of the citizens' rights and liberties, in his capacity of member of this committee. Committee No. 1 is dominated by engineers (60% of the members), while Committee No. 3 is dominated by teachers (66.66% of the members). Hence, it has been observed that, generally, there is a proper, adequate correspondence between the occupational *status* of the members of a specialized Committee and the profile of that Committee.

The attributions of the Council's Committees (*"Výbory"*) in the Czech legislation are similar to the ones exerted by their Romanian counterparts: they are the initial ferment of decision-making, by drafting the resolution for designed local projects, by initiating or approving inquiries and investigations at the local level in specialized field and problems, by deciding on various issues raised for debate by the Council. In the organizational scheme, nevertheless, the place of the Council's Committees is not subject to a different regulation apart from the one of the Municipal Council itself. For the town of Česká Lípa, during the 2010-2014 mandate, there were ten specialized Committees, each formed of a President, a Secretary, members ad experts: the Financial Committee (composed of a president, a secretary-expert, and eight experts), the Audit Committee (with a president, one local councilor, seven experts, and a secretary-expert), Committee on Education and Training (presided by a municipal councilor, and composed of eight experts and a secretary-expert), the Committee for Culture and Tourism (headed by a municipal councilor, formed of eight experts and a secretary-expert), the Committee for the Environment (presided by the Greens' representative in the Municipal Council, and composed of eight experts and a secretary-expert), the Committee for the Development of the City and Monuments (with a municipal councilor as President, one local councilor, seven experts, and a secretary-expert), the Committee for Social Policy (chaired by a local councilor, with three local councilors and five experts, and a secretary-expert), the Claims and the Liquidation Committee (presided by a municipal councilor, two other municipal councilors and six experts as members, and a secretary-expert), the Committee on the Rental and Sale of Real Estate (headed by a municipal councilor, with two municipal councilors and six experts as members, and a secretary-expert), and the Committee for Sport (with a municipal councilor as a Chairman; twelve members-experts, and a secretary-expert). One major novelty for the Czech case is the fact that, within each Committee, politically non-affiliated technocrats can become additional members; therefore, each of the Council's Committee benefits of the expertise of some professionals who are not members of the Local Council. In addition, other citizens, members of the community can become members of a Committee; it is compulsory, nevertheless, that the Committee be chaired by a local councilor. However, similar to the Romanian case, the unchangeable profile of the Council's Committees during four electoral cycles (1998-2012) would imply that the needs and problems of the town remained largely the same.

As in all cases, the Municipal Council in Oleśnica functions in standing Committees, gathered regularly (usually, once per week), and, in special cases, in extraordinary Committees. The evolution of the standing committees of the City Council is largely linear, with no significant modifications or transformations, meaning not necessarily the fact that the priorities or the needs of the community of Oleśnica did not change considerably over time, but rather translating the lack of imagination from the part of the municipal councilors concerning the redesign of their workings under the form of the Council's standing committees, along with a series of legal limitations in reshaping the structure of the these committees. For the 2010-2014 mandate, one of the most important such committees for the Council in Oleśnica was the "Revision Committee" ("*Komisja Rewizyjna*"), having as President municipal councillor Paweł Bielański, and the following membership: municipal councilors Marcin Karczewicz, Damian Siedlecki, and Grzegorz Żyła. The Committee for Economic and Legal Affairs ("*Komisja Ekonomiczno-Prawna*") was chaired by municipal councilor Zbigniew Nagórny, and was composed of other five municipal councilors: Wojciech Brym, Beata Krzesińska, Małgorzata Lipska, Józefa Stefani, and Janina Szczuraszek. This committee was one dominated by women, with a 66.6% female presence. Damian Siedlecki was the President of the Spatial Governance Committee and Municipal Equipment ("*Komisja Ładu Przestrzennego i Urządzeń Komunalnych*"), while the other members were municipal councilors Tadeusz Żółkiewski (serving, at the same time, as the Vice-chair of the Municipal Council), Adam Wójcik (serving, at the same time, as the President of the Council's Committee on Sports and Recreation), Wiesław Piechówka (serving, at the same time, as the Chair of the Municipal Council), Robert Sarna, Józef Stojanowski (serving, at the same time, as the President of the Council's Committee on Health and Social Welfare), and Aleksander Chrzanowski; the Spatial Governance Committee was an exclusively male one, being perceived as occasioning the most technical discussions (concerning particularly infrastructural development). The Municipal Council's Committee for Education, Culture and Regional Heritage ("*Komisja Oświaty, Kultury i Dziedzictwa Regionalnego*") was presided by municipal councilor Józef Stojanowski, and its composition included municipal councilors Piotr Pawłowski, Wojciech Brym, Małgorzata Lipska, Grzegorz Żyła, Janina Szczuraszek (three of the most active members of the Council in Oleśnica), Grażyna Siednienko, Jacek Malczewski, and Wiesław Piechówka (the Chair of the Municipal Council). To some extent surprisingly, this Committee, whose profile would traditionally "recommend" a more vigorous presence of women, was, yet again, dominated by men (66.6% of the membership). The Municipal Council's Committee on Health and Social Welfare (*"Komisja Zdrowia i Opieki Społecznej"*) had municipal councilor Beata Krzesińska acting as President – the only woman acting as president for a Council Committee in the case of Oleśnica, for the 2010-2014 mandate –, and was formed of municipal councilors Tadeusz Żółkiewski (Vice-chair of the Municipal Council), Grażyna Siednienko, Wojciech Bartnik (the second Vice-chair of the Municipal Council of Oleśnica), Józefa Stefani, and Piotr Pawłowski. Finally, the Council's Committee on Sports and Recreation (*"Komisja Sportu i Rekreacji"*) was presided by municipal councilor Adam Wójcik, and included Vice-chair of the Municipal Council Wojciech Bartnik, municipal councilors Aleksander Chrzanowski, Jacek Malczewski, Marcin Karczewicz, Paweł Bielański, Robert Sarna (one of the youngest municipal councilors of Oleśnica).

The Local Council in Gyula works in ordinary and extraordinary sessions, but its activity takes place in committees. Following the local elections of October 2014, resulting in the constitution of the Body of Representatives, four Committees of the Local Council of Gyula were established. The Council's Committee on Economic Resources (*"Gazdasági Erőforrások Bizottsága"*) had the following composition: Galbács Mihály (as president), Balogh Lajos, Ökrös István, Szalai György, Dinya Imre, Kvaszné Kónya Gabriella, and Veres András. The Local Council's Committee on Culture and Education (*"Oktatási és Kulturális Bizottság"*) was composed of seven councilors: Durkó Károly (acting as president), Galbács Mihály, Mittag Mónika, Torma Béla, Cziczeri Noémi, Szabó Ferenc, and Vigné Fábián Diána. The Committee on Human and Social Policy (*"Humán és Társadalompolitikai Bizottság"*) was formed of five councilors, with Kiss Tamásné acting as president, and Balogh Lajos, Szabó Károly, Baranyai Tamás, and Kóra János, as standing members. The Council's Committee on Procurement (*"Közbeszerzési Bizottság"*) was a seven-person body, gathering councilors Ökrös István (president), Szabó Károly, Szalai György, Torma Béla, Csizmadia Imre, Czirok Sándor, and Szalai Katalin. The organization of the committees of the Local Council in Gyula was, to some extent, seemingly superfluous, the scope of these bodies covering a too vast range of aspects and spheres of activity, even for a small-to-medium-sized town, as Gyula is.

In the Slovak case, the Municipal Council nominates the "head of the administrative office", a key position in the local administrative dynamics of the Slovak Republic, entrusted with the preparation of municipal matters adopted by the Council and with the promotion of public servants of the local *apparatus*. In the Slovak local government system, the "head of office" position is complementary to that of the mayor: while the former is the "appointed leader", the later is the "elected leader", in a unique system of dual local executive leadership; if the former is the "civil servant" *par excellence*, the later is

100

"the politician", appealing to the popular vote. The Municipal Council in Slovakia can set up bodies of temporary or permanent character, of advisory or initiative nature, so-called "executive committees" (*"mestský úrad"*): being composed of municipal councilors, other local civil servants (appointed by the Council), and inhabitants of the town, these "executive committees" are entrusted by the Council with specific tasks on specific competence areas. These "executive committees" are similar to the committees of the Local Councils in Romania or Hungary, but, in addition, they include concerned citizens and trained servants for a more adequate policy response to the community's needs.

For the 2012-2016 mandate, the Council's Committee for Finances, Management of Urban Property and Regional Development (*"Komisia MsZ finančná, správy mestského majetku a regionálneho rozvoja"*) comprised councilors Ján Krtík (president), Ivan Murín, Ján Janáč, and Erika Sulinová, and citizens Alexander Bačík (engineer), Ivan Dobrovolný (engineer), and Svetozár Krnáč (engineer). The Committee for Social Matters and Housing (*"Komisia MsZ sociálna a bytová"*) consisted of councilor Gabriel Földi (president), and citizens Marek Földesi (physician), Anna Filipová, Oľga Szalmová, Andrea Haluzová, and Alžbeta Kušnieriková (typically, the Committee of the Council with an overwhelming presence of women). The Committee for transport, traffic management and urban roads, construction and maintenance of roads (*"Komisia MsZ dopravy a správy mestských komunikácií, výstavby a ÚP"*) was composed of councilor Štefan Kalocsay, and citizens Rastislav Kasan (jurist, president), Marcel Mäsiar (engineer), Jozef Bielek (engineer), and Tibor Dávid. The Council's Committee for Environment and Municipal Affairs (*"Komisia MsZ životného prostredia, komunálnych vecí"*) had the following membership: councilors Gabriel Mančík and Juraj Braun, and citizens Roman Karaffa (doctor in Engineering, president), Jozef Kubovič, and Ľuboš Baran. The Committee for Education and Youth (*"Komisia MsZ vzdelávania a mládeže"*) consisted of councilors Roman Salinka (president) and Martina Gašparová, and citizens Ervín Szalma, Peter Benček (Masters' graduates) and Lenka Kluchová (doctor in pedagogy). Municipal councilor Miloš Zaujec (president), and citizens Simona Hudecová, Monika Coková, Roman Ďurčat (engineer), and Juraj Gergely, composed the Municipal Committee on Culture (*"Komisia MsZ kultúry"*). Municipal councilors Mária Kuriačková (president), Ladislav Lutovský, and Ján Koštrna, and citizens Miroslav Králik (engineer), Gabriel Sirotňák (engineer), Martin Paukovič, and Tomáš Krištof, formed the composition of the Council's Committee on Sport (*"Komisia MsZ športu"*). The Committee for Trade, Services, and Tourism (*"Komisia MsZ obchodu, služieb a cestovného ruchu"*) was composed of municipal councilors Alena Frtúsová, MPH (president), and citizens Csaba Tolnai, Igor Éder (doctor in pedagogy), Karol Szép (engineer), and Eva Sleziaková (engineer). The Council's First Committee for the Facilitation of Requests, the Needs and Interests of Urban Dwellers (*"Komisia pre zabezpečovanie požiadaviek, potrieb a záujmov obyvateľov meststkej*") had, as membership, municipal councilor Roman Salinka (president), and citizens Roland Petrík, Roman Nappel, Elena Krajkovičová (engineer), Zuzana Kleinová (engineer), Edita Capalajová, and Anna Kozmová. The Second Committee for the Facilitation of Requests, the Needs and Interests of Urban Dwellers ("*Komisia pre zabezpečovanie požiadaviek, potrieb a záujmov obyvateľov meststkej*") was composed exclusively of citizens: Alexander Bačík (engineer, president), Jana Varinská, Michaela Kováčiková (engineer), Marian Török, and Zuzana Gregáňová. The Third Committee for the Facilitation of Requests, the Needs and Interests of Urban Dwellers ("*Komisia pre zabezpečovanie požiadaviek, potrieb a záujmov obyvateľov meststkej*") encompassed one municipal councilor as president, Štefan Kalocsay, and citizens Silvia Bankóová (engineer), Mária Molnárová, Zuzana Trňanová, Jana Vargová (another Committee dominated by women). The Fourth Committee for the Facilitation of Requests, the Needs and Interests of Urban Dwellers ("*Komisia pre zabezpečovanie požiadaviek, potrieb a záujmov obyvateľov meststkej*") included municipal councilor Ján Janáč (president), and citizens Miroslava Mituníková (engineer), Slavomír Tóth, Milan Limberg, and Ladislav Morvay. Finally, the Committee for the Insurance of the Protection of the Public Interest in the Acts of the Mayor and of the Municipal Council ("*Komisia MsZ na zabezpečovanie ochrany verejného záujmu pri vykone funkcie primátora mesta a poslancov MsZ*") was the largest in membership: councilors Ján Janáč (president), Juraj Braun, Ivan Murín, and Miloš Zaujec, and citizens Igor Éder (doctor in pedagogy), Rastislav Kasan (jurist), Petra Števková, and Csaba Tolnai. The four similar committees on the "needs and interests of urban dwellers" work on five respective constituencies of the town.

Article 48, paragraph (2) of the Statute of the Municipal Council of Targovishte establishes five standing committees: the Council's Committee on Municipal Property, Economic Policy, Finance, Budget, Taxes and Fees ("*Общинска собственост, икономическа политика, финанси, бюджет, данъци и такси*"); the Committee on Territorial Arrangement and Development of Settlements, Integration, Environment, Transport, and Agricultural Policy ("*Териториално-селищно устройство и развитие на населените места, евроинтеграция, околна среда, тра нспорт и аграрна политика*"); the Committee on Education, Culture, Heritage, and Religion ("*Образование, култура, културно-историческо наследство, вероизповедания*"); the Committee on Health, Social Policy, Non-governmental Organizations and Development of Civil Society, Sports, and Tourism ("*Здравеопазване, социална политика, неправителствени организации /НПО / и развитие на гражданско общество, спорт, туризъм*"); the Council's Committee on Legality, Decision Control, the Protection of Public Order and Establishing Conflict of Interests ("*Законност, контрол на реш енията, опазване на обществения ред и установяване на конфликт на интереси*") (The Statute of the Municipal Council of Targovishte, Article 48, paragraph (2)). At the time of the fieldwork, during the 2011-2015 mandate, the Municipal Council's Committee on Municipal Ownership, Economic Policy, Finance, Budget, and Taxes gathered eleven members: Panaiot Jordanov Dimitrov (chairman), Tahir Dzhemalov Tahirov (as deputy-chairman), Hamdi Mehmedov Iliyazov, Sevim Myustedzheb Ali, Arnel Alyaydin Yacoub, Nikola Stoyanov Naydenov, Krassimir Mitev Mirev, Tanju Georgiev Tanev, Plamen Vladimirov Belkolev, Ivaylo Pavlov Parvanov, Desislava Petrova Evgenieva. The Committee on Territorial Planning and Urban Development, Integration, Environment, Transport, and Agricultural Policy was formed of seven municipal councilors: Alexandrov Emil Dimitrov (acting as chairman), Svetoslav Ivanov Savchev (acting as deputy-chairman), Aynur Mehmet Arif, Jordan Panayotov Shivarov, Nevena Yaroslavova Stanimirova, Damian Ivanov Nedialkov, and Imre Ismetova Mehmedova. The Committee on Education, Culture, Heritage, and Religion had seven members: Damian Ivanov Nedialkov (as chairman), Darina Kostov (as deputy-chairman), Ercan Aliyev Bekteshev, Ilia Iliev Svetlozarov, Aneta Ivanova Koumanova, Svetoslav Ivanov Savchev, and Teodora Tomova Metodieva. The membership of the Committee on Health, Social Policy, Non-governmental Organizations and Development of Civil Society, Sports, and Tourism comprised seven members: Dimcho Todorov Dimov (as chairman), Plamen Vladimirov Belkolev (as deputy-chairman), Ercan Aliyev Bekteshev, Nikolay Zlatkov Miltchev, Stoynev Hristo Haralampiev, Tanner Ismailov Ahmedov, and Hussein Mustafov Cherkezov. Finally, the Council's Committee on Legality, Decision Control, the Protection of Public Order and Establishing Conflict of Interests consisted of seven councilors: Sunay Kemalova Hasanov (chairman), Hristo Haralampiev Stoynev (as deputy-chairman), Turhan Bilal Hadzhiibryamolu, Rumen Ivanov Takorov, Plamen Vladimirov Belkolev, Ivaylo Pavlov Parvanov, and Teodora Petkova Vladimirova. Neither the membership, nor the profile of the five Council's standing committees necessarily translate any focused or specialized approach to the needs and demands of the community; generally, they are formed following the existing legislation regulating the activity of Municipal Councils, while their membership was highly heterogeneous, at the time of the fieldwork (i.e. there was no synonymity or mere convergence between the training or profession of the councilors forming a committee and its profile). The composition of the standing and temporary committees is formed exclusively by municipal councilors (similarly to the Romanian and Hungarian cases), with no citizenship participation and no specialized administrative civil servants. As an addition to the activity of the committees, an "Advisory Board" ("консултативен съвет") of five councilors, for support in drafting and discussing policy directions at the local level, is formed; the 2011-2015 composition of this "advisory board" was: Hamdi Mehmedov Iliyazov (having Ercan Aliyev Bekteshev as deputy), Panaiot Jordanov Dimitrov (with Hristo Haralampiev Stoynev as deputy), Krassimir

Mitev Mirev (with Ilya Iliev Svetlozarov as deputy), Tanju Georgiev Tanev (and Plamen Vladimirov Belkolev acting as deputy), and Ivaylo Pavlov Parvanov (having Svetoslav Ivanov Savchev acting as deputy). The importance of this "advisory board" is yet to be considered in the entire architecture of local legislative in Targovishte: its meetings are not clearly established in the Statute of the Municipal Council, its attributions are vague, purely consultative, at times doubling or unnecessarily replicating the attributions of the committees themselves. Article 19 of the Statute of the Municipal Council of Targovishte details over the competences of the "Advisory Council": "(1) At the suggestion of the political forces represented in the Council, the Municipal Council can elect, by one ballot, an Advisory Board comprising representatives of the Council, within two months of the constitution of the Municipal Council. [...] (3) The Advisory Board: (a) assists the Chairmen [of the Municipal Council] in preparing the draft agenda of the meetings; (b) supports the work of the committees and of municipal councilors; (c) performs other tasks assigned by the Chairman of the Municipal Council; (d) creates the necessary conditions for the activity of the municipal councilors and the committees; (e) monitors compliance with this Statute." (The Statute of the Municipal Council of Targovishte, Article 19, paragraphs (1) and (3) [additions mine])

c)   The adoption of the local budget

The fiscal capacity of a municipality is dependent on its capacity to manage the tax base for every locally collected tax. This is the reason why, the local authorities should have also the competence and the prerogatives to manage, to update, and to develop such tax base, without being dependent on central power. A case in point is the property tax (and additional, linked, taxes, e.g. inheritance tax, donation tax, tax on property purchase, etc.), which cannot be properly collected in the absence of a centralized, systematized database of the exact outlook of the inhabitants' immobile properties at one point. Such a comprehensive database can only come with a suitable informational infrastructure and a correspondingly skilled, qualified personnel. Based on the Hungarian case of decentralization, the study authored by Tamás Horváth develops on what the scholars considers of paramount importance and preceding administrative decentralization, though tightly linked to fiscal decentralization: the "service decentralization", which could alleviate the local budgetary burden. Indeed, four processes or *phenomena* are highlighted by Horváth, in the attempt to explain how would leadership change with the advance of "service decentralization": (a) "the increased role of the nonprofit sector in the provision of social services", especially in the region of East-Central Europe, where welfare and social services are central to the prioritization strategy of local political elites; (b) "the reemergence of churches and private charity organizations at the local level", dominantly in Catholic countries or communities, such as the Polish ones; (3) "the gradual creation of a system of sector-neutral funding by the state" (meaning, basically, that the state should be willing to finance whichever entity, either the local authorities or the nongovernmental organizations, is providing public services for the town); and (4) "the partial introduction of market conditions in community consumption" (Horváth 1998: 45-46) (this *desideratum* has been partly achieved in the Hungarian, the Polish, and the Czech cases of local government, in which, due to the externalization of the social services provision to private entities, special boards or single-purpose committees, composed of both citizens and local councilors and functionaries, have been formed to curtail abuses and to supervise the service provision process) While the dynamic described by Horváth might be fortunate and desirable in the logic of market economy and democratization, the service decentralization process has been marked by a series of deficiencies, in practice; they refer dominantly to the quite frequent scenario of the overlapping, at the local level, of key-positions in one individual in both the municipality and the private service-provider, hence hampering the establishment of prices following the logic of the free market, rather than that of the monopoly. Moreover, oftentimes, the local government is virtually unable to provide even basic social services to its community, even if willing to do so, for the large majority of locally-owned companies and service-providing agencies has succumbed during the first instances of transition. In a sense, the local authorities are actually obligated to call in private organizations in services delivery for their community. Therefore, essentially, service decentralization for ECE countries is necessary – and, to some extent, inevitable –, but its initial objectives (those of freeing the local market, of democratizing decision-making through citizen-formed boards for supervising services delivery, of meaningfully engaging the civil society organizations and the NGOs in social services provision, etc.) have been perverted through personalized local politics, nepotism, client-patron linkages, a quite problematic system of public-private incompatibilities of local elected officials and an equally problematic legal framework of public auctions within the municipalities, resulting in a general sense of distrust, defencelessness and disappointment among the citizens.

Economist Ash Amin reiterates the problems of local and regional development (seen from the European perspective of "regionalization" efforts), localized at the level of elites: "The linkage made with economic development is that local political power and voice facilitates the formation of a decision-making and decision-implementing community able to develop and sustain an economic agenda of its own. [...] Governance, especially in the institutionally thin regions, has always been in the hands of elite coalitions, and the resulting institutional *sclerosis* has been a source of economic failure by acting as a block on innovation and the wider distribution of resources and opportunity."

(Amin 1999: 372-373 [italics added]) Indeed, in what concerns the dynamics of decentralization and regionalization, local political elites are central and vital in decision-making particularly on the economic development and infrastructural advance of their communities; the manner in which these elites prioritize at the local level, the fashion in which they themselves see their own impact, role and extent of power, is crucial for the establishment of a meaningful local policy agenda.

Nonetheless, the form and the conditions under which local leaders and authorities can intervene in local economic development, outside the exigencies of the market, are more or less narrowly or broadly defined: if, in Western continental Europe, the local authorities are profoundly involved in drafting developmental strategies locally implemented, in Northern Europe, restrictions are imposed on the implication of the local political elite in the locally-established businesses (see, for an interesting comparison, Marcou 1993: 191-235).

Among the most important functions of the Local Council, along with the election of the Deputy Mayor(s) and the approval of the organizational structure of the local administration, the approval of the local budget represents the third most significant issue the municipality confronts with. Even though the process of elaborating the budget belongs to the mayor and to the financial departments of the local administration, the responsibility of voting and then modifying the budgetary revenues and expenditures is with the Local Council. The Annexes no. 8 presents a simplified version of the Budget of the Town Hall of Tecuci on 2010, voted by the Local Council on the 10th of March 2010. Until December 2010, the budget of the town of Tecuci suffered six modifications, voted and approved by the Local Council. Generally, the budgetary rectifications were generated by various grants and funds from the central administration; the town was fortunate, in this sense, mainly due to the fact the Mayor shared the same political affiliation (the Liberal-Democratic one) with the existing government. The budget of the Town-Hall of Tecuci slightly increased gradually during the latest years: 56.974 thousand of lei in 2008, 60.800 thousand of lei in 2009 (a 6.71% increase), 66.084 thousand of lei in 2010 (a 8.69% increase). It should be observed that the deficit and the surplus are equal to zero, a situation which is in accordance with the existing legislation, any deficit being forbidden by law and any surplus being redistributed by the central administration. In the case of revenues, the largest sums came from the fiscal revenues (80.14%), particularly from taxes on goods and services (51.83%). On the other hand, the local budgetary expenditure was polarized primarily around education (45.57%), housing, services and public development (13.44%), public authorities and external actions (9.22%) and social insurance and assistance (8.77%). This distribution of budgetary priorities largely coincided with the hierarchical significance the local councilors attribute to the various domains of activity in the town: 24.52% of the councilors considered that economic development should be granted the greatest importance by the local

106

administration. Moreover, while the largest amount of funds were reserved for education, housing and public development and public authorities – 77% of the total expenditures –, the members of the Local Council assessed that, actually, efficient and effective measures were taken in such spheres as social services (including housing and unemployment) (20.83% of the local councilors), culture, sport, recreation and youth activities (20.83% of the local councilors) and public improvements (14.58% of the local councilors). These parallelisms are instrumental in evaluating the manner in which the priorities of the local political elites are, eventually, reflected in the future distribution of money and initiation of public policies at the local level, within specific spheres of competence. It should also be mentioned that, in the case local budgetary resources prove to be insufficient, "local budgets may contract loans from the current account of the State Treasury to cover certain shortfalls; they can also benefit from the special purpose transfers from the state budget or they can apply for loans from commercial banks or from other credit institutions" (Pop 2018: 81). These "special purpose transfers" from the central budget have been both one of the survival mechanisms for much impoverished, small municipalities in Romania, but also a mechanism for party rewarding mayors and local councilors sharing the same affiliation to the governing party. Surely, this propensity of governments being "more likely to disburse funds to territories with local leaders politically aligned with them" (Coman 2020: 206), particularly when the institutional and legal contexts are prone to generate such behaviors (e.g. where levels of decentralization are low, and the Local Council has no significant authority), are rather commonplace in Europe, and are by no means specific to Romania or to "consolidating democracies" (see, for instance, Coman 2020).

As in the Romanian case, the adoption of the local budget is among the most important prerogatives of the Municipal Councils in the Czech Republic. Karel Lacina and Zdena Vajdova explain the complex procedure of adopting the budget at the local level in the Czech lands: "The preparation of the municipal budget is a long process that usually is divided into several stages. The first is the preparation of the basic framework of the budget, reflecting real economic growth or decline of the municipality. This stage is followed by an assessment of expected revenues and expenditures, including those of municipal companies financed from its budget (so-called 'budgetary' and 'contributory' organizations […]). The preparation of the first draft of the municipal budget is accomplished by the finance department in large towns and by the whole office in smaller villages. Discussion on this draft by the municipal office is the third stage of the process. The budget proposal is completed in cooperation with other departments of the municipal office and then is discussed by the council and by the public. Afterwards, the municipal council adopts the budget. The municipal board [i.e. the executive instance at the local level, the administrative support of the Mayor] is responsible not only for budget preparation [...], but also for evaluation of the utilization of budgetary resources from the previous fiscal year. Audits are conducting either by private auditing companies at the expense of the municipality or by the district office [i.e. what would be loosely the equivalent of the County Council in Romania, the regional *forum* of decision], in which case the audit is free of charge." (Lacina and Vajdova 2000/2004: 278) In Annexes no. 8, a simplified version of the Budget of the Municipality of Česká Lípa on 2011, the latest adopted by the Municipal Council on the 23rd of January 2011, is presented. The budget suffered a series of transformations from January onwards, generally referring to rectifications and grants from and for the "budgetary" and "contributory" companies. Due to a larger decentralization, funds from the central administration are extremely rare, a situation which would minimize the effects of political bias from the central authorities to the local distribution of funds. The evolution of the magnitude of the municipal budget suffered only minor modifications from 2008 to 2011, being fairly stable due to the economic crisis affecting even small communities and their revenues. Generally, in the case of revenues, the most significant sums were provided by: the fiscal revenues (79.04%), particularly from taxes on goods and services (68.30%). The municipal budgetary expenditure gravitated especially around education (57.89%), social services and public development (32.56%) – two domains that coincided with the grading delivered by the municipal councilors when asked about the significance of particular spheres in the administration of the municipality. Therefore, the councilors' vision on priorities corresponded, like in the case of Tecuci, with the budgetary distribution of funds.

Following the Polish legislation on local budgeting, one can differentiate among three main types of sources of local revenues: (1) own revenues, (2) general state grants (or transfers), and (3) special state grants. The first category of revenues refers to local taxes (especially property tax) and shared taxes (percetages of the personal income tax and corporate income tax). While for the first category of state transfers, local authorities can independently decide their use, for the second category of state grants, the state mandates their employ, specifically for some domain. Generally, the Polish local governments mark the highest level of fiscal autonomy (i.e. the independent capacity of constructing a local budget mainly from own resources, rather than from state transfers, whose impact is less significant) in the region of East-Central Europe. On an analysis of the pressure exerted by macroeconomy (particularly, the national GDP and the global financial crises) on local budgeting, Guziejewska and Walerysiak-Grzechowska (2020) warn that "[t]he local ownership of these revenues is, however, strongly questioned based on the argument that municipalities, counties and voivodeships have no influence on how the taxes are designed, nor do they directly control revenues from them. [But, a]s far as the sustainability of local revenues is concerned, the property tax as a local source and general grants as an external source of funding are crucial."

(Guziejewska and Walerysiak-Grzechowska 2020: 45) Similarly, in a comparative research on the Romanian and the Polish administrative capacity in triggering fiscal decentralization, Alexandru and Guziejewska point out that: "While local governments' own revenues represent a considerable proportion of their total incomes in Romania, their finances are still strongly dependent on the central government. [...] Poland's rates were more favorable, but the country's local finance system is criticized for a large number of revenue transfers from the state budget and for local shares of PIT (Personal Income Tax) and CIT (Corporate Income Tax) revenues with the status of local authorities' own revenues." (Alexandru and Guziejewska 2020: 128)

The local budget in the Hungarian case is generally composed of four main elements, out of which the most important are those revenues that are independently collected, through local taxes determined and imposed by decision of the Local Council; the other elements refer to shared revenues (i.e. that portion of national taxes that is yearly determined by the national legislative as being devolved to the local authorities), to mandatory grants and subsidies from the national budget (determined, as well, by the national Parliament, usually taking into account the demographic magnitude of municipalities), and to capital investment finance (e.g. targeted grants, or deficit financing, similar to the Bulgarian system of "Intergovernmental Transfers")[50]. As in the majority of cases analyzed here, the largest proportion of local budgetary expenditure is devoted to social benefits. Essentially, Hungary keeps confronting the same problems of low fiscal capacity of impoverished local communities, as detailed by G. Kovács: "Due to the decentralization process, local governments' revenues decreased significantly in the last two decades in real value, while the level and scope of services provided did not decrease at the same time. Therefore, local governments, which are short of revenues, have had to perform what is probably one of their most important tasks: to develop their resource absorption and fundraising capacity, which would ensure the necessary financial tools to implement development. One of the methods of using outside resources is borrowing, among which fund acquisition *via* local government bond issuance should be listed." (Kovacs 2015: 258) Despite the recent developments, the typical problems of decentralization for the region of East-Central Europe persisted in the Hungarian case, as well: "In Hungary, the concession of local political autonomy preceded the separation of local budgets from the central government budgeting system. As a result, local governments lack a financially sustainable revenue base and have been forced to sell assets to cover recurrent costs (raising the prospect that the social safety net – for which local governments bear major responsibility – will run out of funds in the near future)." (Dillinger 1994: 9) While rejecting the "splitting country" development hypothesis, according to which Hungary is markedly separated into a "winner",

---

50   See, for the local budgeting in Hungary, Szalai, Zay, Högye, Barati, and Berczik 2002: 329-396.

well-developed Western region, and a "loser" less-developed Eastern part, László Faragó admits the fact that the North-Eastern part of the country is lagging behind the Western one:

> "[D]ifferent, territorially separated communities have to face both internal and external difficulties (lack of resources, problems with adapting *[sic!]* to a new situation on the one hand, and changes in the world market and central regulation, on the other) and are not equally capable of mobilizing their internal resources or attract external resources in order to achieve their objectives. These differences in regional conditions and their consequences may appear in various forms. They can be expressed in the price of real estate, the availability of suitable labour, expected return on investment, etc." (Farago 1999: 316 [additions mine])

One should easily notice that the Hungarian town under scrutiny here, Gyula, lies in the Eastern, less developed region of the country, confronting the developmental problems aptly identified by Faragó.

In accordance with art. 9 of the Slovak Act no. 583 of 2004 on Budget Rules for Local Government, the drafting of a local budget becomes the full responsibility of towns and villages.

> "Since the 1st of January 2007, the municipalities have the obligation of drawing up a multi-annual budget, encompassing budgetary exercise for the next three years. In Slovakia, the budget of the regions and municipalities, which have their own revenues, can be checked only by an auditor (*"hlavný kontrolór"*). But the auditor is appointed by the mayor, with the approval of the Council, which may lead them to favor certain political parties in performing their work." (Malikova 2003: 3 [italics added])

Additionally, the attributions and tasks encompassed by the large range of prerogatives granted to the local and regional authorities require a skilled and qualified personnel, which is oftentimes absent, particularly in very small municipalities, usually municipalities smaller than Levice.

As already identified by Juraj Nemec et al. (2000), the main problem of today's administrative organization in Slovakia is a high degree of territorial and administrative fragmentation, a "highly nonintegrated structure", in which each small settlement of less than one thousand inhabitants bears municipality status (over 33% of the Slovak municipalities); although this fragmentation and atomization can have its uncontestable advantages (e.g. the closeness between the local authorities and their constituencies, a more direct relation between the local elite and the community, the citizen), they produce, in practice, an impossibility to actually make decentralization functioning, for a great, fully-fledged transfer of responsibilities to particularly small communities is quite limited by the actual capacities of the local authorities there (including shortages of financial resources and qualified civil servants). This is especially the reason why the 2001 wave of local administrative reforms hinted at the region as an important unit of administration, in an attempt to encourage (particularly) economic cooperation among small municipalities. At the beginning of 2000s, an average of 40.2% from the local budgets of these municipalities was derived from the state (either through taxes collected nationally, or through capital transfers, block grants, etc.) (Nemec, Bercik, and Kuklis 2000: 305), which resulted in communities that were only around 60% financially autonomous from the state. It was also the case of Levice. This percentage is nevertheless satisfactory for the region of East-Central Europe, placing the case of Slovakia, in respect to the extent of fiscal decentralization, among the highest places, alongside the Czech Republic and Poland.

Quite clearly, the impact of decentralization on a relatively small country should be perceived outside the exclusively territorial paradigm: the consequences of the decentralizing process in Slovakia – required, indeed, by the democratization and the accession to the European Union – should be seen in a different light for service demand and delivery for the citizens, as differently from the Polish, the Romanian, or the Bulgarian cases, where the decentralization was viewed as imperative due particularly to a better territorial distribution and administration. Even so, the benefits of decentralization on Slovakian administration should not be disconsidered or overlooked:

"Thanks to the decentralization process and taxation reform, self-governance bodies acquired extensive decision-making powers as well as necessary funding to perform them. In 2009, however, most self-governance bodies struggled with serious financial problems caused by the global economic crisis, particularly a perceptible decline in tax revenues. Their situation was not made any easier by the central administration, which failed to adequately address their complaints and legitimate demands." (Meseznikov, Kollar, and Vasecka 2010: 478)

Despite the various developments during the last two decades,

"the system of public services [in Slovakia] is very unstable. Due to allocative and technical inefficiency, large internal debt for services and supplies provided by public sector industries has been incurred. [...] The system must be stabilized before the further transfer of responsibilities to self-government can occur." (Nemec, Bercik, and Kuklis 2000: 310 [additions mine])

Central to the discussion on local budgeting and fiscal capacity of the municipalities in Bulgaria is the mechanism of "intergovernmental transfers". G. Thcavdarova et al. explain the system of Intergovernmental Transfers, at work in the fiscal relations between the central authorities and the local ones in Bulgaria:

"The Council of Ministers and the National Association of Municipalities signed a Cooperation Agreement, whereby both parties agreed to decentralized local government and to increase the financial independence of municipalities. Both the Fiscal Decentralization Concept and the Program for its implementation were adopted in 2002. As a result, the reform of local finances allowed for [...] the clear distinction between the local and central responsibilities for the public services. [...]

Prevailing state functions are administration, defense, public order and security, social insurance and social care, and economic activities; prevailing municipal functions include housing and public utilities, while functions as education, healthcare, and culture are mixed." (Thcavdarova, Ivanoc and Savov 2000: 36)

One can easily discern, from the so-called "Intergovernmental Transfers System" functioning in Bulgaria, that the range of spheres in which the local expenditures are covered through this mechanism (i.e. those "state-delegated" spheres) is particularly broad, almost inviting municipalities to use, for their expenses, the transfers from the state budget, and to profit accordingly from series of supplemental subsidies. Additional drawbacks resulted from this highly centralized local administrative construct: (a) the instability of the actual amounts of the transfers (representing, at time, even one third of the total central government expenditure (Thcavdarova, Ivanoc and Savov 2000: 37)); (b) the unpredictability of state subsidies allocation among municipalities (resulting in obvious discretionary distributions, along party affiliations or personal ties); (c) the complexity of the sources of state subsidies to the local level, which favor already rich communities, through the shared personal income tax, the "patent" tax, the "general state subsidies" (i.e. provided without restrictions, unconditionally), the "targeted state subsidies" (i.e. conditional, provided for specific projects on social assistance, healthcare, ecological recovery, and capital investments), and the "extraordinary state subsidies" (i.e. unconditional, unplanned, distributed on oftentimes vague or nontransparent basis, with the scope of helping those municipalities in extremely grave financial contexts). Although the system of "Intergovernmental Transfers" is meant to have a "gap-filling", "equalization" effect on those communities with very feeble tax basis for the personal income tax (the logic is that the more incapable to provide jobs and development a municipality is, the fewer taxes can actually raise, the poorer it gets), the arbitrary manner in which the state subsidies and transfers are distributed, on a too wide range of spheres and competences, determines the impoverishment of the local communities and their perpetual and preserved incapacity to form an independent budget. As a matter of fact, low fiscal capacity is frequently a characteristic of Eastern countries, and, consequently, is to be featured in Romania, as well. In a quite interesting longitudinal study, Desislava Stoilova shows that fiscal capacity and the ability to independently form a budget of small-to-medium-sized municipalities in Bulgaria (as is the case of Targovishte, the case in point here) reached, in 2007, 43% (out of which, only 13.42% are represented by tax revenues), whereas the system of intergovernmental transfers provides 55.1% of the budget of a Bulgarian municipality, on average (the rest being represented by various borrowing) (Stoilova 2008: 7, Table 3: "Local Government Revenue Structure (%), 1991-2007"; see also Ivanov, Tchavdarova, Savov, and Stanev 2002: 167-217; and Davey and Péteri 2006: 585-598). It is the Local Taxes and Fees Act of 1998 that establishes the fashion in which the local authorities can put together the budget, in a country in which the municipalities are quite unable to freely decide on the tax rates imposed on their inhabitants: the law enlarged the fiscal scope of the local authorities, allowing them to autonomously adopt tax rates for local impositions within a certain, legally established, range. Subsequent improvements in the fiscal capacity of small-to-medium-sized municipalities were made possible after significant modifications of the Local Budgets Act, in 2003:

> "Since 2003, local governments have been given full discretion over local fees and service prices [...]. Municipalities can charge local population and business for domestic waste; for the use of marketplaces, fairs, sidewalks, and roadbeds; for the use of nursery homes, kindergartens, social care homes, camps, hostels, and other municipal social services; for extraction of quarried materials; for technical and administrative services; for purchase of grave plots; tourist charges; and other local charges as regulated by law." (Stoilova 2008: 8)

The same deficiencies in the management of financial resources at the level of municipalities are identified and reiterated by a *plethora* of scholars and observers; it is the case of Elena Iankova, who, analyzing the performance of business-government partnership in the period of Bulgarian pre-accession to the EU, concludes that

> "[a]s self-governing authorities, the municipalities have their own resources and are relatively free to dispose of them. However, about half of municipal investment expenditures are financed through central budget subsidies. [...] The formation of municipal revenues remained fairly centralized. Therefore, local authorities were not considered reliable partners in the cofinancing of projects within the pre-accession instruments and the prospective structural and cohesion funds. Issues included the lack of separate investment budgets of municipalities, the legal opportunity to redirect earmarked investment subsidies to cover operating costs, the limited predictability of subsidies and municipal revenues in general, and others." (Iankova 2009: 216-217)

What is more, apart from technical and political deficiencies of the fiscal decentralization in Bulgaria, "weak local administrative capacity and widespread corruption have so far thwarted the process of catching up with the rest" (Nikolova 2010: 682)[51] of Europe and, more importantly, with the consolidated democracies of the West.

---

51 See, also, a very compelling analysis on the Bulgarian local government in Ananieva 2002: 80-88.

Social Biography of the members of the Local / Municipal Councils in Tecuci, Česká Lípa, Oleśnica, Gyula, Targovishte, and Levice

The social biography of the local political elites can be perceived as "a set of social resources which are transformed in official positions and in influence, positions and influence that are not available those who do not possess such resources. The access to the political class demands the employ with increased ability of the personal resources […]." (Stoica 2003: 107) Moreover, as Harasymiw has aptly observed, "the composition of political elites is relevant to the content of public policies" (Harasymiw 1984: 3), the social background of the members of the local elite being partly responsible for the policy priorities for their community. Hence, the social characteristics of the members of the local political elite and, equally, of the Local Council constituted, in an initial phase, components of eligibility in the candidates' recruitment and party nomination processes. The impact of the socio-economic background (or what Lewin labels "environment"[52]) determines future behavior and value orientation, particularly in the case of the "leading few".

Studying local elites in East and West Germany, the local elites' social background and the West German "colonization" of ideas and values into the East, Thomas Cusack reiterates three "visions or theoretical images of political elites within democracies", taking into account primarily the access to power and the ways and means to become part of the elite: (1) the classical perspective of class-based formed elite, where access to elite is highly restricted to the upper socio-economical categories (and where the father's occupation and family background are crucial to accession to elite *status*); (2) the so-called "meritocratic" view, according to which restriction to elite is underpinned by extensive training and education and the acquisition of skills and qualifications, with two variants: (2.a) the "elitist" one, in which the "classical" perspective is reinforced, through the very fact that better training and education are restricted to the upper classes and, as a result, elite positions are, yet again, restricted to the upper classes, and (2.b) the "democratic" one, in which the merits of modernity are brought on scene, for formal equality and equal opportunity presumably allow every individual with personal abilities to acquire high education, such that the access to elite is particularly broad and open for all social categories and backgrounds, provided that they have the required qualifications; (3) the "participatory-democratic" perspective, where elite positions are occupied, with no restriction of birth or special competences, by any

---

52 See, in this sense, the bases of the "field theory" or "Gestalt" psychology, in Lewin 1951.

citizen concerned by, interested in, or motivated by political issues relevant to the community in which one lives, either by being voted or named by community (or through whatever formal mechanism of accessing elite positions) (Cusack 2003: 5-6). In his study of elites in developing India, Anup Kumar Dash acknowledges the importance of the analysis of political elites' background:

"An analysis of the social composition of the elite involves the description of the social background variables of the incumbents of elite positions. Although the social background approach in social research has come to us with a long lineage and a history of diverse applications, its employment in elite analysis, however, has usually had rather a specific purpose, i.e. to relate background variables as contexts of elite socialization experiences to elite attitudes. Background *data* are not only associated with but also serve to explain and forecast attitudinal distribution. Therefore, information about social background characteristics are a prerequisite for an explanatory analysis of elite attitudes." (Dash 1994: 44)

The assertion at work in any study of elite background and socio-demographic profiling is that

"leadership, social background and recruitment patterns will facilitate understanding of the political system because [one can infer] from them a good deal about the system's homogeneity and dominant values, about elite-elite relationships and about elite-mass relationships. [...] The analysis of social background variables, in this sense, represents an attempt to classify the context of the aggregate socialization experiences in which elite attitudes are formed in order to explain the collective orientations of members of influential social circles [...]." (Edinger and Searing 1967: 430 [additions mine])

How "elitist" is the local political elite in Tecuci, Česká Lípa, Oleśnica, Gyula, Targovishte, and Levice?

Following Eldersveld (*Political Elites in Democratic Societies*), the present research asks the question of how "elitist" is the local political elite in Tecuci, Česká Lípa, Oleśnica, Gyula, Targovishte, and Levice? This does not exclusively refer to the economical status the members of the Local / Municipal Council display, but also to their general perceptions regarding such democratic features as citizen participation, social mobility, economic equality, etc. and to a level of congruence between their values and perceptions and those of the people they represent, those of the electorate. One major indicator analyzed here is the fathers' occupation53 of the members of the Municipal Councils, in

---

53 Father's occupation, along with race and sex, have been considered "the most salient characteristics" in respect to the construction of elites' personal biographies, group profile, and to the analysis of "passive representativeness" in the American bibliography

order to further assess the degree of social mobility within the local political elite. Moreover, the social background of a local representative can provide a hint concerning his / her perceptions towards the poor sectors of the population, towards the socially disadvantaged, etc. In the case of Tecuci, according to the answers in the questionnaire provided by the members of the Local Council, the majority of the local councilors (78.94%) came from a lower or working class-based family. In such cases, their fathers have / had only a lower to middle educational level (with only four or eight graduated classes, with an elementary education). For Česká Lípa, the Council comprised largely individuals coming from lower and working-class families (68%), with a very slight difference from Tecuci. For the Municipal Council of Oleśnica, the percentage of councilors coming from a lower-class background was the lowest, and in a striking divergence in comparison to the other five cases: only 28.57% had a lower or working-class background. By contrast, 71.42% of the membership of the Body of Representatives in Gyula had a lower-class family background. The proportions of local councilors coming from working- or lower-class families were equally high for the cases of the Municipal Council in Levice and the Local Council in Targovishte: 70.83%, and 81.81%, respectively, the Bulgarian case being, actually, the one in which the highest percentage of members of the Council were coming from lower-class families. Hence, one can conclude that there existed a significant degree of social mobility among the members of the five Local Councils, with large majorities of them coming from poor, less educated families, with the exception of the paradigmatic Polish case. As a result, in the specific cases of the local political elites in Tecuci, Česká Lípa, Gyula, Levice, Targovishte, and their social and occupational background, the "independence" model, advanced by Robert Putnam, generally applied, as opposed to the "agglutination" model, proposed by Harold Lasswell, specific – to some extent – to the case of the local political elites in Oleśnica, as there was no immediate correlation between a specific social class and the members of the political elite. The application of "independence" model in the case of local political elites in Tecuci, Česká Lípa, Gyula, Levice, and Targovishte, demonstrated a predominately ascendant social mobility of the members of the Local Councils, a phenomenon which characterized 84.21% of the local councilors in Tecuci, 68% of the municipal councilors in Česká Lípa, 64.28% of the municipal councilors in Gyula, 70.83% of the municipal councilors in Levice, and an overwhelmingly 84.84% of the local councilors in Targovishte. There was no case, among the local councilors in all of the six cases, of descendingly mobile from a social perspective, and only three cases (15.78%) for Tecuci, eight cases (32%) for Česká Lípa, five cases

---

(See, in this sense, Coleman Selden 1997: 46-48.). Some of the most representative studies of father's occupation for elite groups, conducted particularly in the United States, are: Daley 1984: 4-15; Davis and West 1984: 16-30; Meier 1975: 526-542; Meier and Nigro 1976: 458-469; Smith 1980: 1-13.

(35.71%) for Gyula, seven cases (29.16%) for Levice, and five cases (15.15%) for Targovishte, of socially immobile. The only outlier here was the membership of the Municipal Council of Oleśnica, where 42.85% of the councilors were socially stagnant. Using Boudon's formula (Boudon 1997/1992, 178) for the calculation of the rate of ascendant social mobility of local political elite,

$$AM = \frac{\sum n_{ij} \times 100}{N}$$

$AM = \frac{16 \times 100}{19} = 84.21$ (for Tecuci),

$AM = \frac{17 \times 100}{25} = 68$ (for Česká Lípa),

$AM = \frac{12 \times 100}{21} = 57.14$ (for Oleśnica),

$AM = \frac{9 \times 100}{14} = 64.28$ (for Gyula),

$AM = \frac{28 \times 100}{33} = 84.84$ (for Targovishte), and

$AM = \frac{17 \times 100}{24} = 70.83$ (for Levice),

it resulted that 84.21% of the members of the Local Council in Tecuci, 68% of the members of the Municipal Council in Česká Lípa, only 57.14% of the members of the Municipal Council in Oleśnica, 64.28% of the members of the Body of Representatives in Gyula, 84.84% of the members of the Local Council in Targovishte, and 70.83% of the members of the Municipal Council in Levice, were, socially and occupationally, in an ascendant position in comparison to their fathers.

Another hypothesis was tested and only partly verified in the six cases selected: it is generally assumed that "[t]he later the newcomers started [in politics], the greater part of them came from upper, or upper-middle class families." (Lengyel 2007: 8) From the *calculi* undertaken, it resulted that this conjecture was not necessarily accurate for the cases selected, since generally the youngest wings of the Councils were coming from upper *strata*. The overwhelming proportion of members of the five Municipal Councils that were ascendantly mobile is not surprising in the context of five countries, Romania, the Czech Republic, Hungary, the Slovak Republic, and Bulgaria, undergoing a regime change in 1989 and, subsequently, gradual social developments generally under an intermediate form of "last should be first" and "everyone steps ahead", a combination which in practice resulted into a veritable "some get

117

ahead" (Kolosi and Róna-Tas 1992). Actually, especially in Romania and Bulgaria, the high level of ascendant social mobility among the local elites is due to the fact that the large mass of the population was rural-based or proletarian during state socialism, which generated, after 1989, a great wave of young individuals who aspired to a better-positioned social and occupational *status* in respect to their worker or peasant fathers. Moreover, for the political climate prior to 1989, the "healthy" social origin for acceding to the political elite was the lower class one, hence the regime itself encouraged the lower-class provenience. A slightly lower rate of ascendant social mobility was to be encountered among the members of the Municipal Councils in Česká Lípa, Levice, Gyula, and, especially, Oleśnica, due also to the initial social *status* of their families of origin: slightly fewer working or peasant families, more middle-class background. In socialist Czechoslovakia, for instance, especially in the years prior to the "Prague Spring" (1968), on the background of political and socio-economic reforms, *détente* and apparent relaxation, a sort of middle class, "*petite bourgeoisie*" started to gradually develop, hence breaking the social monopoly of the working class. A small fragment of the present political elite originates in these families of "*petite bourgeoisie*": in the cases of Česká Lípa and Levice, the proportions were 28% and 25.01%, respectively, of the total number of local councilors. On the other hand, studying the rise of the gentry in interwar Poland and its afterwards conservation in communist and postcommunist Poland, historian Longina Jakubowska aptly suggests that the strong, "dominant and dominating" culture and organizational form of the Polish middle-class has been preserved, particularly locally, for the simple reason this class managed to perpetually convert its capital (whatever its nature) in order "to adapt to any new political order" (Jakubowska 2013: 45-69); expectedly, then, a significant portion of the local councilors in Oleśnica (47.61%) came from a well-preserved middle class. Another 23.8% of the municipal councilors in Oleśnica had an upper-class background. In the case of the Body of Representatives of Gyula, a significant portion of the members were descendents of lower and working-class families (71.42%), while 21.42% of the councilors were coming from middle class families; another 7.14% of the councilors originated from upper class families. The proportion of councilors born and raised in upper class families was the second highest in the case of Gyula, among the six cases. This can partly be explained by two historical realities: firstly, the town of Gyula has been an important cultural center throughout the period of the Austro-Hungarian Empire, and an equally profitable place of smart entrepreneurs, which, in the long run, resulted in an enriched *stratum*; secondly, the period following János Kádár's accession to power, the co-called "Goulash Communism", meant a time of perceived liberalization especially in economic terms, which generated at least a preservation of old socio-economical hierarchies at the local level. The fact that the *ancien régime* allowed for a feeble individual private economic initiative determined

118

the preservation of the existing "*petite bourgeoisie*", similarly to the Czech case, or for the "*embourgeoisement*" of the segments of the working class; indeed, as opposed to the Czech case, Hungary entered state socialism with a least powerful middle class, simply because the interwar Czech Republic was one of the most industrialized nations in the world, whereas Hungary was torn by the loss of 72% of the territory and 64% of its population, following the Treaty of Trianon (1919).

The case of Targovishte resembled the case of Tecuci, in the socio-demographical outlook of the Municipal Council: the overwhelming majority of the local councilors came from lower class backgrounds (81.81%), with only 12.12% descending from middle-class families, and 6.06% from upper-class familial contexts. Surely, the explanation for this distribution lies in the socio-economic peculiarities of pre-communist and communist Bulgaria, another nation of peasants *par excellence*; naturally, then, the clear majority of local elected representatives in Targovishte would come from peasant families, taking into consideration the impact agriculture has in today's economic makeup of the town. Among the lowest percentage of municipal councilors of lower-class background (70.83%) was registered in the case of the Slovak town of Levice: historically, Levice had been and continues to be a less industrialized community than the Czech town of Česká Lípa, and, even through more agriculture-oriented, the town preserved a "*petite bourgeoisie*", specific to Central Europe, due to the significant proportion of intellectuals in the community. This is particularly the reason why one quarter of the municipal councilors had middle-class backgrounds, coming from families of intellectuals or small entrepreneurs. Only 4.16% of the councilors in Levice had upper-class background, surprisingly the lowest percentage among the six cases.

The social mobility was expressed also by the educational level of the members of the Local Council and by the degree of rural-urban mobility. A series of scholars, from Putnam and Lasswell to Keller and Eldersveld, emphasize the importance of education for adhering to the political elite. On the other hand, recent studies have shown that, "[o]n average, citizens are midly, but not significantly, less inclined to vote for elite-educated politicians" (Gift & Lastra-Anadón 2018), an apparent impact of the populist, "from-among-the-people" type of candidates. This part of the research project has tried to identify similarities of socio-economic nature between the members of the legislative local political elite, hence establishing a pattern, a prototype, a profile of the local / municipal councilor in Tecuci, Česká Lípa, Oleśnica, Gyula, Levice, and Targovishte, respectively, from a socio-economic perspective. From the data gathered through the website of the Town halls and through the questionnaire, it was concluded that there was no cohesion – or, only a partial one – among the members of each of the six Local / Municipal Councils, from a social and economic standpoint. They pertained to different social strata and to different economic layers. As the case studies referred to small towns, of

119

30,000 inhabitants to 40,000 inhabitants, with constant and strong connections with the surrounding rural area (predominantly in the case of Tecuci, Gyula, and Targovishte, less so in the case of Česká Lípa, Oleśnica, or Levice), the degree of rural-urban of the local political elite was also taken into consideration, when assessing the social mobility of the said social group.

Concerning the occupational status, for Tecuci, the majority of the local councilors were engineers (45%), followed by those members of the Council being teachers (20%). Among the councilors, there were also lawyers and public notaries (15%), one physician, a mechanic and a welder. What was peculiar to the case of the Local Council in Tecuci was the presence, among the local councilors, of two persons with unusual occupations for the current practice of politics: welder and mechanic. Their presence among the local political elites could indicate a broadening of the access to politics for each occupational category, for each social status. This was not entirely so, as the two cases were administrators or directors of highly profitable firms in Tecuci, hence financially independent individuals. For Česká Lípa, the majority of the municipal councilors were, again, engineers (44%), extremely similar to the Romanian and the Bulgarian cases. What follows was a remarkably proportionate, equal distribution of seats in the Municipal Council among three types of professionals, which were to be found in all the other five cases, as well (and, generally, in almost every decision-making body): teachers, lawyers and physicians, each with 12% of the seats. The Municipal Council of Targovishte was another case of engineer-dominated assembly: 45.45% of the councilors were engineers, while 18.18% were teachers. 12.12% of the councilors in Targovishte were mechanics, and, together with another two members (6.06%) who were technicians, constituted the relatively small group of local elected representatives with no university training. This was actually the largest portion (18.18% of the Council), among the six cases selected, of local councilors bearing no formal university training. The fourth most common occupation in the Council of Targovishte was that of physician (9.09%), an interesting presence in all six Councils, for the very reason that this species of intellectuals is not a traditional occupation prone to enter politics, due to the limited availability for political matters. Yet again, a position in the Local Council is by no means a particularly demanding office (legally, a Council should meet at least once in two months, and the meetings of the Committees are not strictly regulated), but is rather a part-time job, allowing for those intellectuals with quite engaging professions to enter local politics. Another 6.06% of the Council was constituted by graduates of law studies (jurists, lawyers, notaries, etc.), and one councilor (3.03%) was architect. The Local Councils of Levice and Gyula were slight atypical regarding the professional and occupational distribution: the two bodies partially broke the predominance of engineers. For the Municipal Council in Levice, the dominance was divided between engineers (29.16%) and teachers (29.16%), while another significant segment was represented by physicians

(20.83%). The Slovak Municipal Council was the one comprising the largest proportion of physicians. The professional distribution of the Council in Levice included also: jurists (8.33%), technicians (8.33% of the members), and an IT expert (4.16% of the members), an occupation present also in the case of Česká Lípa (again, an indication that less traditional occupations are absorbed in the political "game"). Similarly, the majority of the councilors in Levice were engineers, graduates of technical or technological studies, the rest being physicians and teachers. The dominance of engineers in the Municipal Council of Levice was telling for the pragmatic overtones springing from the sketch of the "ideal municipal councilor": a significant proportion of the members of the Council in Levice pointed to a rather "down-to-earth" approach on how a representative of the local authority, of the community, should look like and should act. The predominance, in this respect, lies with: the inclination towards the development strategies and plan for the local community, dedication for the increase in the inhabitants' welfare locally, etc. On the other hand, the Body of Representatives in Gyula was dominated by teachers (the other exception, along the Municipal Council in Oleśnica, in which the engineers did not represent a majority), 28.57% of the councilors. The next two largest groups were those of engineers and jurists (both gathering 21.42% of the councilors, in each case). The Local Council of Gyula comprised also the largest proportion of jurists, among the six cases, whose average presence in the Councils was around 12%, and the largest proportion of architects (7.14%). Physicians bore a 14.28% presence in the Council of Gyula, while 7.14% of the members were technicians.

The dominant occupational status of the local councilors generates an influence over the public policies and decisions that are considered a priority for adoption in the Council. Hence, in the specific case of the six Local / Municipal Councils, the fact that the majority of its members had been trained in technical or technological fields and were engineers might have determined the general inclination of the Councils to vote projects concerning improvements in infrastructure. In addition, such occupations as engineer, teacher or jurist, are associated with a high social status, especially in the context of a rather small community. The large proportion of engineers (most of them directors or administrators of local firms, in the case of Tecuci and Targovishte) and of teachers would suggest that these are the occupations most suitable in association with the practice of politics at local level, for individuals working in such fields enjoy flexible timetables and extensive leisure time for additional activities, like politics. On the other hand, for the Municipal Councils of Česká Lípa, Levice, and Oleśnica, the peculiarity laid in the fact that, among the municipal councilors, individuals with 21st century-specific types of occupations or with quite atypical ones for political pursuits managed to penetrate the lines of the local political elite: among the members, one could find rather modern occupational statuses, such as a psychologist, musician, painter, or even two IT experts. To the long list of engineers, other technical-like occupations were added: electrician, mechanic, technician (yet other unusual occupations for doing politics), or architect.

In respect to the birth place of the local political elite, in the Romanian town, the largest number of councilors was from Tecuci (55%); there were, however, councilors born in the neighboring towns and villages (Mărăşeşti, Barcea, Cosmeşti, Matca, Nicoreşti, Corod) – a significant percentage of 47.36% of the total number of members of the Local Council; among them, 77% were rural-born, while 22% were urban-born. For the members of the Municipal Council of Česká Lípa, a significant majority was from the town they represented locally (68%), with other councilors being born in surrounding places (32% of the total number of members in the Municipal Council): 16% were rural-born, another 16% were urban-born. For the members of the Municipal Council in Oleśnica, the largest proportion (57.14%) was born in the town they governed at the time of the research. Less than a quarter of the Polish municipal councilors (23.8%) were rurally born, whereas another 19.04% were born in another town neighboring Oleśnica (usually, Wrocław). The Body of Representatives in Gyula displayed a similar composition: 64.28% of the local councilors were born in Gyula, whereas 35.71% were born in the countryside. The category of councilors born in another town was lacking. The Slovak case of Levice had a Municipal Council whose urban-rural composition largely resembled the other five cases, especially that of Česká Lípa: the largest majority of municipal councilors (62.5%) were born in the town they represented; another 16.66% of the Council was also urban-born, but outside Levice, while another 20.83% were born in one of the neighboring villages. Finally, the Local Council of Targovishte presented the following rural-urban composition: the autochtonous councilors represented 51.51% of the total make-up of the Council, whereas an impressive 39.39% were born in the rural are; the remaining 9.09% had their origins in other towns or cities in Bulgaria. The variable of the place of birth of the local political elites is an indicator that provides an image about the degree of social mobility, about the level of modernization (Stoica 2003: 113), about the easiness of migrating from rural to urban areas. Generally, it is assumed that urban-born elites hold rather "modern" views, they are more open to change, while the rural-born elite is inclined to conservative and traditionalist perspectives. The place of birth has also an impact on the local political elites' geographical identification. One can easily observe the proportion of rural-born councilors decreasing dramatically in the case of Česká Lípa (a difference of more than 23%, in comparison to the most rural-based Council, that of Targovishte); the explanation was rather simplistic and twofold: firstly, the level of urbanization for the six countries whose towns are analyzed here is different and it is in conspicuous favor for the Czech Republic; second, the specificity of decentralization in the Czech Republic, in its second, consolidation-phase, led to the situation in which many small villages were transformed and became neighborhoods of the town around which they had previously gravitated (therefore, persons born in such spaces are now perceived as urban-born). On average, it should be highlighted that the rural-urban mobility among the members of the local political elites in the cases under scrutiny was seemingly limited, for only 28.76% of the municipal councilors were coming from a rural background, whereas the vast majority of the members of the Local Councils (71.22%) were born in towns and cities. This situation is, to some extent, problematic, taking into consideration the close relationships with the rural area in most of the six instances, which should have been prone to generate extensive rural-urban mobility. It might equally be the case that people born in the countryside seeking public office aim at bigger arenas, such as politics at the regional or the central level, the stake at the local level being perceived as rather insignificant.

Even though the objects of the present analysis were six small towns, dominated by agricultural and commercial activities and, to some extent, by tourism (especially in the case of Česká Lípa and Gyula), the members of the Local Councils were, in their majority (89% in Tecuci, 96% in Česká Lípa, 66.66% in Oleśnica, 92.85% in Gyula, 95.83% in Levice, and 81.81% in Targovishte), highly educated individuals, graduates of superior studies. The large number of intellectuals in the Local Councils proved the reality that the educational level functions as the most important prerequisite in both the selection of candidates by the local branches of the parties and in the election of public officials by the electorate. This situation is particularly interesting, especially considering the fact that either of the six towns is far from being university-based urban settlement. Actually, at the time of the research, the intellectuals represented a minority among the entire populations of Tecuci (7.47%), Česká Lípa (6.74%), Oleśnica (13%), Gyula (12.9%), Levice (19.83%), and Targovishte (8.98%). From the empirical studies undertaken in Western democracies, it has been revealed that further questions should be addressed in regard to the topic of the variable education for the analysis of political elites: what type of education is more compatible to the position of power in the political hierarchy? More important that the quantitative aspect of education (i.e. how many years a member of the political elite had spent in the educational system), what degree of specialization is required for a political path and what degree of specialization makes involvement in politics virtually impossible? The cases of the highly educated members of the Municipal Councils of Česká Lípa and Levice tended to suggests that, irrespective of the level of specialization provided by a series of post-graduate or advanced studies undertaken by the majority of the members of these two Municipal Councils, a political career, even in a rather part-time fashion (the position of a municipal councilor is by no means soliciting and demanding), remains perfectly compatible with whatever higher level of education. Nevertheless, on the other hand, the developments within the elite configurations in Western democracies show that, in response to both the community's demands and the selection's prerequisites imposed by the party, the "technocratic" model of elite loses weight, the technical studies being overwhelmed by the growing importance of business and legal studies for the local political elite. For the cases of Tecuci and Targovishte, it was interesting that none of the members of these two Local Councils had managerial or business training – they were overwhelmingly graduates of technical studies –, though they conducted, administrated or managed quite profitable local business; hence, in a somehow deviant manner, they corresponded to the general trend among the Western elites. Surprisingly, the legal studies were generally neglected by the local selectorates in the six towns; hence, the members of the Municipal Councils who were lawyers, notaries or held other legal offices were rather sporadic: the average mean of their presence in the six Councils was 12.97%. The case of the Slovak town of Levice appeared similar to the Czech case of Česká Lípa, particularly in terms of passive representativeness and elite outlook (i.e. self-identification). This similarity was especially striking in what concerned the social origins and the educational level of the members of the Municipal Council: as in the case of the Council in Česká Lípa – where the majority of local representatives were graduates of advanced or specialized superior studies –, the large majority of the municipal councilors of Levice were either graduates of Masters' studies or PhD. Generally, the importance and the perceived value of a "superior education" persisted for all the Municipal Councils scrutinized here.

Four of the local councilors of Tecuci were women (Cristea Daniela, Dimitriu Doina, Paraschiv Elena, Tiron Viorica); however, the large majority, 80% of the councilors were males. This proportion showed a clearly male-dominated local political elite, with a profound underrepresentation of the female segment of the population, and proved a still traditionalistic manner of thought in the process of recruitment, by excluding women from local administration. Nevertheless, the percentage of 20% female composition in the Local Council was a start for broader women's participation in politics in the future, especially at the local level. The four women who were, at the time of the research, in the Local Council of Tecuci had those occupations traditionally specific to women: teacher and physician. The average age of the women members of the Local Council was 58.5 years old, higher than the one of male component in the same forum (50.7 years old), which proved that the women's access to politics happens rather late for the former. The four members were highly respected individuals within the community. In the Municipality of Česká Lípa, the representation of the women displayed itself as significantly improved in comparison to the case of Tecuci: out of 25 members of the Municipal Council, 10 were women, accounting for an impressive 40%. The Council seemed thusly deprived of remote, traditional preconceptions that would otherwise favor the severe underrepresentation of women. The female local councilors of Česká Lípa held the most diverse occupations, from traditional ones (physician, teacher) to more authority-yielding ones (engineer, lawyer) and modern ones (IT expert). The average age of the women comprising the Municipal Council was 48.5 years old – with an impressive 10 years gap in comparison to the female local councilors of Tecuci! –, nevertheless, still higher than the one of male local councilors (46.4 years old), which indicates that the accession of women to the political life remains slightly harder that the men's (the difference was smaller than the one of the Local Council in Tecuci, thus not really insurmountable in the years to come and with the advance of democratic consolidation at the local level). Similarly, the dominance of men in the Municipal Council of Oleśnica was conspicuous, as only 23.8% of the membership of the Council was represented by women (Beata Krzesińska, Małgorzata Lipska, Grażyna Siednienko, Józefa Stefani, and Janina Szczuraszek); the proportion was in the limits of women' representation in politics at the local level. The lowest representation of women among the six local Councils was to be found in the case of the Body of Representatives of Gyula, where only two members were women (14.28% of the local councilors); moreover, they had been elected on the "safe lists" of the dominant party, FIDESZ. Both of them were teachers, an occupation traditionally associated with women, especially at the local level. On the other hand, the second highest proportion of women in the local representative body appeared in the case of the Slovak town of Levice: 29.16% of the municipal councilors were women. According to Soňa Čapková, the representation of women in Slovakia at the local level is significantly higher than either regional or national level (Capkova 2010: 552-576), but remains quite unsatisfactory as compared to the levels of female representation in politics in the consolidated democracies of the West. The representation of women in the Municipal Council of Targovishte was in the average limits set up by the overall female representation at the local level in the region of Eastern and Central Europe: 21.21% of the councilors were women. In the Bulgarian case, women were – surprisingly enough – elected on the lists of right-wing parties.

The age of local councilors of Tecuci varied from 33 years old (in the case of Tiberiu-Codruţ Manoiliu) to 72 years old (in the case of the eldest councilor, Chivu Neculai). In Česká Lípa, the youngest municipal councilor was 27 years old (Martin Prokeš), while the eldest was 67 years old (Jaromír Štrumfa). For Oleśnica, the youngest municipal councilor was 32 years old (Adam Wójcik), whereas the eldest councilor was 66 years old (Wojciech Bartnik). The age range in the case of the Body of Representatives in Gyula started at 39 years old (Norbert Alt), and ended at 68 years old (with György Szalai). The age of the municipal councilors in Levice ranged from 32 years old (Martina Gašparová, the youngest woman in the six samples analyzed here) to 69 years old (with Igor Varga). Finally, the Local Council of Targovishte was composed of individuals of 37 years old (the youngest local councilor, Tanju Georgiev Tanev) and of 68 years old (the eldest councilor, Aynur Mehmet Arif). Even though, apparently, for Tecuci, for instance, the difference was striking, the largest part of the Local Council was composed of persons of 40-50 years old (30%) and 50-60 years old (25%). The average age of the local political elite – as studied in the Local Council – in Tecuci was 52.4 years old, the highest among the six cases. For the Municipal Council of Česká Lípa, the age distribution was fairer, although a stable majority belonged to the age category of 50-59 (40%), similar to the case of Tecuci; the average age in the Czech case was 47.24 years old, expectedly lower than that of the local political elite in Tecuci. The average age of the municipal councilors in Oleśnica was 51.35 years old, as the largest percentage of the Council's membership was to be found, as in all the six cases, in the 50-59-year-old category. The average age in the Hungarian case of Gyula was 50.1 years old, while the lowest average age, for the six Local / Municipal Councils selected, was to be registered in the case of the Slovak Council of Levice: 48.5 years old. The average age for the Local Council of Targovishte was 51.6 years old. Age is instrumental in the selection and election of political elites, being a mark of maturity, seriousness, stability, constancy. Generally, older members of the political elite are synonymous with greater professional and political experience, proving outstanding reputation – i.e. married, with children, with a stable job, with an acknowledged career – in front of an electorate living in a rather small community. Moreover, mature, middle-aged individuals embrace those perceptions which are not too obsolete and remote (specific to the elder political elite who lived and worked in the previous totalitarian regime), but not too superfluous and volatile (specific to the young political elite). To some extent, middle-aged local political elite is realistic and pragmatic, being freed of both idealism of the youngest and of traditionalism and conservatism of the eldest. At the same time, the six examples provided here were quite dissimilar to the general age trend for the local elites in East-Central Europe: regularly, regime changes are prone to open the way towards political power for younger personnel than the one representing the *ancien régime*, somehow intrinsically to the process of "elite circulation" specific to radical, irreversible political transformations. As a result, the average age of the local councilors in the East-Central European constituencies results as being dominantly below 45 years old[54]. This was surely not the case for the six examples selected, as both elite groups averaged above 45, with 2.24 points (in the case of Česká Lípa), 7.4 points (in the case

---

54 For a comprehensive analysis of the age structure of local councilors in the Czech Republic, Poland, Hungary and Slovakia, see Baldersheim and Illner 1996: 11. In 1992-1996 – thus, at the beginning of the transition to democracy in the region –, the average age of a local councilor was as follows: 44 – for Hungary; 44.4 – for the Czech Republic, and 45.7 – for Slovakia. Fifteen years after, in the Czech case at least, the average age increase 2.84 points, at 47.24 years old. Conversely, the average age of the local political elite for the Romanian case – 52.4 – is the closest to the Sweden case, which is a highly developed, consolidated democracy.

of Tecuci), 6.35 points (in the case of Oleśnica), 5.1 points (in the case of Gyula), 6.6 points (in the case of Targovishte), and only 3.5 points (in the case of Levice). This discrepancy might be explained through either a maturation of the local political elites, as compared to the situation registered in the early 90s, or through a limited "elite circulation" after 1989 (for the case of Česká Lípa, Oleśnica, Levice, and Gyula) or, better, a full-fledged "elite reproduction" (for the case of Tecuci and Targovishte). From the inquiry undertaken in the social biographies of the members of the six Municipal Councils, it seemed that the valid hypothesis was that the "selectorates" were inclined to nominate candidates who appeared familiar (i.e. incumbent) to the electorate, while the electorate itself had an immanent propensity to vote for the membership in the Municipal Councils exactly those candidates who possessed a certain political and professional experience, a certain level of financial independence – acquired only with a certain age!

Concerning the marital status, 84.21% of the local councilors in Tecuci were married, while a significant percentage of 10.52% was widow, mainly due to the increased age the majority of the councilors had; these were the highest scores, among the six cases, for both the married and the widow councilors. 5.26% of the councilors were unmarried. The Local Council of Targovishte displayed a similar marital distribution: 81.81% of its members were married, 9.09% was widow, 6.06% was unmarried, but 3.03% of the councilors was divorced, a category absent in the case of Tecuci. The marital status is instrumental in the recruitment process, because the condition of being married is generally associated with the stability of a traditional familiar model. On the other hand, in such small towns as Tecuci and Targovishte, the status of divorced (characteristic to none of the members of the Local Council in Tecuci), along with the consensual union, were perceived negatively by the rest of the community. As a matter of fact, the *status* of consensual union or civil partnership was completely absent for all of the six cases, marking the fact that this marital position was undesirable for elected public office, especially in small towns, where conservative views regarding personal life are still dominant. Perceptions were slightly different only in the cases of Česká Lípa and Levice, more open-minded in respect to the matrimonial status of the local representatives. Even though the largest majority of the local elite in both Česká Lípa and Levice was married (68%, and 66.66%, respectively), another significant proportion (20%, and 20.83%, respectively) was unmarried (simply because the local elites in the two cases were younger than the one in Tecuci, for instance). The traditionally "undesired" marital status for a candidate for local representation, i.e. divorced, was to be found in the case of the Municipal Council of Česká Lípa and that of the Municipal Council of Levice in a "permissible" proportion of 8% and 8.33%, respectively (these were actually the highest proportions on divorced local councilors out of the six cases); only 4% of the municipal councilors in Česká Lípa, and 4.16% of the municipal councilors in

Levice were widowed. The striking proportion of unmarried members was to be partially explained by the fact that around 40% of the populations themselves in the two towns were unmarried, making thus a young, unmarried candidate appealing to a seemingly unmarried electorate. Nevertheless, the two representative bodies preserved a sign of traditionalist biasness: no member of the local political elites was involved in consensual marital union. A partly similar case to the ones in the Czech and the Slovak Republic was the Hungarian one of Gyula: in terms of matrimonial outlook of the Body of Representatives, the lowest level of married councilors was to be encountered here (only 64.28%), 14.28% of the councilors were unmarried, 7.14% was divorced, and another 14.28% was widowed. As opposed to the Hungarian case, as a profoundly religious constituency, Oleśnica refused the marital *status* of divorced for its local elected representatives. Typically, instead, 66.66% of the municipal councilors were married, whereas the young segment of the Council was revealed through a 19.04% proportion of unmarried councilors; a significant proportion of 14.28% were widow councilors.

Finally, the introduction of religion as a variable in studying local political elites in Tecuci, Česká Lípa, Oleśnica, Gyula, Levice, and Targovishte was initially considered debatable, particularly due to the low relevance assigned to it, to the atheistic character of the local political elite in Česká Lípa, to the high "nondeclared" rates in religious demographics in the populations of the towns of Gyula and Levice, and to the high non-response rate expected in the questionnaire. The primary suppositions proved wrong: the overwhelming majority of the local councilors answered the religion-related question at the end of the questionnaire, and it was further assessed that the adherence to a specific religion was actually relevant at least in the case of Tecuci, Targovishte, and Oleśnica, by shaping the views, the perceptions and the attitudes of the local political elites. Firstly, in the case of Tecuci, the overwhelming proportion of local councilors who labeled themselves "Christian Orthodox", 100%, was explainable particularly in a community which is itself 98.32% Orthodox, hence, religiously homogeneous. Conversely, the most heterogeneous community of Targovishte resulted in a more heterogeneous Local Council, in which, although the majority was held by the Christian Orthodox (63.63%), the Turkish representatives identified themselves as "Muslims" (36.36% of the local councilors). Secondly, there existed a fragile correlation between the (formal) belonging to the Christian-Orthodox Church of the local councilors and the qualities they cherished the most to a local councilor; among such qualities, fairness and altruism could be associated to the fact the members of the Local Councils all adhered to the Orthodox dogma, but this is not necessarily so. The same logic could be maintained for Oleśnica, a neatly Roman-Catholic community; no wonder, then, that 71.42% of the municipal councilors identified themselves as "Catholics", although, as opposed to the cases of Tecuci and Targovishte, a significant percentage of 28.57% of the municipal councilors labeled themselves either as "free thinkers", "atheists", or refused to declare their confession. The case of the local political elite in Česká Lípa was much more complex: more than 84% of the municipal councilors were atheists, hence no such correlation between religious affiliations and subsequent attitudes, behaviors, values embraced could be reasonably demonstrated. An encouraging representation of the Roman Catholics (16% of the local councilors) was laudable in the context in which only 9% of the population were Catholics. The population of the town itself was in an approximately 78% atheistic, though it seemed, from the overrepresentation of the Catholics, that affinity to the typically Christian teachings of morality, modesty and correctness (to which the majority of the councilors aspired) was still important in selecting candidates. For the cases of both Gyula and Levice, the distribution of confessions in the local legislative assemblies was more complex, mirroring, to some extent, the religious diversity within the two communities. For the Municipal Council of Levice, the highest proportion (75%) identified itself as "Roman-Catholics", and another 12.5% adhered to the Calvinist dogma. A rising Neoprotestant group in the Council comprised 4.16% of its members, and the group of atheists counted 8.33% of the councilors. This situation was later to be translated in the partial abandonment of the dominance of an ethical model of the local councilors, and the adoption of a pragmatic stance in self-identification among the Slovak municipal councilors, through the proportion of atheists and neoprotestants (generally characterized by an increased pragmatism and lack of ceremony and ritualism) in the Municipal Council of Levice. Similarly, the Body of Representatives in Gyula was divided among Roman-Catholics (35.71% of the councilors) and Calvinists (35.71%). But, somehow translating the religious confusion and the confessional upheaval of the community, the Body of Representatives in Gyula comprised also Lutherans (7.14%) and an important segment of irreligious, atheists, or non-declared (21,42% of the councilors).

It should be also mentioned the fact that only six of the respondents out of the six samples had relatives engaged in politics or government, which would contradict the hypothesis advanced by K. Prewitt about the families engaged in political activities that would generate an inevitable interest towards politics to those individuals raised in such *milieus* ("the hypothesis of supra-exposure") (Prewitt 1965: 105). As long as the local councilors were the only ones in their families to be engaged in politics, a supra-exposure to political issues within their families was excluded, and, further, Prewitt's hypothesis was refuted in the case of either the local political elites in Tecuci, Česká Lípa, Gyula, Levice, or (partly) Targovishte and Oleśnica. Moreover, the fact that the large majority of municipal councilors in the six cases was ascendantly mobile *vis-á-vis* their fathers was a proxy for the absence of other relatives involved in politics: the only partial exceptions were one member of the Local Council in Tecuci, three municipal councilors in Targovishte, and two municipal councilors in Oleśnica, who placed their brothers and wives within the parties which supported them, following their elections in the Council, or who evolved in families in which politics has been previously practiced at the central level (as in the Polish case).

All in all, according to the composition of the Local Council of Tecuci at the time of the research, and, hence indirectly, according to the general preferences of the majority of voters in Tecuci, the portrayal of the ideal local councilor would include the following features: the profile of the member of Tecuci Local Council indicated a man born in Tecuci, who graduated technical or technological university studies – therefore, an engineer –, of approximately 52 years old, married, Christian-orthodox (even though not a devoted practitioner), coming from a lower, working-class or peasant family (having, as a result, no other relatives involved in politics), but being himself a member of the middle class with an average income of approximately 42,891 lei yearly, involved in local private business in the sphere of commerce and food industry. For the Municipal Council of Česká Lípa, the portrait of the ideal municipal councilor would look as follows: a man born in Česká Lípa, who graduated technical Masters' or advanced studies, a member of the middle class, an engineer of 47 years old, married, atheist (even though informally subscribing to the Christian-like moral construct), with a lower or working class background, with no relatives engaged in politics. Therefore, the two "ideal" profiles largely coincided. For the Municipal Council in Oleśica, the councilor was, averagely, a man born in Oleśnica, who graduated humanist university studies (generally, a teacher), of 50.2 years old, married, Christian-Catholic (and a devoted practitioner), coming from a middle class *milieu*, but with no other relatives involved in politics, himself part of the middle class and former activist in the civil society. For the Municipal Council in Gyula, the portrait of the councilor read generally as follows: a man born in Gyula, a graduate of humanist or social sciences university studies, of 51.35 years old, married, Christian-Protestant (though not a devoted practitioner), coming from a middle class background (the "*petite-bourgeoisie*") and being himself a member of the middle class, with no relatives engaged in politics. The municipal councilor in Targovishte was, on average, a man born outside Targovishte, usually in the neighboring rural area of the town, a graduate of technical or technological university studies (i.e. an engineer or a technician), of around 51.6 years old, married, Christian-Orthodox (without being a devoted practitioner, although observing the general rites and symbols of Orthodoxy, particularly in opposition to the Muslims), originating from a lower, oftentimes peasant family (consequently, with no family tradition in politics, although sometimes attaching to his / her political position offices in the local bureaucratic *apparatus* of the town for closed relatives), but evolving as a member of the local middle class (although, frequently perceived rather as an "upper-middle class", due particularly to his / her notoriety and to the economic prominence in the town). The municipal councilor in Levice was a man born and raised in Levice, a graduate of technical or technological advanced university studies (overwhelmingly, a Masters' graduate), a Roman-Catholic (and, usually, a devotee of the Catholic rites), married, a member of the middle class, with a lower or working class background, an engineer of 48.5 years old, formally without any relatives engaged in politics, either locally or nationally.

Patterns of Recruitment[55]

The process of political recruitment is defined generically as "a process by which individuals are inducted into active political roles" (Marvick 1976: 29). Prewitt discusses "recruitment" (often interchangeable with "selection") in similar terms: "We have saved the term 'recruitment', in particular, to describe the processes grooming an even smaller group within the active *stratum* for public office." (Prewitt 1970: 107) For Czudnowski, political recruitment is "the process by which individuals or groups of individuals are induced into active political roles" (Czudnowski 1975: 155). Prewitt further suggests that a shift from political "selection" to "political recruitment" is important for illustrating the societal and political realities: "from the vocabulary of socialization and mobilization to the vocabulary of sponsorship, nomination, apprenticeship, and winnowing" marks the "shift from extramural to intramural processes" (Prewitt 1970: 107). V.O. Key stresses the central importance of recruitment (and, more importantly, of self recruitment) in the overall study of democratic politics:

> "The longer one frets with the puzzle of how democratic regimes manage to function, the more plausible it appears that a substantial part of the explanation is to be found in the motives that actuate the leadership echelon, the values that it holds, in the rules of the political game to which it adheres, in the expectations which it entertains about its own *status* in society, and perhaps in some of the objective circumstances, both material and institutional, in which it functions."
> (Key, Jr. 1961: 537)

Harasymiw pushes forth the importance of elite recruitment, by defining it in terms of the "critical links between society and polity": "Recruitment is the important link between social structure and political elite role, and between changes in the two" (Harasymiw 1984: xv and 2), since "the study of [the elite] recruitment contributes to one facet of the understanding of politics and political change." (Harasymiw 1984: 3) Dwaine Marvick postulates that "[t]he study of political recruitment is in an important sense equivalent to the study of political performance – or governance – itself." (Marvick 1976: 29) William Zartman even argues that Pareto's and Mosca's "elite circulation" refers specifically to political recruitment (Zartman 1974: 465-488). Moreover, the significance of the patterns of recruitment designed and employed by the "selec-

---

55 See, for one of the most comprehensive analysis of patterns of recruitment and candidate selection, Hazan and Rahat 2010: esp. 19-89: the two Israeli scholars discuss recruitment on four dimensions: (a) "candidacy" (i.e. criteria of eligibility), (b) "the selectorate", (c) the degree of party "centralization/ decentralization", and (d) "the appointment/ voting method". Equally instrumental in the analysis of recruitment is Gallagher and Marsh 1988.

tors" is enormous: the patterns of elite recruitment can "influence the kind of policies that will be enacted, accelerate or retard changes, effect the distribution of *status* and prestige, and influence the stability of the system." (Seligman 1964: 612-613) While it is difficult to demonstrate the fashion in which the "selectors" conducting the recruitment, being socialized in a certain "system", accustomed with particular mores of selection, can effectively influence, through their actions, the "stability of the system", the manner in which elite recruitment is undertaken virtually shapes the political elite. According to Peppa Norris, there are three main levels of political recruitment: the self-selection (i.e. the interest and the disposition, the inclination to enter into politics), the selection as candidate by a party and the selection by the electorate (i.e. the election as public official) (Norris 1996: 196). Norris employs the same three-staged process of recruitment, her labeling evolving slight different: (1) "certification" (essentially, *criteria* for eligibility, as extracted from electoral legislation, party statutes, and, most importantly, from "informal social norms"); (2) "nomination" (i.e. "the supply of eligibles seeking office and the demand from selectors when deciding who is nominated"), and (3) "election"; the three stages are imagined as a "progressive game of 'musical chairs': many are eligible, few are nominated, and even fewer succeed." (Norris 2006: 89)

The first step in the recruitment process is the self-selection, the decision of a person to enter into politics, the "initial recruitment" (Jacob 1962: 703-716)[56]. The motivation for getting involved into politics was different from each case of local councilor to another. One of the most comprehensive *matrix* of motivations in self-selection process is constructed by James Payne and Olivier Woshinsky, who discriminate among six basic "emotional needs" which determine ordinary people to enter politics; in their model, various motivations generate different behaviors only joining the rank-and-file of politics and afterwards (Payne and Woshinsky 1972: 518-546). Concretely, (1) the need for "adulation" seeks for "personal pride" in politics and describes a gregarian behavior, with the emphasis put on electoral campaigns, during which the personal reputation of the candidate is fully displayed. (2) The "*status*" model considers that "success" is the emotional need to be satisfied in politics, whereas the subsequent behavior of the candidate is that of a person constantly preoccupied with his political career, generally cynical in what regards the others' motivations and politics in general. (3) The "programme" model accounts for the need of the candidate to solve the political problems; as a consequence, his behavior is one interested in the substance of both the public policies and the political process, being more preoccupied of stability,

---

56 Jacob differentiates between "initial recruitment" and "political promotion". He further discriminates between "circulation into the political system" (i.e. from external non-political position into political positions), and "circulation within the political system" (i.e. from lower-level to higher-level positions).

good governance, and favorable to compromise and negotiation. (4) The motivation in the fourth case is "the mission", the need to "identify with a certain cause", in which case the successful candidate is concentrated on ideology, deploying a rather missionary zeal and fully dedicated to social transformation, in a somehow revolutionary endeavor. (5) The "obligation" model distinguishes a candidate that seeks the "sense of civic duty": it is the traditional, though rather idealistic, pathway an ordinary citizen, preoccupied by his community needs and grievances, decides to enter politics to solve the problems of the community, but, due to the fact that he was moralistically driven into politics, he will be more inclined towards normative principles – sometimes, in the detriment of actual, concrete results; he exposes an aversion towards politics and towards negotiations and compromises, being dedicated to some ethical stances that would otherwise forbid compromise. Finally, the "game" model discusses the exercise of attributions in the political competence as a "satisfied need", generating a behavior that is "preoccupied with strategies and tactics; he [the successful candidate] enjoys the political *maneuvers* and manipulation; he has a detached vision upon the political 'game', although he supports its general rules." (Payne and Woshinsky 1972: 518-546 [additions mine]). Another, more recent, theory on the desirable traits a candidate to the political elite status should possess takes into account even biological traits (appearance), together with personality traits (such as extraversion, openness, agreeableness, conscientiousness) in measuring the leader's "emergence" and "effectiveness" (i.e. success) (see the "ascription-actuality theory of leadership" in Wyatt and Silvester 2018). In *Political Elites in Modern Societies*, S. Eldersveld uses, for his study of political activists in Detroit, a matrix of motivation for self-selection in politics that includes eleven motives for getting involved in politics (Eldersveld 1989: 33); the present research uses ten of them. According to the responses provided through the questionnaire, for Tecuci, the large majority of the local councilors, 42.85%, the main motivation for being part of the political spectrum was the sentiment of obligation towards the community. Other motivational aspects for politics pointed out by the members of the Local Council were: the desire to influence the governmental policies (28.57%), the desire to establish friendships and social contacts (19.04%) and the desire to be prestigious, acknowledged as influential within the community (4.76%). For Česká Lípa, the motivations to get involved into politics seemed similar to those of the local political elite of Tecuci: the very sentiment of obligation to the municipality occupied a prime place (53.65% of responses, even greater than in the Romanian case), and was followed by: the desire to influence the policies of the government (only 19.51%), even the desire to establish social friendships and contacts (9.75%), politics as a way of life (7.31%) and, sincerely enough, the possibility of building a personal career in politics (4.87%) (three of the motivational resorts that would not be sincerely spelled out by the political elite in Tecuci, for instance). For the members of the

Municipal Council in Oleśnica, the most important motivational drive for entering the public service was, by far, the very feeling of obligation towards the community (52.94% of the responses). Although this motivation covered the majority of the answers, three other reasons determined the Polish municipal councilors to enter politics: the establishment of social friendships and contacts (17.64% of the answers), the very fun and excitement of politics (another 17.64% of the answers), and politics being a way of life (11.76%). The percentage of those Polish local councilors motivated primarily by the very feeling of obligation towards the community naturally increased when the question targeted specifically the local level (61.11% of the answers). Interestingly enough, the motivation of politics as indispensable, as a way of life, increased, as well, at the local level (22.22%). Hence, the Municipal Council of Oleśnica corresponded to a clearly "obligation" model of self-selection, completed by a "game" model. When discussing the level of self-selection, the *palette* of possibilities for selection, as presented previously by Payne and Woshinsky, was reduced in the case of Gyula: a slight majority of the body of representatives (29.41%) considered the desire to influence the policies of the government as the main motivation to become involved in politics (the sole case among the six in which such a motivation dominated), whereas an equal share was divided between the second most preferred motivations, i.e. the very feeling of obligation towards the community and the desire to establish social friendships and contacts (each of them gathering 23.52% of the answers). Another 17.64% of the answers of the local councilors pointed to the desire for recognition in the community as the main trigger for entering politics, and 5.88% of the answers indicated the possibility of building a personal career in politics. This last type of answer might be a hint for the proportion of reelection and incumbency in the Local Council of Gyula, for an inclination towards constructing a political career was directly linked to the desire to run for another mandate, further resulting in a high degree of incumbency in the local legislative assembly. Consequently, it seems that the cardinal incentives for political participation coincided, in the case of the members of the Local Council in Gyula, with a combination among a "programme" model, focused on the desire to change the governmental policy lines, and the "*status*" and "obligation" models, in which the tendency to establish politically-charged connections was intertwined with the acclaimed sense of obligation to one's own constituency. Slight differences could be observed when the question on entering into politics specifically referred to the involvement in the local matters, as elected representative: the component of "mission" appeared, under the form of "politics is my life" (4.16% of the responses), while the desire for recognition and the component of "adulation" significantly lost importance at the local level (4.16% of the responses, 13.5 points lower than the answer to the more general question of self-selection). This is especially so due to the fact that the local elected representatives in a small-to-medium-sized town are already quite notorious, either as economic potentates or as "social leaders" (teachers, lawyers, physicians – the traditional "intellectuals of the community"); hence, there is no need to overcompensate for social *status*, as opposed to politics conducted at the national level, where the need and the desire for recognition exists and is frequently vital for the perpetuation in power. The importance of social contacts and friendships decreased, as well, when turning a position at the local level. Quite paradoxically, the motivation of establishing contacts and friendships was associated to the frequency of interactions between the members of the Local Council and the group of supporters and close friends. As mentioned, this type of interactions is particularly significant for the reelection process. For the Municipal Council of Levice, the central motivation for self-selection remained the feeling of obligation towards the town, with clearly the highest proportion of this one motivation among the six cases: 67.85% of the answers. Yet, the "obligation" model in the case of Levice decreased significantly when self-selection referred to the personal case of entering politics at the local level (only 41.37% of the answers). Hence, the rich rhetoric of the "obligation" in initial selection transformed into a more pragmatic, down-to-earth approach at the local level: as a result, the importance of the desire to influence the policies of the government increased from the general level (14.28% of the answers) to the local, grass-roots one (27.58% of the answers). Other motivations for being involved in politics for the members of the Municipal Council in Levice referred to: the desire to build a personal career in politics (7.14% of the answers), to establish social contacts (3.57%), the fun and excitement of politics (3.57%), or the desire for recognition in the community (3.57%). It should be observed that an incipient "adulation" model of self-selection appeared in the Slovak case. Finally, self-selection into politics of the local councilors of Targovishte took the following form: a domination of the "obligation" model (the very feeling of obligation towards the community – 36.58% of the answers), coupled with the "programme" model (the desire to influence the governmental policies – 29.26% of the answers, similar to the Romanian and the Hungarian cases), completed by the desire to establish contacts (17.31%), and by the Bulgarian-specific loyalty towards the doctrine of a certain party (7.31% of the answers, generally, and 4.44%, at the local level, a motivational drive quite surprising, taking into account the lack of party institutionalization and party affiliation at the local level in Bulgaria and in this part of Europe, more generally). Building a personal career in politics and the desire for recognition in the community (both 4.87% of the answers) completed the self-selection profile in the Bulgarian case with an "adulation" facet. It seems obvious that the responses gathered through the questionnaire did not express the true, complete and complex motivational mechanisms behind the decision of the members of the Local / Municipal Councils to become involved in politics, but it offered "a perspective at least on the image these people would like to have in the eyes of the citizens" (Stoica 2003: 129).

In 1982, Timothy Bledsoe employed seven motivational triggers for studying self-selection for the members of City Councils in the United States; the result of his scheme is a quite convincing taxonomy of local councilors: (1) the *"Politicos"* (i.e. those councilors who see themselves as "politicians", and their position in the Council as a political activity); (2) the *"Apoliticals"* (i.e. those councilors who do not perceive themselves as "politicians", and their position in the Council as being politically loaded, expressing a rather disinterested attitude towards politics in general); (3) the *"Community-regarding"* group (i.e. those councilors who "seek city office for altruistic reasons with no conception of selfish gain or advancement"); (4) the *"Self-regarding"* group (i.e. those councilors who enter local politics with the intent of personal enrichment); (5) the *"Locals"* (i.e. those councilors for whom politics is a means to help the community, but, more concretely, the close ones, friends, neighbors, etc.); (6) the *"Partisans"* (i.e. those councilors for whom politics is actually "party politics", for whom politics is about ideas, abstractions, conceptions, principles, not necessarily about concrete individuals or groups whose grievances are to be addressed locally); (7) the *"Particularists"* (i.e. those councilors who entered politics for solving or working on a particular, specific issue, regarding to which they feel dissatisfied, preoccupied, or to which they are emotionally attached); (8) the *"Non-particularists"* (i.e. those councilors who are "more universalistic in their concerns" at the local level). After inquiring into the motivational drives to enter politics and the socio-political trajectories of the local / municipal councilors in the six towns selected, this study concluded that: (1) the members of the Local Council of Tecuci and those of the Municipal Council in Targovishte were "politicos", at the rhetorical level, they appeared "community-regarding", although, through the prism of their interactions, they were rather "self-regarding" (with an important component of economic self-interest), more "partisans" in the support they received in (re)election, but "local" in the practical affairs of the community, especially in terms of informal links with neighbors and close friends, and "non-particularists"; (2) the members of the Municipal Council of Česká Lípa were generally "politicos" (due especially to the significant gap between them and the rest of the community and to the previous experiences of central or regional public office, of some of the local councilors), although largely "community-regarding", quite "partisans" (for they remained within party-politics logic, even at the local level), and "non-particularists"; (3) the members of the Municipal Council of Oleśnica were rather "apoliticals" (for, at least declaratively, they preserved a sort of closeness to the community, perceiving themselves as part and parcel of that community, rather than politicians), committed "community-regarding" (having worked previously for the betterment of their community), clearly "locals" (with overwhelmingly local cultural-geographical self-determination and with no party attachment, preferring the interaction with friends, supporters, and neighborhood groups), and, to some extent, "particularists", focused primarily on education and social policy issues; (4) the members of the Body of Representatives in Gyula were, in their majority, "politicos" (although some members of the Council, namely those in the "Friends of Gyula" group, were overtly "apoliticals"), and "community-regarding", profoundly "partisans" (actually, dividing the Council into two "Fidesz"-dominated vs. Socialist-dominated camps, alongside the seemingly outsiders of the "Friends of Gyula"), and rather "non-particularists", generalist in the construction of local policy agenda; (5) the members of the Municipal Council in Levice were generally "apoliticals" (seeing themselves as members of the community they happened to govern for a limited period of time), "community-regarding" (most of them "pillars" of the community, by their profession and experience in public office), conspicuously "locals" (with no party attachments, but a concern for the development of the town), and "non-particularists" (coming from different backgrounds, experiences, and professions, though without being able to impose a specific policy line on the local agenda). Bledsoe's taxonomy is underpinned by Harold Zink's fivefold typology of city councilors in the United States:

> "There is the member who belongs to the ranks of political organizations [...]. [T]here is the business or professional type who reflects the views of the business and professional men of his city [...]. [T]here is the member who occupies a seat for whatever he can personally get out of it. [...] A fourth somewhat common type of member is the member who wants to use the council as a stepping stone to higher political office. [...] A fifth type, not too common in many cities, is the public-spirited citizen who has no expectation of private gain." (Zink 1939: 296)

In his study of local legislators in Connecticut, Barber isolates four types of local politicians, according to the triggers of self-recruitment (operationalized through their desire to run for another mandate) and the degree of adaptation (operationalized through the amount of "energy" they consecrate to the public office, i.e. legislative or policy initiatives, presence in the sessions of the Council and committees, etc.). The result is a fourfold taxonomy: (a) the "Reluctants" (i.e. the local politicians with low energy and no desire for reelection); (b) the "Advertisers" (i.e. the local politicians with high energy and no desire for reelection); (c) the "Spectators" (i.e. the local politicians with low energy, but with a desire for reelection); (d) the "Lawmakers" (i.e. the local politicians with high energy and with a strong desire for reelection) (Barber 1965).

Moreover, it is generally perceived that citizens are closer to the local administration, especially in small communities: they trust their representatives, the local authorities are the first ones to be able to solve citizens' problems. There persists, in this sense, the danger that personalistic types of relation between the citizens and the representatives of the local administration are to be established easier and, hence, personal favors to dominate upon universal, coherent policies. For hampering such developments, a particularly important role is played by the local mass-media. Usually, the local publications and news-oriented websites in Tecuci, for instance, were, in their majority, extremely critical and caustic to the individuals composing the Local Council and to their actions (see "*Favor*", "*Semnal T*" in regard to Dănăilă Vasile, Coman Valentin or Butunoi Liviu). The hostile attitude of the press would discourage any motivation of getting involved into politics. In addition, despite the general perception that politics is financially profitable and, therefore, money and economic benefits would constitute the main motivation for joining politics, the actual situation (based on the gathered data) is quite different. In fact, those who entered the local political arena in Tecuci or Targovishte, for example, were those who were already financially self-sustaining, those who were part of the local economic elites of the town. Those who are willing to aspire to a seat in the Local Council need to have the resources to finance their electoral campaign; moreover, the local councilor's indemnity (e.g. 500 lei per month, for Tecuci; no indemnity for Oleśnica), was and continues to be rather symbolic and it could not represent a financial incentive for a person gaining from 30,000 to 100,000 lei yearly.

The issue of the desire to be reelected is inherent when discussing aspects of self-selection. Actually, the political system seeks a certain degree of stability and professionalization of political elite, while, at the same time, encouraging the change of elites and the change of perspectives. Generally, the political system aimed at the *equilibrium* between oligarchic, atomized structures and discontinuous and anarchical structures. According to the responses in the questionnaire, the large majority of the local / municipal councilors in Tecuci (52.94%), Česká Lípa (63.63%), Gyula (71.42%), Levice (62.5%), and Targovishte (54.54%) expressed their desire to run for another mandate and to get reelected. The only exception in this respect was represented by the members of the Municipal Council of Oleśnica, among whom uncertainty (61.11% of the answers), rather than the desire for incumbency (only 38.88% of the answers), dominated. On the other hand, 23.52% (in Tecuci), 13.63% (Česká Lípa), 28.57% (in Gyula), 25% (in Levice), and 39.39% (in Targovishte) of the local councilors would not have run for another seat in the Local (Municipal) Council; this category included mostly the women in the Local Councils, the youngest and the eldest members of the six forums. Another 23.52% of the members of the Local Council in Tecuci, 22.72% of the members of the Municipal Council in Česká Lípa, 12.5% of the members of the Municipal Council in Levice, and 6.06% of the members of the Local Council in Targovishte, did not state their desire to get reelected. As many of the local councilors occupied, at the same time, leading positions in organizational structure of the local branch of the parties – Presidents, Vice-presidents, members of the Permanent / Political Bureau –, being the ones to form and to purpose the lists of candidates for the Local Council, it was expected that their very desire to run again for a position of local councilor to be the single criterion in having their names at the top of such lists. Actually, since 8 local councilors (i.e. 42.1% of the local councilors) in Tecuci, 12 municipal councilors (i.e. 48% of the municipal councilors) in Česká Lípa, 12 municipal councilors (i.e. 57.14% of the municipal councilors) in Oleśnica, 7 municipal councilors (i.e. 50% of the municipal councilors) in Gyula, 17 municipal councilors (i.e. an impressive 70.83% of the municipal councilors) in Levice, and 14 local councilors (i.e. 42.42% of the local councilors) in Targovishte were reelected, the self-selection seemed a successful recipe for all the six Municipal Councils under scrutiny (particularly for Levice), with a rate of replacement of only 57.9% (Tecuci), 52% (Česká Lípa), 42.86% (Oleśnica), 50% (Gyula), 29.17% (Levice), and 57.58% (Targovishte), respectively, in the Local Councils, that would suggest the beginning of stability and professionalization on the deliberative branch of the local administration.

At the secondary level, that of selection by the party, one should bear in mind that the region of East-Central Europe has been permanently marked, during the transition period, by frequent splits, mergers, and electoral alliances[57], hence tracking the party history of an individual can prove to be problematic, especially at the local level, where party allegiances are especially volatile, changeable, if not altogether insignificant. Moreover, "[t]he conditions of modern party activity, elitist attitudes on the part of many party leaders in [E]astern Europe, and the reluctance of the public to join them combined to give the members that parties have enrolled a relatively marginal role within the organization as a whole." (Lewis 2000: 103) Locally, the post-communist parties adopted a loose organization, their membership being composed of individuals of high social capital.

At the time of the research, all the members of the Local Councils in Tecuci and Targovishte, of the Municipal Council in Česká Lípa, and of the Body of Representatives in Gyula, had been recruited as candidates in an intramural manner, i.e. from within the party. This could be translated by the fact that the support and selection by a political party of a candidate are *sine qua non* conditions for getting elected in a public position. The members of the Municipal Councils in Oleśnica and Levice had been recruited either intramurally, but, most importantly, in an extramural fashion, i.e. from outside the party, without the party. Generally, each of the four parties represented in the Local Council of Tecuci, the eight parties represented in the Municipal Council of Česká Lípa, the three parties represented in the Municipal Council of Oleśnica, the three parties and a local association represented in the Body of Representatives of Gyula, the two parties represented in the Municipal Council of Levice, and the five parties represented in the Local Council of Targovishte imposed, according to their statutes, the same requirements for a future candidate to a seat in the six Municipal Councils. Therefore, for being nominated as candidate, a member (1) should have paid his / her levy on a monthly basis; (2)

---

57 See, in this respect, Bugajski 2002. The volume contains an impressive database of parties in post-communist Eastern Europe.

should be a militant (i.e. a member of the party that is actively involved in the life of its organizations, in its activities and functioning), evaluated according to his / her efficiency in political activity and his / her competence (The Statute of the Liberal-Democrat Party, Title V. *The Carrier in PDL: The Management of Carrier and Candidature in PDL*, p. 28, and the Statute of the TOP 09, Sections 5, *Members' Obligations*, and 7. *Organizational Structure of the Party*), before being selected by the party; (2) should enjoy the support of all members of the Local Branch of the party; (3) should have his / her candidature approved by the Local Branch of the party, which is nevertheless obliged to advance a list of candidates for a public position. In the case of Liberal-Democratic Party (Romania), for instance, the list of candidates for mayor and local councilors was proposed by the Local Permanent Bureau and was approved by the Local Coordination Council. The party militant aspiring to a local elective position was analyzed according to its "file", containing his / her activity within the party and the personal competence, as registered by the Secretariat for human resources, militants and the management of career (SRUMGC) of PD-L. In the case of the National Liberal Party (Romania), the TOP 09 Party (the Czech Republic), FIDESZ (Hungary), and the GOP – "Movement for the Rights and Freedoms" (Bulgaria), an initial proposition of candidates is made by the district organizations and by the organizations at the level of polling stations. The lists of candidates are gathered by the Local Political Bureau; the final list is proposed by the Local Political Bureau / Local Committee, is approved by the Local General Assembly, which submits it, for finalization and validation, to the County Political Bureau / County Committee and to the Territorial Permanent Delegation (The Statute of the National Liberal Party, Chapter V. *The organizational structure at local, communal, town and municipality levels*, art. 38, p. 10); therefore, the candidates of PNL (Romania), TOP 09 (the Czech Republic), FIDESZ (Hungary), and the GOP – "Movement for the Rights and Freedoms" (Bulgaria) must enjoy a broader support, including that at the county level. Moreover, the Local Political Bureau / Local Committee is the one to prepare the selection of candidates for local elections and to organize the electoral campaigns. The Permanent Delegations of PNL and FIDESZ, respectively, and the Executive Committees of TOP 09 and GOP – "Movement for the Rights and Freedoms", respectively, are the organisms that validate the lists of *criteria* for the selection of candidates, even at the local level; the application of this list is compulsory for the local organizations of the party. In the cases of the Social Democratic Party (Romania) and of the Bulgarian Socialist Party, a member of the party aspiring for a seat in the Local Council should have at least one year of membership (The Statute of the Social-Democratic Party, Chapter III. *Organizational Structure and the Leading Bodies of PSD. The Electoral Procedure and the Competences*, Article 18, paragraph 10) – proving, therefore, a minimum level of party loyalty –, he/she should prove political experience, professionalism, "prestige and moral authority within both the party and the society". The Bureau and the Council of the Local Organization of the party propose, from among the party members, the candidates for local elected positions. The list of candidates is finalized by the Executive Committee of the Council of the County Organization. The electoral campaign of the candidates is organized and coordinated by the Executive Committee of the Municipal Branch. In April 2015, the National Council of the Bulgarian Socialist Party has adopted a new set of eligibility *criteria* for candidates in local elections; hence, BSP included even an assessment mechanism for evaluating the activity of mayors and municipal councilors nominated or supported by the Bulgarian Socialist Party, for reviewing the perspective of a second nomination: "Preference [is] given to people with political responsibility, wide general [administrative] knowledge, and team-leading skills". The principles of "renewal and succession" are also considered in supporting a certain candidate. Yet again, one can discern from the very *criteria* put forward by the central branch that incumbency is not expressly favored by the national "selectorates", but rather a sense of continuity, coupled with a spirit of collegiality, a candidate's trait seen indispensable for both the selectorate and the candidate himself / herself. A commitment to "social values" is also required, alongside what is labeled in the BSP Statute as "high professionalism", particularly in matter of public administration and "public authority" (BSP Statute), hence a certain experience in administration.

One could commonsensically observe that a first conspicuous difference between the six municipal councils was the degree of party diversity within their composition. Of course, according to the electoral formula and at the time of the research, the majority of the members of the Local Council of Tecuci were members of the Liberal-Democratic Party (45%), followed by the Social-Democrats (20%) and Liberals (20%). In the Local Council of Tecuci, there were also representatives of the Green Party – Scorta Mihai-Mișu, Manoliu Tiberiu-Codruț and Dănăilă Vasile-Pazvante –, accounting for 15% of the overall number of councilors. Though smaller, the Local Council in Tecuci permitted only to those parties that were central on the national political scene to recruit and appoint for candidacy qualified individuals to run in local elections; the exception of the Green Party, virtually insignificant in the national political arena (with no representation in the Parliament) was not, as already mentioned, a matter of the support for and allegiance to the "green" ideology of the party at the local level (which was, by all means, absent and which posed difficulties for voters in understanding if "green" was an ecologist reference or a legionary one…), but a clear proof of the popularity his leader enjoyed within the town. The situation was less personalized and more diverse in Česká Lípa: 25 councilors represented no less than eight political movements, some of them bearing a specificity to the region in which the town is situated (SLK, for instance, had started as a regional, localized movement, though, at the time of the research, it enjoyed parliamentary representation: 8% of the members in

142

the Municipal Council). The ideological loyalties were thusly diversified, from left-wing allegiances (ČSSD, which bore a feeble leverage of 28% of the members of the Council; KSČM, holding only 12% of the seats), center, populist and center-right movements (ODS, with 20% of the seats; TOP 09 and Public Affairs Party, with 12% of the members each; *"Suverenita, blok Jana Bobošíková"* Party, which held 4% of the municipal seats), to parties promoting green, universalist, postmodern obsessions of the 21st century (e.g. the Green Party had a 4% representation in the Council). While the ideological *spectrum* was richly and beautifully represented within the Municipal Council of Česká Lípa, the proportional representation of gender within the Municipal Council was another priority in Czech politics at the local level.

As in the Romanian case, the support of the party in running for a seat in the Municipal Council in Bulgaria is imperiously necessary: none of the members of the Municipal Council in Targovishte had run as independent candidate. Following local elections in 2015, the Municipal Council in Targovishte was dominantly right-wing oriented (over 60% of its members belonged to right-oriented parties), although no less than five parties were represented in the Council. The Movement for Rights and Freedoms (*ДПС, "Движение за права и свободи"*), the liberal-centrist party of Bulgaria representing the Muslim community of Turks, enjoyed a broad representation in the Municipal Council of Targovishte, due particularly to the geographical positioning of the province (in the eastern part of the country), where a significant Turkish community resides: while nationally, it gathered 12.5% of the parliamentary seats (being the third most important party, as membership and representation), in Targovishte, The Movement for Rights and Freedoms controlled 36.36% of the seats (Aynur Mehmet Arif, Ercan Aliyev Bekteshev, Imre Ismetova Mehmedova, Sevim Myustedzheb Ali, Sunay Kemalova Hasanov, Tanner Ismailov Ahmedov, Tahir Dzhemalov Tahirov, Vladimirova Teodora Petkova, Metodieva Teodora Tomova, Hatice Idriz Alieva, Hamdi Mehmedov Iliyazov, Hussein Mustafov Cherkezov). GERB (*"ГЕРБ"*, *"Граждани за европейско развитие на България"*, *"Graždani za evropejsko razvitie na Bălgarija"*, literally translated as "Citizens for European Development of Bulgaria"), the Bulgarian Prime Minister's party, a centre-right political formation, held 35% of the seats in the national Parliament, and a similar 30.30% of the seats in the Municipal Council of Targovishte (Anet Ivanova Koumanova, Arnel Alyaydin Yacoub, Darina Kostov, Dimcho Todorov Dimov, Jordan Panayotov Shivarov, Nevena Yaroslavova Stanimirova, Nikola Stoyanov Naydenov, Panaiot Jordanov Dimitrov, Turhan Bilal Hadzhiibryamolu, Stoynev Hristo Haralampiev). On the left side, a splinter from the Bulgarian Socialist Party, the "Alternative for Bulgarian Revival" (ABC, *"АБВ"*, *"Алтернатива за българско възраждане"*, *"Alternativa za balgarsko vazrazhdane"*), a centre-left political party, holding 4.58% of the seats in the National Assembly, won 2 seats (6.06%) in the Municipal Council of Targovishte in 2015 (Ivaylo Pavlov

143

Parvanov, and Savchev Svetoslav Ivanov). The main left-wing party, the Bulgarian Socialist Party (BSP, or "the Centenarian", *"Българска социалистическа партия"*, *"БСП"*; *"Bulgarska sotsialisticheska partiya"*), seen as the successor party of the Communists (still retaining the first position, as membership), controlled 15.41% of the seats in the Bulgarian Parliament, and 18.18% of the seats in the Municipal Council of Targovishte (Evgenieva Desislava Petrova, Alexandrov Emil Dimitrov, Iliya Iliev Svetlozarov, Krassimir Mitev Mirev, Nikolay Zlatkov Miltchev, Rumen Ivanov Takorov). The only local party, "United for Targovishte" (*"Обединени за Търговище"*), gathered only 9.09% of the votes, and was represented in the Council by Damian Nedialkov Ivanov, Plamen Vladimirov Belkolev, and Tanju Georgiev Tanev.

Generally, "non-partisan elections" or "extramural" candidate selection are seen as a "means to recruit superior candidates for municipal office and to insulate municipalities from irrelevant state and national partisan issues" (Cassel 2003: 239), particularly when the level of decentralization and financial independence from the center increases. In an "extramural" logic of selection, candidates for local leadership positions "prefer to present themselves during electoral campaigns as independent because being a party candidate in mayoral [and Local Council] elections substantially decreases the chance of re-election" (Majchierkiewicz 2020: 288 [additions mine]). Contrarily, the absence of party labels on the ballots at the local level is perceived as "reduc[ing] the responsibility of the rulers to the ruled by promoting issueless elections and favoring election of incumbents and other 'name' candidates." (Cassel 2003: 239 [additions mine]) Indeed, this assertion was verifiable for the six cases analyzed here, for incumbency levels increased in the context of nonpartisan elections at the local level (e.g. the case of Levice and Oleśnica). The extent to which the socio-demographical or the value-orientation profile of the local elite changed in the context of a "nonpartisan election" was difficult to assess, although it might be commonsensical to observe that "social notables" (e.g. teachers, social workers, physicians, lawyers, etc.) – to use a Dahlian terminology – predominated in those local elections in which party labels and support were irrelevant: the social "standing" was particularly important in "nonpartisan elections" locally. Equally, the extent to which policy prioritization at the local level suffers important modifications, when the municipal councilors are elected without party support, is problematic in measurement, for the simple reason a series of other interconnected variables are interposed (e.g. decentralization level, "ideal" profile, etc.). Indeed, "[p]artisan elections do appear to provide better access to local office to persons who are not community elites" (Cassel 2003: 240 [additions mine]): from the six cases under scrutiny, it has been observed that people born outside the town stood better chances to gain a seat in the Local Council when backed by a political party (this was primarily the case of the local councilors in Tecuci and Targovishte). In effect, however, the local branches of the national parties supported only those candidates that were eligible from the prism of their economic standing within the community, the candidates' place of birth or their social *status* being quite irrelevant in nomination for a seat in the Municipal Council. The extent to which "nonpartisan elections are issueless in nature" and that they result in "more efficient administration of municipalities" (Cassel 2003: 240) are yet again beyond the scope of the present enquiry, although a series of observations were drawn in reference to the latter assessment when discussing the manner of prioritization of municipal councilors; nonetheless, the direct linkage between nonpartisan elections and more efficient governance exceeds the objective of this study, and it can only be discussed through the interposed variable of decentralization: it is not necessarily the fact that the members of the Municipal Council are non-affiliated that makes a local administration more efficient and more issue-focused, but rather the exogenous factor of the level of decentralization specific to a municipality (resulting in the actual fiscal independence and the maneuver space of local authorities to initiate and conduct changes locally) that deems an administration more efficient in addressing the needs of the community. Finally, the issue of electoral competitiveness at the local level in partisan elections remains to be inquired: in all respects, the local elections are perceived as "second-level" elections. One, particularly compelling, argument is that, as a rule, local elections – apart, maybe, from the elections for the European Parliament – stir the least interest at the ballots, and are consequently seen as "second-order" elections (see, for instance, Rallings and Trasher 2005: 584-597; Heath, McLean, Taylor, and Curtice 1999: 389-414; Giebler 2014: 115-138). It is hence evident that local elections concentrate lower levels of voter's turnout generally. While the "second-orderness" of local elections might be compensated by the "community" effect, the very character of these elections in most of East-Central Europe presupposes less competitive campaigns and means debating issues that are perceived as "less important"[58] (even though they usually refer to some specific aspects of inhabitants' everyday life).

Paweł Swianiewicz identifies at least three sources of independent candidates and extramural selection in Polish local elections: (a) "crypto-partisans" (i.e. candidates who speculate on the negative reputation of political parties and on the positive image of technocratic, rather than political, model of local leader, among the constituency's perceptions, and decide to run independently in the elections; sometimes, even a problem of definition and party identification appears at the local level, when candidates stand as independent in elections, even though being formal members of a party, or when candidates stand on local party lists for the Council, even without being formal members of the party on the list of which they run); (b) "local parties" (i.e. small, but stable, local groups of "concerned citizens", but internally hierarchically organized

---

58 "Perhaps the most important aspect of second-order elections is that there is less at stake" (Reif and Schmitt, 1980: 9).

like a political party, decide to present a list of candidates in the elections for the Local Council, although the formal *status* of these groups is different from that of a typical political party; a movement similar to Hungarian and Czech local civic groups which presented candidates in local elections, such as the "Friends of Gyula", in the town analyzed here, or "Mayors of Liberec region" – SLK; such groups, though created under the influence of a very popular, notorious, charismatic leader, existed in the Czech case, as well, "*Suverenita, blok Jana Bobošíková*" Party being the example in Česká Lípa); and (c) "real independent" (Swianiewicz 2010: 497) candidates, usually backed by rather loose (with no groups hierarchy resembling a political party), more or less organizationally stable, locally formed coalitions of citizens.

Indeed, the party affiliation of the local councilors in Levice – and, more generally, in Slovakia – was insignificant, even though a very important proportion of the members of the Municipal Council were supported by a certain political party. Up to the administrative reform – and, oftentimes, even several years after the administrative and tax reforms –, the distribution of funds from the central government to the local authorities based on the party membership of the mayors and the municipal councilors has been maintained. On the other hand, although the large majority of municipal councilors in Česká Lípa were party affiliated, Illner stresses that party allegiances are quite insignificant at the level of Czech small-to-medium-sized towns, as well:

> "While in the regions and the larger cities politics is similar to the national political scene, with the national political parties playing the dominant role, the situation is different in small cities […]. There, party politicization is usually weak or entirely absent and cleavages develop around locally relevant (and locally circumscribed) interests and issues represented by local actors – interests which seldom translate into the programmes and policies advocated [nationally]. In local elections such actors appear usually as independent candidates, local movements, local parties, and coalitions thereof." (Illner 2011: 515)

Equally important in the recruitment process, the electoral *formula* based on which the local representatives are elected in the Council generates its own repercussions. The largest majority of Local / Municipal Councils are elected according to a proportional representation *formula*, on party lists or independent candidates' lists. For example, Gyula elects its Body of Representatives through a *calculus* specific to those municipalities having more than 10,000 inhabitants: the electoral method is rather a mixed one, as 60% of the councilors are elected through simple plurality system in individual electoral constituencies, whilst 40% of the councilors are elected through a proportional representation system among candidates on "compensation lists"; these "compensation lists" usually comprise names of party-backed candidates. Therefore, this mixed electoral system allows for both independent candidates and for candidates backed by strong political parties to successfully run for a seat in the Local Council. A drawback has been scored for this electoral system in local politics after FIDESZ's accession to power, when the new governing co-alition passed an ordinance increasing the threshold from 4 to 5%, shortening the period for a candidate to collect "proposing coupons" (legal request for candidacy), and increasing the minimum number of these "coupons", all of which hindered the small parties to successfully propose candidates for the Lo-cal Council (Szente 2013: 159 and n. 21).

At the end of the day, either centrally or locally, "[i]n complex liberal de-mocracies leaders are embedded in, and their effectiveness significantly de-pends upon, political elites [...]. Leaders with forceful images are in important degree creations of elites – horses they ride to power" (Higley and Pakulski 2007: 6). In this respect, it is the group of political elite-*cum*-oligarchy who selects and forms the new leadership; consequently, a look on selectorates and party leaders is particularly instrumental. E.E. Schattschneider radically con-cludes that: "[H]e who can make the nominations is the owner of the party." (Schattschneider 1942: 100) In general terms, this owner can be "party organ-izations, the personal *cliques*, the groups of dignitaries [...] involved in the selection of candidates and in their presentation to constituencies." (Best and Cotta 2000: 7) Analyzing the manner in which the recruitment of the candi-dates of the Local (Municipal) Council was done in the six cases under scrutiny here, it was observed that three types of party selectorates[59] operated in this process:

- the national selectorates: the Permanent Delegation (in Romania, Bul-garia, Hungary) and the Executive Committee (in the Czech Republic, the Slovak Republic) of the party which established the general criteria in the selection of candidates;
- the county / regional selectorates: County Political Bureau and the Terri-torial Permanent Delegation (in Romania, Bulgaria, Hungary) and Re-gional Committee and the County Committee (in the Czech Republic, the Slovak Republic) which validated the list of candidates for local public offices;
- the local (municipal) selectorates: probably the most important in this pro-cess were the deliberative (Local Coordination Council, Local General Assembly, Council of the Local Organization, etc., in Romania, Bulgaria, Hungary; Local Assembly, in the Czech Republic, the Slovak Republic) and the executive (Local Permanent Bureau, Local Political Bureau, Bu-reau of the Local Organization, etc., in Romania, Bulgaria, Hungary; Lo-cal Committee, in the Czech Republic, the Slovak Republic) organisms within the local branch of the party. The Local Bureaus had the responsi-bility of proposing names of candidates. The composition of such bureaus is particularly significant, for their members are those who actually gen-erate a certain type of local political elite.

---

59   See, for the pioneering usage of the term "selectorate" in reference to the elitist studies, Paterson 1967.

Especially at the local level, the role of the selectorates for the candidates' future nomination and career can be assessed by one additional indicator: the degree of "political proximity" the candidate enjoys in respect to his / her selector. Other types of proximities to a prominent political figure at the local (or, usefully enough, at the country / regional / district) level are "professional" and "family" proximity. The case of "family proximity" was not particularly illustrative for the local elites in either of the six cases, since only six members in all of the six Municipal Councils had relatives engaged in politics. On the other hand, the case of "professional proximity" worked quite interestingly particularly in reference to the local elites in Tecuci and Targovishte, since it did not refer to the professional *status* of the members of the two Local Councils, but rather to their "occupational *status*": in their everyday activities, especially in their business relations, the members interacted with the political leaders of the town, who were, in their turn, local businessmen. Thanks to a rather special form of "professional proximity" – to be coined as "occupational proximity" –, the would-be local councilors became part of the political elite. It was, for instance, the example of such local councilors as Petru Papuc, Liviu Butunoi or Costică Florea (for Tecuci), or Plamen Vladimirov Belkolev, Tahir Dzhemalov Tahirov, or Turhan Bilal Hadzhiibryamolu (for Targovishte).

When further discussing *criteria* of eligibility for the candidates for the Local / Municipal Council, of course, the widest, most basic *criteria* of eligibility – rather than basis for candidate selection – are the ones inscribed in the Constitutions of the six respective countries. For the Czech case, for instance, the Constitution of the Czech Republic and the Act No. 152 / 1994 on the Elections to the Municipal Council and Local Referendums are examples of such documents establishing the very general eligibility *criteria* for any elected public office: every citizen of the Czech Republic with permanent residence in the municipality, 18 years of age on the last day of elections, may stand in elections to the Municipal Council[60].Indeed, while inquiring into the causes for low political involvement into local politics of American citizens, Timothy Bledsoe manages to isolate, at least *prima facie*, three main sets of *criteria* of eligibility, others than the legally established ones: (a) a certain social *status* (meaning, primarily, that the potential candidate should be essentially part of the majority

---

60 Unless there is an electoral obstacle, e.g. citizens deprived of their capacity to act in legal matters, citizens serving a prison sentence, etc. An English translation of the Act No. 152/1994 is to be found in Structure and Operation of Local and Regional Democracy: Czech Republic (2nd ed.), a publication of the Council of Europe and the Steering Committee on Local and Regional Authorities, Council of Europe Publishing, Strasbourg (France), 1998/ 2001, pp. 13-14. The office of municipal councilor is incompatible with other function in the local apparatus: employee of the municipal office, member of the state administration authority with competencies over the local government area (financial offices, commissioned municipal offices), etc. Nevertheless, a local councilor can hold, at the same time, other elective offices (MP, senator, member of District Assembly, etc.).

148

group, in terms of ethnicity, or of a socially "favorable" group, in terms of education, gender, age, marital *status*, income, family background, etc.); (b) "political stimulation" (i.e. "the required exposure to political stimuli necessary for substantial political involvement", such as informal party affiliation, or experience in public positions, etc.); (3) part in a "significant channel of political entry" (Bledsoe 1993: 63) (e.g. membership in a political party, in a community organization, in local boards, commissions, committees, associations, part of a certain legal profession, etc.). Whereas the first two thresholds a potential candidate should overcome in order to become a certain candidate for a local position are applicable in ECE, the third one is problematic when contextualized for the East-Central European realities, for local "civism", or local "social awareness", is a societal trait still in its infancy in the region.

During an initial phase, components of eligibility[61] in the candidates' recruitment and party nomination processes, for the specific cases of the Local Councils of Tecuci and Targovishte, of the Body of Representatives of Gyula, and the Municipal Councils of Česká Lípa, Oleśnica, and Levice, were the following:

- educational level and occupational status: Another informal eligibility *criterion*, particularly in the Czech and the Slovak cases, is the educational level of the would-be candidates: a highly-trained, knowledgeable, skilled candidate is seen as "the bearer of progressive ideas" (Eyerman 1990: 91), an "articulator of needs and interests" (Eyerman 1990: 92), sometimes, the non-ideological critic. In the process of recruitment of local political elites, the high educational level of the would-be candidates is extremely important, even for the selection at local level. Hence, the general perception of the selectorates is that "the expertise and the wisdom would lead to the 'best' [i.e. the correct] political decisions." (Stoica 2003: 119 [additions mine]) Moreover, the group of intellectuals was a majority group within the social hierarchy of the six towns, which would inherently qualify those who graduated university studies as an elite. The overrepresentation of a certain occupation – that of engineer – in most of the Local Councils would indicate a preference of the local selectorates for candidates with technical and technological training and expertise. The presence of teachers among the local councilors could be associated with the importance the selectorates assign to education. In addition, both engineers and teachers enjoyed a traditional prestige within the community. For the cases of Česká Lípa and Levice, the most striking element was the remarkably high educational capital of the two Municipal Councils (graduates of Master and PhD programmes), which would evidently imply that

---

61 Those criteria of eligibility contained in electoral laws – such as Romanian citizenship, the age over 18 years old, with a permanent residence in Romania – were presumed as inherent from the beginning. Even through necessary, they are by no means sufficient in the candidates' recruitment process.

the level of education of the candidates had been of paramount importance for the selectorates, and for the electors. The importance of highly-educated individuals in the Municipal Councils is almost self-evident for the "selectorates" in Poland, Slovakia, or the Czech Republic:

"Intellectuals help societies talk about their problems. [...] Intellectuals are key democratic agents as they stimulate informed discussion about pressing social problems, fulfilling this role by cultivating *civility* in public life and promoting the *subversion* of restrictive common sense." (Goldfarb 1998: 1 [italics in original])

- high level of financial independence: 73.68% of the local councilors in Tecuci, and 75.75% of the local councilors in Targovishte were involved in the business area. They were either administrators or directors of their own firms or they worked as consultants, jurists or engineers in the firms of their close relatives (wives, sons or daughters). The majority of these firms were highly profitable businesses in both Tecuci and Targovishte (chains of restaurants or pharmacies, notary public bureaus, furniture firm, small commercial firms such as food stores and department stores, etc.), making their owners and administrators very powerful and influential individuals. Due to their reputation, to their capacity in gathering supporters and voters and to their ability in self-funding the electoral campaign, such persons were prone to be nominated for a seat in the Local Council. In this sense, probably the most notable case was the one of Costică Florea of PD-L, with virtually no record of party activity and no significant experience in public institutions; even so, what was clearly striking to this particular member of the Local Council of Tecuci was his annual income, about two times the income of the next richest local councilor and more than 32 times the revenue of the poorest one. Petru Papuc from PNL came close to the above-mentioned example, once more due to his commercial activities within the town. Nevertheless, as already pointed out, the situation was commonplace for Tecuci and Targovishte, since the local branches of the main parties, largely sustained from partisans' and sympathizers' donations, were incapable to financially support the campaigns of would-be councilors and thusly required from the candidates the payment of their own campaign and greetingly welcomed businessmen who wished a political position within the community. The situation was largely different in Česká Lípa, where, even though a certain degree of financial independence was rather intrinsically required (no unemployed would have ever acceded to a seat in the Municipal Council), the parties were more supportive to their candidates during campaigning for Municipal Council, while candidates themselves acquired financial autonomy and self-sustenance thanks largely to their professional status, not as businessmen (though exceptions were to be encountered, as well).
- incumbency: 42.1% of the members of the Local Council in Tecuci, 48% of the municipal councilors in Česká Lípa, 57.14% of the municipal councilors in Oleśnica, 50% of the municipal councilors in Gyula, an over-

whelming 70.83% of the municipal councilors in Levice, and 42.42% of the local councilors in Targovishte, were at their second, third or fourth mandate as local councilors. Similarly, the continuity of power in the Slovak case was quite clearly expressed through a high level of incumbency of the municipal councilors: 70.83% of the members of the Municipal Council in Levice were at least at their second mandate. In what concerned the recruitment process, the high availability of the existing membership of the Council in Levice for a local elected office (62.5% of the respondents would have run for another mandate) was associated to a high level of self-confidence in reelection, supported, at the same time, by repeated nominations by the local branches of the parties. Incumbency is one of the crucial factors differentiating "established politicians" from "aspiring" ones (Czudnowski 1976: 45-78), for it creates a certain routinization in office, a high familiarity with procedures and the rules of "the game"; "established politicians" are perceived as more reliable, a "sure" choice at the ballot box. This situation guarantees to this proportion a high degree of experience for this public position, a certain easiness in dealing with the responsibilities associated with the position. At large, there is a general trend towards a "closing of the elites" after thirty years since the communist breakdown, a trend that was present for the six selected cases as well: as the high rates of incumbency showed, the willingness of the selectorates in supporting new figures proved to be rather contingent, hence announcing "the closing of the elites" and, with it, the beginning of the "professionalization of politics" at the local level.

- age: While not an eligibility criterion of primary importance, age was significant in the selection of candidates, as certain age categories – mainly 40 to 50 and 50 to 60 – were dominant among the members of all the six Councils. Generally, maturity is associated with a stable family and a sure, comfortable socio-economical situation, with a certain level of prestige and reputation in the community. People in their 50s and 60s had the time to prove something to the community, to provide for their community. This is the reason why the selectorates prefer – even unconsciously – a particular age category. For Česká Lípa and for Levice, the youngsters tended to penetrate more and more the political mindset of the selectorates and to advance as capable candidates.

- an "orthodox" lifestyle, high degree of morality (this was especially true for Tecuci, Oleśnica, and, partly, Targovishte): Under this phrase, features like a universally accepted marital *status* and religion or a clean criminal record are included. Being married and being part of a united family and acknowledging the Christian religious conviction and conduct are two of the characteristics that are, traditionally, positively perceived both by the electorate and by the selectorates, particularly in the case of elected officials in relatively small communities. Moreover, 14.66% of the members of the Local Council of Tecuci, 15.27% of the members of the Municipal Council of Oleśnica, and 19.1% of the members of the Local Council in

Targovishte, mentioned honesty among the first five most important qualities a local councilor should possess; honesty is, again, associated with an "orthodox", desirable conduit of living. Others named similar features: altruism (1.33%, 4.61%, and 1.12% of the answers, respectively) or modesty (1.33%, and 1.12% of the answers, respectively). It seems that such moral characteristics would qualify a party militant to be selected for candidacy. Despite the fact that, religiously, the Municipal Councils of Česká Lípa, Levice and Gyula were deprived of definitive affiliations, even the Czech, the Slovak, and the Hungarian selectorates favored, in their candidate selection, the same "orthodox" lifestyle of the candidates: the large majority of the municipal councilors were married, displaying happy families, and were inclined towards an ideal image of the municipal councilors that bore predominantly ethical features: honesty (12.03%, 11.21%, and 13.84% of the responses, respectively), modesty (1.85%, and 0.93% of the answers, respectively), high moral stance (10.18%, 9.34%, and 1.53% of the responses, respectively), courage and bravery (3.7%, 2.8% of the responses, respectively).

- party loyalty and party discipline: The parties require, according to their statutes, a minimum time span of membership. Moreover, in the cases of Tecuci, Česká Lípa, Gyula, and Targovishte, there was no situation, among the members of the above-mentioned four Local Councils, of extra-mural selection (i.e. recruitment of candidates from outside the party): all the local councilors in the four cases were recruited on the list of candidates from within the party. Nevertheless, this was relatively important for the selection of candidates particularly for the Local Council in Tecuci, as there were several situations in which on the list proposed by the Local Bureaus names of party switchers were to be found. In the Local Council of Tecuci, the members themselves tended to value party loyalty (2.66% of the responses), as did the members of the Municipal Councils of Česká Lípa (1.85% of the responses), the members of the Body of Representative of Gyula (1.53% of the answers), and the members of the Local Council of Targovishte (the highest percentage – 3.37% of the answers). By contrast, the perceived importance of party loyalty for the members of the Municipal Councils in Oleśnica and Levice – the large majority of them selected in an extramural fashion – registered the lowest values (1.38% and 0.93% of the answers, respectively).

Prestige and reputation are equally important in the patterns of recruitment and party nomination process at the local level, especially in the context of a small town, more often than not preserving patrimonial and surveillance-like societal features. Reputation may be given by the matrimonial *status* – proved by the large proportion of married individuals among the local councilors, 84.21% for Tecuci, 68% for Česká Lípa, 66.66% for Oleśnica, 64.28% for Gyula, 66.66% for Levice, and 81.81% for Targovishte –, by the embraced religion – 100% of the members of the Local Council in Tecuci – and by the degree of financial independence. Local notoriety was, in the cases of Tecuci and Targovishte, the resultant of non-political activities, namely business activities: at the local level, the citizens consider that business notoriety of the majority of the local councilors is linked primarily to the fact that these economic and political notabilities are first and foremost job-providers for the community, hence their notoriety increases accordingly, exponentially. Therefore, many of the local councilors in Tecuci and Targovishte – in Česká Lípa, Oleśnica, Gyula, and Levice, as well, but due largely to reasons related to their professional *status* or to their prominent party activity and party seniority – exerted an additional high-profile social role, usually roles prone to increased prestige and local visibility. Either job-providers and some sort of local *mecena* (for Tecuci and Targovishte), cultural prominent figures (for Oleśnica and Levice), or professional notabilities and political "experts" (for Česká Lípa and Gyula), the local political elite in the six cases enjoyed a significant level of notoriety working as part of the candidate's credential, as booster for nomination assets. Equally significant in the realm of prestige and reputation at the local level are the so-called "apprenticeship positions", i.e. those institutional or non-institutional positions, partisan or non-partisan *loci* a candidate or an elected official holds that are politically relevant for occupying or maintaining in the targeted office an individual capable of exercising a series of adequate social-economic traits. These apprenticeship positions referred generally to such offices as director of local educational establishments (e.g. Viorica Tiron, Elena Paraschiv), private administrators or managers of publicly owned spots (e.g. Vasile Dănăilă), members of the leadership of local (branches of) political parties (e.g. Vasile Diaconu, Petr Skokan, etc.) and former public officials at the national, regional or local levels (e.g. Jiří Kočandrle).

In Tecuci, in terms of professional preference of the local selectorates, in the local elections of 2008, the Social-Democratic Party proposed, as candidates for the Local Council, a list including people working in educational and healthcare systems, along with engineers. Subsequently, in the Local Council resulting out of the elections, the party whose councilors were the most diversified from an occupational status perspective was PSD. Actually, the Social Democrats had the sole local councilor who was a physician. There was one party whose members in the Local Council were none of them engineers: the Green Party. In addition, this particular party advanced two (out of its total of three) councilors who had occupations following a technical-professional education (i.e. an average or under-average level of education), having not graduated high-school, but a "professional school": one local councilor from the Green Party was a mechanic, the other was a welder. It was observed that 47% of the local councilors were not born in Tecuci, but in the neighboring rural area. The parties having the largest portions of councilors coming from the neighboring villages were the Social-Democratic Party (with a ratio of 2/2, i.e. half of the Social-Democrats councilors were rural-based, half – urban-based) and – surprisingly – the National Liberal Party (with an equal ratio of 2/2, i.e. 50% of the Liberal councilors were rural-based and another one coming from a neighboring town, Mărăşeşti). The other two parties represented in the Local Council had similar rural-urban ratios: 3/5 (37.5% coming from villages) for the Liberal-Democratic Party and ½ for the Green Party (33% of the Green Party' councilors coming from rural area).

In terms of party allegiances, the Municipal Council of Česká Lípa was a remarkably heterogeneous organism, at the time of the research. It gathered individuals, representatives of different legitimacy, diversely selected and, subsequently, exhibiting various allegiances and political loyalties. As a result, the composition of the Municipal Council of Česká Lípa counted: (1) 7 councilors belonging to the Czech Party of Social-Democracy (ČSSD: Karel Bubeník, Martin Hájek, Petr Máška, Jana Rychtaříková, Jaromír Štrumfa, Jaroslav Ulbrich, Romana Žatecká); (2) 5 councilors of the Civil Democratic Party (ODS: Jana Jansová Kalousová, Hana Moudrá, Eva Stehlíková, Jan Stejskal, Karel Tejnora); (3) 3 councilors of the "TOP 09" Party (Karel Heller, Anna Kobosilová, Jiří Kočandrle); (4) 3 members of the Public Affairs Party (VV: Antonín Lačný, Jiřina Mimrová, Petr Skokan); (5) 3 members of the Communist Party of Bohemia and Moravia (KSČM: Marie Nedvědová, Oldřich Panc, Jana Zejdová); (6) 2 members of the political movement "Mayors of Liberec region" (SLK: Martin Prokeš, Tomáš Vlček); (7) 1 member of the Green Party (SZ: Miroslav Hudec), and (8) 1 member of "Suverenita, blok Jana Bobošíková" Party (Věra Strnadová). In Česká Lípa, during the elections of 2010, the Czech Party of Social Democracy favored diversity in terms of the age and occupation of the candidates; its representatives in the Municipal Council were probably the most diverse, from age (33 to 59 years old) to occupation (engineers to the IT expert). Its insistence on engineers was nevertheless notable. The opposing and main rival, the Civil Democratic Party opted for two typical occupational statuses in candidate selection, engineer and teacher, and for elder candidates (an average of 50.8 years old, one of the highest, as opposed to ČSSD's 49.42 years old). ODS presented probably the most classical type of candidate selection, similar to the one practiced by the selectorates for Tecuci. TOP 09 and Public Affairs Party favored engineers as well, and an average age ranging from 43 (TOP 09) to 49.66 years old (VV). The Communist Party preferred lawyers, while "Suverenita, blok Jana Bobošíková" Party betted for a young woman. The political movement "Mayors of Liberec region" scored as the party with the lowest age average (29 years old) – and the proposition of a young musician as a viable candidate – , while the Green Party was the party with the highest age average (60 years old) and a psychologist.

The overwhelming majority of the Local Council in Gyula (71.42% of the seats) was dominated by FIDESZ-KDNP party, the governing coalition at the national level. FIDESZ-KDNP is a coalition between FDESZ – Hungarian

154

Civic Alliance (*Magyar Polgári Szövetség*) and its satellite partner, the Christian Democratic People's Party (KDNP, *Kereszténydemokrata Néppárt*), a national conservative, right-wing political formation, presently in control of a supermajority on the national, regional, and local political scene (52.73% of the seats in the National Assembly, following the elections of 2010). DK-EGYÜTT-PM-MSZP (*"Összefogás"*, translated as "unity") represents a super-coalition at the local level, formed in order to counter the overwhelming victory of FIDESZ-KDNP: the left-wing alliance consists of the Hungarian Socialist Party (MSZP, *Magyar Szocialista Párt*) – enjoying 14.57% of the seats in the national parliament, in 2010-2014) –, *Együtt (Együtt – A Korszakváltók Pártja*, translated as "Together – Party for a New Era") – a quite young social-liberal party, developed initially from three civil society organizations, controlling only 1% of the parliamentary seats –, the Democratic Coalition (DK, *Demokratikus Koalíció*) – a centre-left political formation, formed as a splinter from MSZP, holding 2.01% of the seats in the National Assembly, in 2010-2014 –, and "Dialogue for Hungary" (PM, *Párbeszéd Magyarországért*) – Hungary's green liberal political party, initiated in 2013, and holding another 1% of the parliamentary seats[62]. In the case of the Local Council in Gyula, the political formation DK-EGYÜTT-PM-MSZP gathered a quite feeble 7.14% of the seats, with only one councilor voting in the Council (Bod Tamás). Another 7.14% of the seats in the Local Council of Gyula were won by JOBBIK party (with local councilor Csengeri Lajos as sole representative of the party within the Council); JOBBIK (*Jobbik Magyarországért Mozgalom*, translated as "Movement for a Better Hungary") is Hungary's radical nationalistic, conservative, extreme-right, Christian-oriented party, the third most powerful political party in the country, controlling 12.06% of the seats in the National Assembly (for the 2010-2014 mandate). *"Városbarátok"* literally means "city's friends", and it does not represent a political party *per se*; two local councilors in Gyula (Durkó Károly István and Szalai György), representing 14.28% of the Local Council, were elected under this banner. The context for this *"Városbarátok"* was complicated in Gyula, for both local councilors were not politically affiliated, though not quite independently elected, for they enjoyed the backing of this seemingly odd formation. It might be hypothesized that their election in the Local Council has been extramural, as they have been supported in the elections through this non-party mechanism called "the Friends of the City". *"Városbarátok"* developed in Gyula from a group of "concerned citizens" and local civil society organizations. The initial scope of this formation was to

---

62 The left-wing broad alliance DK-EGYÜTT-PM-MSZP, became "DK-EGYÜTT-PM-MSZP-MLP", after the Hungarian Liberal Party (Magyar Liberális Párt, MLP) joined the coalition; a centre-left party (at least declaratively), MLP held another 1% of the seats in the national legislature (for the 2010-2014 mandate). The party was not part of the alliance at the time of the latest local elections in Hungary, when the Local Council in Gyula, analyzed here, had been elected.

oversee and to keep a tight check on the quality of the public works effectuated in the town, to exercise a citizens' control over the municipal spending, to fight for fiscal "relaxation" for local artisans, craftsmen, entrepreneurs, etc. The agenda of the "Town's Friends" has significantly evolved; it gradually included: the rights of the retired, intelligent waste disposal, the improvement of the monitoring system of European funds for local SMEs, the support for the implementation of free transport to school program for the pupils from the rural surrounding area of Gyula, the preservation of old buildings and historical monuments, etc. The ideological orientation of *"Városbarátok"* is quite uncertain (the program of this group includes support for people with disabilities, but proposes, at the same time, a "pre-Trianon" economic mechanism, linking Gyula to Arad); the program displays a rather backward-looking, oriented towards the revival of the old outlook of the town, i.e. the development of the traditional gastronomy (e.g. the Gyula sausages and the town's own variant of brandy), together with the revitalization of the balneo tourism (including the tourism-linked infrastructure), aimed at reaffirming the regional role of the town.

Law no. 346 of 1990 on Local Government Elections in Slovakia stipulates the general level *criteria* of eligibility: a candidate to the position of local councilor may be any citizen with the right to vote: every citizen of the Slovak Republic eighteen years of age by the day of the elections, with permanent residence in the given municipality has the right to run in the elections for municipal self-government organs. The age limit for the office of mayor is twenty-five years old (Slovak National Council Act No. 346 of 1990 on Local Government Elections). Following the local elections of 2014, the Slovak Democratic and Christian Union – Democratic Party (SDKÚ-DS, *"Kresťanskodemokratické hnutie Sloboda a Solidarita Slovenská demokratická a kresťanská únia – Demokratická strana"*), a centre-right, liberal-conservative and Christian democratic political alliance, a political formation with no representation in the national Parliament, gathered 16.66% of the seats in the Municipal Council of Levice (Juraj Braun, Richard Strákoš, Ivan Murín, and Miloš Zaujec). At the opposite pole, Direction – Social Democracy (SMER-SD, *"SMER – Sociálna demokracia"*), having controlled one-third of the seats in the National Council, had eight representatives in the Municipal Council of Levice (33.33% of the seats), replicating the score at the national level. Nonetheless, 50% of the municipal councilors were independently elected, hence confirming a trend in East-Central Europe, namely that, in local politics, party affiliation is futile, if existent, when it comes to elections and the subsequent management of the town. In the case of both Oleśnica and Levice (the two Municipal Councils which were largely formed of independent councilors), one could easily notice that the average age for obtaining a seat in the Council for the party non-affiliated was slightly higher, as compared to those local councilors selected *via* a traditional, party-support manner (e.g. in Oleśnica, the average age of an independent councilor was 53.5 years old, whereas a party-backed municipal councilor was, on average, 50.22 years old).

The last test to be taken by an individual seeking to be elected for a seat in the Local Council is his / her selection by the electorate, by the voters of the town. In this sense, prestige and a positive reputation are particularly important. This situation would favor those candidates who are influential – especially through their businesses (restaurants, pharmacies, groceries, etc.) –, but also those who are respected within the community, due to their occupational *status* (particularly teachers and physicians). Moreover, the fact that a significant segment of the local councilors in all six municipalities was reelected would indicate that those persons enjoy a significant level of popular support and trust. Finally, for those local councilors who are elected on party lists, the score of a certain party at the national level is vital in the elections of the members of the Local / Municipal Council. Hence, for instance, in the 2008-2012 mandate, the most numerous councilors in Tecuci (8 – 42.1%) were coming from PD-L, the then-governing party, while the opposition parties had, in the Council, an equal number of representatives: 4 – 21.05% each. The special case of the Green Party (having 15.78% of the seats in the Council), a non-parliamentary party with extremely low scores at the national level, was explained through the reputation and the popularity the leader of its local branch enjoyed within the community. There was a clear categorical majority of the Liberal-Democratic Party in the Local Council of Tecuci. A similar case was to be encountered for the Body of Representatives in Gyula, unequivocally dominated by the FIDESZ-supported municipal councilors. In the Municipal Council of Česká Lípa, by contrast, the feeble majority was held by the Czech Party of Social Democracy (7 – 28%), followed closely by the Civil Democratic Party (5 – 20%). The fact that the Czech local political arena permitted and enabled much many parties to propose, advance and support candidates for the Municipal Council suggests a greater openness of the Czech political scene, but it also points, to some extent, to the maturity of the Romanian political scene and its closeness: hence, the political scene at the local level, in the special case of Tecuci, in accordance to the results of the elections of 2008 for the formation of the Local Council, displayed the very dominance of the three great parties at the national level – plus a political movement whose locomotive was a local economic potentate –, which further indicates the inability, the incapacity of the small, localized to advance and to sustain candidates even in the circumscribed space of the community in which they function. These movements and organizations born and operating at the local level are virtually incapacitated, in the Romanian case, unless some local economic notables seeking political recognition and office attach their names to these formations, strongly financing their activity during electoral campaigns and frequently for a quite limited time span. To some extent, hence, the candidates select themselves, with the approval of the regional branches of the party. Conversely, the existence of the Czech regional party "Mayors of Liberec Region", SLK, demonstrated that, in the case of Česká Lípa, the political scene was yet to mature, still allowing for the moment, the appearance of new political formations that could actually present and support candidates at the local level, candidates who were afterwards elected. Surely, SLK might not enjoy the same resources as the top national political competitors (e.g. ODC, CSSD and TOP 09), nevertheless it still managed to mobilize votes and to attract popular support. The same could be held for the case of the regional party MK – "United for Targovishte", having a feeble, but encouraging representation in the Local Council of Targovishte, and for the case of the local *quasi*-political association "*Városbarátok*" which held two seats within the Body of Representatives in Gyula.

While referring to the British case of party affiliations at the local level, Patrick Dunleavy is right in pointing out that, in the absence of a genuine electoral competition locally, the electoral responsiveness of the local political elites is surpassed by the government performance at the central level (Dunleavy 1980: 138-139); this is particularly so for states with a profound tradition of centralism, and, for the region of East-Central Europe, this dynamic appears manifest in the less decentralized countries, where levels of satisfaction or disenchantment with cabinet performance is usually translated into voting patterns at the local level, irrespective of the actual performance or achievements of the local authorities. These party-motivated shifts are telling for the importance of party affiliation in a candidature in the Local Council in countries like Romania and Bulgaria[63].

Finally, for identifying the qualities that ideally a local councilor should possess, qualities that could constitute eligibility *criteria* for both the parties and the electorate, the questionnaire included an open question addressing the issue. After comprehensively scrutinizing the ones in power, the recent scholarly generally agreed on five models[64] that might account for specific "qualities" in defining and identifying elites. The assemblage of these models pledges to the fact that a normative-descriptive reconciliation was intended, although in an overwhelmingly descriptive fashion[65]. The "ethical model" of

---

63 In this respect, illuminating was the great shift towards a new mayor and an overwhelmingly new composition of the Local Council in Tecuci, following the local elections of 2012, when, in the context of a acute disenchantment with the governing party and of the rise of a strong opposing electoral alliance (the Social-Liberal Union), the mayor and the majority of the Council missed another mandate, despite performing fairly well throughout two subsequent mandates (particularly, in infrastructure developments).

64 The fivefold model of values of the political elite was firstly used by Prewitt 1970, but it has been employed ever since (and subsequently modified and altered) in numerous empirical studies of the 70s-90s.

65 This is particularly the reason why this book coins the recent (i.e. post-Wright-Mills) empirical drive in studying and defining political elites as "neo-descriptive", since it

political elite refers to such qualities as: correctness, honesty, fairness, altruism, modesty, high moral standards, verticality and seriousness, courage and bravery, punctuality. The "technocratic model" of political elite takes into consideration such attributes as: political experience, political will, expertise and training, intelligence, patience / rapid reaction, enthusiasm and imagination. The "pragmatic model" of political elite is respective to such features as: dedication to the constituency's (state's) improvement plans, devotion and respect for the community / country, desire to change, the capacity to identify development opportunities for the community / country, vision, perspective, initiative, persuasion skills, capacity to compromise and negotiate, dialog-oriented, intuition, social sensitivity, care for the citizen, economic independence, leadership skills. The "political model" subscribes to the following qualities: oratorical skills, rhetoric, political loyalty, incorruptibility, interest detachment (objectivity), collegiality and team spirit. The "gender model" refers to the gender quality. The results largely coincided to an "ethical model", with features such as honesty (justness, correctness, fairness, truthfulness) (14.66% of the answers for Tecuci, 12.03% of the answers for Česká Lípa, 15.27% of the answers for Oleśnica, 13.84% of the answers for Gyula, 11.21% of the answers for Levice, and an impressive 19.1% of the answers for Targovishte), moral verticality, seriousness, personal disciplie, sobriety (5.33% for Tecuci, an impressive and telling 10.18% for Česká Lípa, 2.77% for Oleśnica, the lowest 1.53% for Gyula, 9.34% for Levice, and 6.74% for Targovishte), altruism and selflessness (1.33% of the answers for Tecuci, 5.55% for Oleśnica, 4.61% for Gyula, and 1.12% for Targovishte) and modesty (1.33% of the responses for Tecuci, 1.85% of the responses for Česká Lípa, 0.93% of the answers for Levice, and 1.12% of the answers for Targovishte), courage and bravery (3.7% for Česká Lípa, and 2.8% for Levice), punctuality (very similar results for Česká Lípa, 0.92%, and for Levice, 0.93%) among the most important qualities a local councilor should have. The technocratic model was equally valued by the local councilors: a significant number pointed out such characteristics as training and expertise (4% of the answers for Tecuci, 4.62% for Česká Lípa, 1.38% for Oleśnica, 1.53% for Gyula, 3.73% for Levice, and 4.49% for Targovishte), and political experience and political will (5.33% for Tecuci, 6.48% for Česká Lípa, 1.38% for Oleśnica, 1.53% for Gyula, 5.6% for Levice, and 6.74% for Targovishte), reliability and solidity (5.55% for Oleśnica, and 4.61% for Gyula), effectiveness and competence (2.77% of the answers for Oleśnica, 1.53% of the answers for Gyula, a telling 9.34% of the answers for Levice), intelligence and wisdom (6.48% of the answers for Česká Lípa, 4.16% of the answers for Oleśnica, 3.07% of the answers for Gyula, and 5.6% of the answers for Levice), patience or rapid reaction (1.85% for Česká Lípa, and 0.93% for Levice), and enthusiasm, imagination, creativity, and innovation (1.85% of the

---

admits the necessity of introducing the "ethical model", in spite of the fact that the inquiries are in themselves largely descriptive, exploratory.

answers for Česká Lípa, 5.55% of the answers for Oleśnica, 4.61% of the answers for Gyula, and 0.93% of the answers for Levice) as the hallmark of the technocratic model. Those local councilors mentioning the dedication to the town's improvement plans, devotion, desire to change, and respect for the community (12% for Tecuci, a falling 8.33% for Česká Lípa, 4.61% for Gyula, 7.47% for Levice, and a surprising, but encouraging, 15.73% for Targovishte), involvement, diligence, commitment, assertiveness, industry (6.94% of the answers for Oleśnica, and 6.15% of the answers for Gyula), determination, consistency, consequence (2.77% for Oleśnica, and 1.53% for Gyula), thoroughness (1.38% for Oleśnica, and 1.53% for Gyula), the capacity to identify development opportunities for the town, vision, perspective (6.66% for Tecuci, 10.18% for Česká Lípa, 1.38% for Oleśnica, 1.53% for Gyula, 9.34% for Levice, and 7.86% for Targovishte), the initiative and enactment (1.33% for Tecuci, a similar 1.85% for Česká Lípa, 1.38% for Oleśnica, 1.53% for Gyula, 0.93% for Levice, and 1.12% for Targovishte), the persuasion skills, the capacity to compromise, cooperate, and negotiate, dialogue-orientation, non-conflictual stance (1.33% for Tecuci, a more significant 7.4% for Česká Lípa, 8.33% for Oleśnica, 7.69% for Gyula, 6.54% for Levice, and only 1.12% for Targovishte), intuition (0.92% for Česká Lípa, and 0.92% for Levice), openness to others, tolerance, broadmindedness (particularly, in the case of Oleśnica – 9.71% of the answers –, and Gyula – 9.23% of the answers), social sensitivity, social activity, care for the citizen, the spirit of social justice, and social-problem awareness (3.7% for Česká Lípa, the highest – 11.11% – for Oleśnica, 10.76% for Gyula, and 2.8% for Levice), economic independence (1.85% for Česká Lípa, 0.93% for Levice, and an expected 4.49% for Targovishte), leadership skills (2.77% for Česká Lípa, 4.61% for Gyula, and 1,86% for Levice), accountability, responsibility, responsiveness (5.55% of the answers for Oleśnica, and 4.61% of the answers for Gyula), etc. favored the pragmatic model. Finally, the political model was constructed through the following qualities: party loyalty (2.66% of the answers for Tecuci, 1.85% of the answers for Česká Lípa, 1.38% of the answers for Oleśnica, 1.53% of the answers for Gyula, only 0.93% of the answers for Levice, and 3.37% of the answers for Targovishte), oratorical skills (1.33% for Tecuci, 0.92% for Česká Lípa, 0.93% for Levice, and 1.12% for Targovishte), incorruptibility (5.33% of the answers for Tecuci, 4.62% of the answers for Česká Lípa, 3.07% of the answers for Gyula, 3.73% of the answers for Levice, and a surprising 6.74% of the answers for Targovishte), interest detachment and objectivity (2.66% for Tecuci, a similar 2.77% for both Česká Lípa and Oleśnica, 1.53% for Gyula, 1.86% for Levice, and 3.37% for Targovishte), political independence (relevant only for Oleśnica – 1.38% of the answers –, for Gyula – 1.53% of the answers –, and, most clearly, for Levice – 8.41% of the answers), but, most important, team spirit and collegiality (12% of the responses in the case of Tecuci, and 15.73% of the responses in the case of Targovishte, as opposed to

2.77% of the responses in the case of Česká Lípa, 1.38% of the responses in the case of Oleśnica, 1.53% of the responses in the case of Gyula, and 1.86% of the responses in the case of Levice). The gender model was not used by the present study, as no local councilor perceived the gender differences as being important in sketching the ideal profile of a member of the Local Council. Generally, for the Local Council of Tecuci, the dominant models were the political (24% of the answers), and the ethical ones (22.65% of the answers). For the Municipal Council of Česká Lípa, the prevalent models were the ethical (28.68% of the answers) and the pragmatic ones (27.77% of the answers). For the Municipal Council of Oleśnica, the model of paramount importance in the councilors' ranking was the pragmatic one (48.56% of the answers), followed by the ethical one (23.59% of the answers); the political model ranked the lowest among all the six Local Councils (6.91% of the answers). For the Body of Representatives of Gyula, the dominant model was the pragmatic one (ranking the highest among the six cases: 53.84% of the answers), followed, at a considerable distance, by the ethical one (20% of the answers). For the Municipal Council in Levice, the model that prevailed among the councilors' perceptions on themselves was the pragmatic model (30.84% of the answers), but the technocratic (26.16% of the answers, the highest percentage for the six cases) and the ethical ones (25.23% of the answers) followed quite closely. For the Local Council of Targovishte, the portrait of the "ideal local councilor" seen through the eyes of the councilors themselves was equally divided between the pragmatic model (30.33% of the answers), and the political model (30.33% of the answers), although the ethical model, as well, played a significant role (28.08% of the answers).

In what concerns matters of composing the ideal portrait of a local / municipal councilor, one should not overlook the "canonical" sketch of a politician drawn by Herbert Jacob, for whom "the need for prestige, power, nurturance, exhibitionism (being in the public spotlight) and avoidance-of-friendship compose the most salient traits of *homo politicus*." (Jacob 1962: 708) Firstly, in opposition to what Jacob describes, for the cases scrutinized here, the individuals entering local politics through the means of a popular vote were quite well-known within the community, due either to their economic preeminence, to their position within a rather small community (teachers, lawyers, physicians), or to their prior involvement in reform groups (especially for the Polish case). This study contends that entering local politics, for the groups of local councilors analyzed here, was a matter of adding influence to their initial standing within the community, either for their own personal interest (improving business contacts, establishing business deals, creating the appropriate legal environment for perpetuating their own endeavors), or for the general interest of the community (improving social benefits for a certain social category or segment, pushing for economic recovery and infrastructure developments, preserving public security, pursuing cultural activities, putting forward the promotion of minority rights, etc.).

Interactions with other groups and institutions. Networks of interactions

Politics is about personal interaction: between individuals perceiving the same goal, between those pursuing different aims; between institutions, between institutions and other groups, between institutions and the citizen, etc. Ultimately, the politician, by the very nature of its occupation, is obliged to interact with other individuals, with groups, with institutions. In fact, the interactions, links, or connections of a local political elite, their nature and their complexity, are indicators in assessing the degree of integration of this particular group within the existing societal framework, i.e. "[a] high frequency of interactions can be seen as an indicator of a solid integration of the political elite" (Stoica 2003: 153). As a result, the activities and actions of the political elite become viable and meaningful for society. A series of scholars have convincingly argued that political elite is a very coherent, homogenous group of individuals, establishing strong unbreakable connections with some other groups. Famously, C. Wright-Mills argues, in his *The Power Elite*, that the political elite (the "political directorate") is tightly linked to the economical (the "corporate chief tenets") and military elites (the "war lords"). The connections, Wright-Mills further contends, go back to the childhood of the members of these elites; the members of these three groups shared the same family and educational backgrounds; established links since high-school or college and, since then, they preserved the same personal relations: they meet in rather informal than formal fashion, there are even psychological similarities between them (e.g. their behavior is the same in contexts of crisis) (Wright-Mills 1956).

Caught in interstices, as "an ecology of games" (Long 1958: 251), the local community, the town, is "a polity, an economy, a society [which] presents itself as an order in which expectations are met and functions performed" (Long 1958: 251), essentially through constant interactions and linkages. Classical theoreticians (predominantly, Mosca 1939, and Michels 1962/1911) describe the political elites' integration as being the clearest illustrated by a high level of frequency of their interactions with other groups and institutions, and by a dense network of political power. In this respect, Mosca and Michels and, afterwards, Meisel, describe the elites as a unitary, coherent group, characterized by an extreme degree of cohesion. Meisel (1962: 4) concludes that elites bear essentially "the 3Cs": group consciousness, coherence, conspiracy. This is particularly the reason why the elite group is perceived as a whole, the central piece of the power relations and the independent variable of government interactions. Generally, the unitary elite fulfills the requirements of the "3 Cs" to the extent in which it possesses – paraphrasing a Marxist vocabulary – "elite group consciousness". Elite "group consciousness" represents more than the exclusivist and exclusive formula of club, caste, of solidarity among members, of identity of values, interest, ideas, origins, attitudes, behaviors, oftentimes, even priorities. Moreover, the elite has, as primary capacity, the preservation of self-perpetuation, for the simple reason that the elite group find its origin out of a very narrow and fragile segment of the society: the unitary elite is exclusive, so it does not receive members through a "liberal" and "democratic" equation (i.e. from all social *strata*, classes and categories). Its members are those "privileged" from a social standpoint, the fittest, the strong ones, the repositories of resources (wealth, abilities, acquaintances, power, prestige, influence, etc.). A cohesive elite is essentially an autonomous elite, as well, enjoying independence in its actions and, at the same time, irresponsive before anybody else for the consequences of these actions. Adhering to an evidently critical perspective and to a descriptive approach, the "Italian classical elitists" equate the elite to a sectarian, unitary, coherent, irresponsible, autonomous social construction. Of a special importance for the present study, the classical theory of elites perceives the elite as an isolated social group, its interactions and contacts being almost exclusively intra-elite ones, and the power networks including only rarely other "nodes" (other groups outside the elite, namely components of the "civil society").

In the study of regime change and transition, renowned scholars on political elites John Higley and Michael Burton differentiate between "ideocratically united" and "ideocratically disunited" elites (i.e. when the context is characterized "by ruthless, often violent interelite conflicts[; e]lite factions deeply distrust each other, interpersonal relations do not extend across factional lines, and factions do not cooperate to contain societal divisions or to avoid political crises" (Burton and Higley 1987: 296)[66]). But this dichotomy is most illuminating for the case of the former Soviet republics, while the states of former "Sovietized Europe" represent classic cases in which "regime changes are closely associated with crises, [...] elites are the critical actors in crises and thus in regime change" (Dogan and Higley 1998: 248). The centrality of political elites in regime change and transition in the region of East-Central Europe is conspicuous: "[...] political elites continue to figure heavily in studies of communist breakdowns and the postcommunist regimes which have emerged in Eastern Europe." (Burton and Higley 1997: 153) The elites who display a significant degree of unity and cohesion can be united on the basis of one of the two fundaments: (a) ideologically united elites, and (b) consensually united elites. The first are the revolutionary elites, unified around an ideal, elites who do not accept compromise, but they access leadership positions only after they suppress the elites that preceded them; the consensual ones access governing

---

66   The two scholars refine their initial dichotomy in further distinguishing between a "disunified national elite" and a "consensually unified national elite", or among the "pluralistic" ("consensually unified") type, the "totalitarian" ("ideologically unified") type, and the "divided" ("disunified") type (Burton and Higley 1989: 17-32, esp. 17-19).

positions as a result of a compromise, of a negotiation, in the circumstances of some fundamental changes and of some profound structural and attitudinal transformations, and their unity is realized around some values – prerequisites of the good functioning of the political system (Burton and Higley 1987: 219-238; Higley and Burton 2006).

Once with the advance of the poliarchy studies (see, most famously, Dahl 1961), the perspective on the elite as a unitary group loses its consistency, making room for some analyses which develop on the basis of pluralism inside the elite group, which is seen as a fragmented one, divided among different ideologies, diverse interests and priorities, divergent socio-demographical biographies and value and attitudinal orientations. Moreover, the elite fragmentation appears as central in the explicative attempts of the non-violent revolutions in East-Central Europe at the end of the 1980s and the beginning of the 1990s (see, for instance, Kitschelt, Mansfeldova, Markowski, and Tóka 1999; Szelényi and Szelényi 1995: 615-638; Linz and Stepan 1996). The present study favors a particularly dynamic approach, in which every individual belonging, positionally, to the elite group is treated as a part *per se* of a local network of power, establishing and maintaining a series of interactions, in his numerous capacities and social roles (neighbor, entrepreneur, member of some religious or ethnic community, etc.). On the other hand, the scholars of democratic elites switch the center of research on the elites' plurality of ideas, of interests, of values, of attitudes, and behavioral models, concluding that the democratic leaders constitute a fairly fragmented group, a grouping of factions, frequently bearing divergent interests (given also by the representation, the responsiveness, and the accountability the elite group owes to those who owe their very political power resource, namely the electorate), of various backgrounds. Consequently, the network of power which forms at the level of one government (either central, regional, or local) has, as its "nodes", both the political elites and elites of other nature (which preserve their central position in the scheme), and other groups and institutions which are not part of the elite (civic groups, citizens groups, reform groups, religious or ethnic groups, trade unions, and other professional organizations, employers' organizations and different economic organizations, media, supporters, administrative institutions, etc.). In such an inextricable scheme, the decisional time spans expand, for decision regarding public policies and governance, generally, is the outcome of a negotiation, which is both intra- and extra-elite one (Dahl 1971). Interactions and contacts with the different portions of the society significantly intensify – for they are imperiously necessary in a democratic construct –, the degree of interaction of elites within the society increasing proportionally. The elite, for the scholars who followed Schumpeter (Schumpeter 1942), cease to be an isolated one – precisely because of the fact that, only by opening to the society and by permanent interacting with it, with the price of assuming the governmental responsibility, the democratic elite can preserve and reproduce itself (Shipman, Edmunds, and Turner 2018: 177-206).

Hence, the network of power – or the "iron triangle" (Wright-Mills 1956), as it appears in the classical elite theory – constitute an adjacent mark to the institutional analysis. Following Wright-Mills, Domhoff and Dye develop a theory of elite network of power involving the "power structure" (i.e. the "network of organizations and roles responsible for maintaining the general social structure and shaping new policies within a society" or a community), and the "power elite" (i.e. the "small set of people who are the individual actors within that power structure, who also share direct, informal access to other elite actors in their sphere of influence" (Domhoff and Dye 1987: 9)). Boissevain and Mitchell (1973) discuss the networks of power exactly from the structural-functionalist perspective, even though they construct their hypothesis on the basis of individual attitudes and behaviors of the network's actors, behaviors which would influence the actions and the roles within the network. Nonetheless, the study of the networks of power and of the elites' interactions presupposes a dynamic – rather than a static – approach on the actors' roles within the network: the actors within the network (the nodes) are essentially dependent among each other, hence each of the actors is influenced primarily by the interactions and the contacts he establishes and maintains. In addition, in the continuous mutations of the network, between influence and domination, the networks of power are permanently rebuilt, are ultimately dynamic. While studying and inquiring into methods of participative and collaborative local governance in Western Europe, Tony Bovaird et al. set five groups with which the local authorities establish interactions for such endeavors: the "citizens (as individuals), voluntary sector, including trade unions, political parties and community organizations, business, media, higher levels of government / Parliament, including international levels" (Bovaird, Löffler, and Parrado-Díez 2002: 13); these groups are central in the construction of the network of power at the local level, for the good governance of the community. Equally, the analysis of the networks of power in transitional societies, in developing societies and in consolidating democracies, is all the more important so as, in these contexts, the degree of institutionalization is low and, consequently, the informal, personalized relations are dominant. Additionally, recent studies on local leadership's interactions in Eastern and Central Europe and West Balkans have shown that, due to the lack of formal, regulated activities and interactions local elites could employ in their influence capacity at the national level (such as lobbying), clientelism and a sort of a "hidden leadership" (Liddle, Gibney, Sotarauta, and Beer 2016) are flourishing (Merkaj, Lucchetti, and Fiorillo 2020). In the study of political elites in Russia, before and immediately after the fall of communism, Anton Steen (1997) finds the analysis of the networks of power quite fortuity for his case, defining the network as "an unstructured, less stable link", which complements two consecrated models of impersonal decision-making: the constitutional model (i.e. power belongs to the government, legitimized by an assembly formed as a result of the popular vote), and the corporatist model (i.e. power divides, in a liberal fashion, among the governmental leaders and key-groups, interests groups, in an institutionalized, predictable, stable formula). Similarly, in a collection of essays on power networks in Sweden, Gergei M. Farkas concludes that three are the major spheres of interests for the study of elite interactions and their networks of power: (i) the degree of elite integration; (ii) the distribution of elite power; (iii) the significance of those informal, personal relations among elites (Farkas 2012: 11).

Surely, the level of integration of elites within the society is based equally on the frequency of the interactions which the said elite establishes and preserve, and on the density of the networks of power which they create in their extension. The level of interaction of elites refers to "the fundamental question of whether the elite in a particular social setting is united into one cohesive social unit or fragmented into several loosely connected elite factions" (Higley, Hoffmann-Lange, Kadushin, and Moore 1991: 35-53). The distribution of power essentially means "who has the power over whom?", and it includes the dichotomy between influence and dominance. With respect to the role of the elites' informal, personal relations, such a role often refers to the interconnectivity given by friendships, kinships, and marital relations, but also to the construction of "social capital". Matthew O. Jackson (2010) analyzes an exponential case for the importance of relations and interactions for the ascendancy of a certain elite group and for the monopolization of power: the rise of the Medici family in Renaissance Italy. Although, initially, possessing less wealth and capacity of political decision-making as compared to the other oligarchies of Florence, Cosimo de Medici gradually consolidated and extended his network of power through marriages with the other potentates of the city, through kinships by alliance[67], through lineages, through economic exchanges, and through patronage. In effect, the monopolization of power in the network means that: if one considers $P(ij)$ as the number of those paths (i.e. the link between two nodes) that are the shortest connecting the node (the actor) i with the node (the actor) j, and $Pk(ij)$ as the number of those paths where the actor (the node) k intercede, then the node k monopolizes the network as $Pk(ij)$ is greater. The logic of the monopolization of the network by an actor subscribes to the idea of "All roads lead to Rome": an actor of the sort the Medici family was in Renaissance Florence succeeds in dominating the network initially from the position of an "interposed", an "intermediary", or of a "connector node".

---

67   See Padgett and Ansell (1993: 1259-1319), who describe the networks of marriages within the great families in Florence of 1430s. The two historians show that, a far cry from the economic power and the influence on the political legislator, the establishment and the maintenance of some links with key-actors in the economy of the network of power made that the Medici family outperform the influence of the Strozzi family, more economically and politically potent.

Hence, for a marginal actor to establish an interaction or a contact with another actor of the network, the former should first establish a link with the "connector node"; the more numerous these situations, the more consolidated the position of the "connector node" becomes, for this node comes to monopolize the network. One should bear in mind also that such a situation presupposes that the interaction with the "connector node" (for relating with another node/actor) is the simplest manner (or the shortest path) for establishing the targeted contact. Consequently, either the direct, unmediated contact is inaccessible, or the "connector node" creates the conditions for this contact to be intermediated. Although this study concerns only unmediated relations between the members of the Municipal Council (the local political elite) and other groups – this is, to some extent, explicable through the small demographics of the towns-case studies (30,000-40,000 inhabitants) –, too frequently, such relations are mediated by a specialized *apparatus*, a quite consistent one formed by functionaries. The fashion in which the local councilors interact with other groups within or without the community is not strictly regulated by the legislations concerning local administrations, hence this analysis considers only the egocentric networks (namely, those centered on a political actor, that of the elite group), though one should not neglect those (initially, almost invisible) groups which ensure the link between the elites and other groups, which ensure (or hinder) the communication between the actors of the network, which facilitate (or curtail) the leaders assuming responsibilities and their scrutiny by the governed (precisely from this perspective, Stoica adds to the study of Iaşi's political elites' interactions and networks, the group of public servants (Stoica 2003: 153-177)).

A series of distinctions are useful in the methodological construction of the networks of power and of the interactions and contacts of the local political elite. The first dichotomy refers to (a) the institutionalized, formalized, impersonal interactions, and to (b) the uninstitutionalized, personalized, informal interactions. As a rule, even in the consolidated democracies, those contacts formed and maintained outside the institutional framework, the personal contacts bear a particularly important significance within the recruitment process of elites, in the construction of priorities at the local level, in the channeling of grievances of the various groups towards the government, etc. In such a climate, the relationships between the elite and the groups of supporters and friends, neighbours, etc. are developed. On the other hand, in less institutionalized contexts, where the rules of the democratic "game" have not been yet completely internalized, the dominance of the informal interactions translates patronage relations, clientelism, nepotism, etc. As the development of democratic institutions is still in its infancy and as the efficiency of institutions and of impersonal relations (in the Weberian sense) is still quite low for the countries of the former "Sovietized Europe", the personal, informal interactions become crucial for the effective advance of the interests and the grievances of some key-groups within the network.

	The type of interaction	
	Closed	Open
The decision-making form Consensual		
Conflictual		

Virgil Stoica (2003: 154) proposes four "ideal types", associating to the variable of problem the variable of the type of interaction of local elite. Hence, the first type describes an elite of "classical" type, a club-type elite, a unitary elite, who decides in a consensual manner (*recte*, relatively fast time spans for decision-making), but who is, in turn, isolated, closed towards the rest of the societal segments, with an evidently low frequency of exterior interactions. The second type draws on an open elite, who preserves relations with the rest of the society, with the ones whom they govern, and who – surprisingly – does not meet conflictual relations with the various groups and institutions it intersects. Such a circumstance, in which the time spans of decision-making are low and the governing process is rapidly developed – even in the situation in which the frequency of contacts with the other segments of the society is high –, coincides rather with Putnam's *desideratum*, in which, in a democratic climate, the continuous, frequent, and coherent interaction of elites with the governed generates a communality of values, principles, and even interests. In practice, the scenario is quite remote, being rather characteristic for the client-patron type of government or for the interactions with such groups as the supporters, neighbours, family – interactions which are important for reelections, for instance. Indeed, this type of interactions provide for what Healey et al. coin as "institutional capital" (Healey, Cars, Madanipour, and de Magalhães 2002: 6-28) (a peculiar relational combination among intellectual, social, and political capital). This type is, to some extent, characteristic for small towns, for "in the simpler context of the small city, political interaction reduces opposition potential, while in the complex larger cities, political interaction intensifies it." (Eulau and Prewitt 1973: 147) The third type is peculiar to the closed, but pluralistic elite, a rather conflictual elite in the government process. It is the poliarhic elite, the dahlian-modeled one, who, although is a distinguished caste, having a strong "group consciousness" and symbolically and representatively distancing itself from the rest of the society which it governs, does not display unity, is rather fragmentary in interests and priorities, is factionalist. The fourth instance refers to the democratic elite of Schumpeterian type, the "ideal" model of democratic elite and of decision-making, of government: the democratic elite has to interact with a multitude of groups and institutions, which inevitably generates conflicts among interests, attitudes, priorities, behaviors. Henceforth, the conflict becomes a constant and a necessity of democratic government, and the democratic governing elite fragments itself along the landmarks of interests clashing in such a conflict.

The present study favored a factor analysis having as variables the level of geographical isolation of the local elites (i.e. the frequency of interactions with groups and institutions from within the community), and the level of elite isolation of the local elites (i.e. the frequency of the interactions with groups and instances from within the political elite). For the first type, namely the local elite isolated both geographically and politically, is an extremely rare case in the proposed typology, for it is characteristic to those communities with a significant degree of decentralization, where local leaders subscribe themselves almost completely to the development plans and to the government of the municipality which it represents, and the large palette of responsibilities and attributions allows it to have only sporadic interactions with the regional or central elite. Moreover, even in the process of political recruitment of local elites, the role played by local or national elites is considerably diminished, the local party branches or local parties themselves playing the main role in recruitment. The exemplary cases for the present study were Česká Lípa and Oleśnica, where the average score of isolation was significant (both as geographical and as elite isolation). A second type is the local elite isolated from a spatial standpoint, but open from an elite standpoint; the type corresponds to a situation in which the government is decentralized, although the local elite displays a high level of "group consciousness", the distance between those who govern and the governed being considerable, and, consequently, the representativeness – low. The third case superposes on a geographically opened, but elitistically closed, local elite. The cases exemplified in the present study were those of the towns of Tecuci and Targovishte, where the local elite developed in a context characterized by a centralized government, the local leaders' attributions and responsibilities being profoundly affected (hence, the feeling of political and decisional impotence). For such an elite, the frequency of interactions initiated and developed outside the community it leads correlates with a great distance between the local elite and the members of the community, rather due to the "group consciousness" than due to the lack of representativeness in respect to the constituency. The closed elite from an elite point of view, but open from a geographical point of view, is dependent on the resources of the center, to whom it feels subordinated, indebted; as a matter of fact, the central elites are those who ensure the recruitment and the support of the local ones.

		The level of elite isolation	
		Isolated elites	Open elites
The level of geographical isolation	Isolated elites		
	Open elites		

The present study retains the tradition recorded by the analysis of the networks of power – a tradition developed around the adjuvant concepts of "interaction", "contact", "link", "node", "connection", "path", etc. –, starting from the first decades of the 20th century. The first research endeavors in the sphere of networks of power appeared with the "Harvard School" in the '30s-'40s, and with the studies undertaken by Mayo (1933) and Homans (1951). However, central and genuinely impressive stand the multiple pioneering research conducted by Robert Warner, in the so-called "Yankee City", starting 1941 and ending with a synthesis published in 1963. After the Harvard School, a series of works written in a socio-metric note follows, so that the research concerning the nature and the structure of the networks of power is based on a rather geometrical, graphical, visual, *formula*, of matrix-styled type: Moreno (1934) and Lewin (1951) inaugurate sociometry in the analysis of the networks of power and of the political elites' interactions with other groups and institutions, but the epitome of sociometry on this field is reached once with the collective writings of statistician Cartwright and mathematician Harary (Harary, Norman, and Cartwright 1965). Only in the '50s – '70s, the profoundly mathematical and conspicuously quantitative paradigm starts its evolution on a descending path, once with the developments and the perspectives brought by "the anthropological school of Manchester", exponential, in this respect, being the contributions in the field of the networks of power signed by Nadel (1957) and Granovetter (1974). The analysis of the elite-centered networks of power recalibrates in the '70s, the peak decade for the political elites studies, a decade which will not be outperformed even by the literature dedicated to the reforming, regime change initiating elites in East-Central Europe, at the end of the 1980s.

Before proceeding to the empirical analysis of the elites' interactions and of the networks of power at the local level in the small-to-medium-sized towns of East-Central Europe, a series of conceptual clarifications are seen as necessary. The notion of "interaction" (or "contact") refers both to the positive vectors (support) and to the negative ones (contestation, critique). Consequently, although a high number of contacts undoubtedly reflects the degree of integration of elites within the society / community, the same frequency does not represent a marker of the governed' support for the government. Also, in the view of evaluating the level of elite integration, a high level of interactions should be pondered by the intra-elite number of contacts and by that of non-formal, family-typed contacts (relatives, neighbors, supporters, etc.). Even so, the interactions – particularly, the extra-elite ones – which the elites established, maintain, entertain, develop, constitute a reliable marker for the government dynamics and an essential one for evaluating coordination and decision-making, especially at the community level. The elites' interaction with a diversity of groups and institutions leads the ones who govern to acknowledge and assume the interests of the societal segments, but also to a communality (minimal, at least) of values, for often the interactions is underpinned and develops

171

in a mutually agreeable formula (Putnam 1973: 80). Higley and Pakulski reiterate the basic principle of "elite integration": there is

"a consensus among the otherwise widely differentiated elite groups that, despite their disagreements in ideologies and policy issues, they stick to the democratic rules of the [democratic] game. [...] In a democratic society elite unity is not to be confused with elite homogeneity, elite unity exists in conditions of wide elite differentiation: in sum, the unity is about the basic procedures." (Higley and Pakulski 1992: 104-119 [additions mine])

Additionally, the prospects of the formation and perpetuation of an elite that is "unified in defence of democratic institutions" are seen by the two scholars, at the beginning of the 1990s, as: (a) the "best" in Poland and Hungary, (b) "less good" in Czechoslovakia, (c) "poor" in Romania, Bulgaria, and Albania, and (d) "virtually nonexistent" in the former Yugoslav republics (Higley and Pakulski 1992: 104-119). Interestingly enough, out of the states enumerated above, the situation for those in the former "Sovietized Europe" are pertinently assessed in a quite a similar vein to Kitschelt's assessments on the three types of communist dictatorships, to be explained below, in the explanatory section.

The political interaction is defined by Robert Vance Presthus, in his ample study *Elites in the Policy Process*, strictly as "face-to-face contacts with legislatives and functionaries" (Presthus 1974: 176). In the quite compelling study on the Russian elites after the communist breakdown, *Political Elites and the New Russia: The Power Basis of Yeltsin's and Putin's Regimes*, Anton Steen perceives "the network" as "a continuum along which the elite interaction can be organized in various ways" (Steen 2003: 146). In addition, Van Warden attached to the notion of "network of power" a series of characteristic features generically named as "dimensions": the number of participants in the network (i.e. the number of "nodes"), the participants' identity, the function of the network (i.e. information exchange or decision-making), the degree of formalization (institutionalization) (van Waarden 1992: 29-52).

Similar observations stand true in the case of the networks of power, as well. Hence, most frequently, the density of the network of power does not mirror a synonimity of interests, but, *au contraire*, can suggest a permanent contestation, tension, pressure between the elite and the contact groups. Essentially, if an optimal proportion of tension, opposition, control, scrutiny, *critique* and pressure, is maintained, the network of power presents the characteristic traits of a poliarchy; surely, on the other hand, if the high density of the network is given, in overwhelming proportions, by contacts and interactions of negative vector, the government become unstable and illegitimate. A government described by a network of interactions of preponderantly positive vectors does not denote, in itself, a democratic government, but rather an ideal, improbable one, for the sources of contestation and opposition in a democracy are central for the logic of government. Where, within the network of local power, there are no "nodes" of contestation and pressure towards the elites, the society /

community is not only atomized in respect to the government, but, most frequently, such a network describes relations of patronage and clientelism between the elites and the governed. A second problem should be imperatively
tackled, in the case of the networks of power: the limitation of the analysis of
the network. Lauman et al. (Lauman, Marsden, and Prensky 1992: 61-87) recall that the literature conventionally differentiates between: (a) the "realist"
approach (which is often associated to the positional perspective of identifying
and analyzing elites, such that it suffices to institutionally isolate the elite
group, and, afterwards, forming the network is perceived also on institutional
bases), and (b) the "nominalist" approach (which is associated to the reputational perspective of identifying and analyzing elites, the recomposition of the
network being done on the basis of the frequency and the direction of the elites'
contacts, even if these contacts circumvent a formal, institutional framework).
As the perspective of this study is a dynamic one, in the analysis of the networks for the elites of the six case studies, the "nominalist" approach was predominantly employed. There is also the possibility of limiting the network by
dint of a certain legislative domain or of a certain sphere of activity ("*policy
domain power network*"), within which the local political elite can decide
(Knoke and Laumann 1982: 255-270). Henceforth, each domain of activity at
the local level and the decision-making manner within that domain generate a
new network of power. The density of the network was computed following a
formula consecrated by Petru Iluț and Irina Culic (1997: 113-133):

$$D_E = \frac{(\Sigma \Sigma z_{ij})}{(n_{E2} - n_E)},$$

in which n_E – the number of elements within the network, i – the central actor
of the network (in this case, the local political elite, formed positionally by the
members of the Municipal / Local Councils in the six towns, the case-studies
of this contribution), j – one of the actors in the network, with the exception of
the central actor,

$\Sigma \Sigma z_{ij}$ – the contacts and interactions from the multitude of potential contacts of the actor i with the actors of his / her egocentric network[68].

Aberbach, Putnam, and Rockman (1981) highlight a series of extremely
important aspects for the study of the networks of power in Western Europe,
with implications especially in the analysis of the local elites' interactions and
networks. Firstly, the density of the network does not constitute a suitable indicator for the situations in which the spatial proximity is an obstacle for the
nodes' similarly, the density within a certain sector of the network can translate
even the very spatial proximity, but not the coherence of the relations.

---

68   A "egocentric network" is that network in which the central actor (recte that with whom
     the most numerous contacts are established) can be conspicuously identified, that who
     is evident without supplementary mathematical computations (See Iluț and Culic 1997).

Generally, though, the density of the network signifies the fact that the elites work together with the other groups for resolving problems, for establishing the agenda of priorities, and, sometimes, in decision-making. Secondly, the density of the network among the different tiers of government (local, regional, central elites) can signify various dependences, although it is specific to Western Europe and cannot be correlated with the indicators of democratic or efficient governance (even for the relationships between the political elite and the administrative, bureaucratic, technocratic elite): in states such as the United States or Germany, the frequency of the interactions among different levels of the elite, or between these and the administrative elite, denotes close and frequent relationships, while the same type of interaction superposes on some distant and less frequent relations, in the case of Great Britain and of the Netherlands. But the density of the network is but one of its features. One supplementary distinction is instrumental, in the case of elites' interactions and of the networks of power: that between "domination" and "influence". Knoke, following the observations noted by Gamson (1968: 60), defines "influence" as that type of relation in which "one actor provides information to another with the intention of altering the latter's actions" (Knoke 1993: 24). On the other hand, "dominance" is that type of relations in which "one actor controls the behavior of another actor by offering or withholding some benefit or harm" (Knoke 1993: 25).

A last problem discussed here – although not the last on the list of methodological problems concerning the construction of network of power – is that of identifying the key-actors with whom the local political elite establishes and maintains interactions and contacts of indisputable importance. In identifying the key-actors of the network of power, four techniques are generally employed (Stoica 2002; Stoica 2003; Knoke 1993: 23-45): (1) the positional approach (the identification of actors placed, at a certain moment, in positions of power or decision); (2) the decisional approach (the identification of actors who participate in decision-making or who influence directly the decision-making process, following the poliarhic dahlian model); (3) the reputational approach (the identification of actors who are seen as decisional by those observers or those elements of the network who bear the necessary information regarding the networks of power, following the model imposed by Floyd Hunter, in the 1950s); (4) the relational approach (the identification of actors who, though do not enjoy a special prestige or are less known to the other actors of the network, establish and maintain essential relations for the network of power, even outside the network per se). This study concentrates on thirteen groups with whom the local political elite is supposed to establish and preserve interactions, contacts and connections, within the community and outside it. The isolation of the thirteen groups is by no means exhaustive, but constitutes a selection based on Samuel Eldersveld's empirical contribution on the political activists' interactions in Ann Arbour, Michigan, in the 1970s, and published as "Lecture II" in his acclaimed *Political Elites in Modern Societies* (1989). These thirteen groups are: (a) business groups, (b) neighbourhood groups, (c) civic and reform groups, (d) religious groups, (e) ethnic groups, (f) trade unions, (g) close friends and supporters, (h) local media, (i) other elected officials at the local level, (j) elected officials at the central level (senators, MPs, etc.), (k) other town administrators (mayors, deputy mayors), (l) county / region / province administrators (prefects, sub-prefects, voievodes, *kraj*-s, etc.), and (m) the members of the national executive (ministers, secretaries of state, etc.).

The techniques of influence and domination exerted by each of these groups are beyond the scope of this study, although, depending on the frequency of the local elites' interactions with each of these groups, assessments could be made on the type of interaction: influence or domination. From the methodological standpoint, in the empirical study of the political elites' interactions and contacts, and in the drawing of the networks of power, a series of other dilemmas appears, among which one should remark: the necessity of a very great number of nodes within the network, even at the local level, and, as a result, the unfeasible character of drawing the network of power under the classical, consecrated forms (matrixes, sociograms, other graphical images, etc.). For the analysis of interactions and the networks of power, two aspects of particular importance should be kept in mind, especially at the local level: the general characteristics of interactions and the form of the networks of power are determined by the specific characteristics of each group / individual / node, but also by the institutional *formula* – i.e. the context, the climate, together with the topography and the physical-biological and socio-economical *milieu* – which precedes the formation of contacts, and, afterwards, that of networks; on the other hand, the dynamics of the network, once formed, influences and determines especially the perceptions, the attitudes, the value orientations, the behaviors of the nodes (groups and individuals), which can become either characteristics of the network, or just temporary indicators for a given situation. Boissevain identifies two major types of characteristics of the social networks: (a) those which concern the interaction (the actor's multiplicity, the relational content, the relational form, the sense and the intensity of the interaction), and (b) those which concern the structure (the dimension and the density of the network, the actor's centrality, the existence of *cliques*) (Boissevain 1989: 557-558). Petru Iluț defines "the network" as "regularities in the configurations of relations established among the different elements of a social system" (1997: 114). In effect, these "regularities" are only apparent, for the dynamics of the network and the multiplicity of the interactions and contacts of the elites (even the local ones) only seldom allow for regularities.

The *problématique* of the drawing of the networks of power inherently contains also a spatial dimension: the question is being addressed of placing of the different actors within the network, either further or closer to the main node, i.e. the elite group. Normally, the spatial, geographical localization of the network's nodes in respect to the center is done on the basis of the frequency of the contacts between two actors or of the intensity of the interaction between the two: two actors frequently and intensely interacting should be placed one next to the other, being represented as two juxtaposed nodes, while actors only occasionally or rarely establishing contacts with the political elite should be graphically translated as marginal nodes of the network, distanced from the main node. The graphical, spatial representation of the network thusly acquires two supplementary traits: (a) "the sectorial differentiation", and (b) "the integrative centrality" (Laumann and Pappi 1976: 142). The studies on local elites involving the construction of networks of power (illustrative, in this sense, are those conducted by Laumann and Pappi (1976), in a medium-sized German town, and Galaskiewicz's (1979) comparative study on two American towns) conclude that the ordinary graphic of the local network of power is similar to a (bicycle) wheel or to a sphere, with the intensification of contacts and links once with the advance to the center. Such a structure allows for the network to be sectorially analyzed:

> "The centre is dominated by the governmental actors with the most comprehensive mandates of policies; the first circle is dominated by the big interests special for certain sectors; and the peripheries are occupied by minor petitioners. In fact, the interest groups taken as a whole serve as intermediate communication filters which link the peripheries to the center." (Laumann and Pappi 1976: 245)

On the other hand, predominantly in the economic sector in which a profoundly liberal, minimalist vision dominates (and the state is caught in a *laissez-faire* formula), the network of power encounters a "sphere with empty middle or hollow core" form: is what Heinz et al. conclude in their study on the connections the representatives of the business *milieu* in Washington maintain with 72 local notabilities, in decision-making in four major spheres (agriculture, energy, health, and work); the private businesses interact only marginally with the political notables, and these interactions are founded exclusively on client-patron dynamics, on economic ideologies, and on party lineages. In the logic of the "sphere with a hollow core" (Heinz, Laumann, Salisbury, and Nelson 1990: 356-390), the governmental mediators and bureaucratized, impersonal procedures are thusly avoided, in favor of sanctified, informal, personalized contacts, of some "shortcuts" at the fringe of legality in decision-making. The existence of "informal contacts" and the perpetuation of informality in the elite network formation in ECE are to be seen as part of a genuine "culture of informality": on the one hand, informality is "functional and mainly a result of transition", and, on the other hand, it is "embedded in the national culture and / or a leftover from communism" (Grødeland 2007: 217-252). What the cited studies reveal is the fact that identifying the contacts and interactions of the group of political elites with other groups and institutions and, afterwards, drawing of the network of power for the elite group, represent markers for the analysis of the decision-making process: "The network analyses of elite structures are ultimately useful only in so far they improve our understanding of the way in which elites interact for arriving to decisions regarding public policies." (Knoke 1993: 34-35). Therefore, if the connections the political elite establishes and maintains are not translated in sketching the public agenda and in the decision-making process, the very existence and importance of these links are profoundly questionable.

In the study of the networks of elite interaction, the present research starts from C. Wright-Mills's very observation regarding the tight, almost intimate connectivity among the political elite ("the political directorate"), the economic one ("the chief tenants"), and the military one ("the war lords") (Wright-Mills 1956). Indeed, Wright-Mills extremely compellingly argues the fact that the political elite is a very coherent, homogeneous group, composed of individuals establishing strong, unbreakable connections with certain, equally powerful, groups. The intimate links among the three elite groups, Mills highlights, dates from the childhood of these elites' members; the representatives of the three elite groups share the same family origins and educational backgrounds; they establish links as early as the high-school or university period, and, from that moment on, they preserve the same personal relations: they meet in a rather informal, than formal, manner; there are even psychological resemblances among the members of the three elite groups (for instance, their behavior is similar in times of crisis). While closely observing Mills's famous conclusions on "the power elite", Medding suggests that "in spite of the importance of an elite's origins, background, and related sociological characteristics, these alone do not explain the level of interaction or integration which occurs within and among leadership groups" (Medding 1982: 404). It is, to some extent, debatable if either the social-economical profile and the family background determine further interactions, or the established contacts and interactions influence a certain socio-economic *status*.

Despite its allegedly universal applicability and the empirically verifiable truth, this pattern was only partially considered by this study on local political elites in the small-to-medium-sized communities in East-Central Europe. The main objective remained that of constructing a hierarchy and a classification of thirteen groups with which a local councilor is prone to maintain stable links: business groups, neighbours groups, civic and reform groups, religious groups, ethnic groups, trade unions, close friends and supporters, local media, other local elected officials, the central legislatives (MPs, senators), other town administrators (mayors, deputy mayors), county / regional administrators (prefects, voievods, etc.), and members of the central executives (ministers, secretaries of state, etc.). The selection of these thirteen groups was based on the second lecture of S. Eldersveld's study, *Political Elites in Modern Societies* (1989: 62) (nine, out of his fifteen groups, were employed by the present analysis, while the other four, added by this study, came as a logical result of the legal realities, empirically observed, in the six analyzed countries). Moreover, according to the resulting grading of the significance of these interactions, one could attempt an assessment regarding the manner in which the local councilors guide their interests and coordinate their activities, within the communities they lead. Thusly, this evaluation implied a rather dynamic model, in which the members of the six Local Councils were asked to answer to the question about their interactions with other groups, in their capacity as individuals (i.e. as businessmen, as neighbors, as members of some families, as influential persons within the community, as persons who try to change for the better the existing situation of their towns, etc.), and not exclusively as members of the Municipal Councils (at this point, the positional approach was temporarily abandoned). After all, it is the "individual agency, in the ongoing flow of relations and actions, [who] re-enacts and reforms power structures through acknowledging them or deliberately seeking to change them" (Healey, Cameron, Davoudi, Graham, and Madanipour 1995: 14). As a result, the six Municipal Councils ceased to be perceived and studied as comprehensive, unified local institutions, which established a series of formal contacts, in a legal and conventional manner, with other institutions and groups of individuals; rather, the councilors themselves were seen as six groups of individuals, part of the local political elite, each of these individuals maintaining and forming networks of interactions with other different groups. Moreover, when trying to advance their own or their community's interests, these people become dependent on certain groups or persons, therefore establishing inevitable interactions. Generally, in their attempt to consolidate their reputation and power, their influence and control, local political elites, as a unitary group, establish, inevitably or deliberately, networks of interactions with various other groups.

Eventually, two important differentiations were operated among the thirteen selected groups: (a) one was that between those interactions with groups from within the political elite (those usually formal, rather specialized, connections, bearing a personal nature, as well; e.g. town administrators, other elected officials, county / region / district administrators, the members of the national legislative and executive, etc.), and those interactions with groups from outside the political elite (those more personal, frequently informal, connections; e.g. the business groups, ethnic and religious groups, supporters, neighbors, civic groups, unions, local media, etc.); (b) the other one, equally instrumental, was that between the interactions established and developed exclusively or predominantly within the town for which a group of persons constituted a local political elite (the "internal" ones; e.g. those with supporters, neighbors, unions, local media, etc.), and the interactions underpinned and developed outside the town (the "external" ones, generally at the regional and the national levels). Due to the contingencies of the present attempt in studying local political elites in the six towns, no assessment was made concerning the

178

nature (positive or negative connections) and the complexity of interactions that the members of the six Local / Municipal Councils established.

From the collected *data*, following the administration of the questionnaire on the members of the Municipal / Local Councils of the six towns, one could observe a profound inclination towards the local level of the political elites of these communities. Markers differed, though not significantly, which suggested, on the one hand, an evident tendency of geographical isolation of the local elite, and, on the other hand, a focus of interests and priorities on the led communities. The most frequent interactions with the central / regional institutions and with political elites from outside the community were maintained by the members of the Local Council in Tecuci (12.17%), followed by the councilors of Targovishte (6.47%), the least decentralized cases out the six ones; as such, regarding the centralized government and administrative organization *formulae*, the local elites find themselves obligated to increase the number of interactions with the central and regional elites, whom they "owe" a translation, into the local, of the decisions taken at the central level. The dependency to the central level is found also in the recruitment *formulae* of local elites, and in the absence of strong, well-rounded local party branches, capable of independently supporting candidates. The frequency of interaction with the elites from outside the community significantly decreases as the mechanisms of decentralization start to operate, the lowest scores being characteristic for the Czech case (Česká Lípa – 1.58%) and the Polish case (Oleśnica – 2.63%), where a rather pragmatic elite detached itself from the centre in order to independently operate changes in the development of the governed communities.

For the consolidating democracies and the transitional democracies, keygroups for the democratic government appear as extremely weak in action, the pressure upon and possible interactions with local elites being virtually inexistent. This is the case of trade unions and of other professional organizations, of civic and reform groups, sometimes of ethnic and religious groups. It is thusly natural that the interactions with these groups to be found in a conspicuously insufficient proportion in those communities in which the rules of the "democratic game", the democratic values, principles, and institutional logic are in the process of internalization. Only in the Czech case (and, only partially, in the Polish one – 21.05% –, the Hungarian case – 20.35% –, and the Slovak case – 23.23%), the contacts with the civic and reform groups acquired a significant frequency (25.39%), and could represent a nodal point of the scheme of interactions with the local elite. Indeed, during the transitional period and with increased decentralization, local elites became "tied to public officials and civil servants, whose loyalty had been turned away from the central hierarchy towards local networks and clubs of influential people working between" (Piana 2016/2010: 205). The case of Oleśnica was a peculiar case, for the increased frequency of interactions between the Municipal Council and the organized civil society (21.05%) was due to the occupational origin of the present local elite: part of the existing Council's membership came from the ranks of the civil society, previously being members of some local reform organizations, particularly in the sphere of education and instruction. These connections were maintained and facilitated a permanence and a consistency in the local elite's interactions with those citizens organized in civic groups.

The contacts with the neighbourhood groups, as well as those with supporters and friends constitute two categories of particular importance for the dynamic of reelection (and, hence, for the preservation of local elites[69]). The Polish case was, yet again, telling, as the contacts with the neighbours, the supporters, and friends dominated the *palette* of interactions of the members of the Municipal Council (49.99%). Through these groups, the representative of local power can collect grievances, can articulate interests, can establish priorities and a working agenda to be consequently presented and advanced in the Council's meetings. Consequently, although seemingly marginal, the interactions with supporters, friends, and neighbours bear a double importance: essential role in reelection and the preservation of the local elite (particularly, in the case of extramural recruitment, as it is the case, as a matter of fact, of the Municipal Council of Oleśnica), and a role in the direct conveyance of grievances, needs, interests, exigencies, and of control from the part of the members of the community. Similar to the interactions with the traditionally contesting groups (i.e. the reform groups, the civic groups), the local elites' interactions with the mass-media are, more often than not, generators of pressures, oppositions, tensions, contestation. The initial working hypothesis is that, in a democratic climate, within the community, the political elite's interactions with the local media are based on pressures similar to the ones exerted by the relations with the reform groups. Nonetheless, for the consolidating democracies, the contacts with the press, particularly at the local level, can develop under the form of a patronage, as well, the elite's predominance over the local information means, through sponsorships and funding, either direct or indirect, conspicuous or veiled, hence becoming rather the rule than the exception of a "backwardness"[70] residue. East-Central Europe postulates local relations between the two groups which are oftentimes informal, dominance-styled, poorly institutionalized. The interactions with the business groups, with the economic elite – from within or from outside the governed constituency – constitute a major point in the construction of the local elites' agenda of priorities, for the development strategies of the town which they govern. A constant and coherent interaction with the local group of entrepreneurs or with the potential

---

69 One can easily observe, for that matter, that, in those cases in which the interaction with these three types of groups presented a higher share, the reelection rate was higher: 42.1% (for Tecuci), 48% (for Česká Lípa), 51% (for Oleśnica), 49.6% (for Gyula), 46.6% (for Levice), 41.5% (for Targovishte).
70 For the conceptualization of the notion of "backwardness" for "the second Europe" (Martin Malia), see: Berend 1986: 153-170; Berend 2003; Malia 2006.

external investors appears as *sine qua non* for any efficient local government. On the other hand, it is a plain truism the fact that the informal links the local political elite establishes and maintains with the economic elite cannot be controlled – in what concerns their orientation and content – by the citizens; as such – and especially in the case of decentralized elites, where no restrictive downwards accountability mechanism exists –, the contacts between the two elite groups can generate changes in influence and power, changes that can only fragilely be controlled by the upwards accountability mechanisms, exerted by the town's citizens (mechanisms which, indeed, are functional precisely in decentralized contexts). Moreover, for the cases of consolidating democracies, the patronage and "sponsorship" structures can be easily reproduced, forasmuch as the overlapping of local political elites on the economic elites can appear in situations of fragile institutionalization. Such a circumstance was characteristic for the cases of elites in Tecuci and Targovishte, where local councilors interacted with (especially local) businessmen and entrepreneurs, precisely because the former were themselves members of the economic elite: 19.51% of the interactions of the political elite in Tecuci, and 14.28% of those of the political elite in Targovishte were linked to the economic elite, while the significantly decentralized elites of Česká Lípa and Oleśnica recorded considerably lower proportions of contacts with the business groups (7.93% out of the total of contacts, in the Czech case, and 13.15% of the contacts, in the Polish case), although their frequency was constant. If the weight, in the case of the two towns and in the case of the towns of Gyula (10.65%) and Levice (8.23%), suggested a relation founded on influence, on the other hand, in the case of the towns of Tecuci and Targovishte, the intercrescence between the local political elite and the economic one, and the intensity of the relations between the Local Councils and the business group translated a relationship based on dominance. The decisions approved in the Councils were profoundly influenced by the councilors' capacity as entrepreneurs, firm administrators or managers, employers. What is more, Robert Vance Presthus highlights the importance of the link between the economic elite and the political one in what concerns the construction of the public policy agenda: "Closely allied with time spent in political interaction as a criterion is the priority which groups ascribe to 'influencing government'." (Presthus 1974: 177) Focusing on the American case and the theory of "growth machine", Alan Harding contends that urban coalitions and strong contacts between the local political elites and the business groups are central to the initial development of the town or the city; such linkages are dominant over the "planning bureaucracies, political parties, and elected officials, pushing for urban policies supportive" (Harding 1994: 357) of their economic endeavors and personal benefit. The overlapping of socio-political elites with the economic ones, under the form of the overlap of "social notables" (i.e. the social upper class) on the "economic notables" (i.e. the leaders of the business community), at least at the local level, has been aptly observed in the case of an established democracy, for the American town of New Haven: the initial and acclaimed conclusions of Dahl's *Who Governs?*, concerning the clear separation between the political elites and the economic ones and the lack of any pressure of the latter upon the former, are "reexamined" and profoundly revised by Domhoff's *Who Really Rules?*, which concludes that the intertwined relations between the two elite groups is irreversible and extremely important for the development of the community[71].

A particular case is represented by the contacts of the local / municipal councilors with minority groups (ethnic and religious ones). For the "consociational", consensual model of democracy – as it appears in Lijphart's works (primarily, in Lijphart 1999) –, such interactions constitute the foundation of an "ideal type" of democratic governance meant to accommodate the interests of some quite diverse groups, which act in a fragmented society / community, a society / community of pluralities and (especially ethnic and religious) diversity. In addition, the groups of ethnic and religious minorities can act as ones of the most powerful sources of pressure, contestation, and *critique*, even for the local government. Surely and expectedly, those ethnically and religiously homogeneous communities are to be governed by local elites with weak, rare, circumstantial, or occasional interactions with the groups of religious and ethnic minorities. This was largely also the case of the six towns selected here, where the religious and ethnic groups, out of purely numerical considerations, could not articulate interests and demands directed towards the local government. The frequency of the local political elites' interactions with the ethnic groups was consequently insignificant in all of the six cases: in the case of the town of Tecuci, only 4.87% of the local elites' interactions were established with the ethnic group of the Roma population; in Česká Lípa, only 1.58% of interactions were reserved to the group of Slovak minority; in Gyula, 4.65% of the local elite's interactions were established with the groups of ethnic Romanians (3.2% of the total population of the community), ethnic Germans (3.1% of the population), and Roma (0.3% of the population); in Targovishte, the local councilors' interactions with the ethnic groups (especially, with the ethnic Turks, who constitute 18% of the town's population) comprised 5.19% out of the total of this elite group's interactions (in fact, the highest weight among the six cases); in Levice, the share of the local elite's interactions with the ethnic groups constituted 4.95% from the total of contacts, dominantly with the Hungarian minority, which forms a community of 8.4% of the town's population; finally, the local political elites in Oleśnica did not establish any contact with ethnic groups (despite the fact that a very thin percentage of ethnic Germans does exist in the ethnic composition of the town, following the attainment of the "Recovered Territories", after 1945). Nevertheless, in respect of the

---

71   See the convincing revision of Dahl's Who Governs?, in Domhoff 1978: esp. 3-4.

representation of ethnic groups and their existence as a node of networks of local power, one should remark the Hungarian representation system, for councils of ethnic minorities, formed of inhabitants of the town, function in Gyula, as well as in other towns of the country: their role is rather consultative and formal, bearing a significance primarily in the sphere of the cultural activities of the citadel, but their very existence (which is, as a matter of fact, compulsory, according to the Hungarian legislation on local administration) provides a genuine basis for the representation and crystallization of minority groups' interests at the local level.

On the other hand, the representation, within the network of local political elites' interactions and contacts in the six towns, of the religious groups placed itself on similar indicators, the weight of these groups within the network being even less significant than that of ethnic groups (with an average ratio of 2.83% out of the total of interactions, as opposed to 3.54% of contacts, in the case of ethnic groups). For the case studies discussed here, the proportion (and, inherently, the impact) of the municipal councilors' interactions with the religious groups (oftentimes, minority ones, but also those of the majority) presented itself as the following: for Tecuci, 2.43% of interactions were those with Christian-Orthodox groups and Neo-protestant groups (Adventists, Pentecostals); for Česká Lípa, 3.17% of the local elite's contacts were those with the minority groups of Protestants (Lutherans) and Catholics, although the majority of the members of the Municipal Council and of the town's population identified itself as atheist; for Oleśnica, 2.63% of interactions were constituted by those with the Catholic organizations (which have, to a large extent, a charitable and social scope, as well as a ritualistic and ceremonial one); for Gyula, 2.35% of contacts were established and maintained with diverse religious groups (from Greek-Catholics, Roman-Catholics, to Lutherans), though they were small groups and, thusly, with no notable impact within the network of local power; for Levice, 2.45% of interactions were represented by those with the groups of Catholics and Protestants (Lutherans); finally, for Targovishte, the interactions with the religious groups presented the greatest weight among the six cases (3.89% out of the total of interactions), explicably only through the prism of a certain cultural effervescence between the majority of Christian-Orthodox and the Muslim minority.

Regarding the sketch of the networks of power in the case of each of the six local political elite groups, this study considered only the binomial links (that is, those established between two nodes, the simplest "paths" of the network), underpinning the drawing of the networks on the presumption that the network is of concentric type (the "absolute network" premise, in the framework of which all the "nodes" establish binomial links with the center, but do not establish binomial contacts between them). Taking into consideration the contingencies of this study, the density of each of the six networks was equal to:

$$D(K) = \frac{13}{91} = 0.14,$$

hence, only the links between the thirteen selected groups and the group of municipal councilors were considered, not also the direct interactions established between or among them. The computation of the density represents an extraordinary indicator for the elite group's cohesion and for the level of integration of the political elites within the community / society. For a better image on the centrality of the group of municipal councilors within the network of local power, correlated with the density of the concentrically-typed network, one can calculate the density of one actor's egocentric network, according to the *formula* presented above. Due to the structure of the network and to the limitations of the study, the index of absolute centrality was set at 1, i.e. the proportion of the relations already established within the network which involved the actor i (the members of the Municipal Council) was 100%.

Conclusively, according to the answers delivered through the questionnaire, the most frequent contacts the members of the Local Councils in the two former "patrimonial communist dictatorships" established and developed are those with the business groups, hence interactions that were outside the traditional sphere of competence of the political elite, placed at the border between those connections that took place exclusively within the town and those developed outside the town, because the local councilors developed relations with various business groups, be they local, regional or national ones. Approximately the same importance was given to the interactions with other local elected representatives, but this situation was predictable, since the local councilors met with their colleagues normally at least five times per month (one ordinary session of the Local Council and four meetings of the specialized Committees). This result could be coupled with the fact that these local councilors valued collegiality as one of the most important characteristics of a member of the Local Council. Another frequent interaction of the members of all the six Local / Municipal Councils was that with close friends and the group of supporters: essential part in their reelection, the interaction with the group of supporters and friends is, nevertheless, a connection outside the political elite group, less specialized and informal, a local-based one. In fact, frequently, the formal meetings of the local councilors with members of the political elite outside the town (other town and county administrators, MPs, members of the Cabinet) were extremely rare, almost inexistent. This outcome would suggest an extremely isolated local political elite, incapable or uninterested in advancing the problems of the town to superior layers of the political elite, for resolution. Local-based contacts, even though necessary, are not sufficient in solving the problems of the community one represents. The internal links between segments of the political elites at different layers were unstable for the studied samples, which proved an evident difficulty in solving problems, especially those for which power at the local level was insufficient. Moreover, the em-

184

phasis put on personal connections (neighbors, friends, supporters, other local councilors, so colleagues), in the detriment of the interactions with local civil society (organized reform groups, religious groups, unions, mass-media) pointed to the incomplete institutionalization and to the lack of impersonality of society, especially in the case of Tecuci and Targovishte, based on favors, not on coherent policies from the representatives of the local political elite.

For the case of the members of the Municipal Councils in Česká Lípa and Levice, fortunately enough, the most frequent interactions were entertained with civic and reform groups, a type of interaction that is generally outside the political elite sphere, since the civic and reform groups are apolitical groups, and take place and function within the town, simply because the scope and the range of action and influence of such groups is contingent to a specific, limited space. Nevertheless, this type of interaction, though sometimes highly formalized, is of paramount importance to the profile of a consolidated democracy and their predominance in the case of the small municipalities of Česká Lípa and Levice demonstrated once more the democratic propensity of the local political elite in the two cases. The dissimilarity with the Local Councils of Tecuci and Targovishte was conspicuous, as civic and reform groups were in themselves a virtual rarity for the organizational landscape of these two towns. On the other hand, the networks established with the local media by municipal councilors in Česká Lípa and Levice – hence another relation that takes place outside the local political elite sphere, though functioning within the limits of the town – presupposed bilateral benefits, i.e. on the one hand, the proper transmission and dissemination of valuable information from the local decision-making elite to the masses of citizens and, on the other hand, a certain increase in the notoriety, popularity and prestige capital for the local elite, for conveniently assuring a positive reputation within the community and thusly a new mandate of municipal councilor. If this dependency worked beautifully, no wonder the high incumbency rate for all the six cases under scrutiny here, since press and media coverage could surely help reelection. Pivotal in reelection are the relations with the groups of supporters and friends. Striking was another mark of profound localism for the local political elites in Česká Lípa and Levice: virtually no relation was established with the political elite at the regional and national levels, probably partly due to the practiced decentralization and devolution.

Values embraced by the local political elite

An analysis of the opinions and attitudes adopted by the local political elite is instrumental and paramount in the description of this group. In reference to the views, perceptions, opinions, and attitudes of the local political elite, Robert Putnam (1976: 80) identifies four major orientations in the attitudes of this type of elite: cognitive orientations (predispositions based on which individuals interpret the existing reality; e.g. the attitudes regarding the social conflict); normative orientations (assessments regarding the way the society should be; e.g. the attitudes, ideologically motivated, towards the economical equality); interpersonal orientations (perceptions about the other segments of the political elite); stylistic orientations ("structural characteristics of the beliefs systems of the political elite" (Stoica 2003: 179)). Certain values embraced by the representatives of the local political elite can be explained by their social background: for instance, it is expected that those coming from lower class families are inclined to favor economic equality. Other values are acquired in the process of socialization (i.e. the type of education, the episodes of primary socialization, etc.). Following Putman's conception of "value orientation", sociologist Robin M. Williams identifies "major value orientations" (see, more importantly, Williams, Jr. 1952) (e.g. equality, individual freedom, efficiency, progress, practicability, humanitarianism, etc.), with a significant impact on policymaking. For instance, a value orientation dominated by equality among the membership of the local political elite may lead to a favoring of social security topics as preeminent on the political agenda of the community. Similarly, a value orientation divergent from (political) conflict may result in discouraging those contacts and the general impact of pressure-generating and contesting groups, s.o.a.s.f.

In the complex study of the values and their impact on participation and "activeness" at the local level, "The International Studies of Values in Politics" project developed, at the beginning of the 1970s, a framework of variables influencing leaders' attitudes towards "innovative change" and prioritization strategy; the importance of these variables is indisputable for the present discussion: (a) the degree of local autonomy in a political system (hence, the level of decentralization, specific to a certain community); (b) a country's level of economic development (or, the rate of growth, nationally); and (c) cultural traditions, peculiar to a society or a community, either political-ideological or social. (The International Studies of Values in Politics Project 1971) Indeed, this study puts a great emphasis on the mutual, bivalent relation between the degree of decentralization (hence, the political-administrative framework) and the value-cultural orientations of the local political elites.

In focusing on the conduct of public servants and elected officials, Thomas and Cynthia Lynch speak of a "democratic morality" or "the ethical spirit of

186

public administration", translated through benevolence and the pursuit of the "common good", and through a series of four values with a special significance in the discussion this book advances, for they deal with the manner in which the municipal councilors perceived themselves or thought of the public position they held: (a) "the commitment [...] to continued economic and social progress", (b) "the need for civic virtue", (c) "the role [of the leaders] in curbing the excesses and inadequacies of the market system", and (d) "the importance of public trust in leading [the community]" (Lynch and Lynch 2009: 7-8)[72]. In the Lynchs' view, the public servant and the elected official "must have the character virtues of optimism, courage, humility, and a willingness to offer compromise" (Lynch and Lynch 2009: 13)[73].

The present research evaluated the attitudes of the local political elite – i.e. of the members of the Local Councils in Tecuci and Targovishte, of the Municipal Councils of Česká Lípa, Oleśnica, and Levice, and of the Body of Representatives in Gyula, respectively – towards seven values: four of them referred to the fundaments of the democratic construct and they were quantified by question no. 9 in the administered questionnaire: citizen participation; gradual, innovative change; the importance of the political conflict; economic equality. The four variables selected in the understanding of the value charge of democracy have been thusly chosen as to comprise both the procedural-instrumental definition of democracy (putting emphasis on citizen participation and the existence of political conflict), and the substantive definition of democracy (focusing on economic equality)[74]. The attitudes of the members of the Local Councils towards the state intervention in economy were also taken into consideration, while a sixth value referred to local autonomy and decentralization, two processes permanently on the agenda of the post-communist governments, with a special emphasis for the situation of decentralization in the states of former "Sovietized Europe". Finally, the seventh value analyzed in the responses provided by the local / municipal councilors of Tecuci, Česká Lípa, Oleśnica, Gyula, Levice, and Targovishte, was their local / national (central) orientation, their geographical identification with a certain cultural-territorial unit (the native village / town; the municipality of Tecuci, Česká Lípa, Oleśnica, Gyula, Levice, and Targovishte, respectively; the regions of Moldavia, Liberec, Lower Silesia, Békés, Nitria, and Targovishte, respectively; Romania, the Czech Republic, Poland, Hungary, the Slovak Republic, and

---

72 In their argument in favor of "democratic ethics" in public administration, the Lynchs draw from: Appleby 1952; and Appleby 1965: 333-347.
73 Bailey (1965/1964: 283-298) labels the last one as "fairness tempered by charity", but Bailey adds "patience, honesty, loyalty, cheerfulness, courtesy, humility", some of which can be easily found in the portrait constructed by the six groups of municipal councilors when asked about the qualities a local elected official should ideally possess.
74 See, in this respect, a plea for the instrumental conception of democracy, Burton 1992: 1-37, esp. 2-3.

Bulgaria, respectively; Central Europe; or Europe). The attitudes towards state intervention in economy and local autonomy and decentralization were quantified through attitudinal intensity scale (I strongly agree with – I agree with – I partially agree with – I disagree with – I strongly disagree with – Don't know / don't answer).

According to the answers delivered by the local councilors, within a democracy, the most valued features were those of citizen participation (35.29% of the local councilors of Tecuci, an overwhelming 59.09% of the municipal councilors of Česká Lípa, 36.84% of the municipal councilors of Oleśnica, 33.33% of the municipal councilors of Gyula, 57.14% of the municipal councilors of Levice, and 35.48% of the local councilors of Targovishte), the avoidance of political conflict (35.29% of the local councilors in Tecuci, 31.59% of the municipal councilors in Oleśnica, and 35.48% of the local councilors in Targovishte) and innovative, gradual, piecemeal change (29.41% of the local councilors in Tecuci, 18.18% of the municipal councilors in Česká Lípa, 15.78% of the municipal councilors in Oleśnica, 16.66% of the municipal councilors in Gyula, 19.04% of the municipal councilors in Levice, and 29.03% of the local councilors in Targovishte). Generally, the citizen participation was the most cherished value for the municipal councilors in the six cases, with an average score of 42.86% of the total number of answers. The idea of gradual, peaceful, innovative change, associated with a democratic regime, was considered of paramount importance only by an average of 21.35% of the total number of respondents. Conflict avoidance was not a democratic priority for the municipal councilors in Česká Lípa and Levice (9.09%, and 9.52% of the respondents, respectively), although conflict avoidance scored the second most important democratic benefit (24.32% of the total number of answers for the six cases) among the four selected. Economic equality was credited as central for 13.63% of the councilors in Česká Lípa, 15.78% in Oleśnica, a quarter of the local representatives in Gyula, and another 14.28% of the municipal councilors in Levice, mainly due to the presence of some strong leftist side within these Councils, including social democrats and communists. More important, in the case of Tecuci and Targovishte, was the fact that none of the respondents representing the local political elites perceived economic equality as central to a democratic construct; this attitude proved a clear-cut break with the practices of encouraging economic equality of the *ancien régime*, at least at the rhetorical, declarative level. Moreover, it showed that, once an individual acquired a high social and occupational *status*, he / she tends to strongly reject economic equality, in favor of a principle based on merit or competition, on which they had gained the differentiation from the masses. Hence, a clear rejection of two values was observed among the local councilors: that of economic equality (only 11.44% of the total number of answers in the six cases) and that of political conflict. The avoidance of political conflict seemed beneficial for democracy and for the general good, from the

188

standpoint of the majority of local councilors in Tecuci, Oleśnica, Targovishte, and, partly, Gyula. As unusually as it might appear, among the members of these Local / Municipal Councils, there was an irreducible contradiction between what Dahl labeled "political participation" and "political contestation" (Dahl 1984: 31), between "political liberty" (expressed in conflict) and "political equality" (expressed in participation) (Aberbach, Putnam, and Rockman 1981: 172-173). Democracy – and, particularly, "urban" democracy – encounters two major forms of citizen participation, although this study did not include such a differentiation in the analysis of elite value orientations: (a) the "elite-directed" form of participation, and (b) the "elite-challenging" form of participation (Gabriel 2000: 187-259, esp. 204-248, citing the famous Inglehart 1979). This study referred almost exclusively to "elite-directed", conventional, traditional forms of citizen participation, from voting in local elections to participation in the Local Council's monthly meetings.

An uncertainty dominated the attitudes of the local councilors in the six municipalities in regard to the state intervention in economy, particularly on the background of economic crisis in which the research was conducted (2011-2016): a strong majority in Tecuci (52.94%) and Targovishte (51.61%) only partially agreed with economic interventionism, expressing a position which defined them as moderates. On the other hand, 23.52% of the local councilors in Tecuci, 36.36% of the municipal councilors in Česká Lípa, 29.41% of the municipal councilors in Oleśnica, 27.27% of the municipal councilor in Gyula, 38.09% of the municipal councilors in Levice, and another 22.58% of the local councilors in Targovishte did agree with the intervention of the state in economy, especially in the context and in the time of the research, governed by a financial-economic crisis; marks of this interventionism had already been implemented at the national level and they were perceived as beneficial for 23.52% of the local councilors in Tecuci, for instance (most of them, members of the governing party). The trend was even stronger among the municipal councilors of Česká Lípa: 27.7% of them partially agreed with state intervention in economy, and 36.36% bluntly stated that they agreed with interventionism (the leftist core of the Municipal Council here was once again present); furthermore, 4.54% of the councilors in Česká Lípa, an impressive 17.64% of the councilors in Oleśnica, an equally impressive 18.18% of the councilors in Gyula, 4.76% of the councilors in Levice, and 3.22% of the local councilors in Targovishte, declared themselves in strong favor for economic intervention, seen as a stabilizing factor. On the contrary, a minority of 17.64% of the members of the Local Council of Tecuci, 22.72% of the members of the Municipal Council of Česká Lípa, only 5.88% of the municipal councilors in Oleśnica, 9.09% of the municipal councilors in Gyula, 19.04% of the councilors in Levice, and a strong 16.12% of the local councilors in Targovishte, disagreed with the interventionist policies. Another 5.88% in Tecuci, 9.09% in Česká Lípa, 11.76% in Oleśnica, 9.09% in Gyula, 9.52% in Levice, and 6.45% in

Targovishte, voiced strong negative attitudes towards the state intervention in economy. Those local councilors holding negative views regarding economic interventionism largely coincided with the segment of the local political elite that managed highly successful local businesses and, consequently, was concerned that governmental policies could breach private individual initiative in economy, or with the segment of the local political elite holding strong right-wing, *laissez-faire* positions. No strong agreement with state interventionism in economy was recorded among the responses in Tecuci, indicating a rightist majority within the Council. On the other hand, the fact that most of the members of the Local Councils in Tecuci and Targovishte, and of the Municipal Councils in Oleśnica and Gyula, placed their answers in the middle of the intensity scale, allegedly "partially agreeing" with the state intervention in economy, was rather telling for the lack of knowledge and the associated general confusion among the members of the local political elite regarding the advantages and the drawbacks, the implication of the state intervention in economy: it might be rather the case that, trying the avoid an answer of "Don't know / Don't answer", the so-called "moderates" favored a middle-ground answer.

A strong inclination towards local autonomy and decentralization was manifested by the local political elite in all of the six Local / Municipal Councils under scrutiny here. One important digression is necessary at this point: the collocation "local autonomy", though present in any piece of legislation of East-Central European countries after 1989 – in a vigorous *impetus* of catching up with the West, following a "path dependency"[75] –, comprises two principal dimensions (Vetter 2007: 90-91): (1) the "legal" dimension (i.e. the construction of "the municipalities' *spectrum* of functions and the freedom they have in making decisions about delivering public services" (Vetter 2007: 90), and (2) the "political" dimension (i.e. the construction of "the type of influence municipalities have on higher decision-making level in order to foster their interests there" (Vetter 2007: 90, following Page 1991: 13 and 42). First and foremost, for the principle of "local autonomy" to transcend formal, legislative scripts, "the need for both sides in the central-local relationship to recognize each other as governments" (Elliott 1981: 96) is central in any pursuit of local government. This mutual acknowledgement presupposes, of course, a historical legacy of grass-roots, bottom-up decentralization and a sense of autonomous community, developed outside and beyond the legal provisions inscribed

---

75 The topic of "path dependency" has been discussed most vigorously by Kitschelt, Mansfeldova, Markowski, and Tóka 1999. Nicole Gallina (2007: 75-91) associates "path dependency" to a series of developments in the ECE political elites' behavior prior and following the EU accession: "[...] ECE political elites have internalized a 'negative political culture' including unethical behavior and an egoistic struggle for political power contradicting the principles of liberal democracy." See, for further analysis, Gallina 2008.

in foundational acts. But all the six cases under scrutiny here – Romania, the Czech Republic, Poland, Hungary, the Slovak Republic, Bulgaria – are typical cases of top-down, downwards decentralization, with no indisputable legacy of autarchic, independent local, communal government. How, then, can such bilateral recognition be possible if the local autonomy is seen as granted by the central authorities to the local ones?

Both interpretations of "local autonomy" were considered in the selection of it as value or principle to be evaluated when analyzing the six Local / Municipal Councils and their members, and when administering the questionnaire. All in all, "local autonomy" might be equated with "local discretion", with the successful delivery by the local authorities of overall well-being for the political and social community, founded on the increased proximity of municipalities to their citizens:

> "If the state is important at all, then the local state has intrinsic importance because it is a key point of contact for most citizens with the *apparatus* of the national state structure, whether in federal or unitary political systems. Further, the local state is the point at which many public / private controversies and interactions become manifest to citizens and officials. The local state is typically responsible for the implementation of many centrally formulated programmes and hence frequently for arbitration between public and private interests." (Gurr and King 1987: 49-50)[76]

Pierre defines "local autonomy" as "consisting of the maximization of local government policy-making powers, revenue-raising powers and implementation capacities. Autonomy is constrained by central state policy and actions, local and national economic trends and local political and social interests." (Pierre 1990: 38) Quite similarly, Page and Goldsmith conceptualize "local autonomy" as "discretion" of the local authorities in decision-making process, the independence action of the said in respect to the regional and central authorities:

> "Discretion refers to the ability of actors within local government to make decisions about the type and level of services it delivers within the formal statutory and

---

76 Gurr and King discuss two dimensions determining the degree of autonomy: (1) the first type of local autonomy refers to local economic and social factors (e.g. "the extent of business establishments, the limits of local tax revenue, unemployment, activities of local political organizations, and social movements or interest groups in the sense of veto players, who aim to influence the local agenda"), and (2) the second type of local autonomy is defined as "the degree of local discretion resulting from the independence from higher political level [...] [being] determined by constitutional protection, the allocation of resources or political pressure."

administrative framework for local service delivery, and about how that service is provided and financed." (Page and Goldsmith 1987: 5)[77]

Interestingly enough, Page makes recourse to a conceptual, etymologic mutation, by labeling "the *spectrum* of responsibilities and the discretion in providing local services" as "legal localism", whereas the "access to national decision-makers with the goal of representing local interests" is coined "political localism" (Page 1991: 13 and 42). This book adds to the legal and political localism an identity-geographical localism, but it discusses it, not as a priority of the local political elites in the six case-studies, but as a value embraced by the said elite groups. A clear majority of 64.7% of the local councilors in Tecuci, a less evident majority of 40.9% of the municipal councilors in Česká Lípa, 43.75% of the municipal councilors in Oleśnica, 40% of the municipal councilors in Gyula, a more reluctant portion of 38.09% of the municipal councilors in Levice, and a powerful majority of 64.51% of the local councilors in Targovishte, expressed agreement with the principle of decentralization. Another 11.76% in Tecuci, a quarter in Oleśnica, 30% in Gyula, 4.76% in Levice, 9.67% in Targovishte, strongly and enthusiastically agreed with the said principle. Indeed, there was an unrestrained enthusiasm and general agreement regarding the "normative desirability" of decentralization and "local government as one that is close to local communities and that can best engage, represent, and serve the grassroots" (Lankina and Hudalla, with Wollmann 2008: 6) While inquiring into the Romanian case of decentralization during the 1990s and the beginning of 2000s, Felix Jakob reiterates the same enthusiasm manifested among the local elites in Tecuci:

> "The merits of decentralization have never been openly questioned by the central government or by any political parties, and local government reform has been confirmed repeatedly as a prime objective and integral part of the economic transition strategy. But large segments of the government administration appear to believe that maintaining the *status quo* or even reinforcing the mechanisms of central control over the local government system is, for the time being, preferable to stronger local government." (Jakob 1995: 229)

Moderates concerning the issue of local autonomy and decentralization (most probably, realistically assessing the costs the local administration would face in such a context) were included in the 23.52% of the local councilors in Tecuci, a more convincing 36.36% of the local councilors in Česká Lípa, 25% of the municipal councilors in Oleśnica, 30% of the municipal councilors in Gyula, 33.33% of the municipal councilors in Levice, and another 22.58% of the local councilors in Targovishte, who only partially agreed with this principle, characterizing many countries of Western Europe. It is interesting to

---

77 Elander (1991: 33) adds a third dimension of "local autonomy" including factors determining "the way community interests are represented and heard at higher levels of government."

observe that none of the members of the Local Councils in Tecuci, Gyula, and Targovishte disagreed with the tendency towards local autonomy and decentralization, which proved a clear and definitive acceptance of these values among the studied segment of the local political elite. Having lived already the experience, the benefits and the drawbacks of decentralization, none of the municipal councilors in Česká Lípa, Oleśnica, and partly in Gyula and Levice, had a strong negative reaction toward the issue, though, in the case of Česká Lípa, none manifested a strong positive reaction either, judging more objectively the matter, with a greater degree of awareness. Some of the councilors in Česká Lípa (22.72%), in Oleśnica (6.25%), and in Levice (23.8%), more vehement and rather disappointed by the present status of decentralization, were simply disagreeing with the principle overall. It became evident that the initial enthusiasm of the local elite in Česká Lípa, for instance, had disappeared in favor of a rather cold mindedness regarding the issue of decentralization and devolution. Actually, in discussing the Czech case of local government and decentralization, Gorzelak isolates six "myths" on local government in the countries of former "Sovietized Europe", myths that produced overemphasized expectations and unjustified enthusiasm about the benefits of decentralization, on the one hand, and that generated a trend towards "re-centralization" at the central level: (1) "the myth of local autonomy" (i.e. "unrealistic expectations toward the potential of local autonomy and the rejection of any central involvement in local affairs"); (2) "the myth of prosperity" (i.e. "the belief that economic autarky will guarantee the prosperity of local communities"); (3) "the myth of property" (i.e. "the belief that the restoration of municipal property will in itself guarantee local development"); (4) "the myth of omnipotence" (i.e. "the belief that municipalities are both entitled to and capable of deciding all local problems by themselves"); (5) "the myth of eagerness" (i.e. "the belief that zeal can compensate for knowledge and skills in local politics and administration"); and (6) "the myth of stabilization" (i.e. "the belief that stable conditions are what local governments should and can attempt to reach") (Gorzelak 1992: 204-209).

Finally, out of the responses gathered after the questionnaires had been filled in, it resulted that the large majority of the members of the six Local Councils, regardless of their place of birth, identified themselves primarily with the town they represented, the municipalities of Tecuci, Česká Lípa, Oleśnica, Gyula, Levice, and Targovishte, respectively, the places where they lived, where they worked and where they had established the most numerous contacts and connections. The tendency towards localism (more pronounced among the local elites of Česká Lípa – 80.76% – and of Levice – 80% – than in the ones of Gyula – 53.84% –, Oleśnica – 55% –, Targovishte – 63.88% –, or Tecuci – 63.63%) was evident and it was further emphasized by the exclusiveness of local interactions the local councilors in almost all the six municipalities formed and developed, despite the fact that approximately 47%, 32%,

193

43%, 36%, 37%, and 48% of them were not born in Tecuci, Česká Lípa, Oleśnica, Gyula, Levice, and Targovishte, respectively. There was a more or less fragile tendency towards centralism, as only 18.18% of the members of the Local Council in Tecuci, 15% of the members of the Municipal Council in Oleśnica, 15.38% of the members of the Body of Representatives in Gyula, 4% of the members of the Municipal Council in Levice, and 19.44% of the members of the Local Council in Targovishte (the highest proportion of national identification, among the six cases) identified themselves, first and foremost, with Romania, Poland, Hungary, Slovakia, or Bulgaria, respectively, not with the town in which they lived. Equal percentages (9.09% for Tecuci, 11.53% for Česká Lípa, 15% for Oleśnica, 15.38% for Gyula, 8% for Levice, and 8.33% for Targovishte) were attributed to those segments of the local political elite who identified themselves primarily with the town / commune / village in which they had been born and in which they had experienced the process of primary socialization, and to those who identified themselves with the region of Moldavia (9.09% for Tecuci), Liberec-Bohemia (11.53% for Česká Lípa), Lower Silesia (10% for Oleśnica), Békés (7.69% for Gyula), Nitria (8% for Levice), and Targovishte (8.33% for Targovishte), respectively, manifesting thusly a regional inclination and an identification with the cultural patterns the region displayed. There was no European or even Central European identification among the local councilors, with the partial exceptions of 5% of the municipal councilors in Oleśnica, and 7.69% of the municipal councilors in Gyula, who held an "European" identification. Probably due to an increased level of decentralization, the local political elite in Česká Lípa had an almost absent inclination towards centralism, since the decision-making mechanisms were, by that time, in the hands of the local power: while 11.53% still identified themselves with the place in which they had been born, in a purely localist manner, 3.84% and 7.69% identified themselves at best with the regions of Liberec and Bohemia, respectively, but clear signs of centralism were absent for the local councilors of Česká Lípa (no respondent identified himself / herself primarily with his / her country, with the collocation "Central Europe" or with Europe (famously enough, Czechs are one of the most Euroskeptic EU members, no surprise, then, that no local councilor in Česká Lípa identified with Europe).

In a quite compelling and revealing study on the outlook of local leaders in Lithuania after 1990, Arvydas Matulionis, Svajone Mikene, and Rimantas Rauleckas link the geographical or "local-global" self-identification of the local political elite to the party affiliation: generally, their study contends, left-wing dominance on the local political *spectrum* is corresponding to a largely local self-identification, while right-wing party prevalence will indicate a national cultural-geographical self-identification, due especially to the drive to national revitalization and restoration, characteristic for the newly-independent Baltic states in the early 1990s (Matulionis, Mikene, and Rauleckas 2006: 101-

142). Moreover, as in the case of the six local elite groups under scrutiny here, the study on Lithuanian local leadership concludes that "[w]ider geopolitical identities than the national level do not show any signs of being internalized, as processes of globalization would suggest" (Matulionis, Mikene, and Rauleckas 2006: 135).

As a conclusion, by using the framework of classification based on partic-ipation-conflict acceptance and economic equality-interventionism acceptance provided by Virgil Stoica in *Cine conduce Iaşiul?*, it could be observed that: (1) the majority of the local councilors in Tecuci fell into the category of the "populists" (accepting citizen participation, but rejecting political conflict and seeking avoidance of conflict), and in that of "statists-anti-egalitarians" (par-tially accepting state intervention in economy, but rejecting economic equal-ity); (2) the majority of the municipal councilors in Česká Lípa could be cate-gorized as "democrats" (accepting both citizen participation and political con-flict) and "statists-egalitarians" (clearly accepting state intervention in econ-omy and partially desiring economic equality); (3) the majority of the munici-pal councilors in Oleśnica could be labeled as "populists" (embracing citizen participation, but refuting political conflict in the conduct of the community), and "statists-egalitarians" (partially accepting interventionism in economy, and partially favoring economic equality in a democratic construct); (4) the majority of the municipal councilors in Gyula could be coined still as "popu-lists" (wholeheartedly accepting the participation of citizens in the public life of the town, but partially favoring conflict avoidance in local politics), and as "statists-egalitarians" (the clearest case: accepting the state intervention in economy and supporting the *desideratum* of economic equality as a feature of democracy, hence the general idea of the "welfare society"); (5) the majority of the municipal councilors in Levice could be characterized as "democrats" (accepting both citizen participation and political conflict) and "statists-egali-tarians" (clearly accepting state intervention in economy, particularly in times of crisis, and partially accepting economic equality); and (6) the majority of the local councilors in Targovishte fell into the category of the "populists" (ac-cepting citizen participation, but rejecting political conflict and seeking avoid-ance of conflict) and in that of "statists-anti-egalitarians" (partially accepting state intervention in economy, but clearly rejecting economic equality).

According to the answers delivered by the local councilors, within a de-mocracy, the most valued features were those of citizen participation (with an average level of acceptance of 42.86%), and, surprisingly, conflict avoidance (an average level of acceptance of 24.32%). Gradual change was placed on an average level of acceptance of 21.35%. Economic equality and conflict avoid-ance posed some interesting problems to the value orientations of these elites. Firstly, there was a clear rejection of economic equality among the local coun-cilors of Tecuci and Targovishte, which could be translated by a syndrome of total detachment, expressed rhetorically, from the *ancién régime*. Secondly, for the local councilors of Tecuci, Oleśnica, and Targovishte, conflict avoidance was significant, which would hint to a monolithical behavior inside the Council.

The answers provided in the questionnaire by the members of the Municipal Councils in Tecuci, Česká Lípa, Oleśnica, Gyula, Levice, and Targovishte, in respect to the state intervention in economy and to the prospects of further decentralization and local autonomy, sketched: (a) a local leadership in Tecuci and in Targovishte who was very enthusiastic about decentralization (sometimes, without actually being aware of the whole *palette* of responsibilities that increased decentralization usually generates), but quite undecided to the idea of the interventionist state (partly because the political elite coincided with the economic elite, and locally, it became easier to act as private entrepreneurs, though enjoying the state subsidies); (b) a local leadership in Česká Lípa who presented a real skepticism in respect to an already significantly decentralized distribution of power, and generally favorable to the state intervention in economy, particularly in times of crisis; (c) a local leadership in Oleśnica who was much in favor of both the protectionist state and of increased decentralization and local autonomy (with significant proportion of respondents being "strongly in favor" of the two); and (d) a local leadership in Gyula and in Levice who generally held a positive stance towards increased decentralization and its benefits, and a rather cautious stance regarding the state intervention in economy, partly because of the government's attitude in respect to the most recent financial crisis.

196

Priorities of the local political elite

The local political elite is formed, after all, to lead, to decide upon and to implement public policies, through which the general good of citizens to be attained. Generally, it is perceived that the local political class should provide for the town and its citizens. The priorities of the local political elites in what concerns the municipal public policies in different domains represent an instrument for describing their orientations, their perceptions regarding the problems the town – i.e. the geographical space where they exert their influence and power – and their views regarding the capabilities in finding solutions for such problems. Solving public problems is also a matter of popular perception and of reputation for local political elites.

The study and the administered questionnaire differentiated between four forms of prioritization: (a) spheres to which a special importance should be granted (political responsiveness and policy prognosis); (b) spheres in which considerable measures could be taken at the local level (political / policy power and responsibility); (c) spheres in which effective measures had already been taken (political accountability and policy diagnosis), and (d) spheres in which the local councilor exerted a personal influence (personal responsibility and influence).

The following observations were meant to identify and to sketch the public agenda of the members of the Local Councils in Tecuci and Targovishte, of the Municipal Council in Česká Lípa, Oleśnica, and Levice, and of the Body of Representative in Gyula, by pointing out, based on the answers provided in the questionnaires, their priorities in solving certain problems the six towns confronted with and by stressing the level of importance they assessed to different local problems.

From the responses delivered to the open question concerning the identification of the main problem the towns confronted with, it was observed that there was an uniformization of perceptions among the members of the six Local / Municipal Councils: 15.78% (for Tecuci), 26.92% (for Česká Lípa), 28.57% (for both Oleśnica and Gyula), 28% (for Levice), and 15.15% (for Targovishte) of them considered that the principal problem of their towns was represented by the ever increasing rate of unemployment and the general lack of job opportunities for the inhabitants of their town. This main community problem was coupled with the lack of funds and investments in the town (a problem actually hinting to the poor fiscal capacity of these six municipalities): 42.1% of the answers for Tecuci, 23.07% of the answers for Česká Lípa, 23.8% of the answers for Oleśnica, 21.42% of the answers for Gyula, 24% of the answers for Levice, and 42.42% of the answers for Targovishte. It should be noticed that exactly for those towns with the poorest fiscal capacity (Tecuci, Targovishte, and Levice), the local political elites identified the lack of funds and

197

investments as particularly stringent. Taking into account that part of this research has been undertaken during the economic crisis (2010-2014), some of the members of the Local Councils pointed to it as the main problem their town confronted with: 26.92% of the responses in the case of Česká Lípa, 4.76% of the responses in the case of Oleśnica, 7.14% of the responses in the case of Gyula, and 12% of the responses in the case of Levice. Therefore, the perception of the financial crisis and of its repercussions at the local level, among the local political elite, was extremely different, depending primarily on the time of the research. The lack of modernization, of development opportunities, and the existence of a dysfunctional, remote and inefficient infrastructure, posed additional problems on the wellbeing of the town, from the local councilors' perspective, in the case of Tecuci (5.26% of the answers) and of Targovishte (3.03% of the answers); for both Tecuci and Targovishte, similar percentages were assigned to the perceived general lack of perspectives. As for Tecuci and for Targovishte, the major problem of the towns that the local political elites were worried about was actually the lack of funding and investments. The lack of social cohesion, social sensitivity, and of social dialogue within the community was problematic for almost all the six local elite groups: 10.52% of the answers for Tecuci, 15.38% of the answers for Česká Lípa, 16% of the answers for Levice, and 9.09% of the answers for Targovishte. This issue, but also the rest of the problems mentioned in the questionnaire by the local councilors, are rather common to the great majority of local administrations in the region of East-Central Europe, alike; they are not specific to these towns, but they were, indeed, stringent for the local administrations of Tecuci, Česká Lípa, Oleśnica, Gyula, Levice, and Targovishte. As observed, the six communities confronted the same problems, but their perceived magnitude was different for the six municipalities. Other problems identified by the local political elites in the six towns were: problems in healthcare services (4.76% of the answers for Oleśnica, and 7.14% of the answers for Gyula), social exclusion (a quite significant problem for some communities: 4.76% of the responses for Oleśnica, 7.14% of the responses for Gyula, 12% of the responses for Levice), populism (4.76% of the responses for Oleśnica, 9.09% of the responses for Targovishte), etc.

Another issue raised by the present study was that of assuming responsibility for the resolution of the problems the town confronted with, at different layers of administration (local, regional, national). The distribution of responsibilities in solving the local problems, as seen by the local councilors, reshaped the structure of their agenda. According to the responses provided through the questionnaire by the members of the Local Councils of Tecuci and Targovishte, those of the Municipal Councils of Česká Lípa, Oleśnica, and Levice, and those of the Body of Representatives in Gyula, they considered that sufficient political power at the local level existed only for taking significant measures in the following domains: for Tecuci, culture, sport, recreation and youth activities (20.33% of the respondents), social services (18.64% of the local councilors), public improvements (13.55% of the respondents) and education (13.55%) (The municipal budget on 2010 seemed to be structured on these major lines, a situation that proved that local administration was capable of dealing with these problems). Even though 24.52% of them assesed that a special attention should be given to economic development, 16.98% to public safety and 16.98% to public improvements, these measures (except the issue of public improvements) could not be taken at the local level, for the local authorities were incapable and powerless when dealing with such problems. The situation was quite similar in the case of the perceived power the members of the Local Council in Targovishte had in solving the problems of the town they governed; their perception was that political power to effectuate change existed only in such spheres as: culture, sport, and recreational activities (21.91% of the answers), social services (17.8% of the answers), education and public improvements (13.69% of the answers in both cases). Only 5.47% of the local councilors of Targovishte assessed there was sufficient power at the local level to trigger economic development, and only 6.84% of them thought the same in respect to the improvement of minorities rights and interethnic relations, a particularly stringent issue, especially for a town as Targovishte, accommodating an important Turkish minority. For Česká Lípa, public improvements (26.98% of the local councilors – such an answer was due especially to an increased degree of devolution), social services (23.8% of the respondents), public safety (18.04% of the respondents) and even economic development (14.28% of the respondents) seemed to have transcended the line between those spheres of significance and those spheres in which effective change at the local level could be taken. Particularly due to the extended prerogatives the process of administrative decentralization provides, the municipal councilors of Česká Lípa seemed much more confident in their capacity to solve the more pressing issues of the community. For the municipality of Oleśnica, which enjoyed a significant degree of decentralization, the distribution of responsibilities for the local level was quite differently assessed: the municipal councilors estimated that sufficient power existed at the local level to effectuate changes in: education (25.64% of the answers), economic development (20.51% of the answers), and healthcare (15.38% of the answers). The picture for local responsiveness and responsibility was even "brighter" from the perspective of the municipal representatives in Gyula: they considered that there was sufficient political power locally for triggering change in those key areas for the wellbeing of the town, such as: education (25.71% of the responses), economic development (22.85% of the responses), healthcare (14.28% of the responses), and social services (14.28% of the answers). Caught in the realities of a small town in a small country, the municipal councilors of Levice assumed responsibility at the local level for equally important areas: public improvements (27.41% of the answers, the highest percentage among the six cases), social services (24.19% of the answers, again the highest ratio among the selected cases), and public safety (17.74% of the answers). It is laudable how, irrespective of the fact Levice is a small community and that the Slovak decentralization has been problematic, its local elite group acknowledged and assumed responsibility for such "hard-core" domains of public life.

The least of concerns for the local political elites in Tecuci, Levice, and Targovishte seemed to be the issue of pollution: 1.88% of the local councilors in Tecuci, 1.63% of the municipal councilors in Levice, and 2.98% of the local councilors in Targovishte considered it as a veritable problem for the town, especially in the context of a small community and of a contract between the local administration and a national firm, which ensured, during the last years, the recycling process of waste in the town. The least significant spheres for the local political elite of Česká Lípa were, equally, pollution, minority' rights (since there is virtually no ethnic diversity in the socio-demographical structure of the town, similar to the 1.63% score of significance assigned by the local political elites in Levice) and town's recreational activities (each with a 1.66% score of significance). No wonder that these aspects were degraded in the hierarchical priority scaling of these local elites, since economic crisis had seemed to have captured the entire preoccupations of the municipal councilors of Česká Lípa, Levice, and, partly, Gyula.

The members of the Local Councils of Tecuci and Targovishte admitted that, actually, significant and efficient measures had been operated only in the spheres of social services (20.83%, and 20.96% of the answers, respectively) – generated particularly by a continuous increase from the population in the demand of such services as housing or unemployment assistance –, culture, sport, youth and recreation activities (20.83%, and 22.58% of the answers, respectively) and, again, public improvements (14.58%, and 14.51% of the respondents, respectively), while the gravest problems of their towns (economic development, lack of opportunities, etc), even though acknowledged by the local political elites, had been constantly avoided. The local councilors of Česká Lípa, Levice, Oleśnica, and Gyula evaluated that effective and efficient measures had been taken in the fields of culture, sport, recreation and youth activities (23.07% of the respondents, in a similar manner to the case of Tecuci; 21.56%, 23.8%, 23.68% of the answers, respectively), public safety (23.07%, 21.56%, 4.76%, and 2.63% of the answers, respectively) and, like in Tecuci and Targovishte, public improvements (19.23%, 19.6%, 26.19%, and 26.31% of the answers, respectively), even though on a background of economic depression.

There were no significant variations in accordance to age in the identification of the major problem the towns confronted with.

Generally, when asked about a particular domain in which each of the local councilor would have been able to exert his / her own personal influence in the resolution of problems, the responses suggested a pattern: each local councilor found himself / herself influential in domains that coincided with their professional and occupational expertise (e.g. a teacher would have assessed his / her major influence in the educational domain, while an engineer considered himself influential in solving problems in the sphere of public improvements); or each local councilor found himself / herself influential in those spheres that coincided with the domains of interest for the specialized committee whose member the local councilor was (e.g. a local councilor member of the Committee no. 5 in Tecuci, for local public administration, for juridical issues, for the observance of public order and for the observance and promotion of the citizens' rights and liberties, usually answered that he / she could exert his / her influence in the domains of public safety or the rights of minorities and inter-ethnical relations, etc.). The domain in which the majority of the local councilors of Tecuci (33.33%) and of Targovishte (36.17%) found themselves influential was that of public improvements, mainly because many of them were engineers and their occupational *status* imprinted them expertise in this domain. The sphere in which the majority of the municipal councilors of Česká Lípa (35.48%) and of Levice (33.33%) felt somehow influential was, similarly, the public improvements one, once again due simply to their main technical training. The sphere of activity at the local level in which the members of the Municipal Council of Oleśnica (27.02%), and those of the Body of Representatives in Gyula (27.27%) considered themselves as being influential was the "soft" domain of culture, sport, and youth and recreational activities, due primarily to their professional background. Nevertheless, in a general trend, the members of the Local Councils acknowledged their personal influence in the resolution of some of the town's problems in a specialized manner, in a way that took into consideration almost exclusively the educational training, the occupation and the acquired expertise in a single domain. This highly subjective assessment regarding personal influence of the local councilors shows a tendency towards a technocratic model of the local political elite. In the case of Tecuci and of Targovishte, many local councilors (21.21%, and 21.27%, respectively) considered themselves influential in the solution of problems regarding economic development, probably because they were conducting successful private businesses in the town. There were, of course, some sporadic exceptions: in the case of Česká Lípa, councilor Karel Heller, an engineer himself, was part of multiple Committees, including Audit and Education ones.

Much of the results gathered from the administration of the questionnaire regarding the priorities of the local elites in the Romanian and the Bulgarian cases were similar to the observations drawn on the local leadership in the former Soviet republics (see, for instance, Snapkovskii 1999: 113-114). The similarities refer primarily to the reluctance in assuming responsibility for the local public matter, on the simple basis that the representatives of the political elite at the local level considered they were deprived of the authority, influence and effective power to actually undertake meaningful actions for solving the problems of the community they represented. If, in the case of the former Soviet republics, dominantly Belarus and Ukraine, the sequence of pendulating periods of liberal democracy and authoritarianism generated the local authorities' conviction that they lacked the "power" to determine change in their towns and that their efficiency was remarkably low, for the Romanian and the Bulgarian cases following the communist breakdown, there has been a continuous, perennial preoccupation for increased devolution, externalization of the public services to the local authorities, and a permanent attempt to greater, comprehensive decentralization. As a consequence, the resemblance was quite curious and inexplicable at the first glance, though hinting to the unwillingness of the Romanian and the Bulgarian local political elite – especially in small-to-medium-sized communities – to assume the responsibilities and the full range of prerogatives and attributions springing from their institutional position. A long history of centralism and an equally consistent series of rather unsuccessful essays of decentralization after 1989 bred a less responsible local elite, one who is less responsive to the needs and the problems of their communities and who traditionally transfers the accountability and responsiveness towards the central authorities, on the consecrated fundament that it is deficient in effective "power". As a matter of fact, this is partly accurate, notwithstanding the alleged dominance of the "local autonomy", the implementation of decentralization became synonymous with the impoverishment of the local administrations and their subsequent impotence[78] of the local leadership in dealing with immediate needs of the community: the externalization of the public services from the central government to the local authorities signified the almost exclusive administration by the municipalities of such crucial establishments as schools, high schools, hospitals, cultural foyers, museums, theaters, cinemas, etc.; the maintenance of these settings, the infrastructural workings entered in the main attributions of the municipalities, which lost the overwhelming financial, budgetary support of the centre and became obliged to extract more diligently and meaningfully taxes from its citizens, from the local firms and from renting publicly owned property. For instance, in 2010-2011, Tecuci received only 2.23% of its revenues from the state budget, while, prior to the administrative reforms leading to increased decentralization, the town had received up to 40% from the state budget. Conversely, the capacity to support the service infrastructure of the town was severely contingent upon the local authorities' capability to extract taxes, while, at the same time, the ability to attract European structural funds for regional development was equally limited, generating, in the case of Tecuci for example, only 2.98% of the revenues (in 2010). Therefore, these were, at the time of the research, the main sources of frustration of the local councilors in respect to their "power" to effectuate positive, meaningful change within their communities.

---

78 For this specific wording for the self-perceived inability of the local leaders to effectuate change in their communities, see Martinsen 1995: 330-361.

On the other hand, in a quite compelling – and one of the very few, Eng-lish-written – study to discuss the local issues and public perceptions in me-dium-sized towns in the Czech Republic, Daniel Hanšpach argues that priori-tization at the level of the town of Liberec differs markedly from the inhabit-ants' perceptions regarding the fields to which a special concern should be given: if the local authorities put a special emphasis on infrastructural improve-ments, economic recovery, and public safety, the inhabitants of Liberec are more preoccupied by environmental issues, availability of housing and public safety (Hanšpach 1997). Hence, it should be noted the sharp difference in "sub-stantive representation" of local priorities between the rulers and the ruled. Nevertheless, though indicative for the cases scrutinized here, Hanšpach's study on local perceptions in Liberec cannot be generalized for the whole coun-try (so as to comprise the case of Česká Lípa) or for the whole region of ECE (so as to comprise the six cases under scrutiny in this study).

A special attention should be paid on those indicators of policy prognosis and policy power / responsibility. Hence, though the elites in Tecuci and in Targovishte assigned an increased importance to the so-called "hard" spheres of competence in local government (public improvements – 16.98% and 16.41%, respectively; public safety – 16.98% and 16.41%, respectively –, and economic development – 24.52% and 23.88%, respectively), the said consid-ered that there resided power to implement changes locally only in such rather "soft" domains as: culture, sport and recreation / youth activities (20.33% and 21.91%, respectively) and social services (18.64% and 17.8%, respectively). A sentiment of political impotence among those cases of less-decentralized elites was persistent: although they had identified quite clearly and pertinently the spheres in which important measures should be taken locally, they were either unwilling or irresponsible to operate changes for their communities in key spheres, vital for the development of their constituencies. Conversely, for Česká Lípa, Levice, and Oleśnica – three cases in which significant degrees of decentralization improved the level of responsibility at the level of local policy and comprehensive and effective prioritization –, the local political elites tended to confound the spheres in which a special importance should be granted with those spheres in which considerable measures could be taken at the local level: public improvements (24.19% to 26.98%, for Česká Lípa; 24.59% to 27.41%, for Levice, and 11.9%, for both indicators, in the case of Oleśnica), social services (30.64% to 23.8%, for Česká Lípa; 29.5% to 24.19%, for Levice; and 16.66%, for both indicators for Oleśnica), economic develop-ment (22.58% to 14.28%, for Česká Lípa; 21.31% to 14.51%, for Levice; and 16.66%, for both indicators in the case of Oleśnica). Measures already operated have been undertaken in "hard" spheres, as well: public improvements and so-cial services (19.23% and 25%, respectively, for Česká Lípa; 19.6% and 23.52%, respectively, for Levice; 21.19% and 19.04%, respectively, for Oleśnica). Once more, the policy responsibility and prioritization were indicated as higher for the highly decentralized local political elites.

Somehow expectedly, the local focus of decision-makers diverged from such policy domains as pollution and interethnic relations and minority rights. First, given the absence of significant minority groups (with the partial exceptions of Targovishte and Gyula), the need for policy in this sphere was proportionally decreasing. Secondly, the importance of environmental matters and pollution in developing countries – as was the case with those in East-Central Europe – was yet a topic of debate; moreover, in small urban settings, the matter of pollution did not pose considerable hardship in decision-making, though perceived as a liability.

One other element in reference to the priorities of the local political elites in the six selected towns discusses the manner in which the local councilors accommodated their existing social / professional / occupational *status* to their acquired political role, the status of "local political elite". Generally, there are six possible scenarios (Ştefan 2004: 132-133) in the issue of accommodating previous social role with newly-acquired political roles: (1) "temporarily suspension" of the social / professional function, and, in the future, going back to it once the political role is over; (2) "a challenge", since the councilor has reached a peak in his social role and needed a new challenge and, consequently chose to act in a political capacity; (3) "visibility" (to some extent, the reverse of "challenge" solution: the councilor plans to use the relations, the networks of power, the visibility and the political experience acquired during the exercise of the political role in the advance of his social-professional career; (4) "definite end" of the social position previously held and the starting of a new professional path once the political role is ended in its turn; (5) "new profession", thus the complete abandonment of the previous professional position and the total dedication to a political career, in an overlapping between social and political roles and in an attempt to "professionalization of politics", and (6) "business and politics" at the same time, exerting both the social and the political roles. As already noted, the position of municipal councilor is clearly a part-time activity, especially in the case of the Council in Česká Lípa, where the members met quite rarely in ordinary sessions and slightly more frequently in the specialized Committees. Moreover, particularly in the case of the Councils in Tecuci and Targovishte, a significant portion of the local councilors had long abandoned their profession (which they practiced, as a general rule, only during the communist period) in favor of more profitable business activities; nonetheless, once involved into politics, none of them renounced their current activities, either as businessmen (managers, administrators of firms) or as professionals (in the case of those outside the economic, profit-making undertakings). The overwhelming majority of them, in the cases of Česká Lípa and Levice fitted the profile of politics as a "challenge", in the cases of Gyula and Oleśnica, they corresponded to a combination of "visibility" and "temporary suspension" profiles of politics, while for the cases of Tecuci and Targovishte, the pattern was that of "business and politics".

When concerning the area of social assistance (from unemployment benefits, housing, retirement pensions, child services, etc.), Hungary is a special case, displaying interesting features in the manner of distributing responsibilities between the central and the local. In practice, the responsibilities of the local authorities in this sphere are limited:

> "Local governments are then responsible for meeting the needs of those inadequately served by the central welfare system. Central and local governments' responsibilities for social assistance vary, with the central government responsible for setting guidelines for minimum incomes of pensioners and the unemployed and local governments tasked with establishing need, determining eligibility, establishing assistance levels, and funding outlays." (Bird, Wallich and Péteri 1995: 78)

As a result,

> "[t]here may thus be substantial differences across localities in the level of welfare provided, as well as in eligibility *criteria*, depending on the resources available to the locality. [...] [This probably is the reason why i]t has been said that Hungary has 3,200 different social assistance policies." (Fábián and Straussman 1994: 271-280 [additions mine])

In their compelling attempt to explain and put forward a "city-county consolidation" ("C3") model, Suzanne Leland, Hurt Thurmaier et al. isolate a series of steps (or "parts") in the process they study, among them, the initial one referring to "elite agenda setting" (Lelard and Thurmaier 2004: 11). Concretely, Leland et al. deal with the likeliness of city-county consolidation, when local political elites prioritize in the sense of supporting and sustaining a policy of re-approaching the neighboring area to the municipality with the purpose of furthering economic development. This developmental strategy was intrinsic, though not always explicit, for such municipalities as Tecuci, Targovishte, and Česká Lípa. When discussing the drafting of local agenda of priorities, the Local / Municipal Council, as a whole, should be considered as well. Eulau and Prewitt identify, in this respect, governing "styles" (i.e. "the informal ways in which the council approaches its governing tasks") and "practices"; the latter refer to "exchange", "bargaining", "compromise", "coalition formation", and "ministration" (Eulau and Prewitt 1973: 109-113). "Cosponsorship", "opinion leadership", "friendship", "respect", "expertise", "opposition potential", "stratification" are only five examples of the Local Council's relational properties of political import. The governing styles identified by the two American scholars for Local / Municipal Councils are: (1) the "benevolent" style (a "residual" type, imbedded in the fiber of the "nonpartisan" local politics, according to which the "council works for the good of the city and its citizens; its work is a public service and serving on the council is not a matter of self-interest; the council is open to suggestions from its members, the city staff, and local citizens, but though responsive, it leaves the initiative to others"), (2) the "pragmatic" style (in which the Council's emphasis in decision-making lies on "planning, meeting problems before they arise, following external standards, and coming to efficient, economically sound, and technically competent decisions"), (3) the "political" style (according to which the Council is perceived by its members as "an arena in which a political game is played, where advantages may be derived from going along or obstructing, where differences in *status* and power are seen as important, where there is more emphasis on policy payoffs that may benefit the individual councilman or his particular clientele") (Eulau and Prewitt 1973: 119-120). Partial examples for the "benevolent" style of local leadership were the Municipal Councils in Oleśnica and Levice; examples for the "pragmatic" style of local leadership were the Municipal Council in Česká Lípa and the Body of Representatives in Gyula, whereas examples for the "political" style of local leadership were the Local Councils in Tecuci and Targovishte.

In one of the most empirically compelling and theoretically comprehensive case-studies on local government in East-Central Europe, the book authored by Martin Hořák presents generally the distribution of competences between the two main tiers of administration, central and local, following the initiation of the democratic transition process:

> "In the sphere of social services including health, welfare, and education, responsibilities are usually shared with the national government, although the degree of municipal responsibility varies across the region. [...] In all cases, however, national governments have retained significant control over the regulation of service standards, so municipalities typically have little say in policy making. By contrast, in the sphere of physical goods and services – such as physical planning, roads, and public infrastructure – local councils often have primary responsibility for policymaking as well as delivery [...]." (Hořák 2007: 29)

Nevertheless, in practice, the distribution seemed distorted from "the norm", because local councilors in the six countries under scrutiny here seemed preoccupied of and particularly focused on social services, education, and cultural activities in the communities they governed; the focus on infrastructural developments and planning represented only partial exceptions for the Czech, the Slovak, and the Polish cases. Engaged in a comparative endeavor on local government in Western Europe, Chandler explains the general prioritization path at the local level: "Local authorities, therefore, tend to be responsible for tasks such as social services, education, housing and recreation." (Chandler 1993: 191) Indeed, this was substantiated by the findings in this study, which reiterated the overwhelming focus of the members of the six Local / Municipal Councils on matters of social welfare, education, recreation, and culture. Hence, it appeares that, as a rule, the local authorities are to perform efficiently and effectively in those rather "soft" spheres of activity. Nevertheless, the tendency towards improvements in "hard" spheres of activities among the members of the Municipal Councils of those more decentralized towns (Oleśnica, Česká Lípa, and, to some extent, Levice) was evident, especially in opposition to the inclination of the local councilors of less decentralized towns (primarily, Tecuci and Targovishte) for "soft" spheres: indicators of political responsiveness for the latter were coalesced around cultural and recreational activities, whereas the former diverged towards infrastructural improvements, education, social services. The distribution of political responsibility and political responsiveness is heavily influenced by the level of decentralization characteristic to a community, to the degree of discretion a local elected official or a civil servant is allowed, to the budgetary capacity a municipality can independently create.

Representativeness of the Local / Municipal Council

One of the central issues observed by the present research project is the degree in which the local representatives, the elected members of the Local / Munici-pal Council were truly representative for the entire population of the town, for their electorate. The representativeness was analyzed by Peterson, by consid-ering three dimensions: formal representation, descriptive (passive) represen-tation, substantive (active) representation (Peterson 1970: 491). In fact, through the legitimacy granted by the electorate and its vote, a public official is considered "the representative" of a certain constituency. This is formal rep-resentation. Being elected by the inhabitants of Tecuci, Česká Lípa, Oleśnica, Gyula, Levice, or Targovishte, all the members of the six Local / Municipal Councils, were representatives of the citizens of Tecuci, Česká Lípa, Oleśnica, Gyula, Levice, and Targovishte, respectively. Passive (descriptive) represen-tation represents the main focus of the present section of the research. It refers to the socio-demographical resemblance between the electorate and the mem-bers of the Local Council; according to such principle of representation, the public officials are representative for the citizens only if they bear similar oc-cupational statuses, places of birth, gender, age, economic statuses, educational levels with the different segments of the electorate. The Local Council should, hence, be a socio-demographical mirror of the population of the town. Finally, the substantive (active) representation defines representation through the sim-ilarities of perception, views, attitudes, opinions, between the electorate and the elected officials. All opinions existing in the community should be properly represented within the Local Council. Lester Seligman differentiates between "symbolic" and "instrumental" representation (Seligman 1971: 16), in which the "symbolic" representation describes a formal form of delegating political power to the would-be "political elite", while "instrumental" representation re-fers to the active, executive type, in which the citizen, being unable to exercise comprehensive political power, due to various, countless reasons, transfers his share of the *res publica* to a representative, in a "minimalist", "procedural", Schumpeterian fashion.

The "representative process" or the process of representation is "better to the extent that it establishes and renews connection between constituents and representative[s], and among members of the constituency" (Young 2000: 128 [additions mine]). Jane Mansbridge advances one of the most important and comprehensive refinements of the classical theories of representation, by dis-tinguishing among four types of representation (Mansbridge 2003: 515-528; see, also, more frequently cited, Mansbridge 1998): (1) "promissory represen-tation" (i.e. the classical, traditional, typical model of representation, in which "the principal", the elector, keeps some measure of control over "the agent", the elected, the ruler; the *criteria* for democratic accountability are "singular", "dyadic", "aggregative" (Mansbridge 2003: 515), and district-based; the concept of power is perceived through a "forward-looking intentionality" (Mansbridge 2003: 516); the "mandate" view of the representative in Manin, Przeworski, and Stokes 1991: 29-54); (2) "anticipatory representation" (i.e. a model of representation in which "the agent", the representative, "tries to please the voter not of the past but of the future" (Mansbridge 2003: 517), hence, thinking about the "retrospective voting" the "agent" undertakes in elections; the concept of power is perceived through a "backward-looking" reaction; the "accountability" view of the representative in Manin et al., or similar to Arnold's "alternative control model" (Arnold 1993/1977: 401-416), though more "interactive and more continually reflexive" (Mansbridge 2003: 515); the *criteria* for democratic accountability appropriate for this type of representation are "systemic", "deliberative", and "plural" (Mansbridge 2003: 515); the "agent" educates, even manipulates, the "principle", the dialogue between the two being constant); (3) "self-referential representation" or "gyroscopic representation" (i.e. a model of representation similar to Bernstein's "initial selection" (Bernstein 1989), Kingdon's "representation by recruitment" (Kingdon 1981), or Stimson, MacKuen, and Erikson's "electoral replacement" (1995: 543-565)[79]: a model in which "voters [s]elect representatives who, *without* external incentives, can be relatively accurately assumed to act in ways the voter approves" (Mansbridge 2003: 520 [italics in original, additions mine]), essentially the opposite model to the "anticipatory" one; the "agent", the representative is not primarily accountable to his / her constituency, to the voters, but rather to his / her own beliefs, principles, convictions; the *criteria* for democratic accountability – or, more accurately, predictability – appropriate for this type of representation are equally "systemic", "deliberative", and "plural", and consist in: "deliberation at authorization", "ease of maintenance and removal", and "legislative deliberation" (Mansbridge 2003: 522) and discretion; in a sub-model of "self-referential representation", labeled "party discipline" sub-model, the representative guides his / her actions according to the set of principles or commitments imposed by the party to which (s)he adheres; different from both Burke's "mandate" or "trustee" form of representation, because it puts a great emphasis not on the "statesman" characteristic of the representative, but rather on specific personal, ethical features the representative possesses; the dialogue "principal" – "agent" is nonexistent); (4) "surrogate representation" (i.e. a model of representation in which "the principal" has no constituency or electoral relation with "the agent"; essentially, "non-territorial"

---

79 For Stimson et al., "dynamic representation" implies that "[i]f public opinion changes and then public policy responds", something, to some extent, similar to Mansbridge's "anticipatory representation". Two mechanisms of policy responsiveness are identified: (a) "elections change the government's political composition, which is then reflected in new policy", and (b) "policymakers calculate future (mainly electoral) implications of current public views and act accordingly" (p. 543).

representation; "collective representation" in Weissberg (1978: 535-547), or "institutional representation" in Jackson and King (1989: 1143-1164), or, to some extent, "virtual representation" in Burke; a model of representation based fundamentally on "contributors" (in money), not on "voters", for the accountability relationship is inexistent between "the agent" and the "surrogate constituency", though it can be turned into "responsibility", if the latter is formed of a minority identifiable with the former; a type of representation meant to resolve two democratic shortcomings: (a) "adversary fairness" – i.e. "providing proportional representation to conflicting interests" –, and (b) "deliberative efficacy" – i.e. "providing some representation for relevant perspectives on a decision" (Mansbridge 2003: 524); the *criteria* for democratic accountability appropriate for this type of representation are, yet again, "systemic", "deliberative", and "plural").

More recently, Wessels distinguishes three levels of representation, based on the question regarding whom the representative addresses: (1) "the geographical dimension", (2) "the group dimension" (from religious and ethnic, to economic or ideological groups), and (3) "the individual dimension" (Wessels 2007: 839). In the specific case of the study of the six municipalities, a mixture of geographical representation (expressed under the form of cultural-geographical self-identification of the municipal councilors), and group representation (expressed under the form of the local councilors' contacts and interactions with other groups) was considered by this study.

When questioning and measuring degrees of representativeness, the most frequently cited name is that of British scholar J. Donald Kingsley, one of the first to comprehensively discuss the concept of "representative bureaucracy". His contribution, dated 1944, concludes that "[n]o group can safely be entrusted with power who do not themselves mirror the dominant forces in society" (Kingsley 1944: 282), who do not "share the same backgrounds and hold similar social views" (Kingsley 1944: 273) with the people represented, for, generally, this social representativeness would easily entail more responsible and responsive public officials towards the public needs, political desires and grievances of the electorate[80]. Nonetheless, Kingsley's work is dedicated to the public servants in governmental agencies in highly developed, consolidated democracies (such as Great Britain, a well-known "class-based society", resulting in a similarly "class-based politics"), without actually covering the problem of representation and representativeness for "elected officials" (i.e. those directly responsive to and responsible in front of the people) in consolidating democracies (i.e. those democracies without a very clearly distinguishable middle class, but with a quite clear gap between the lower and the upper

---

80 Even though it concerns the "bureaucracy" in its classical sense – and, thusly, it does not refer specifically to the issue of representativeness of the "elected official" –, the account in Coleman Selden 1997, presents a genuinely important contribution to the study of representation, representativeness and responsiveness.

class). The conditions of democracy are different for Kingsley's discussion and the one proposed here, determining seemingly different interpretations and accounts on the concepts revolving around "representation". This observation holds true in all the other explorations of the 1940s and the 1950s on representation "soil": David Levitan, for instance, develops on the *desideratum* of socio-demographic representation in post-war United States, among the public bureaucracy, leading to a more favorable citizenry towards the activity of governmental agencies, oftentimes perceived as intrusive (Levitan 1946: 562-598; see, esp. 570-591); Norton Long, while studying the same post-war American bureaucracy (Long 2010/1949: 97-104), comes to the conclusion that increased socio-demographic representation leads to increasing discretion granted to the group displaying such a degree of representation in respect to the *populus*, making the group more accessible in the citizens' eyes; a renowned scholar of public administration, Paul Van Riper tentatively assumes that

> "when civil servants hold attitudes similar to those of the people whom they represent, their decisions will resemble decisions those they represent would have made under comparable circumstances." (Van Riper 1958, quoted in Coleman Selden 1997: 72)

It was only in the 1980s that the distinction employed in this book had been advanced: Frederick Mosher differentiates between "passive" and "active" representation (Mosher 1982). As will be elaborated further, "passive representation" hints to "the origin of individuals and the degree to which, collectively, they mirror the whole society" (Mosher 1982: 12), namely a simple measurement of indices of: education, family income, family social class, race, religion, father's occupation, etc. On the other hand, "active representation" points to "the interests and the desires of groups" to which a certain sociodemographic similarity is shared by the ones in power. While the "passive" representation is retained as supreme by Mosher over the "active" one and the link between the two types is intrinsically presupposed – i.e. a certain socioeconomic background is prone to determine a certain kind of value, attitude, and behavioral orientation –, the distinction becomes prominent in public administration studies only with its development by Kenneth J. Meier, who suggests that a passively representative elite (or, more generically, holders of power) intrinsically suggests a symbolic dedication to equality and to the equal accession to power[81]. In the same line, Guinier argues that passive representativeness implies at least the fact that certain segments of the elite group had experienced the same type of socialization as the analogous segments in the population (Guinier 1994), which would, in turn, mean that the gap between the rulers and the ruled is somewhat overcome through a seemingly shared set

---

81 The same conjecture has been supported by Gallas 1985: 25-31; Wise 1990: 567-575; and Kellough 1990: 83-92, although all contributions refer to the state apparatus, not the elected officials.

of values and attitudes prescribing for predictable behaviors in decision-making. Nevertheless, lacking any statistical or empirical backing for the perceived connection between social background, values and attitudes, and behavior, or, else, between "passive" and "active" representation of the elite in respect to its "constituency", the direct evidence of this link has been constantly challenged and under intense scrutiny. Hence, as regards the conceptions of "representation" and "representativeness", following Sally Coleman Selden, three "ages" can be distinguished in the study thereof: (a) the focus on "passive" (demographic) representation[82], as buster of democratic practice, through various empirical research on race, sex, age, place of birth, education, etc. (e.g. the famous investigations on employment levels in public bodies of women and individuals belonging to different ethnic minority groups); (b) the focus on those "policy-relevant" attitudinal orientations prone to predict or to provide an explanation for various elite behaviors on the public scene (i.e. the age in which "active" representativeness" begins to take precedence over the "passive" one, in what concerns the studies of representation)[83]; (3) the focus on explaining the connection between "passive" and "active" representativeness[84], in the case of "policy outputs and outcomes" (Coleman Selden 1997: 44).

Although the focus on "active" representativeness can indicate, to a greater extent, explanations and interpretations for policy orientations and agenda setting, the predilection of exploring indicators of "passive" representativeness – indeed, easier to operate in the process of data collection and data analysis – becomes of prime importance when inquiring into those "characteristics [that] are politically relevant" (Pitkin 1967: 87) for elite reproduction. This was, *inter alia*, one of the objectives of the first part of the empirical inquiry of this book, namely the identification of those features and traits, at the level of personal biographies, an individual should possess in order to be a member of the local political elite. This book employs the "representation index" to measure passive representativeness, simply computed as follows:

---

82 Illustrative for this "age" are: Dye and Renick 1981: 475-486; Eisinger 1982: 380-392; Welch, Karnig, and Eribes 1983: 660-673; Stein 1985: 78-89; Stein 1986: 694-713; Stein 1994: 181-191; Riccucci 1986: 3-15; Saltzstein 1986: 140-164; Mladenka 1989: 391-407; Mladenka 1989: 165-191; Mladenka 1991: 532-548; Kellough 1990: 557-566; Kellough and Elliot 1992: 1-11; Kim 1993: 52-66; Kim and Mengistu 1994: 161-179; Cornwell and Kellough 1994: 265-270; Lewis and Nice 1994: 393-410.

83 The most representative attempts for this "age" of studies on representation are: Garnham 1975: 44-51; Meier and Nigro 1976: 458-469; Rosenbloom and Featherstonhaugh 1977: 878-882; Rosenbloom and Kinnard 1977: 35-60; Thompson 1978: 325-347.

84 Commonly cited studies for this orientation in the general "representation studies" branch are, among others: Meier and Stewart, Jr. 1992: 157-171; Meier 1993: 393-414; Hindera 1990; Hindera 1993: 95-108; Hindera 1993: 415-429.

representation index

$$= \frac{\% \; of \; a \; group \; within \; the \; elite \; group \; (i.\, e.\, Municipal \; Council)}{\% \; of \; a \; group \; within \; the \; relevant \; population}$$

The present research limits its observations only to the descriptive representation of the Local Councils in Tecuci and Targovishte, of the Municipal Councils in Česká Lípa, Oleśnica, and Levice, and of the Body of Representatives in Gyula, emphasizing the similarities and differences between the socio-demographical features of the local councilors and the electorate (i.e. the populations of Tecuci, Česká Lípa, Oleśnica, Gyula, Levice, and Targovishte, respectively). Hence, the following characteristics were taken into account when sketching the degree of representativeness of the Local Council: nationality, gender, level of education, age, religion, matrimonial status and place of birth.

a) Nationality[85]

The towns of Tecuci, Česká Lípa, Oleśnica, and Gyula, are highly homogenous in respect to ethnic structure of the population: 96.13% of the population living in Tecuci is Romanian, 93.06% of the population in Česká Lípa is Czech, 87% of the population living in Oleśnica is Polish, 83.4% of the population living in Gyula is Hungarian. In Tecuci, the largest minority is represented by the Roma population, but even the Roma community accounts for only 3.65% of the total population. As a consequence, the Local Council of Tecuci was, in its entirety, of Romanian nationality. Even though the Roma minority was not represented in the Council, the representation of nationality of the electorate was fairly expressed in the Council. In Česká Lípa, the largest minority is the Slovaks, but they represent a feeble 2.07% of the population. Even so, the Slovak minority was the only one represented in the Municipal Council, enjoying a slightly overrepresentation of 8% of the members of the Municipal Council, the rest of 92% being, as expected, of Czech nationality. All the members of the Municipal Council in Oleśnica were Polish, although the population of the town comprises small communities of Germans (the ones remaining in Poland, after the so-called "Recovered Territories", in which Oleśnica is situated, were given to post-war Poland), of Tatars and Lithuanians (more or less forcefully moved to these territories during the communist dictatorship), but, given the small magnitude of these communities, they were not represented in the Municipal Council.

The case of Hungary is particularly important in accommodating the needs and representing the interests of the ethnic minorities at the local level, through

85   See Annexes No. 4.1.

the setting up of a system of consultative councils of minority groups. Their importance in local decision-making is subject to debates, in the everyday practice of local government in Hungary, the focus of their contribution being especially linked to cultural events and the promotion of minority rights locally. For the municipality of Gyula, all the members of the Body of Representatives were Hungarians; the other nationalities of the town – Romanians (3.1% of the population, due primarily to the geographical proximity to Romania), Germans (3.1% of the population), and Roma (0.3% of the population of the town) – were not represented in the local legislative assembly, exactly because mechanisms of representation for national minorities exised by the means of the above-mentioned local "consultative councils".

Taking into consideration its positioning in the country (i.e. several miles from the Hungarian border), and its history (the town has been part of Hungary, up to the Treaty of Trianon, and again, between 1938 to 1945, with a population of 89% Hungarian, at the time when it was restored to Czechoslovakia), Levice cannot pretend to be a neatly homogeneous community in ethnic terms: although 77.66% of the population in the town is Slovak, there is also an important Hungarian community (comprising 9.13% of Levice's population), and an equally significant group of what has been labeled in the Slovak census *data* as "unidentified" (11.57%, i.e. people who either refused to mentioned their ethnicity or they do not subscribed to a strict ethnic categorization). This group might be problematic in statistics, but it represents quite an interesting trend (dominantly, indeed, in Western Europe) of referring to ethnicity and national identity in rather "postmodern" (i.e. fluid, evanescent) terms. Within the Municipal Council, two members (Gabriel Földi and Štefan Kalocsay) had Hungarian roots, which resulted in a 8% representation of the Hungarian minority in the Council, a proportion closely resembling the proportion in the overall population of the town. The other ten groups present in the ethnic structure of the town were not represented in the Municipal Council.

A significant demographic characteristic of Targovishte is an important migration of ethnic Turks from the region of Targovishte, which resulted in an increasingly homogenized population in the town, from an ethnic point of view: in a particularly destabilizing and disturbing demographic situation, 79.4% of the population in the town is Bulgarian, whereas the remaining Turkish minority gathers only 17.7% of the community. Even in the context of a perpetually declining minority, Targovishte is the most ethnically heterogeneous town among the six cases analyzed here: the Roma community comprises 1.8% of the population, while other ethnic groups, together with the non-definable and the "undeclared", make up 5.3% of the town's population. Due to the traditional importance of the Turkish minority for the town, this ethnic group – despite the fact that the Bulgarian constitutional makeup does not allow for the political expression of ethnic minorities – was overrepresented within the Municipal Council of Targovishte: 36.36% of the members of the

Council were representatives of the Turkish minority, although the proportion of this minority in the constituency is below 18%.

b)   Gender[86]

The situation was completely different in the case of representativeness of the six Local Councils based on gender differences. Discrepancies were more obvious for Tecuci and Targovishte: while around 52% of the electorate is female, in the two Councils only 21.05%, and 21.21%, respectively, of the members were women. The conspicuous disparities were somehow attenuated in the case of Česká Lípa: 51.41% of the population of the town is female and in the Council 40% of the seats were held by women. The improvement in Česká Lípa was evident and important, the highest representation of women among the six cases. Overall, even though an increasingly significant proportion, the women remain under-represented in politics, even at the local level.

The representation of women in the Council of Levice failed to score a record among the selected cases: 29.16% of the Council's membership was composed of women (whereas 52.36% of the population is composed of women), a ratio that placed Levice within the average representation of women in the Municipal Council among the six cases selected here. Hence, demographically, the representativeness among the female population of the town was lacking in this case, as in the other five cases: 52.36% of the population of Levice is constituted by women, which generated a clear underrepresentation for this demographic sector.

The same disparities of female underrepresentation in the Municipal Council were preserved in the case of the local legislative assemblies in Oleśnica and Gyula, in which the lowest female representation was sadly achieved: for Oleśnica, 19.04% of the Municipal Council was composed of women, whereas the town's population comprises 52.4% women; for Gyula, while 52.36% of the population of the town is represented by women, only 14.28% were represented in the Body of Representatives, the local legislative body with the lowest representation of women among the six cases under scrutiny.

---

86   See Annexes No. 4.3.

c)   Educational level[87]

In Tecuci, the population of the town displays a complex distribution, on multiple layers, of the educational level. The electorate contains: the segment of those who have only a primary education (16.81% of the total population); the segment of those who have only an inferior secondary education (*gymnasium*) (21.93% of the population); the segment of those who graduated high-school or professional studies (41.8% of the population); the small percentage of those who graduated post-high-school studies of various types (4.14%); another, small, part of intellectuals (accounting for only 7.47% of the population of the town) and, at the opposite side, the segment of those who have no graduated level of education and the illiterates (7.79%). The educational structure of the Local Council was simpler, hence excluding from representation many of the categories mentioned above, on different basis (for instance, it is clear why the small segment of the illiterates or that of those with a primary education cannot be represented in the Council). In the Council, 89.48% of the members were intellectuals – as opposed to 7.47% in the population – which indicated an evident overrepresentation of those who had graduated university studies. Only 10.52% of the local councilors had a superior secondary education (high school or professional-technical studies), while, in the population, this category represents actually the most significant part, from an educational perspective (41.8%). One observation could be drawn from this distribution: even though the public position they occupy (that of members in the Local Council) does not require necessarily a superior education, the local councilors (and their selectorates, as well) perceive the level of university studies as a *sine qua non* condition for acquiring and being effective in that official position. This is mainly the reason why large segments of the town's population are under-represented in the Council or are simply not represented at all.

In the Czech Republic, the educational system comprises several subsequent layers of training and advance expertise, a system that is translated for the town of Česká Lípa in the following fashion: the layer of those who have no graduated level of education (0.37% of the total population of the town); the layer of those who have only a primary education (24.13% of the population); the layer of the secondary education, subdivided in those who graduated superior secondary education (high-school studies; 39.83% of the population) and those who graduated only inferior secondary education (gymnasium: 24.31%); the layer of the post-high-school studies (3.13% of the population), and finally, the layer of those who graduated superior or advanced studies (university studies: only 6.74% of the population). As in the case of Tecuci, there was no surprise that some of these layers had no representation in the Municipal Council (those with no graduated studies, those who graduated only

---

87   See Annexes No. 4.5.

216

primary or inferior secondary studies). What was, nevertheless, striking was the fact that those who graduated from superior secondary education (high-school, vocational, trade, professional studies) were virtually not represented: while this is the segment that constitutes, educationally, the majority of the electorate in Česká Lípa (64.14%), in the Council it was dramatically underrepresented by only 4% of the members. Instead, those holding a diploma from an institution of higher education were clearly overrepresented in the Municipal Council. Moreover, the Municipal Council of Česká Lípa bore an even major discrepancy in terms of educational representativeness: not only that the overwhelming majority had graduated from university studies (i.e. the B.A. studies), but 28% of the total number of municipal councilors were graduates from Master's programmes, 12% were "*MUDr.*", i.e. in the Czech educational system, a type of post-graduate diploma, superior to the Master's one, yet not PhD, and 4% (the psychologist in the Council, Miloslav Hudec) were "*PhDr*". Hence, the gap between the Municipal Council and the population of Česká Lípa was conspicuous regarding educational status, pointing to the fact that the municipal councilors became increasingly specialized, on the trend of technocratic politics, but with rather symbolic representation for the socio-demographical characteristics of the population they represented.

In the Slovak Republic, the educational layers include a pre-university training that is quite unique in its organization, and a university training whose system of degrees is resembling the Czech one. "Basic" education refers to the graduation of at least eight grades; this educational level is specific to 10.61% of the population of the town. Under the general umbrella of "training" (gathering 11.9% of the town's population), people of no particular school-attending education are statistically gathered, whereas "vocational training" consists in those forms of instructions focused on practical aspects (e.g. veterinary technician, hair stylist, mechanic, craftsman, nurse, etc.), following the basic training, and encompassing no more than three years; "vocational training" is particular to 8.01% of the population of Levice. "Full secondary vocational (with GCSE)" level is generally the higher continuation of the vocational training, after the age of 14-16 years old, in disciplines such as pedagogy or theology, an educational level generally assimilated in the secondary education; full secondary vocational (with GCSE) level has been graduated by 2.65% of the town's population. "Secondary (with GCSE)" level (the instruction graduated by the majority of the population of Levice, 22.05%, similarly to the other cases analyzed here) represents the high-school education, of either humanistic and social sciences, or mathematically-associated and natural sciences, a four-year instruction finalized with a rigorous, thorough examination (similar to the GCSE in the United Kingdom or the baccalaureate on the continent). "General secondary" comprises high-school attendees, of theoretical training, who have not passed a final examination; in the population of Levice, the ratio of these individuals is only 6.67%. The label "high professional education" considers post-secondary, post-high-school studies of vocational character (usually, in medicine or in military), characteristic for only 2.29% of the population of Levice. Finally, the tertiary level of education is composed of: Bachelor graduates (4.1% of the population), Masters' graduates (15.07%), and PhDs (0.66%), resulting in a total of 19.83% of the population of Levice being university trained, clearly the highest percentage among the six cases. On the other hand, the proportion of inhabitants with no formal schooling (16.23%) is the highest in Levice among the six cases. In this respect, Levice presents a disparity that can only be explained through social-economic and cultural inquiries exceeding the scope of the present research. These educational *strata* in the population of Levice were only partially represented in the membership of the Municipal Council. As in other cases, the tertiary education was clearly overrepresented: the case of Česká Lípa was, to some extent, replicated, in the case of Levice, the gap between "the rulers" and "the ruled" in terms of education being significant and a particular mark of "elite distinctiveness", since the large majority of the members of the Municipal Council in Levice were graduates of post-university or advanced university studies, Masters' or PhD programmes.

Probably the most important demographic characteristic of recent years Targovishte is an impressive increase in the educational level of the population. The presence in the Municipal Council of highly educated individuals in the community was no surprise: evidently, "[i]t is little wonder then that intellectuals in political parties and movements occupy such a prominent position: they possess skills which mesh neatly with the oligarchical demands of complex organization" (Brym 1980: 36), for indeed, the Municipal Council in Targovishte remotely resembled a local oligarchy. The graduates of university studies were clearly overrepresented in the Local Council (81.81% of the members were university trained), but graduates of superior post-secondary, especially technical, studies in the population of the town were overrepresented, as well, since 6.06% of the members of the Council had graduated post-high-school education. Professional studies were fairly represented, as well, in the Council of Targovishte, as 12.12% of the councilors were professionally trained as mechanics. The fact that other educational levels received passive representation in the Local Council, in the case of Targovishte, could be the expression of accessibility of local politics for other than university trained individuals.

A fair representation of post-high-school studies (7.14% of the municipal councilors) was to be found in the case of the Body of Representatives in Gyula. Although both the Municipal Council in Oleśnica and the Body of Representatives in Gyula maintained the overrepresentation of university-trained segment in the populations of the two towns (66.66% of the Polish councilors, and 92.85% of the Hungarian councilors), in the case of the Council in Oleśnica, high-school graduates, although constituting the majority in the population of the town, received only a 19.04% representation in the Council, whereas the quite sporadic group of graduates of post-secondary studies were overrepresented (14.28% of the membership of the Municipal Council).

d)   Age[88]

The age category most represented in the Local Council of Tecuci was that of 50 to 59 years old (36.84% of the members of the Local Council), followed closely by that of 40 to 49 years old (31.57%). Actually, due to a process which is peculiar to small, provincial communities in Romania – i.e. the aging of the population –, there was a largely fair representation of age variable in the Council, as the second most numerous segment of age in the electorate is that of 50 to 59 years old (15.49% of the population). In the case of 70-79 age category, the representation of the electorate in the Local Council was extremely exact (from a proportional stance): around 5% in both the electorate and in the Local Council. On the other hand, it should be observed that there was virtually no representation of 20-29 age category in the Local Council, even though this category accounts for 16.65% of the town's population, while 30-39 age category was clearly underrepresented (in the population, this segment accounts for 17.2% of the population, in the Council it represented only 5.26% of the members). A slight overrepresentation of 60-69 age category was observed, as well: even though only 8.55% of the population of the town, this segment represented 21.05% of the local councilors. This situation was the result of the patterns of recruitment used by the selectorates, who considered that a stable socio-economic situation of the candidates to a seat in the Local Council could be acquired only with a certain age, after a certain time in which the candidates started to enjoy reputation, prestige and a significant degree of popular trust and support. The younger persons were perceived as still not ready to join the group of the local political elite.

Česká Lípa is among the four urban areas in the Czech Republic where the proportion of elders (over 65 years old) exceeds 10% of the population; it is actually considered one of the most "age friendly" towns in Europe. Within the Municipal Council, nonetheless, this age segment lacked proper representation: only 12% of the municipal councilors were over 60 years old. On the other hand, there was a significant overrepresentation of the category 50-59 years old (only 12.46% in the electorate and 40% in the Council), but this was clearly due to the party selectorates' stratagems). But, most importantly, as opposed to the case of the Local Council in Tecuci, the age categories of young people (especially 20-29 and 30-39), though underrepresented in absolute

---

88   See Annexes No. 4.4.

values, enjoyed a significant representation of 32% of the members of the Municipal Council of Česká Lípa. This situation pointed to a more open-minded approach in selecting candidates at the local level, a more democratic one. Finally, the age category 40-49 was probably the fairest represented in the Municipal Council (14.75% of the population of the town and 16% of the members of the Municipal Council).

Although the average age for the town of Oleśnica is slightly below 40 years old, average age in the Municipal Council of the town was 51.35, a significant age gap between the population and the Council. Needless to say, younger segments in the population were not represented in the legislative *forum*, for only 30-39 years old age segment (14.28% of the members of the Council), 40-49 years old age segment (the largest proportion of the Council: 38.09% of the members of the Council, neatly overrepresented, since the percentage in the total population of the town is only 12.72%), 50-59 years old age segment (clearly overrepresented: 28.57% of the membership of the Council, in comparison to 13.52% in the population), and 60-69 years old age segment (19.04% of the Council's membership) were represented effectively in the Municipal Council of Oleśnica. The age category 20-29 years old, the second most important age category in the population of Oleśnica (23.72% of the population) had no representation in the Council, whereas the most significant age segment in the population, 30-39 years old (17.2% in the population), was slightly underrepresented. By contrast, a slight overrepresentation of the age category 60-69 years old in the Council (since the same age category in the population is around 12.69%) pointed to the fact that both the selectorates and, most importantly, the electorate, preferred a mature local legislative assembly in Oleśnica. Not too mature, though, since the age categories 70-79 years old (6.98% of the total population of the town), and over 80 years old (3.62% of the total population) lacked representation in the Municipal Council. It was important, though, that the Polish case allowed for a more visible representation of the age segment 30-39 years old, the most active category in the work field.

The image of a mature, responsible, well-tempered individual, for the leadership of a rather traditional, small community (as is, generally, the case for all the six towns under scrutiny here) was preserved in the Slovak case also: the age representativeness was by no means fairer, for the age segments of 49 to 69 year-old dominated the membership of the Municipal Council in Levice. Nonetheless, the Municipal Council in Levice recorded the lowest average age among the six cases: 48.5 years old, allowing a feeble representation for those age categories below 50 years old in the population of the town.

The Body of Representatives in Gyula, as well, had one of the lowest average age among the six Councils scrutinized in this book: 50.1 years old. As a matter of fact, the representative assembly in the Hungarian case presented the most uniformly, indeed, representative instance, in terms of age distribution: the most important segment in the population of Gyula, 50-59 years old (15.6% of the population) was slightly overrepresented in Municipal Council, but its representation was fair, since, due to the phenomenon of ageing, especially in smaller towns of East-Central Europe, this particular age category became dominant in the public life of Gyula. Surprisingly, there was a slight underrepresentation for the age category of 40-49 years old (13.2% of the population), but the younger categories (20-29 years old – 10.7% of the population of Gyula –, and 30-39 years old – 14.4% of the population, the second most important segment) received virtually no representation in the Body of Representatives.

Finally, for the Local Council of Targovishte, the overrepresentation of 50-59 years old and 60-69 years old age categories was conspicuous. As a matter of fact, the representative assembly in Targovishte presented one of the highest average age for the six cases: 51.6 years, meaning both that the accession to power at the local level was more difficult for young people in the Bulgarian case, and that important age segments in the population of the town were left completely unrepresented in the age make-up of the Council of Targovishte. Again, it was the case of the age categories of 20-29 years old (12.05% of the population of the town) and 30-39 years old (15.22% of the population, the second most significant age group in the town's demographics). The most important age segment in Targovishte, that of 40-49 years old (16.04% of the total population), received an overrepresentation in the Local Council of Targovishte.

e)   Religion[89]

As in the case of nationality, Tecuci and Oleśnica are highly homogeneous regarding their religious structure: 98.32% of the population in Tecuci is Christian-Orthodox, whereas 96% of the population in Oleśnica is Roman-Catholics. No surprise that 100% of the local councilors in Tecuci were themselves Christian-Orthodox, while 71.42% of the municipal councilors in Oleśnica identified themselves as "Roman-Catholics". As a result, largely, there was a fair representation of the religion of the population in the Local Council of Tecuci, and the Municipal Council of Oleśnica. For the Municipal Council of Oleśnica, the fair representation of the Roman-Catholics in the local legislative assembly was evident: Although a highly homogeneous town in terms of religious affiliations, the population of Oleśnica includes small communities of Catholic-Byzantine Ukrainians, religious groups belonging to the Polish

---

89 See Annexes No. 4.2.

Orthodox Church, a Lutheran community, and Neo-protestant groups, especially Pentecostals.

On the other hand, the Czech Republic is famously known for being one of the countries which register an atheist majority. Therefore, one can state that in Česká Lípa, there is a homogeneity in religious terms, since 78.85% of the population declared itself as "atheist". This segment was, as expected, somehow overrepresented within the Municipal Council, with 84% of the councilors being atheist. A surprisingly fair representation of the Roman-Catholic minority (9.77% of the total population of Česká Lípa) was to be noticed within the Council: up to 16% of the councilors were believers, Roman-Catholic. Other confessions (e.g. Hussite Church, Church of the Czech Brothers, Jehova Witnesses Church, Orthodox Church, etc.) with less than 2% within the total population of the town were not represented in the Municipal Council.

The Body of Representatives in Gyula only partially mirrored the religious diversity of the town. The largest proportion of the population identifies itself as "irreligious" (26.7%), with no stable or clear religious affiliation. This group received a fair representation in the representative body of the town, where 21.42% of the municipal councilors declared no religious affiliation. Apart from "irreligious", another 1.5% of the population of Gyula is atheist, although this group had no representation in the Council, even if the town is especially fragmented in terms of confessional affiliations. The second and the third largest religious groups in the town, the Roman-Catholics (18.4% of the population) and Protestant-Calvinist (17.9% of the population), were, expectedly, overrepresented in the Body of Representatives of Gyula: 35.71% of the membership of the local representative assembly was Catholics, and another 35.71% of the municipal councilors were Protestant-Calvinist. The Lutherans in Gyula were slightly overrepresented (1.6% in the population, compared to 7.14% in the Body of Representatives), whereas the small Orthodox community in the town (comprised mostly of the Romanian minority) lacked representation in the local assembly. Given the religious diversity (or fragmentation) in the town of Gyula, its Body of Representatives provided a relatively fair passive representativeness.

The religious distribution in the town of Levice comprises a majority of Roman-Catholics (50.39% of the population), followed by a significant group of atheists (22.55% of the population) and an equally important segment of Neo-protestant practicing Christians (from Baptists, Chrismatic, Pentecostals, to Jehovah's Witnesses and Adventists of the 7th Day – a total of 14.72% of the population of Levice). Other small religious groups in Levice are: the Protestant-Calvinists (6.22% of the population), the Protestant-Lutherans (3.53%), the Moravian Brethren (1.4%), the Greek Catholics (0.34%), a movement called "*Modrý kríž*" (Blue Cross) (0.26% of the population in Levice, but quite specific to Slovakia), Muslims, Jewish (around 0.55% of the total population of the town). This religious diversity was only partly represented in the

Municipal Council of Levice. The religious group of Catholics was overtly overrepresented in the Municipal Council of Levice, where 75% of the members were themselves Catholics. As in all the cases in which this group was to be found in the religious composition of the town, the atheists were underrepresented, as only 8.33% of the membership of the Council in Levice was atheist. The Calvinists were surprisingly overrepresented in the Municipal Council, 12.5% of its membership adhering to this confessional group. The representation of Neo-protestants in the Council of Levice was, to some extent, surprising: though clearly underrepresented, the Neo-protestants received a 4.16% demographic representation in the local assembly. In spite of the fact the other religious groups were not passively represented in the Municipal Council of Levice, it is encouraging that the Neo-protestants (religious groups that enjoy an increase in membership in East-Central Europe, chiefly due to their strong proselytism) managed to penetrate local political leadership. The philosophy of most of the Neo-protestant groups is rather redistributive, which would have added to the local political elite in Levice a more left-wing stance in decision-making.

Within the Local Council of Targovishte, the distribution of religion mirrored, to some extent, the distribution of ethnicity. Only two religious groups were represented in the Council: that of the Christian-Orthodox and of the Muslims. Quite unexpectedly, the Orthodox were slightly underrepresented in the Local Council of Targovishte, where 63.63% of the membership was Orthodox; in the population of the town, the Orthodox represent around 79.5%. Instead, the Muslims were clearly overrepresented in the local legislative assembly, with 36.36% of the membership of the Council, compared to only around 17.8% of the population of Targovishte. Other small religious groups of the town enjoyed no representation in the Municipal Council: the Catholics, the Neo-protestants (a rising group, in terms of membership), the non-declared, etc. The overrepresentation of Muslims was triggered by other factors, rather than those concerning the fair representation of ethnic and religious minorities (groups that are, as a matter of fact, not officially recognized by the Bulgarian fundamental law); these factors referred to the prominent economic position of the members of the Council within the town, and to the party support the Muslim community enjoyed from the "Movements for Rights and Freedoms".

One could observe that, when dealing with religious indicators in the population, the group of "irreligious", "non-declared", "other", or even "atheists" becomes larger and larger, especially due to the fact that religious affiliation becomes more and more a private matter. Public records of the distribution of religious affiliation in the population are more and more scarce, since even the last European-wide census reserved an open-ended, optional question on the matter of religion. No wonder, then, that, in Gyula, for instance, 29% of the population cannot be religiously identified.

f)   Matrimonial status[90]

The most numerous segment of the electorate in Tecuci is unmarried (47.03%), while those married account for 39.13% of the population. While 3.64% of the population is divorced, 7.01% is widow; only 3.17% are engaged in a consensual union, probably due to the fact that, being a small community, the town still bears traditionalistic traits concerning family and marriage. The distribution of the variable marital status in the Local Council was slightly different: here, the clearly dominant category was that of the married individuals (84.21% of the members of the Local Council), while 10.52% were widow (all of them women). One local councilor (5.26%) was unmarried. The overrepresentation of the married individuals and the underrepresentation of the unmarried ones in the Council was the consequence of the type of recruitment the selectorates used in forming the list of candidates: being married is associated with a stable, "orthodox" family situation, while the unmarried or divorced statuses of the candidates to the position of local councilor can raise questions regarding the candidates' morality, especially in a small community. The proportion of widows in the Council could be explained by the high average age the Local Council displayed.

Perceptions are more diverse in Česká Lípa, more open-minded in respect to the matrimonial status of the local representatives. Even though the largest majority of the local elite in Česká Lípa was married, another significant proportion (20%) was unmarried (simply because the local elite here was younger than the one in Tecuci). The traditionally "undesired" marital status for a candidate for local representation, i.e. divorced, was to be found in the case of the Municipal Council of Česká Lípa in a "permissible" proportion of 8%, naturally under-representative for the entire population of the town (11.2% divorced); only 4% of the municipal councilors were widowed, while in the population the percentage is fairly similar: 5.68%. The striking proportion of unmarried members was to be partially explained by the fact that 41.42% of the population itself is unmarried, making thus a young, unmarried candidate appealing to a seemingly unmarried electorate. Overall, the category of unmarried was underrepresented, while the category of married people was slightly overrepresented (68% in the Council vs. 41.05% in the population). Česká Lípa preserved a sign of traditionalist biasness: no member of the local political elite was involved in consensual marital union, though a feeble 0.63% in the population finds itself in this matrimonial situation.

56.2% of the population above 15 years old in Oleśnica is married, whereas 28.8% of the population is unmarried (given, also, the relatively young population of the town, one of the youngest populations among the six cases). 9.4% of the population of Oleśnica is widow, a marital segment which

---

90   See Annexes No. 4.6.

was overrepresented in the Municipal Council: 14.28% of the municipal councilors were themselves widows. The marital category of the divorced (representing 4.8% of the population) was, expectedly, not represented in the Municipal Council of Oleśnica. Quite clearly, the feeble proportion of inhabitants living in a consensual union (only 0.8% of the population) lacked representation, as well. As in the other cases analyzed here, the married segment of the population in Oleśnica was slightly overrepresented in the Municipal Council (66.66% of the membership of the Council), but the representativeness gap was lower than in the other cases. The lower the representativeness gap was in the case of the unmarried also: even though still underrepresented in the Council (19.04% of the municipal councilors), the unmarried enjoyed a fairer passive representation in the local assembly of Oleśnica, slightly better than in the other six cases.

The matrimonial composition of the population in Gyula presents an important division between the married and the unmarried; the statistical difference between the two marital segments is lower than in other small-to-medium-sized towns: 43.3% of the population is married, while 31.4% of the population is unmarried. A significant segment in the structure of the population is divorced (12.5%), whereas another 12.7% of the population of Gyula is widow. There is no statistic regarding the *de facto* marital *status* of the inhabitants in Gyula, hence no record exists concerning persons over 15 years old involved in consensual union. The matrimonial situation within the Body of Representatives in Gyula differed: while there was no representation of consensual union, the married segment of the population was, once again, overrepresented, with 64.28% of the membership of the legislative assembly being themselves married. The underrepresentation of unmarried in the local assembly was one of the acutest of the six cases: only 14.28% of the municipal councilors were unmarried. The same proportion was represented in the local assembly by the widows, who received thusly a feeble overrepresentation in the local leading *forum*. Quite interestingly, the category of the divorced, though traditionally not represented or, at best, underrepresented in the local decisional bodies, received a feeble, but important, representation in the Body of Representatives in Gyula: 7.14% of its membership belonged to this particular marital segment.

Marital representativeness displayed significant gaps in the case of both Levice and Targovishte. In the former, while the populations of the married and the unmarried in the population of the town is similar, placed somewhere near 41%, in the Municipal Council of Levice, the gap of representativeness was important: whereas 66.66% of the membership was married, only 20.83% was unmarried. The underrepresentation of the unmarried, perceived as unstable and volatile in their lifestyle, was as flagrant as the overrepresentation of the married (seen as possessing a family capital of paramount importance, especially within a small town as Levice). Two counterintuitive aspects should be mentioned in the case of the Municipal Council of Levice and its marital representativeness: the widow were surprisingly underrepresented in the local assembly (6% in the population of the town, as compared to 4.16% in the Council); and the segment of the divorced managed to penetrate the ranks of the local political elite in Levice, as 8.33% of the municipal councilors were divorced, providing a quite fair representation for this marital category. Finally, for the Local Council of Targovishte, probably the most conspicuous representativeness gap concerned the married segment of the population: as an overwhelming 81.81% of the membership of the Council was married, in the population of Targovishte, only 49% is actually married; the gap was of 33 points. The traditionally underrepresented marital statuses were to be found in the case of Targovishte, as well, but the gaps of representativeness were probably the highest among the six cases under scrutiny: the unmarried (6.06% in the Council, as compared to 37% in the population), the divorced (surprisingly represented in the Council by 3.03%), and the consensually united (not represented in the Council). The matrimonial segment of the widows received a fair representation in the Local Council of Targovishte.

As already observed, the general representation of unmarried was weak, especially taking into consideration the fact that, given the average age in the six Municipal Councils exceeded 40 years old, most of the local representatives became married persons by that age. By contrast, also in connection to the municipal councilors' age, the representation of widows in the six local assemblies was fairly distributed, sometimes approaching overrepresentation. One cannot but notice the lack of passive representativeness of the divorced and of the persons living in a consensual union or civil partnership in the six Municipal / Local Councils, even in the context in which both types of marital statuses are currently increasing numerically in the entire region of East-Central Europe. Though the importance of a classical family is gradually vanishing in the region, the image of the traditional family – and of the traditional local political elite, from the marital perspective – was still preserved in the six cases of small-to-medium-sized towns, and enjoyed a broad representation in the local assemblies of these municipalities.

g)   Place of birth[91]

In what regards the place of birth, it was clear that the local political elite was more rural-based that the electorate of Tecuci: only 52.63% of the local councilors had been born in Tecuci, as opposed to 98.42% of the population. It could be said, paradoxically, that the segment of the population born in Tecuci

---

91   See Annexes No. 4.7.

was underrepresented in the Local Council, in favor of those coming from the neighboring rural area: 36.84% of the members of the Local Council of Tecuci had been born in a rural area, while 10.52% had been born in another town (Mărăşeşti). In the electorate, only 1.12% of those presently living in Tecuci were born in a rural place and only 0.33% in another town. Beneficial for the phenomenon of ascendant social mobility, the rural origin of approximately 37% of the local councilors was counterbalanced by the fact that 63.63% of the members of the Local Council identified themselves primarily with Tecuci, regardless of their place of birth.

Moreover, the fact that 36.84% of the members of the Local Council were from the neighboring rural area proved that the rural-urban mobility was a recurrent phenomenon for the local political elite in Tecuci. Particularly due to the fact that Tecuci is a small town, with numerous and constant connections, largely economic ones, with the surrounding villages and communes, significant segments of the rural population, primarily intellectuals, choose to live in the town, hence overcoming the rural-urban gap. The situation is somehow different for the rest of the rural population, who choose to remain in its native commune / village or to migrate in other countries (Italy), for better jobs. As a result, generally, almost half of the members of the Local Council in Tecuci were rural-born individuals, mainly intellectuals (85% of them).

For the Czech case, the same underrepresentation of the ones born in Česká Lípa was to be observed: 97.43% of the population of the town is born here, while only 68% of their representatives were actually born in the same town. On the other hand, there was an overrepresentation in the Council of the feeble proportions of inhabitants born in rural areas (16% in the Council, while only 1.01% in the entire population of the town) and those born in other towns (another 16% of the municipal councils representing only 1.54% of the inhabitants of Česká Lípa). Overall, in what concerned the place of birth of the councilors and their representativeness in this respect, the lack of proportionality was to dominate.

The rural-urban mobility in the case of Oleśnica presents a series of peculiarities, given primarily by the fact that this relatively small town is one of those gravitating around the biggest in Western Poland, Wrocław. Investment projects conducted in Wrocław affect the mobility (essentially, job-generated) in Oleśnica. This is the reason why people coming from the surrounding rural area come to Oleśnica to find jobs in great investment projects; their representation in the Municipal Council of Oleśnica was quite fair, since 23.8% of the members of the Council had been born in one of the neighboring villages. There was even an overrepresentation of the rural-born category in the Council, marking a high level of rural-urban mobility for the Polish local political elite. Similarly, the category of people born in other towns (which does not reach 10% of the population of Oleśnica) was overrepresented in the Municipal Council (19.04% of the councilors had been born in other urban area). Nevertheless – and quite uniquely –, this overrepresentation was done in the detriment of the underrepresentation of the largest segment of the population born in Oleśnica: whereas over 95% of the population of the town is autochthonous, only 57.14% of the municipal councilors had been born in Oleśnica. This necessarily means that the degree of urban-rural mobility among the local political elite in Oleśnica is unmatched by the same indicator in the population of the town.

The same underrepresentation of the autochthonous was to be found in the Hungarian and the Slovak cases analyzed here: the people born and raised in Gyula and Levice, respectively, were generally underrepresented in the local legislative assemblies of the respective town: only 64.28% of the membership of the Body of Representatives in Gyula, and a similar 62.5% of the representatives in Levice, had been born in Gyula and Levice, respectively, as opposed to 96% of the population in Gyula, and 97% of the population in Levice. The segment in the populations of the two towns who are born in another town or city was practically inexistent in the case of the Body of Representative of Gyula, and reached 16.66% in the case of the Municipal Council in Levice. Moreover, even though foreign residents in these towns could run for a seat in the Local Council (courtesy to the six countries' membership in the European Union), the representation in the local assemblies for people born outside the country was inexistent. Again, in the case of Gyula and Levice, the rural-urban mobility indicator for the local political elites was significantly higher than the same indicator in the case of their respective populations.

Targovishte and the vast surrounding rural area have agriculture as main economic occupation (both as industrial crops, from sunflower to tobacco, and as cereals, from wheat to maize and barley, and vines), which contributed 31.2% to the general revenues of the local budget (considerably higher than the average of 13.4% of the budget at the national level)[92]; naturally, the perpetual relations between the town and its neighboring villages – similar to the ones maintained in the case of Tecuci – contribute to this overwhelming importance of agriculture for the town's economy. The same type of relation generates a demographic peculiarity, in the sense that an important segment of the population has been economically and voluntarily displaced from the village to the town. This trend – which is presently in an evident and irrefutable decline – had its impact on the socio-demographic composition of the Municipal Council in Targovishte, where 39.39% of the members had been born outside the town, in one of the neighboring villages.

All in all, the general discussion and the specific analysis of representativeness and representation at the local level bear the *problématique* usually posed by the relations between the few powerful ones and the many, instrumentally (through procedurally) powerless, between the elites and the non-

---

92 A Eurostat statistic of 2011, at https://circabc.europa.eu/webdav/CircaBC/ESTAT/reg-portraits/Information/bg034_geo.htm, last accessed: 13.01.2016.

elites. Hypothetically and normatively, the gap between the leadership and the masses, the elected and the electorate, is somehow bridged and overcome at the local level, since small-to-medium communities are generally closed, sur-veillance-type ones; moreover, the local elites are the first level of power ac-cessible to the ordinary citizen in his quest for problem-solving, in his recourse to authorities. The first interaction of the citizen, as part of the non-elite, with the political leadership is established through the local political elite, which would presuppose that this elite group would be characterized by the greatest degree of representativeness in respect to the electorate, to the voting masses. As shown above, statistically, empirically, rather the reverse was valid, at least in the particular cases of the towns of Tecuci, Česká Lípa, Oleśnica, Gyula, Levice, and Targovishte. At the passive, descriptive, socio-demographical level, the members of the six Local / Municipal Councils were quite dissimilar to their electorate, but this dissonance is relatively natural in the relationships between elites and non-elites, since the Aristotelian perspective of "virtuous" elites has been preserved somehow into the present day in the form of a more educated, more experienced, better trained, mature, urban-based group of in-dividuals in position of power. In the 70s – the years of the "elite theory"'s prominence – Verba and Nie discuss the issue of bridging the *hiatus* between the elites and the masses by reaching different levels of "congruence" (Verba and Nie 1972) (agreement, consonance in decision-making and priority rank-ing) first and foremost within the local community. It is in the key of Verba and Nie's observation that the significance of both participation and represen-tation and representativeness is to be assessed. Nevertheless, besides the eval-uation of the degree of representativeness however passive, the level of some "closeness" between the local community and the local branches of power is beyond the scope and the empirical reach of the present study. Moreover, as it has been rather modestly shown for the six cases in point, this kind of "close-ness" or "congruence" was by all means contingent and largely prescriptive, rather than an empirically valid, descriptive characteristic even at the local level.

The paradigmatic case of Poland: Local Political Elite in Oleśnica: recruitment, priorities, values, socio-economic outlook (A comparison to the local political elites in Tecuci and Česká Lípa)

Poland is a classic case in what concerns the popular expectations immediately after 1989 and the counter-elites' intention to neutralize former communist elites, even at the local level:

> "Rapid decentralization reforms were expected to bring about a replacement of local elites and minimize the danger that state reforms would be sabotaged by local post-communist *nomenklatura*. Quick but intense preparations of the reform resulted" (Swianiewicz 2011: 483)

out of these two initial objectives, aimed, firstly, at decentralization and democratization at the local level, and, afterwards, at regionalization (tailored, more and more apparently, on the neighboring German model of sixteen *"Länder"*). This rapid drive towards decentralization intrinsically triggering democratization led, in turn, to a dissolution of the seat of political responsibility, a dissolution latter intensified by the process of regionalization; citizens tend to get lost when assigning responsibility for policy outcomes among the different tiers of government (León 2018).

At the level of self-selection, one could immediately observe a series of conspicuous differences between the three cases discussed in this section: although the main motivational element that drive individuals to enter politics remained, in the Polish case as well, allegedly the very feeling of obligation towards their community (52.94% of the responses), the other aspects determining the *impetus* to become involved in the affairs of the *res publica* at the local level differed to some extent by the results accounting for the self-selection in the Romanian and the Czech cases. As a consequence, 11.76% of the local councilors in Oleśnica somehow sententiously declared that politics was their way of life, the political practice becoming increasingly a facet of everyday life, an indispensable, inseparable aspect of these councilors' existence. One might correlate this percentage – a novelty of the process of self-selection at the local level in East-Central Europe, since the previous two cases, Tecuci and Česká Lípa, displayed no such answer among their municipal councilors – with the high proportion of incumbency within the Municipal Council of Oleśnica (57.89%): once these councilors professionalized themselves in the service of the community, being continuously present in the Council for even decades, they became accustomed with the political exercise and with the routine of the workings of the Council and its committees. Therefore, from the standpoint of the prolonged incumbency, it appeared rather natural that part of the members of the Council motivated their entering politics by bluntly stating that politics was their way of life. Another discrepancy of the Polish case in comparison to the Romanian and the Czech ones in the field of self-selection was the very fun and excitement of politics (17.64% of the responses) as motivational drive. Once more, it seemed that the previous experiences with the political practice and the incumbency might be correlated with such a response and to its significant proportion among the councilors of Oleśnica: due to the permanent interaction with the political realm, some councilors perceived the exercise of politics as an activity that might provide a sense of excitement, even amusement. The intensity of the bargaining and negotiations presupposed by the governance "game", the dynamism of the electoral and political campaigns, the surprise behind the inherent changes that the actions of other political actors might trigger could produce thrilling sentiments in those interested in entering politics. A significant percentage among the answers provided by the members of the Local Council in Oleśnica regarding the motivational background of self-selection, generally and in each one's particular case, was to be reserved to the response "To establish social friendships and contacts", which would suggest a model of local elite cohesion similar to the one analyzed in Tecuci, accompanied by high appreciation of collegiality, team spirit and dialogue, as attributes a local councilor should first and foremost possess. Conversely, and similarly to the two cases previously inquired, the belief that involvement in politics would help with business contracts was not at all endorsed by the councilors in Oleśnica as a potential motivational factor for getting involved into politics or becoming a member of the Municipal Council, as neither were the desire for recognition within the community, the desire to be close to influential people, building a personal career in politics – despite the fact most of the respondents actually did build a career in being municipal councilors sometimes for more than a decade –, and the loyalty towards the doctrine of a certain party (0% for all the enumerated variants of response). Therefore, it might be concluded that, exactly like in the Czech case, the elite in Oleśnica displayed no concern whatsoever for such assets like prestige, party identification (or, better, ideological identification), privileged economic status (and resulting business ties), a certain informal influence within the community, or, for that matter, carreristic objectives. What was indeed worth pausing upon was not only the fact that responses in Oleśnica were less varied, less dispersed than those in Tecuci and Česká Lípa, but rather compact and trend-like, but, more importantly, the fact that none of the municipal councilors associated the motivation to enter into politics with the desire to influence the policies of the government. This situation appeared as a veritable disparity, quite tortuous for explanation, since, generally, private individuals decide to enter politics particularly driven by the desire to have an influence on the governmental decision-making. As compared to the responses provided by the municipal councilors in Tecuci (34.78%) and Česká Lípa (19.51%), the ones among the members of the Local Council in Oleśnica were strikingly surprising and denoted more than an isolated, locally-entrenched elite, with no permanent and comprehensive links to the elite at the central level – which had been actually observed previously both in Romania and the Czech Republic – ; they suggested the clear confinement of this political elite to its own community, to the needs, the problems and the expectations of the said community, quite awkwardly reserving no interest whatsoever to the policies issued at the central level which, indeed, affect less and less the life of the increasingly decentralized administrative units and municipalities. All in all, one could discern from the responses provided to the questions referring to self-selection by the councilors in Oleśnica the highest level of professionalization of the local political elite in East-Central Europe among the three selected cases. This preliminary observation was straightened by the results to the question regarding the eventuality of incumbency, where no Polish municipal councilor refuted the perspective of another mandate within the Local Council, as opposed to 23.52% in the Romanian case and 13.63% in the Czech case. On the other hand, the largest proportion of respondents in Oleśnica (an impressive 61.11%) were uncertain about (or rather refrained from answering) the prospects of running for another mandate of municipal councilor. The certainty in respect to future incumbency was the lowest for the Polish case (38.88%, as compared to the more conclusive 52.94% in Tecuci and 63.63% in Česká Lípa), which would correlate to the slightly higher electoral volatility characteristic for the Polish democracy, but which, inversely, contradicted the high level of actual, existing incumbency within the Local Council of Oleśnica.

A series of differences might be encountered in what concerned the priorities of the three local elites in Romania, the Czech Republic and Poland. The Municipal Council of Oleśnica considered of the utmost importance such spheres as: education (21.42%), social services (including unemployment and housing) and economic development (each with 16.66% of the responses) and culture, sport, recreation and youth activities (14.28%). As opposed to the previously inquired cases, the Polish municipal councilors were less concerned with activities in the sphere of public improvements (11.9%, as compared to 16.98% in Tecuci and 24.19% in the Czech Republic) and minorities' rights and interethnic relations (0%, understandably, as the population of the town is quite homogeneous in ethnic, religious and national terms, hence such a domain of competence was largely insignificant in the decision-making process at the local level). Conversely, the Council in Oleśnica was slightly more concerned with pollution than the other two (4.76%, as opposed to 1.88% in Tecuci and 1.61% in Česká Lípa), education (21.42%, as compared with 15.09% in Tecuci and only 9.67% in Česká Lípa) and culture and related activities (14.28%, opposing some insignificant 1.88% in Tecuci and 1.61% in Česká Lípa). If one embarked in an inquiry into the professional profile and the occupational *status* of the municipal councilors in Oleśnica, one might find a partial explanation for these results and the discrepancies in respect to the two other Municipal Councils: the large majority of the councilors in Oleśnica were professionals working in public sector frequently as teachers; it might be assumed that working within the educational system, these councilors would have displayed an increased concern for the domains of competence in which they actually had a certain professional competence. This situation might be correlated with the answers to the other questions related to the distribution of priorities at the local level: the spheres of competence in which there existed sufficient political power seated at the local level to operate significant measures and improvements (the same dominance of education – 21.42% of the responses, followed by social services and economic development – 16.66% for each of the answers); the spheres of competence in which efficient and effective measures had already been taken during the last years (culture and culturally-related activities – 23.8%, confirming a trend present already in the two previously inquired cases; and, once more, education – 19.04% of the respondents); the spheres of competence on which one councilor could have exerted a personal influence for the improvement of the situation (culture, sport, recreation and youth activities – 27.02% of the responses; and the recurrent education – 21.62%, both results being in sharp difference to the results obtained in the Czech and the Romanian cases). As a matter of fact, when accounting for the personal influence each of the members of the Municipal Council in Oleśnica bore on particular domains in the functioning of the municipality, the discrepancies with the municipalities of Tecuci and Česká Lípa were conspicuous. Firstly, there was a decreased personal influence when assessing it in respect to: public improvements (21.62% of the responses: though significant, this percentage was the lowest among the three cases selected: 33.33% in Tecuci and 35.48% in Česká Lípa); healthcare (only 2.7%, in comparison with 3.03% and 9.67% in Tecuci and Česká Lípa, respectively); economic development (a warring 2.7%, in striking difference to 21.21% among the councilors of Tecuci and 9.67% among the ones of Česká Lípa). Inversely, personal influence in solving pressing issues for the local community was the highest (and marking considerable differences) in Oleśnica among the three cases when it came to: education (21.62%, as opposed to only 12.9% in the Czech case and 9.09% in the Romanian case), public safety (16.21% of the respondents, in comparison to 12.12% in Tecuci and 3.22% in Česká Lípa) and various cultural activities (a categorical 27.02% of the answers, in marked difference to the resembling 6.06% and 6.45%, in the Romanian and the Czech cases, respectively).

It is important to note that the local elite of Oleśnica was as isolated as the elite groups in the other two cases, in terms of the networks of power and interactions with elite groups at the national level. None of the members of the Municipal Council of Oleśnica established contacts with members of the central administration, i.e. members of the Cabinet (ministers, state secretaries, etc.), state legislators (senators, deputies, MPs) or even with other city or town administrators (mayors, deputy mayors, etc.); only 2.63% of the respondents in the Polish case had interactions with political representatives at the level of the voievodship, i.e. at the district / county level. The frequency of the interactions with other local elected officials was similar: 2.63% of the councilors in Oleśnica established relations with such officials, the lowest percentage among the three cases analyzed (11.11% in the case of Česká Lípa and a more robust 19.51% in Tecuci). Overall, the members of the Municipal Council in Oleśnica were the most isolated group in terms of the networks of power and elite interactions, hence being the most circumscribed elite group among the three cases, only 5.26% of the local councilors establishing contacts with other groups that transcended the limits of their constituencies, the space of their community (as opposed to 31.68% for Tecuci and 12.69% for Česká Lípa). The increased isolation with the Czech and the Polish local political elites was to be explained partially through the prism of the more and more significant degree of decentralization: in both the Czech and the Polish cases, the local elite focused primarily on the immediate issues their communities faced, linking their interests to those of the groups acting within these communities, while the contacts with elites outside the town they represented became increasing sporadic and improbable. On the other hand, the most important relations the local political elite in Oleśnica entertained within the community were those with the neighborhood groups – 39.47% of the responses – and, more significantly, with the civic and reform groups – 21.05%. Comparably, the percentage – and thusly, the importance – assigned to the relations of elites with the neighborhood was the highest in the Polish case and, overall, the highest among all types of groups considered here and among all three cases. The percentage describing the relations with the neighbors was discrepantly higher as compared to the Romanian (12.19%) and the Czech (only 7.93%) cases, a situation which pointed to the strong link, to the closeness between the members of the Municipal Council and their immediate constituency. It is important to mention that, though quite alike in terms of population size, Oleśnica is the smallest among the three towns analyzed here and might be prone to more stable and stronger relations between the local councilors and their neighbors. Moreover, such a type of relations, though they might appear trivial and insignificant in the entire political dynamic, bear a particular role especially in the process of reelection of the local leaders in small-to-medium communities: the very fact that many members of the Municipal Council in Oleśnica were incumbents was one of the most powerful illustrations of the strategic importance of neighborhood groups in the dynamics of political recruitment in small polities. Such an interaction is non-mediated, immediate and probably the simplest form the local leaders can establish with their constituency. The Polish local elite seemed to have understood this key aspect the best. To a considerable distance from the value assigned to the relation with the neighborhood groups, the interactions with the civic and reform groups were perceived to be most frequent for 21.05% of the councilors in Oleśnica. In Oleśnica, a significant part of the members of the Council were professionals employed in the sector of civil society organizations, intimately linked to the activities of various NGOs, particularly in the field of education. In a rather abnormal fashion, therefore, the members of the political elite constituted simultaneously members of the civil society sector. This abnormality found itself reflected in the increased frequency of the links between the Municipal Council and the civic and reform groups, but this type of interactions represents a conspicuous and telling feature of good local governance and of democratic development at the community level: the Polish percentages in this area were similar to the Czech ones (21.05% to 25.39%) and dissimilar to the Romanian case (only 4.87% of the municipal councilors' contacts). Since the population of Oleśnica is fairly homogeneous in ethnic and religious terms, no relations were established with ethnic groups, while only 2.63% represented contacts with the religious groups, founded mainly upon the regular attendance of Catholic masses during Sunday. The proportions for the two indicators among the Polish, the Romanian and the Czech cases were fairly similar (for the religious groups: 2.63%, 2.43% and 3.17%, respectively). The frequency of the relations of the local councilors in Oleśnica with the local media subscribed within the general trend set up by the same type of relations in Tecuci: only 5.26% of the local elites' contacts were established with the local media, resembling 4.87% for the same relationship in Tecuci. In this sense, Česká Lípa presented an outlier, since the contacts with the local media represented 15.87%, three to four times higher than the other two cases. It is commonsensical that, as a rule, the Czech elites are inclined towards a more open and direct relation with the media, the political life becoming quite "tabloid"-ized during recent decades; notwithstanding this inherent tendency, it appears hazardous to hypothesize that this is valid even for the local political elite, even though the popular interest is concentrated upon the private life of the politicians in a surveillance-like community, in which social interactions are more frequent and covers the large part of the community's population. It is worth mentioning as well the fact that the case of Oleśnica encountered the lowest proportion among the three cases studied here regarding the local councilors' interaction with close friends and supporters (10.52%, as compared to 12.69% in Česká Lípa and 17.07% in Tecuci), which might appear in sharp contrast with the high importance attributed by the same elite group to the contacts with the neighborhood. Close friends and supporters represent key elements in the political recruitment and reelection processes, particularly at the local level, where attachments and personal ties are conducive to incumbency within the Municipal Council. Cumulatively indeed, the councilors of the Polish town seemed to have best understood this sort of dynamics: 49.99%, therefore half of their interactions, were established with the neighbors, supporters and friends, as opposed to 29.26% for Tecuci and 20.62% for Česká Lípa. The repercussions of the dominance of those groups among the municipal councilors' links were twofold. On the one hand, it suggested a profound isolation of the members of the Municipal Council to their immediate constituency, with the almost complete neglect of the networks of power at the central or regional level (possibly explainable through an increased degree of decentralization after 1998 that determined intrinsically a local elite more focused, almost circumscribed to the community they represented and led, due to the increased authority and capacity to actually implement changes, rather than pushing and negotiating for them with the central administration). In this sense, such an isolation and a more robust concern for the local matters appears beneficial and the inclination towards establishing contacts with groups in the local councilors' nearest proximity illustrates this situation quite accurately: it is among these groups that the Municipal Council extracts grievances, expressed problems to be dealt with, immediate issues to be solved. Therefore, such relations might be both a valuable and uncontestable resource in political recruitment and reelection procedures and a source of public policies and Council's resolutions. On the other hand, the conspicuous prominence of this type of contacts, rather informal and non-formalized, non-institutionalized, is prone to generate a general absence of *critique* in respect to the political performances of the municipal councilors – or, more precisely, a sort of autism from the part of the members of the Council towards (otherwise immanent) criticisms – and to bear the seeds of *phenomena* located at the margins of political structure – particularly recurrent in the political *compendium* offered by East-Central Europe –, such as patronage and clientelism. While, indeed, the growing frequency of relations with neighborhood groups, with close friends and supporters is instrumental in taking the pulse of the local demands and expectations, these forms of interactions are, at the same time, unlikely to produce criticism directed towards the performances of the members of the Municipal Council and, more often than not, the local councilor has to respond somehow to the unconditional help and support he receives from these groups, strategically placing individuals belonging to such groups within the local administration *apparatus*. Clientelistic practices of this fashion were rather commonplace for Tecuci, where entire streets were inhabited by persons variously linked to the Municipality (working either as local councilors, local civil servants or under the subordination of governmental agencies with local branches in the town), but they could be sporadically encountered in the Polish case, as well: close supporters – frequently, members of the parties represented in the Council – were seen to colonize the local administration, generally undertaking petty jobs, but secured with the very incumbency of their "patrons" in the Council. Expectedly, the "consensual" type of relations dominates among the interactions with close friends, supporters and neighbors. Moreover, yet another aspect appeared problematic in this form of interaction: the 50% of the contacts with supporters, friends, sympathizers and alike was by no means compensated, counterbalanced by the poor 23.68% describing the frequency and importance of the contacts established by the local councilors with two other groups, generally perceived to raise claims and criticism towards the situation of the town, the situation of particular social groups in the composition of the town and towards the political performance of the local elite: the unions (2.63%) and the civic and reform groups (21.05%). The small proportion of interactions with trade unions (a very similar percentage to the one among the local councilors in Tecuci, 2.43%) seemed, in this scheme, quite surprising: clearly, Oleśnica did not possess a tradition of trade unionism so robust as the cities on the shore of the Baltic Sea that had actually triggered such a contestation movement at the end of the 1970s capable to ultimately generating the breakdown of the communist regime in Poland. Though part of the Lower Silesia – a region powerfully industrialized starting as early as the interwar period –, Oleśnica has developed as a small town, with predominantly agricultural activities and, during state socialism, with small factories mainly food-oriented, since the raw materials for the food industry were easily accessible here. Therefore, as in the Romanian case, trade unions at the local level formed rather as loose organizations or appeared as local branches for great organizations usually centrally-based. In such a context, one might argue – even though the major socio-economical problems of the town are linked to the destructive repercussions of deindustrialization – that the connections of the local elite with trade unions are largely insignificant for the very fact that trade unions are inactive and insignificant themselves in both scope and activity within the miniatural picture of the "civil society" in Oleśnica. As a direct consequence, large parts of the town's population facing profound social and economic distress were virtually unrepresented, while the local elite had no partner in the dialogue for improving the situation in probably the most pressing spheres of the community's life: social assistance and economic development. Conversely, the absence of trade unions and, subsequently, of the criticism customarily conveyed by these groups towards the local elite, was, to some extent, counterbalanced by the more comprehensive and dynamic dialogue the members of the Municipal Council in Oleśnica sustained with civic and reform groups (21.05% of the responses). Nevertheless, as previously stated, the relations with the civic organizations appeared problematic, as well, since the municipal councilors themselves were often members of these organizations. This unwary, puzzling arrangement, overlapping might represent a specific feature of small administrative units in East-Central Europe: as a rule, those that initially engaged in civic and reform activities are part of the middle class, with university education (lawyers, teachers, engineers) or professional studies (small businessmen); the fortunate case of Oleśnica demonstrated that these individuals had managed to forge into the local political scene, being recruited as prominent figures in their professions and as belonging to civic and reform bodies. Over time, they became incumbents in the Municipal Council, even though they had firstly operated within the "contestational" side of the public sphere. It was thusly natural that the connection with the civic and reform groups be maintained and represent approximately a quarter of the entire *spectrum* of networks the members of the local political elite established. Finally, the interactions with the business groups might have constituted another source of "contestation" and criticism at the local level towards the political elite of the town. As it has been shown above, the political elite in Tecuci tended to confound itself with the economic one and the local leadership of Oleśnica was *quasi*-synonymous with particular segments of the civic and reform groups. Small business, routinely commerce-oriented, are characteristic for Oleśnica, while several big factories have plummeted in debts, leading eventually to an inescapable default and mounting unemployment for the town's inhabitants. Notwithstanding the economic context in which the town struggled during 2009-2014, the small *foci* of contestation coming from the business groups and from the "economic" elite – which was quite difficult to pinpoint at the moment of the study, as many great investors leaving the community in recent years – did exist and they became apparent in the frequency and significance of this group's interactions with the members of the Municipal Council, accounting for 13.15% of the total number of elite networks and contacts. In addition, this proportion was telling particularly when correlated with the identification – through the eyes of the local councilors – of the main problem their town confronted with: the everincreasing unemployment and the lack of job-generating investments for the citizens of the community. It might be contended that the intensity of contacts with the business groups was an indication of the genuine concern the local elite bore in respect to the welfare of its community.

Major discrepancies with regard to the cherishing of democratic values by the local political elite among the three selected cases are not to be neglected. They might constitute an indication of the fashion in which the concept of "democracy" was understood in each community, an irrefutable validation for the valences the notion of "democracy" connoted and denoted in each political culture. This has been conspicuously showed by the comparison provided for Tecuci and Česká Lípa, a comparison that revealed the Romanian local elite had a clearly, unequivocal anti-egalitarian-statist understanding of democracy, while perceiving citizen participation and conflict avoidance as paramount features within the democratic arrangement; the Czech local elite considered a rather statist-egalitarian perspective on democratic outlook, with an evident emphasis on citizen participation as central feature for democracy and a broad acceptance of conflict as inherent for the democratic practice and rules. The case of Oleśnica, while being closer to the case of Tecuci, presented its own peculiarities. On the one hand, the members of the Municipal Council in the Polish town were slightly anti-egalitarian and overwhelmingly statists, since only 16.66% of the respondents thought of economic equality as an inseparable

238

component of democracy, while a total of 76.46% of the local councilors agreed in various degrees to the state intervention in economy. Even so, the results were not completely conclusive in Oleśnica: for instance, the distribution of the importance of the four values selected in the definition of democracy displayed proportions that expressed a variety of opinions and not a clear-cut perspective, not even a sketched tendency towards one single value: 33.33% of the members of the Municipal Council in Oleśnica valued citizen participation the most in a democracy, but another 33.33% of them perceived conflict avoidance as paramount for any democratic construct; similarly, 16.66% of the local councilors found innovative, gradual change as the most significant feature of democracy, while another 16.66% considered economic equality as the most valued achievement with the installation of democracy. As already observed, the valuing of the four democratic characteristics in the Polish case generally resembled the Romanian case, with the Czech case being quite dissimilar and presenting itself as an outlier in this sense. First, the proportions expressing the evaluation of citizen participation as a democratic value were alike (33.33% for the Polish case and 35.29% for the Romanian case), as are the percentages for conflict avoidance (33.33% and 35.29%, respectively); in opposition, the Czech local elite valued overwhelmingly citizen participation (a clear-cut 59.09% of the respondents), but the valuing of innovative, piecemeal change among the political elite of Česká Lípa – 18.18% of the responses – was somehow resembling to the value for the same democratic feature in Oleśnica, 16.66%. Quite significantly, while there was a clear rejection of economic equality for the members of the Local Council in Tecuci (0%), the percentages for the economic equality as democratic value among the municipal councilors of Česká Lípa and Oleśnica became instrumental in already constructing a trend: 16.66% for the Polish case and 13.63% for the Czech case. Therefore, it might be reasonably hypothesized that, while economic equality as policy fundament might appear as far-fetched, a certain degree of societal welfare is somehow inseparably associated with the democratic *desideratum*[93], it seems an indispensable prerequisite for democratic development; moreover, it is conspicuous that the two "new democracies" that registered the most significant and comprehensive achievements on the *route* of democratic development, Poland and the Czech Republic, are the ones to have properly learned this instrumental lesson and this value internalization translated at the

---

93 The relationship between economic welfare and democratic advance (a rather passive relation, influence-type one, since it is assumed that democracy develops and evolves at a certain level of economic standard for the citizens of the polity) is commonplace in the general study of democratic development and consolidation. Among the scholars who perceived economic welfare as sine qua non for the democratic drive, particularly in the "new democracies", see the renowned seminal work of Lipset 1959: 69-105, but also Heo and Tan 2001: 463-473; Przeworski 2004; Doucouliagos and Ulubaşoğlu 2008: 61-83; Gerring, Bond, Barndt and Moreno 2005: 323-364; Menocal 2007: 1-17.

local level through a political elite who values economic equality and a concern for the citizens' welfare as a part of democracy, even in spite of the communist past that at least rhetorically, declaratively put a great emphasis on the (otherwise dangerous and quite unrealistic) idea of economic equality. Generally, the most valued feature associated with democracy by the local political elite in East-Central European countries was citizen participation, with an overall average of 42.57% of the total population of members of the Municipal Councils studied here; nevertheless, the consensus over the primacy of this value for substantively defining "democracy" was definitely clearest in the case of the Local Council of Česká Lípa, resulting into a more "democratic"[94] local elite in the Czech case. The second most cherished value in a democracy from the prism of the local elite in the three Councils was, expectedly, innovative, gradual change, the capacity of democratic arrangements to intrinsically encapsulate piecemeal, beneficial transformations, generally in a reform-like fashion rather than turbulent, revolutionary manner; gradual change presupposed by a democracy construct gathered an average support of 21.41% among the members of the three Municipal Councils, with slight fluctuations from 16.66%, in the Polish case, to a more robust 29.41%, for the Romanian case. Conflict avoidance ranked the third among the most valued features customarily associated with the democratic *modus operandi*, with significant variations and fluctuations for the three cases selected; the discussion over the conflict avoidance capacity of a democracy was largely open, since it was not clear-cut for the members of the three Municipal Councils whether democracy should either provide an *arena* for clashing interests, opinions, perspectives, policies, conducts or create the channels through which conflict is neutralized and institutionalized. In this sense, the most evident discrepancy was to be seen between the results in the Czech case (a mere 9.09% of the respondents perceived conflict avoidance as paramount for democracy) and the quite similar proportions in the Romanian and Polish cases (a clearly more significant 35.29% and 33.33%, respectively, argued that conflict avoidance is of the utmost importance for any democratic makeup). As a consequence, one might commonsensically contend that the political leadership in Tecuci and Oleśnica displayed a consensual, "consociational" decisional style, focused towards bargaining, compromise, dialogue and negotiation in decision-making, whereas

---

94 The "democratic" political elite is one of the four typologies constructed by Stoica 2003: 203-206. The scholar distinguishes among four types of elites, by triangulated between the level of their acceptance/ rejection of citizen participation as a defining value of democracy and the degree of their acceptance/ rejection of political conflict within a democracy. The resulting types of political elites are: (1) "authoritarianists" (i.e. rejection of both citizen participation and political conflict), (2) "populists" (i.e. acceptance of citizen participation combined with rejection of political conflict), (3) "pluralists" (i.e. rejection of citizen participation associated with acceptance of political conflict), and (4) "democrats" (i.e. acceptance of both citizen participation and political conflict).

the local political elite in Česká Lípa exposed a rather confrontational, conflicting decisional style, oriented towards debate and polemics in decision-making. Overall, conflict avoidance as democratic "virtue" scored 25.9% of the total number of responses collected from within the three Local Councils. Notwithstanding these preliminary observations, the discussion over the actual necessity of conflict avoidance in a democracy and the manner in which this alleged necessity is to be considered by the local political elite remains under scrutiny, though exceeding, for the time being, the immediate scope of this enquiry. Finally, the least valued among the four values proposed for the association with "democracy" was, expectedly, economic equality, with an overall average of 10.09% of the total number of local councilors in the three cases. While the 0% attributed to economic equality in the Council of Tecuci has been explained through the occupational *status* (businessmen, potentiates of the town) of the councilors themselves and to their attempt to detach themselves, at the level of ideas and economic behavior, from the *dicta* of the defunct regime, and while the Council of Česká Lípa was dominated, at the time of the research, by left-wing, socialist and green political parties that might have explained the significance a considerable proportion of the members attributed to economic equality (13.63% of the responses), in the case of Oleśnica, the 16.66% of the responses devoted to economic equality and welfare was determined partly to the professional *status* of the members of the Municipal Council (in small communities, teachers and former / actual non-governmental activists are seen to be traditionally concerned with welfare and social security issues, while intrinsically, sometimes, they bear leftist views), but also to their age (many of them were retired, older persons, politically socialized primarily during the *ancien régime*, in a communist regime that had put a marked emphasis on economic equality and on the elimination / attenuation of differences in the standard of living – otherwise, immanent in any social arrangement – among citizens). When correlating levels of acceptance / rejection of citizen participation with degrees of acceptance / avoidance of political conflict, the local political elites of Oleśnica resulted as the "populist" type of elite, i.e. high levels of acceptance of citizen participation correlated with high levels of avoidance of political conflict, similar to the local elite in Tecuci, but opposed to the "democratic" type, characteristic of Česká Lípa, assimilated to high levels of acceptance of citizen participation coupled with high levels of acceptance of political conflict (calculated, in this case, rather as the rejection of conflict avoidance). Conversely, when correlating the levels of acceptance / rejection of economic equality with levels of acceptance / rejection of the state intervention in economy – correlated on the basic premises that, as a rule, a protectionist state is conducive to welfare –, it resulted that the members of the Municipal Council in Oleśnica could be described rather as "statists-egalitarianists", i.e. relatively high levels of acceptance of economic equality associated to high levels of acceptance of the state intervention in economy, quite similarly to the local political elite in Česká Lípa, but largely dissimilar to the local councilors in Tecuci, who might be coined as "statists-anti-egalitarianists", i.e. relatively high levels of acceptance of the state intervention in economy correlated with clearly high levels of rejection of economic equality. In assessing the protectionist state, its significance in present times and its viability, the members of the Municipal Council in Oleśnica epitomized the overwhelming acceptance of the state intervention in economy: 17.64% of them were strongly agreeing with the protectionist policies – definitely the highest proportion for the clear acceptance among the three cases, with 0% for Tecuci and 4.54% for Česká Lípa –, another 29.41% agreed with the state intervention in economy and yet other 29.41% partially agreed with it. Cumulatively, the local elite of Oleśnica registered the highest level of acceptance towards the protectionist state (76.46% of the members of the Municipal Council agreed, in various degrees, with it, the exact cumulative percentage as in the case of the Local Council of Tecuci, and comparable to the overall proportion for Česká Lípa, i.e. 68.17% of the responses). Oleśnica presented the highest percentage translating strong acceptance to the protectionist state among the three cases (17.64%), which might be partially explained through the timing of the data collecting for the populations surveyed: if the questionnaires for Tecuci were administered in 2010-2011 and those for Česká Lípa in 2011-2012, three years marked by economic recession and world financial crisis, the questionnaires for Oleśnica were administered at the end of 2012 and the beginning of 2013, a period of relative economic revigoration and improvement after five years during which the protectionist state and leftist solutions had proven partly successful. It appeared therefore commonsensical that the Polish local elite would be trustier, more confident in the model of welfare state, since the leftist-oriented responses to crises were perceived as effective yet far. 5.88% of the respondents in Oleśnica did not answer the question. Conversely, a total of 17.64% categorically disagreed with the state intervention in economy, 11.76% of them bearing strong feelings about it. It appeared that the members of the Municipal Council in the Polish case displayed powerful, unequivocal standpoints with regard to the protectionist state, since the topic of the state intervention in economy coalesced, or rather polarized, local councilors in a more consistent proportion (17.64% as strongly accepting and 11.76% as strongly rejecting) towards the *extremis* of the intensity scale proposed for measurement in this case: if, normally, the two poles on the acceptance-rejection scale gathered 5.88% within the Local Council of Tecuci (and only in the "strong rejection" side) and 13.63% for the Municipal Council of Česká Lípa (considerably more in the "strong rejection" part, as well), the Municipal Council of Oleśnica appeared largely dissimilar, for it coupled a 29.4% of the responses, quite surprisingly, preponderantly in the "strong acceptance" area. This discrepancy described, on one hand, a more radical local elite in the Polish case, capable of voicing powerful, clear-cut sentiments and viewpoints in respect to political practices and economic mechanisms, but, at the same time, a more polarized Municipal Council, divided on the lines of attitudinal stance towards the protectionist state. On the other hand, the results suggested a more robust inclination towards welfare solutions to the economic crisis, a tendency to favor the protectionist approaches to the national economy. The statist outlook of the Municipal Council in Oleśnica was thusly conspicuous.

Measuring the perceptions of the local elite towards larger local autonomy and decentralization is instrumental because it provides an insight into the recognition and consideration of various levels of authority in the leadership of the community. Surely, Poland underwent a drive towards increased decentralization after the adoption of the Law on Municipalities in March 1998, a process that culminated with a significant *palette* of attributions and prerogatives at the local level granted by the central administration to the local institutional instances, particularly the Municipal Council. Within the institutional arrangement of the Polish local administration[95], the Municipal Council represents the institution that is popularly elected and the one that emanates the administrative *apparatus* of the Municipality, an *apparatus* led by the Mayor. Therefore, as opposed to the Czech arrangement, the parliamentary model is not replicated at the local level in the Polish case. The largest *palette* of attributions and functions belongs to the Municipal Council which undertook the regulation tasks in most of the spheres of the community life, including social services, public improvements, education, healthcare, cultural and recreation activities. Inversely, there is a side effect to a more comprehensive and extended decentralization: larger local autonomy and decentralization mean primarily an effective say of the municipality on the local budget; as a consequence, it lies in the capacity of the local municipality to properly collect taxes and to efficiently administer the budgetary revenues thusly collected in order to actually effect changes in the various domains of competence under its direct supervision. With greater decentralization come greater authority and the ability to have a tremendous say in the conduct of the community's affairs, but, conversely, it also comes a great deal of responsibility in handling the ever-increasing problems the community confronts with. Balancing the advantages with the drawbacks of decentralization and autonomy at the local level, the members of the Municipal Council of Oleśnica positioned themselves somewhere in between the enthusiasm of the local elite in Tecuci (100% approval of greater decentralization, with various degrees, with a core of 64.7% approving and another 11.76% strongly approving decentralization) and the rather cautious pragmatism of the local elite in Česká Lípa (experienced in both the good points and the disadvantages decentralization presupposes, with 77.26% of the respondents approving or partially approving and another 22.72% disagreeing with larger local autonomy and decentralization granted by the central

---

95 For a quite comprehensive and detailed account on the evolution, benefits, achievements, and drawbacks of decentralization process in Poland, see Kerlin 2005.

authorities). The Polish local political elite displayed a sense of realism, properly understanding the mechanisms encapsulated by decentralizing a greater range of responsibilities in the local authority's sphere of competence, as 43.75% of the municipal councilors generally agreed with decentralization. Worth noting is that the acceptance of the Polish elites towards decentralization was around 44%, significantly less than the case of Tecuci (64.70%), but slightly higher than the Czech case (40.9%). Relevant, as well, was the fact that, in Oleśnica, the municipal councilors displayed the highest proportion of strong acceptance of decentralization and the perspective of autonomous entities in the Polish administrative arrangement: 25% of the respondents, as opposed to none in the case of Česká Lípa and only 11.76% in the case of Tecuci. Hence, the members of the Municipal Council in Oleśnica resulted as the most enthusiastic ones among the three selected cases in respect to decentralization and greater authority and responsibility granted to the local elite. In part, this might be explicable through the success of the 1998 reform of the administrative division of the Polish territory: the 1998 Act inaugurated a stage of local governance unprecedented in the Polish history, opening the way for an efficient distribution of funds and for an effective tax collection at the local level allowing for a comprehensive and more coherent development of the communities. The enthusiasm of the local elites had slightly decreased after the beginning of the economic crisis in 2008, but the reform had a 10-year period to nurture positive effects and to generate socio-economic growth of the local communities to profoundly mark the unequivocal positive evaluation of decentralization, while the economic crisis did not put a definitive imprint on the Polish economy overall, a situation that had made relatively rapid recovery of small communities possible and quite probable. Decentralization worked its charms in Poland, while being partially contested in the Czech Republic and unaccomplished and highly problematic in Romania; this was simply the reason why 25% of the local councilors in Oleśnica were strongly agreeing with its mechanisms and forms of manifestation. The partial acceptance of decentralization and local autonomy in the Polish case was, once again, situated in-between the Czech and the Romanian cases: a quarter of the members of the Municipal Council in Oleśnica expressed partial, rather reserved, approval, the same type of approval characterizing 23.52% of the councilors in Tecuci and 36.36% of those in Česká Lípa. Such a result was analogous to the general trend in the responses provided by the three selected groups: generally, the local elite in Oleśnica qualified as an intermediate group of elites between the Romanian and the Czech elite groups. On the same logic, a very thin proportion of 6.25% of the municipal councilors in Oleśnica bluntly stated that they disagreed with the ideas and the projects of decentralization and local autonomy, being largely disappointed with the feasibility and the efficiency of these projects and with the merits of the ideas; this disapproval was totally absent among the local councilors in Tecuci, but quite present among the councilors in Česká

Lípa (22.72% of the responses); expectedly, no member of the Municipal Council would have totally dismissed the reality of decentralization and the prospect of autonomy, a result that was consistent with the absence of such attitude of rejection for the other two Councils. All in all, the local elite in Oleśnica displayed a generally realistic, pragmatic stance in its evaluation of the importance of decentralization and autonomy – with a total of 93.75% of the councilors agreeing with the two administrative arrangements, in various degrees, as opposed to a feeble 6.25% of mere disagreement –, somewhere in the middle of the intensity axis, between a clearly enthusiastic, rather idealistic elite in Tecuci, in this respect, and a skeptical, slightly disenchanted elite in Česká Lípa. In Oleśnica, decentralization had produced positive effects and a more suitable management at the local level; consequently, the attitudes of the local elite towards it mirrored generally the experience this elite had had with the reality of increased devolution and growing array of authority and responsibility.

The evaluation of the evolution of the community's development, i.e. the direction the town is heading to, might be somehow correlated with the general attitude towards decentralization, devolution of responsibilities, and even local autonomy: these processes tend to generate significant, profound, cross-cutting transformations within small-to-medium municipalities, not exclusively in the area of the administrative organization of the bureaucratic personnel, but also in more concrete fields, such as the administration and management of schools, hospitals, public works, cultural sites, infrastructure, social security, etc. There are actually these developments that inevitably nurture a certain image of the town and, subsequently, a certain projection regarding the future of the community. Given the assessment by the local elites in Oleśnica of the largely successful process of decentralization, as impacted by their own community, their evaluation of the prospective *status* of the town was not surprising: an overwhelming 94.11% of the local councilors bore no reserves concerning the positive evolution of the town, while only 5.88% considered that there would be no major change in this evolution. Quite importantly noting was the fact that none of the members of the Municipal Council believed that Oleśnica was heading in a bad, wrong direction. Comparably, in both the other two cases, a particular level of negative projection appeared in the evaluations of the local elites regarding their towns: larger in Česká Lípa (22.72%), more nuanced in Tecuci (18.75%). However, the perspectives in Oleśnica were completely divergent from the same in the other two cases, and the results described completely different standpoints to the question of the future of the three communities. Concretely, while more than a half of the responses in the Czech case were circumscribed to the answer of stagnant evolution of the town (59.09% for "There is no change"), the proportion decreased with more than a half in the case of Tecuci (25% for "There is no change") and, eventually, becoming four times smaller in the case of Oleśnica (5.88% for "There is no change").

Therefore, the more stagnant projections over the town were to be found in the Czech case, whereas the most dynamic projections were characteristic for Oleśnica, from the perspectives of the local elite governing these towns. These results appeared rather dissonant when correlated with the incumbency level within the Municipal Councils analyzed here. Usually, it might be hypothesized that high levels of incumbency in the Council correspond to a less dynamic, even stagnant evolution of the community; conversely, low levels of incumbency are associated with a more dynamic – for better or for worse – evaluation of the development undergone by the town. This hypothesis was not verifiable to the empirical test of the *data* collected, since the elite group with the highest level of incumbency (Oleśnica, with 57.89% of the members of the Council) embraced an assessment of the direction in which their community was heading that was highly dynamic (94.11% of the responses actually describing a positive evolution); on the other hand, the elite group displaying the highest degree of elite renewal (Tecuci, with 42.1% incumbency in the Council) still bore a proportion of 25% prospective stagnation. The differences were present in the positive evaluation of the future of the community among the three cases: the lowest percentage of local councilors that considered that their town was heading in a good direction was to be encountered in the Czech case (18.18% of the responses), as opposed to the Polish case, in which the percentage expressing the same evaluation increased more than five times (94.11%); the Romanian case was an intermediate one, with 56.25% of the local councilors crediting the fact that the town they ruled was heading in the right direction. Overall, for the totality of the three cases, the positive evaluation of the future evolution of the towns in which the selected elite groups operated was an average of 56.18%, a value coinciding with the same evaluation for Tecuci (56.25%). Inversely, only an average of 13.82% of the members of the three Local Councils considered that their communities were heading in the wrong direction. In this sense, one should stress the conspicuous disparities between the Polish and the Czech cases: in the Czech case, those councilors who envisaged a positive future for the town (18.18%) were overwhelmed by those who evaluated that the direction in which the town was heading was the bad one (22.72%), whereas, in the Polish case, those who credited positive assessment regarding the future of their community were unequivocally unchallenged (there were no answers among the members of the Municipal Council in Oleśnica expressing negative assessments). Lastly, an average of 29.99% of the councilors in the three municipalities saw no change in the evolution of the towns, arguing in favor of a stagnant situation. Yet, it remained unclear what the source for such a deeply-entrenched and categorical enthusiasm concerning the perspectives of their community was in the case of the local councilors of Oleśnica. While, on the one hand, the disenchantment and the general disillusionment of the political elite in Česká Lípa in the face of the challenges posed by the economic crisis to the small-to-medium sized, largely decentralized, self-governing communities were expressed in the form of a skeptical, rather pessimistic perspective on the future development of the town, the explanation for the highly optimistic attitude of the elites in Oleśnica regarding the community's future could only be tentative. For one, this optimism might spring from the elite's capacity of containment of the effects of the economic crisis, that had seemed devastating for other communities. Secondly, such an overwhelmingly positive assessment might be interpreted as mere *desideratum* rather than as an evaluation founded on actual *data* on the prospective development of the town; the enthusiasm based on pure idealism might constitute, as a matter of fact, a suitable, even though quite problematic, explanation, since the same elite group vigorously denounced the unemployment and the lack of investments generating job opportunities as the two main problems its town confronted with. Therefore, the problems did exist and they were more pregnant and neuralgic as ever; when these problems were persistent, it seemed inexplicable the unlimited enthusiasm of the local elite to the future of a town facing so stringent issues. As a matter of fact, the Polish elites claimed more serious problems than the Czech ones, even though the former was five times more confident about the future of their town than the later: compare, for instance, the importance of unemployment to the social sensitivity or the significance of cultural effervescence.

The geographical identification of the local political elite was considered in order to correlate it with the priorities of the ruling groups of small-to-medium communities. It has been already presumed that stronger links, interactions and power networks formed and maintained at the local level suggest localism and, subsequently, a more pronounced focus on the local priorities and on dealing and solving the community's immediate issues and, conversely, an isolation with respect to the national concerns. Similarly, it might be hypothesized that a geographical identification inclined towards localism (i.e. the cases in which the members of the Local Councils identified primarily with their native towns / communes / villages / municipalities, with the town they represented or with the region which they inhabited) is prone to generate an emphasis on local problems, perceived as taking precedence over the "national interests". Quite alike, stressing on a more broadly understood geographical identification (either national – i.e. with the country –, or regionally international – i.e. with the region to which their country is customarily associated or with the continent) is telling for the local elite's openness towards more general, far-reaching, all-encompassing, rather defused issues. Considering these observations, the Municipal Council in Oleśnica expectedly exposed a high degree of localism, as 50% of the members of the Council identified first and foremost with the municipality they politically represented and governed, the town of Oleśnica; another 15% of the councilors bore a particular attachment towards the native town / village, thus making localism in geographical identification a characteristic pertaining to 65% of the Council. Regional identification was featured by only 15% of the councilors: 10% of them expressed belonging to the region of Lower Silesia as a first mark of territorial identification, whereas 5% claimed the identification with the Oleśnica county / province (i.e. a territorial-administrative division specific to the Polish administration, labeled "*powiat*" that is somewhere in-between the municipality, the "*gmina*", and the region, the "*województwa*", the voivodship). Expectedly – and anticipated from the very overview drawn from the results gathered regarding elites' interactions and networks of power –, the least favored geographical association was the international one. None of the councilors identified themselves primarily as East-Central European, which was probably perceived as an invented, unnatural, constructed form of regional identity that exceeded the statist boundaries[96]. Despite the numerous attempts at constructing a regional, East-Central European (or, better, Central European) identity (particularly among the Polish, Czech, Slovak and Hungarian nations, renownedly known as "the Visegrad Group"), such efforts had not penetrated the local level and the rationale of the local elites in the four countries, since the members of the Local Council in Oleśnica claimed no such dimension of geographic and cultural identification. Moreover, many of the councilors still lived under the paradigm of not being associated with something even remotely Eastern, as the younger ones displayed an increased preoccupation of detaching themselves from the communist past, characterized by a persistent association with the East: for that matter, "East-Central European" connoted an empty shell, since the reference to the "East" was automatically refuted, while, with the accession to the European Union in 2004, Poland as a whole should allegedly be a component part of Europe, not even of Central, i.e. Second-ranked, Europe. On the other hand, the national identification remained strong, even though hardly compensating for the powerful localism manifested in the self identification of the members of the Municipal Council in Oleśnica: 15% identified culturally and geographically primarily with Poland, nurturing a sense of national pride and considering the "national interests" taking precedence over the local ones. Finally, a fully-fledged "European identity" was characteristic of a mere 5% of the local councilors in Oleśnica. In comparison with the results for the Romanian and the Czech cases, the Polish case presented a more dispersed range of sources of identification, a multilayered and multifaceted one. At least six layers of geographical and cultural identification were acknowledged and given due consideration by the respondents: there were firstly (1) a native source of identification (at the village or town level – 15%), and (2) a local *per se* identification (with the town which these councilors represented and ruled for – 50%); secondly, there were complementary, rather regional sources of identification, (3) the county / province, the "*powiat*" (5%) and (4) the region,

---

96 After all, what does it mean to be a "East-Central European"? For an in-depth discussion of the valences the collocation "East-Central Europe" bears and for a historical review over the "Second Europe", see Malia 2006: 16-33.

the "*województwa*" (10%); thirdly, there was an almost inherent national source of identification, primarily characterizing a robust 15% of the councilors; and fourthly, there was an additional "European identity" claimed by 5% of the local councilors. The scheme appeared significantly reduced, compressed in the other two cases: in Tecuci, only four types of cultural-geographical identification were considered by the councilors (the native, the local, the regional and the national ones), while, in Česká Lípa, the matrix included four sources as well, though slightly different from the ones considered in the case of Tecuci, due especially to different forms of administrative organization of the territory between the two (native, local, provincial, regional). Definitely, part of the discrepancies among the three cases in respect to the cultural-geographical identification spang from the very administrative arrangements of each of the countries under scrutiny. But the differences lay also in the degree of openness each of the elite groups inquired here actually displayed. Indeed, the level of localism was dominant for all cases, though quite dissimilar as numerical value: 65% in Oleśnica, 72.72% in Tecuci, 92.29% in Česká Lípa; it resulted that, as a matter of fact, the local elite in Oleśnica was the least isolated, which would, to a certain extent, stand against the isolation of the same group when considering their overwhelmingly local connections and networks of power. Generally, the Polish local councilors' understanding of cultural-geographical identity suggested a higher degree of broadness, openmindedness, stressing not exclusively on native / local identification, but rather on a regional one, as well: 10% of the councilors of Oleśnica identified with the region of Lower Silesia, a similar 9.09% of the councilors in Tecuci identified with the region of Moldavia, whereas only 3.84% of the councilors in Česká Lípa identified primarily with the region of Liberec, part of which their municipality is. The nature of the Polish (and, in some degree, the Czech) administrative arrangement of the territory is conducive to the establishment of multifaceted and polyvalent relations between the level of municipality and that of the county (which sometimes overlap) and between the local and the regional / voivodship levels, particularly in the sphere of the division of competences and responsibilities in key areas of local development and management (e.g. public improvements, social services, infrastructure); this very nature of the Polish administration might constitute an explicative insight into the importance the local councilors of Oleśnica credited to the regional identification. In addition, the Polish elite group was the only one among the three cases selected to consider and acknowledge a "European" identification (5% of the responses). Among the three Local Councils, the Romanian local elite was the more inclined towards a national identification (18.18%), in stark opposition to the Czech elite that acknowledged no such source of identification (testifying once more to the extremely localized character of the elite in Česká Lípa); the elite in Oleśnica was close to the Romanian case, with 15% of the councilors considering a national identification and referring to themselves primarily

249

as "Poles" rather than "inhabitants of Oleśnica" or "representatives of Lower Silesia". All in all, the average level of localism among the three cases was 76.67%, that of regionalism mounted to 11.87% of the entire population comprised in the three Municipal Councils, while that of nationalism was 11.06%; the European identification was present only in the Polish case (15% of the responses). It is worth mentioning as well that none of the entire population of the local councilors in the three cases considered an "East-Central European" identity, perceived as a rather pejorative collocation even though projects of regionalizing the countries situated in Eastern and the Central part of the European continent under the banner of "East-Central Europe" had been advanced by the central elites (see, in this sense, the "V4" project).

The satisfaction of the municipal councilors of being inhabitants of the municipality they represented might constitute an indicator of the fashion in which they evaluated their political performance in managing the town's problems. Not surprisingly, the same hardly restrained enthusiasm of the members of the Municipal Council in Oleśnica in respect to the direction in which their community was heading transpired in the evaluation of the satisfaction felt by inhibiting the town: an impressive 47.05% of the councilors felt very satisfied living in Oleśnica and another equally impressive 52.94% declared they were satisfied inhibiting the town. None of the members of the Municipal Council in Oleśnica considered (s)he was unsatisfied or very unsatisfied as an inhabitant of the town. As a result, the entire population of the Council concentrated around higher degrees of satisfaction of living in Oleśnica. This quite unprecedented enthusiasm was unparalleled by any of the other two cases: although the members of the Councils in both Tecuci and Česká Lípa showed high levels of satisfaction as inhabitants of their communities (fairly satisfied was characteristic for 58.82% of the councilors in Tecuci and for 72.72% of those in Česká Lípa), cumulatively it was the Municipal Council of Oleśnica that accounted for the highest percentage of very satisfied elites in respect to the outlook of their community. Comparatively, there was no councilor to be very satisfied of living in Tecuci and a feeble 4.54% of the councilors very satisfied of being part of the community in Česká Lípa; the degree of satisfaction of inhabiting Oleśnica was more than ten times higher than that in the Czech case. In the case of the Local Council of Oleśnica, there was also an almost unnoticeable difference between those very satisfied and those fairly satisfied (5.89%), whereas in the case of Česká Lípa and Tecuci, the difference impressively climbed at 68.18% and 58.82%, respectively; this low difference was a translation of the enthusiasm the local elite in Oleśnica bore for the current and the future situation of their municipality. A reasonable proportion of dissatisfaction in respect to being an inhabitant of the town was inherent within the Municipal Councils of Tecuci (29.41% of the councilors) and of Česká Lípa (22.72% of the councilors); the Romanian case further displayed a sentiment of profound dissatisfaction among the elite inhabiting the town (11.76%), in contrast to the other two cases in which no such strong dissatisfaction was encountered within the elite groups. The strong satisfaction of the Polish local elite towards inhabiting the town and towards the conditions, advantages, benefits and privileges the town could offer was intimately correlated with their assessment of the positive direction in which the town was heading and with their evaluation of their own political performances in crucial, focal areas and sphere of competence at the local level (e.g. public improvements, infrastructure, healthcare, education, cultural & youth & sports activities, social services and public security). Moreover, the confidence and the enthusiasm of the local political elites in Oleśnica were revelatory for a dynamic community, with constant interactions with the surrounding rural area together with which the town forms the mixed "*powiat*". There was also some form of local pride among the members of the Municipal Council that nurtured in this enthusiasm, a propensity towards localism and immediate proximity that stressed on the achievements and the accomplishments the community registered through local governance after the initiation of the decentralization process after 1998. Overall, for the three cases considered here, the average percentage of strong satisfaction in respect to the living in and the conditions of living in a certain small-to-medium community was 17.19% of the entire population of the Councils. The satisfaction as to being an inhabitant of the town represented, expressed by the local councilors, registered an average of 61.49% among the three samples, a percentage that translated a great deal of compliance with the conditions and benefits the towns could provide from the part of the leaders of these three towns. The level of dissatisfaction with inhabiting the three towns exposed an average proportion of 17.37% of the total population of the local councilors; the level of strong dissatisfaction was encountered only in the Romanian case, with an average of 11.76%.

Indeed, the Polish case of local administration and government represents a special instance: Hesse and Goetz contend that

"in sum, [...] local governments and administration in Poland have gone through major upheavals during the past years. The territorial organization of local governance has remained largely unchanged, but there have been far-reaching functional, political, administrative and financial reforms which have begun to transform the role of the local level in the governance of Poland." (Hesse and Goetz 1992: 39)

Concluding Remarks

The similarities between the six cases were unpredictably striking. The six Local / Municipal Councils are similarly organized and they are all the emanations of direct popular vote followed by an applied formula of proportional representation. In addition, once thusly constituted, the selected Councils are the legal bearers of a series of quite resembling attributions, functions and prerogatives at the local level. Following the legal frameworks regulating the outlook and the functioning of the Municipal (Local) Councils in all the six countries selected, one can dichotomously distinguish between general and specific attributions of the local legislative *fora*. In this sense, somehow overcoming the classical distinction, Virgil Stoica designs a fourfold classification of prerogatives and attributions for the Municipal Councils in East-Central Europe: (1) attributions within the sphere of internal organizations of the Local Councils themselves and of their public services; (2) attributions in the field of elaborating, administering and executing the local budget and of establishing the local taxes and budgetary revenues; (3) attributions in the domain of organizing, coordinating and ensuring the economic and socio-cultural activities and activities aimed at observing, protecting and promoting the citizens' rights and liberties, and (4) attributions connected to the local representation and promotion of the community (e.g. the conferring of titles of honor, the cooperation of "twin towns" from abroad and from within the country, etc.) (Stoica 2003: 76-78). At a closer look, one could observe that, generally, the Municipal Council in Česká Lípa faces a larger, more diversified palette of prerogatives, a significantly special place among these tasks being occupied by the election of both the Mayor and the Vice-majors among its members. Therefore, a first important differentiation is actually the position held by each of the six Municipal Councils within the organizational scheme of the towns they represent, within the political configuration favored by the legislation on local affairs in Romania, the Czech Republic, Poland, Hungary, the Slovak Republic, and in Bulgaria, respectively. In the case of Tecuci, Oleśnica (after 1998), Gyula, Levice, and Targovishte, the Mayor, the head of the local administration, is the emanation of the popular vote, while in the case of Česká Lípa, the Mayor and his Vices are the expression, the extension of the Council itself – two models that would illustrate the reproduction of the presidential and parliamentary democracies, respectively, at the local scale. Hence, one would contend, the Municipal Council in Česká Lípa enjoys a central position in the "elective" matters of the local administration, though the Council in the other five cases works as the balancing counterpart of the Mayor's authority, with functions of paramount importance particularly in the field of budget debating and approval. Nevertheless, as in any presidential-like form of legal organization, cleavages and contradictory standpoints may arouse between the two instances, the legislative (i.e. the Local Council) and the executive (i.e. the Mayor) ones, especially in the difficult, problematic context of different, opposable political affiliations of the two institutions. However, as a rule, the Mayor has enjoyed the (political) support of the Local Council, since the popular vote for the Mayor is similar to, and practically doubles, the one for the members of the Council.

Though the patterns – more exactly, the mechanisms – of recruitment are largely alike in the six cases – but, more importantly, in the four cases in which the municipal representatives are selected in an intramural manner –, the results they yielded were dissimilar, the final composition of the six Municipal Councils encountering some marked differences. For once, the three-layered hierarchy of selection appears valid for all the four cases of dominantly intramural, party-based selection (Tecuci, Česká Lípa, Gyula, and Targovishte): the "selectorates" – or the "gate-keepers" – are arranged on three major levels: (1) the national, (2) the regional (or the county level), and (3) the local levels. As expected, the local selectorates play the most important, central role in the actual mural selection of the would-be local councilors. In the case of Tecuci and Targovishte, the networks of power established between the local selectorates and the future candidates for a seat in the Council were particularly significant, since – due mainly to the small magnitude of the town's community – the relations between the two groups went as far as family connections. Therefore, an insistence on personalized politics became more visible and pregnant in the case of the local elites in Tecuci and Targovishte, where connections of nepotism-styled flavor were to be still sporadically encountered, but a tendency towards personalized politics was to be seen in the case of Oleśnica, as well, where the town's notables were quite visible in their activity as municipal councilors. The problem aroused exactly in the sphere of these extremely localized types of relations among elites, that tended to virtually monopolize the entire *palette* of connections the local elite was capable of establishing and cultivating: the power networks of the local political elite in Tecuci and Targovishte were centered on and channeled by the locally-based relations, in an unfortunate misbalance with a more open approach in local affairs favored by the relationships with the central authorities or with homolog officials throughout the country. The conspicuous predominance of local connections, of those created exclusively within the extremely contingent setting of the town, demonstrated the closeness, the enclave character of the local political elites in Tecuci and Targovishte, but the same observation was valid for all the six cases under scrutiny. On the other hand, due to the fact that the political and the economic elites overlapped in the cases of Tecuci and Targovishte, the most consistent elite connections were those with the business entities and groups that might be frequently developed outside the immediate space of the town. Therefore, the same individuals were reluctant in creating and sustaining vaster, airy relations in their capacity as political elite, though, at the same time, establishing business connections that would normally transcend the spatial and structural contingencies of the town in their capacity as economic elite. If C. Wright-Mills describes, for the American society of the 50s, a famous inseparable and inextricable interconnectedness between the political, the economic and the military elites, in Tecuci and in Targovishte, as previously stated, a first problem of analysis aroused when facing the reality of a virtual overlapping between the political and economic local elite: the potentates of the town were at the same time the economic magnates and political leaders. The situation was strikingly different in the other four cases, with very few, sporadic, isolated exceptions: the Municipal Councils here were formed of individuals who, in a large majority, enjoyed a rich political experience in the local officialdom. On the other hand, they represented the middle-class *stratum* of the town, being highly educated, having financial independence, but entertaining no business connections with the economic elite of the community, which constituted a different entity, comprising other individuals. The persistence and the sense of personalized politics, generally favored at the local level, were being gradually lost, being yet not totally absent.

Conspicuous differences and discrepancies were to be spotted in the spheres of the priorities and values the six local elite groups indicated during the survey. While, for the case of Tecuci and Targovishte, there was a persistent preoccupation with the lack of funds and investments, and with opportunities for economic development at the local level, in Česká Lípa, Levice, and Gyula, among the most pressing problems the towns confronted with, the local councilors pointed to the economic crisis (experienced during the research) and, more specifically, to unemployment and to related social problems (including housing, education and healthcare). When asked to pinpoint the major problem in the administration of their community, the six elite groups reacted slightly differently: from the answers received to an open-ended question, one could observe the fact that the local councilors in Tecuci and Targovishte, in their large majority, indicated a certain important problem (i.e. lack of funds and investments)[97], while the municipal councilors in Česká Lípa and Oleśnica produced a great diversity of answers, with only slight agreement on the gravest problem of their town (e.g. for Česká Lípa, 26.92% - for both economic crisis and unemployment). The distribution of the answers demonstrated, at least in respect to the priorities concerning the town, a more cohesive, unified political elite in Tecuci and Targovishte, bearing similar perspectives and visions regarding the problems of their community and the measures to be taken, concentrated around one principal issue to be dealt with at the local level; on

---

97 One should remember the fact that only a handful of questionnaires were filled in in a setting bringing together the councilors, hence favoring some sort of a peer pressure generating similar answers (e.g. during the ordinary sessions of the Local Council or during the sessions of the Council's specialized Committees). The majority of the questionnaires were filled in in settings in which the respondent was outside the direct influence of his peers (work place, home, by phone, etc.).

254

the other hand, the local political elites in Česká Lípa, Oleśnica, Levice and Gyula were more fragmented, rather divided in agreeing on the central problem of the town in which they exerted influence and authority, with no consensus regarding priorities of their actions at the local level.

Explanatory trajectories: the "legacy of the ancien régime"

For the purpose of accounting for the differences between the six selected cases, this book isolates two main explanatory independent variables: (1) the level of administrative decentralization, and (2) the "elite political culture". The collocation "elite political culture" is differently referred to in the literature. Even though almost all the studies tackling the topic of "political culture" revolve around the *spiritus rectore* G. Almond and S. Verba and their pioneering *opus magnum The Civic Culture*, Kenneth Jowitt, for instance, defines "elite political culture" somehow in opposition to what he coins as "regime political culture" and "community political culture": an "elite political culture" is "a set of informal adaptative (behavioral and attitudinal) postures that emerge as response to and consequence of a given elite's identity-forming experiences."[98] For the specific study of political elites, Robert Putnam famously referred to "elite political culture", defined as some form of attitudinal and behavioral aggregates of the elite group, generally constant, hardly changeable, stable ones; the term accounts for "patterns of beliefs and attitudes [prevalent among the members of the political elite] about the economic, political, social, cultural systems" (Putman 1973 [additions mine]). James Anderson (1997: 43-44) cites renowned political scientist Daniel J. Elazar and his description of three types of "political cultures", a considerable and compelling scholarly evolution from the classical Almond and Verba's threefold "parochial" – "subject" – "participant" political cultures: (1) "individualistic" (i.e. in which the government is "an utilitarian device to be used to accomplish what the people wants", while the political elites is only "interested in holding office as a means of controlling government's favors or rewards"), (2) "moralistic" (i.e. in which the government is "a mechanism for advancing the public interest", public service takes precedence over public interest, together with an accepted level of interventionism), and (3) "traditionalistic" political culture (i.e. in which the government is maintainer of the existing social order, in a rather "paternalistic and elitist view of government" (Elazar 1984), the political power is concentrated around an enclosed, small, monolithic political elite, and the citizenry is politically inactive and atomized). In applying the observations drawn from the usage of the concept "elite political culture", one could only wonder if the six selected groups forming the Local Councils of the municipalities of Tecuci and

---

98 "Regime political culture" is "a set of informal adaptative (behavioral and attitudinal) postures that emerge in response to the institutional definition of social, economic, and political life" and "community political culture" is defined as "a set of informal adaptative (behavioral and attitudinal) postures that emerge in response to the institutional definition of social, economic, and political life". See Jowitt 1992: 51-52 and 54-56.

Targovishte, the Municipal Councils of the municipalities Česká Lípa, Oleśnica, and Levice, and the Body of Representatives of the municipality of Gyula, had acquired a sense of group consciousness as an elite; such an "elite consciousness" at the local level is difficult to be operationalized and subsequently measured, but some attemptive endeavors might employ such indicators as the degree of group cohesion, the acknowledgement of some "special" (i.e. specific) traits a local councilor should possess (excepting, of course, the moral, ethical dimension which is by no means one of group or *status* differentiation in the case of elites[99]). Starting from the premises that the elite group is eminently homogeneous, unitary and that the members of such a group are highly aware that they belong to it, sharing resembling social origins and embracing similar values, knowing each other, James Meisel summarizes this form of "elite consciousness" as the rule of the "3Cs": "group consciousness", "coherence" and "conspirativity" (i.e. common intentions) (Meisel 1962: 4). Only in the presence of elite consciousness as a prerequisite, can one speak and comprehensively analyze the "elite political culture". For the specific cases referred to by the book, there was surely a more profound sense of group solidarity (commonly referred to by the respondents as "collegiality" and "team spirit") and cohesion among the members of the Local Councils in Tecuci and Targovishte: they generally thought alike, had the same priorities, embraced the same values, had a largely similar social and family background, they resembled each other, to some extent, even in demographic terms (approximately the same age, same religion, same ethnical homogeneity). However, this is not sufficient: did they feel as belonging to the town's elite, to the upper *strata* of the community? Surprisingly, the members of the Local Councils in Tecuci and Targovishte did display a sense of prominence within the community, if not from an economic standpoint (for those who were the leading entrepreneurs of the town), at least from a reputational point of view (in a small community, such as those analyzed here, the prestige enjoyed due to a well-viewed occupational status – physician, engineer, especially teacher – or due to "great deeds" in the service of the community – for those administrating public spots, for instance – is a particularly important mark of distinguishness conducive to a sense of elitism).

Conversely, for the Municipal Councils of Česká Lípa, Levice, and only partly Gyula, what might have be applied in regard to the "elite political culture" and group consciousness was the paradigm of "democratic elitism" (Higley and Best 2010, and, equally illuminating, Higley and Best 2009)[100],

---

99   Though rhetorically catchy and discursively fashionable, the ethical image of the political elite, in the sweet Aristotelian tradition, is an obsolete one, and its obsoleteness became conspicuous in the literature as early as the beginning of the 20th century, with the famous works of the Italian "elitists", the trio Pareto – Mosca – Michels.

100 For the first mentions of the phrase "democratic elitism", see the renowned works of Bachrach: Bachrach, 1967; and Bachrach and Baratz 1970.

i.e. the more or less natural reconciliation between the democratic *desideratum* of popular sovereignty and the rule by the people and the elitist conception of the actual rule by the few. What was proper for the political elites in Česká Lípa and Levice was particularly this type of approaching the *res publica*, the public, administrative affairs of the community: while being well aware of the position held in the power hierarchy of the town, the local elite here had the tendency of confounding itself with the bulk of the population they represented, at least at a discursive level. Nevertheless, this attitude was conspicuously contradicted by the clear discrepancy and misrepresentation elite – electorate at the descriptive level of education: the high educational level of the political elites of Česká Lípa and Levice, with the large majority of local councilors having graduated post-graduate and even doctoral studies, provided exactly that type of distinctiveness and group consciousness of the members of the Municipal Councils of Česká Lípa and Levice in regard to the population's outlook of their constituencies.

In reference to the study of "elite political culture" *per se*, the book, following Anton Steen's inquiry into the Russian and Baltic post-communist elites (Steen 2007: 79-102), differentiates, at the limited level of attitudinal orientations, among three indicators of such political culture, partially accounting for the differences between the six elite groups discussed here: (1) the "content" of the attitude (i.e. either liberal or more authoritarian-like perspectives), (2) the "level" of expressing the respective attitude (i.e. either "ideological", "policy" or "instrumental" positions and attitude statements), and (3) the "structure" of the attitude (i.e. the degree of attitude cohesion at the group level, that is, "conforming or conflicting within and between elite groups"). Globally, all communities of Tecuci, Česká Lípa, Oleśnica, Gyula, Levice, and Targovishte experienced historically a totalitarian past, accompanied by a corresponding political culture at all of the three levels (regime, elite, community). Even after thirty years since the communist breakdown, the legacy of the *ancien régime* remained persistent. As it has already been observed, the local political elites in Tecuci and Targovishte were rather statist-anti-egalitarian, which appeared rather as a paradox in respect to the outlook of the defunct communist regime: the image of the state as prominent in socio-economical realm was preserved, while a rejection of economic equality was strongly affirmed, exactly in opposition to the aspirations of the former leadership. In the Czech and the Slovak Republics (as former Czechoslovakia) until 1989, the "theme" of the regime was the same (i.e. the communist one), but the "variation" was not a "modernizing-nationalizing"[101], "patrimonial"[102] dictatorship, as in Romania

---

101 The term "modernizing-nationalizing communist dictatorship" belongs to Petrescu 2010: 12, 47-48, 76, 113-118 and 404.
102 For the coining of the term "patrimonial" communist dictatorship, see Kitschelt, Mansfeldova, Markowski, and Tóka 1999: 39.

and Bulgaria, but a "bureaucratic-authoritarian"[103], "welfare"[104] communist dictatorship. Conversely, in Česká Lípa and Levice, the local elites tended to be more inclined to a "welfare-state" approach in conducting local policies, somehow admitting the social benefits of the former regime, without holding a nostalgic stance: this is probably the reason why they fitted into the category of "statist-egalitarians", since a significant proportion of them were concerned with the social problems the community they represented (especially unemployment) and they still cherished economic equality as an indispensable value in democracy. All in all, it is notorious that the six countries whose local elites are here under scrutiny had suffered a regime change in their recent history, which marked a somewhat consistent process of "elite circulation", for the Czech, the Slovak, the Polish, and the Hungarian cases, and a persistent "elite reproduction", for the Romanian and the Bulgarian cases (Szelényi and Szelényi 1995: 615-638). These two parallel developments translated only in fragmentary form at the local level, although they irrefutably generated a more or less radical change in the dominant "elite political culture", especially in respect to the priorities of these groups in their communities: the shift became more conspicuous when observing the personal-oriented priorities of the members of the political elite, definitely transformed in the drive towards a rather ferocious capitalism; economic wellbeing and acquiring financial assets became of paramount importance for the former elite that had recently lost political power in its attempt to reinvent itself into economic potentates, but also for the newly rising elite particularly interested in taking a hold on the sources of power in its fight both for decommunization and democratic, free market development and against the "post-" and "neo-communist" contending elites. The cases of the Czech Republic or Poland, on the one hand, and Romania or Bulgaria, on the other hand, couldn't be more different in this respect: after 1989, while the Czech elites engaged in a so-called "voucher privatization" (Eyal 2000: 50)[105], the Romanian elite was often seen as "neo-communist", the inheritor of the former monolithic Communist Party, hence quite reluctant to the efficient implementation of free market policies. Within the political culture of "transitional elites" in the six countries, transmuted even at the local level, the economic issue of some sort of "additional resources" (i.e. additional

---

103 Kitschelt et al. (1999) distinguish between three main types of communist dictatorship: (1) "national-accommodative" (Poland and Hungary), (2) "bureaucratic-authoritarian" (borrowing a term from Linz and Stepan 1996) (East Germany and Czechoslovakia), and (3) "patrimonial" communist dictatorships (Romania and Bulgaria).

104 The variation "welfare" communist dictatorship was first used in respect to East Germany and Czechoslovakia by Jarausch 1999: 47-69, esp. 59-60.

105 "Voucher privatization" meant that the new government de-nationalized assets to a series of investment funds, funds under the control of the central bank; hence, the Czech privatization was rather limited, the individual, private claims to ownership being largely neglected in the process. This peculiar type of privatization generated a mood of asceticism among the economic elite.

to the political ones) plays a central role. In this regard, Czech scholar Gil Eyal describes globally two patterns of elite transformation in the face of "capitalism", i.e. of the challenges posed by the free market economy, in East-Central Europe:

> "(1) where the *nomenklatura* managed to convert itself into a propertied class *via* 'spontaneous privatization', the result was a system of 'capitalists without capitalism', i.e. a relatively powerful propertied social class thriving in the context of a weak, rudimentary, or even absent capitalist market institutions"; and (2) "where [...] the *nomenklatura* was blocked by an independent *intelligentsia*, the latter began to understand itself and act as a *bildungsbürgertum*, a cultural bourgeoisie in charge of building capitalist institutions. Privatization proceeded more cautiously, and typically produced diffuse ownership rights and *de facto* managerial control. The result was a 'capitalism without capitalists', i.e. developed capital and labor markets, functioning stock exchanges, and budding mechanisms of corporate governance, all administered by the *intelligentsia* in its role as 'cultural bourgeoisie', but without a propertied class." (Eyal 2000: 49-50 [additions mine])

In continuation of Eyal's "capitalism without capitalists and capitalists without capitalism", Lawrence King and Iván Szelényi distinguish a certain fragmentation within the party *nomenklatura*, during the last decade of state socialism, in respect to the possibility of social mobility, and the resulting generational opportunities. As King and Szelényi conclude, it was those middle-ranked and middle-class party officials who accumulated the highest level of frustration, as their social and political ascendant mobility was curtailed by high-level party officials. Nevertheless, in a "partially privatized economic sector" emerging under communism, particularly in the socialist countries of Central Europe, this socio-political *stratum* reoriented its energies towards the economy:

> "To the extent that private enterprise offered higher incomes than party positions, lower-level party officials entered into business, creating a split between them and party elites and also with middle *strata* who continued to devote their efforts to maintaining or advancing their careers within the party. In this way, technocrats in the Eastern European parties who saw their careers and hopes for reform blocked found a new path to advance themselves and to challenge state socialism in the emerging private sector, which is why they abandoned state socialism and became the leading edge of capitalist enterprise." (King and Szelényi 2004; see also Lachmann 2013: esp. 99-101)[106]

While some claims regarding the birth of a "gangster capitalism" in post-communist Czech Republic were raised, the place of a more ferocious, indeed "gangster"-type, capitalism is undoubtedly transitional, developing Romania

---

106 The stellar book, authored by Konrád and Szelényi, written initially as a samizdat essay during 1973-1974, The Intellectuals on the Road to Class Power (1979) represents a mandatory reading for the examination of the counter-elite's position during the last decades of state socialism in Central-Eastern Europe.

and Bulgaria. After successive governmental changes and "elite circulations", the "voucher privatization" of the early '90s has its repercussions in today's representations of the local political elite in the Czech Republic, since, as it has been revealed, middle-aged members of the Municipal Council in Česká Lípa were inclined to favor statist stances, the state intervention in economy, a perennial orientation among the Czech political elite, in the old tradition consecrated by a timid "voucher privatization", recently reinforced by the economic crisis: there is a persistent image of the state being the most efficient manager of firms and the most serious, safe and committed entrepreneur.

Probably, one of the most immediate elements inherited from the defunct regime in the Romanian and the Bulgarian cases, and so facilely transmitted at the local level, where it found a fertile soil to further develop and be perpetuated, is the insistence and perseverance of the political elites to capture the leadership positions in other societal spheres as well, especially the economic and social ones, less the cultural, facets of the community. Not only do the local political elites in Tecuci and Targovishte bore the monopoly on economic activities, but they also led the social life of the town, through their position on the hierarchical scheme of the community (leading physicians, directors of schools, chiefs of administrative committees, administrators of public spots, etc.). On the other hand, in the sphere of regime change and post-communist developments, the difference between the Romanian or the Bulgarian, and the Czech or the Polish cases lies as well in a timing discrepancy: if, in the Czech and the Polish cases, elite change initiated before the systemic, structural change, in the Romanian and the Bulgarian ones, the sequence was rather reversed, since institutional changes were precursor of elite change. At the local level, after thirty years since the communist breakdown, this might be translated through a reluctance of the local political elites in Tecuci and Targovishte towards effective and efficient reforms in crucial domains (such as public improvements, changes in transport, education and healthcare infrastructure), as opposed to a more open approach towards meaningful change in the case of the Municipal Councils of Česká Lípa and Levice, where change started from the membership of the Councils themselves. Moreover, transiting the Municipal Councils from Tecuci and Targovishte to Česká Lípa and Levice, and back, one could observe a monolithic-like elite, highly homogeneous in terms of bio-demographical features, values, priorities and patterns of recruitment, cherishing party loyalty, political experience and collegiality (team spirit) especially, opposing a more heterogeneous elite group, demographically more diverse, with different values and cultural standards, sprung from similar recruitment procedures and embracing the same priorities in respect to the community they represented and governed. Monolithism and the predominance of a "political model" might be reminiscent of the elites of the former regime, while a "pragmatic model" and a fragmented elite group would coincide to a tradition of circulating elites and technocratic "*petite bourgeoisie*" during the period of state socialism. Instead, nowadays, it is the "pragmatic model" of "organizational and personal commitments", of efficiency and effective management, that surpasses the importance of the "political model" of party and ideological loyalty: though the influence of party affiliations and ideological affinities become crucial and even indispensable in the recruitment schemes, they lose their importance in the face of the localized problems the small community confronts with; problem-solving, respect for the community, competence and the capacity to pinpoint development opportunities for the town are those elite features that impose themselves when a group establishes itself as a local political elite.

Hellman pinpoints exactly the "winners" of early transition in East-Central Europe, particularly at the local level; the situation described coincides especially with the Romanian and the Bulgarian cases:

> "[T]he most frequently mentioned obstacles to the progress of economic reform in post-communist transitions have come from very different sources: from enterprise insiders who have become new owners only to strip their firms' assets; [...] from local officials who have prevented market entry in their regions to protect their share of local monopoly rents [...]. These actors can hardly be classified as the short-term losers of economic reform. On the contrary, they were its earliest and its biggest winners." (Hellman 1998: 204)

In former "patrimonial" communist dictatorships, central and local leaders transferred political capital into economic one; in contemporaneity, conversely, local elites transferred economic capital into political one, adding political leverage to an already existent economic one. The extraordinary drive towards increased decentralization after 1989 added to this capital transfer locally, for "[w]ithout doubt, the 1990 local government reform [in ECE] established one of the most liberal systems of local government in Europe" (Balázs 1993: 75).

The variable of the heritage of the communist *ancien régime*, i.e. the "Leninist legacy" (Jowitt 1999: 207-223; Hanson 1995: 306-314), appears central for the present analysis of the differences between the six local elite groups, as significant characteristics of the local political elites in the six selected cases (particularly, segments of the social biography of the members of the Local Councils, the construction and the design of the networks of power and elite interactions, the values embraced by the six elite groups, etc.) were directly and non-intermediated influenced by the outlook the defunct state socialism preserved even in the post-communist, transitional era. Yet, the different cases of "communist dictatorship" and their reverberations into the present-day local elite *milieu* are necessary, though not sufficient, in explaining the complete landscape constructed and shaped by each local political elite in its own community, considering the very fact that a long series of post-communist, transitional structural changes marked indiscriminately and undoubtedly such landscape. This is particularly the reason why the degree of decentralization was equally considered in the concluding remarks of the present study of local political elites in East-Central Europe, a *locus* of constant transitional political-administrative experiments and reforms, of permanent reconfigurations and re-organizations, invariably aimed towards democratic consolidation, i.e. larger and more consistent citizen participation.

Explanatory trajectories: the level of administrative decentralization

This book considers, as one of the most important independent variable accounting for the variations and the discrepancies between the local elites of six fairly similar towns, the degree of decentralization these six communities enjoy. Generally, the most convincing argument for designing and establishing forms of local government, decentralization and greater autonomy at the local or regional levels lies in the *dictum* of increasing citizen participation and bridging the apparently incommensurable gap between the elites and the masses, between the rulers and the ruled, thus making the decision-making process largely accessible to the ordinary citizens. Consequently and normatively, such a logic would inevitably lead to a "local democratic mandate" from the part of each member of the Local Council, i.e. "by being more immediate to local communities, [the representative] can [...] be far more responsive to local wishes than national government[s]" (Copus 2004: 180 [additions mine]).

The *problématique* of the decentralization of public services towards the local communities has represented a perennial preoccupation on the agenda and within the programmes of the postcommunist governments, while its legislative realization and, further, the implementation of such a policy have generated remarkably diverse – here and there, controversial – outcomes: on the one hand, observers and decision-makers praise the benefits of "local autonomy" and independent public policy at the local level, accompanied by a more meaningful citizens' participation, on the other hand, contestations are voiced through the prism of what is seemed to be a gradual "impoverishment" of the small-to-medium-sized municipalities, in the absence of the financial support provided by the state budget. The question of decentralization is much more conspicuous in periods of crisis, as it puts a considerable pressure on the financial situation of the local communities which, in a decentralized and devoluted administrative system – hence in the absence of the significant sums recouped from the state budget –, find themselves obligated to collect appreciable taxes in the local budget from a population increasingly impoverished by the effects of economic fluctuations. In this sense, the degree of *de facto* decentralization is probably the most relevantly illustrated by the average proportion, from the local budget, of all the administrative-territorial units on the area of a state, ensured out of its own, independent sources, by the municipalities themselves: within those states with a decentralized administrative tradition, the budgetary proportion resulting from the collection of taxes from within the local community can constitute up to 60% of the total of the municipality's budgetary revenues (e.g. Poland); on the other hand, countries administratively centralized are situated at the other extreme, encompassing those municipalities exposing serious problems in the management of local finances, collecting under 30% of the budgetary revenues, while the rest of the income emanates from the state budget. This is the case of Romania as well, where the successive attempts of decentralization failed to prepare the small communities (i.e. the communes, the small-to-medium-sized towns) in efficiently collecting and effectively administering the local taxes. Meanwhile, after the 1989 *momentum*, the local communities have been entrusted with increasingly broad administrative attributions (e.g. the administration of schools and hospitals, the management of public security, social welfare, etc.), without them improving somehow the capacity of collecting taxes in an autonomous fashion. Such municipalities confronted an impoverishment of the local political elites' abilities to initiate and implement local development projects (particularly, in the sphere of infrastructural development and of economic growth through investments and attraction of private capital); such a circumstance has the unfortunate "merit" to constitute itself into a fertile soil for unprofitable public vendue, for the exercise of personal influences at the local level, for corruption, and the perpetuation of "patron-client"-styled relations (cf. Grzymała-Busse 2007). In addition, the absence of clear fiscal rules and a limited fiscal decentralization resulted in conspicuous discrepancies in public-sector efficiency between municipalities in East-Central Europe (see, for the period 1995 to 2015, Christl, Köppl-Turyna, and Kucsera 2020).

The notion of "decentralization", as antagonistic to the Janusian notion of "centralization" – "the tendency towards unity" –, suggests "the tendency towards diversity", the diminution – and not the opposite – of centralization, the reduction of power concentration; "administrative decentralization" connotes

> "the existence of some local public persons, appointed by the territory's community, with their own attributions, who directly intervene in the management and the administration of the collectivity's problems, involving *local autonomy*" (Apostol Tofan 2003/2008: 253-255 [italics in original, transl. mine]).

Therefrom ineluctably appears the problem of the degree of decentralization propitious to a democratic construct and to an efficient administration, considering undoubtedly different factors (e.g. the traditions and the history, the area and the population of the state, the dispersion degree of the inhabitants, the economic conditions and the political context, etc.); equally dilemmatic remains also the convenient operationalization of the concept of "decentralization". Adverting on the major discrepancies between "administrative decentralization" and "political decentralization" (that is, federalism, "the most profound form of decentralization", a "major constitutional option, often associated to some exceptional historical circumstances" (Frège 1986: 38)), from a legal perspective, Dana Apostol Tofan discriminates between (a) "territorial decentralization" (i.e. "the existence of some elected authorities, at the level of the territorial-administrative units, authorities that dispose of general material competence"), and (b) "technical decentralization" or "decentralization through services" (i.e. "the existence of some moral persons of public law, that perform specific public services, distinct from the bulk of public services provided for by the state authorities") (Apostol Tofan 2008/2003: 255). Virgil Stoica distinguishes firstly between "centralization" (i.e. that form of organization in which the national unity is of paramount importance, thusly considering that "a strong center can assure the observance of the interests of all groups (either regional, sectorial or ethnic)[107]", and perceiving particularly significant the legislative uniformity and equality of resources available to each of the peripheral units), and "decentralization" (i.e. "the local organization which opposes centralization", stressing on the specific interest of local communities and insuring much more possibilities of citizens' participation and information and concern regarding public affairs and governance) (Stoica 2003: 63-66). Concretely, decentralization needs the simultaneous fulfillment of the following prerequisites: the existence of a local community with its own necessary material means (i.e. a local budget), the existence of local decision-making bodies elected by the community (not by the central authorities, which otherwise exert some sort of administrative endorsement for the limit between local problems and those of general interests not to be breached.) (Fesler 1968: 370-379). A notion that frequently accompanies the discussions regarding the systems of local governance and administration, "de-concentration" describes the situation in which "in a centralized society, decision-making is conferred to those agents of the central authority localized at the local level" (as opposed to "decentralization", i.e. the situation in which decision-making and "the prerogatives of the central authority are conferred to those functionaries who are territorially close to the citizens they govern") (Stoica 2003: 64); subsequently, "de-concentration" is "the distribution of power within a group of similar interests, the political structure constituting hence the interest of a particular group", while "decentralization" is "the distribution of power among groups of different interests, in which at least one group represents the central body" (see the distinction explained in Mawhood 1983). The different types of decentralization bear as *fundamenta* different *criteria*: organizationally, (1) "vertical" (i.e. "the power dispersion to bottom on the chain of authority"), and (2) "horizontal" (i.e. "the transfer of some responsibilities to particular organizations outside the central administrative structure"); structurally, (1) "functional" (i.e. "the recognition of some autonomy of the institutions and public services situated at the local level"), and (2) "territorial" (i.e. "the recognition of some autonomy of the local communities" *per se*). Generally, decentralization is defined as comprising two steps (Stoica 2003: 65-66): (a) "de-concentration" (in its turn, being either of "vertical structure", with an "unintegrated local administration", or of "prefectorial structure", with an "integrated local administration"), and (b) "devolution" (i.e. "the power transfer from the central

---

107 "while a weak one would lead to rivalry and disharmony" (Stoica 2003).

266

government to the regional institutions", as an intermediary stage between the central governance and the local one; the regional institutions are neither sovereign nor federative. Devolution can be either (1) "administrative" – i.e. "the regional institutions only implement the policies decided upon at the center" – , or (2) "legislative" – i.e. "the establishment of elected regional assemblies, invested with political responsibilities and with a certain fiscal independence, a situation which confer them a high degree of maneuver and decision-making in their area of responsibility") (Heywood 1997).

In a quite compelling and empirically challenging research project, coordinated by Daniel Treisman at the UCLA, in 2002, decentralization is distinguished among six layers of conceptualization around 166 countries: (1) "vertical decentralization" (the number of tiers[108] among which the tasks of administration and decision-making are divided); (2) "decisionmaking decentralization" (the fashion in which the decision-making authority is distributed among the different tiers; indeed, the actual number of tiers appears genuinely irrelevant unless each tier is granted decision-making authority and a considerable degree of accountability)[109]; (3) "appointment decentralization" (the level at which officials at different tiers of administration and decision-making are selected (voted / appointed) and dismissed)[110]; (4) "electoral decentralization" (the extent to which direct, popular elections are employed in the selection of decision-makers at each administrative tier); (5) "fiscal decentralization" (the most commonly employed understanding of decentralization[111] and the main focus of analysis in this book; the manner of collecting budgetary matters at each tier of administration, including tax revenues and public expenditure)[112];

---

108 The notion "tier" was conceptualized through a number of three defining characteristics: (1) "it was funded from the public budget", (2) "it had authority to administer a range of public services", and (3) "it had a territorial jurisdiction" (Treisman 2002: 6).

109 Nevertheless, the problem arouses in the very evaluation of the impact each tier posses in the decision-making process: distribution of authority can be understood as that within a given policy area or as that between different domains; the decision-making authority may or may not include the veto power of some tier in the process; various activity domains or policy areas cannot be prioritized in terms of the degree of decision-making authority dissipation or their prioritization differs from municipality to municipality, from region to region, from country to country, etc.

110 The "appointment" type of decentralization tends to admit nuances in the patterns of recruitment of political elites: not only the level at which the political selection occurs is paramount, but also the manner of selection should be properly assessed in order to establish the degree of de facto "appointment decentralization"; in addition, the separation of power at each tier provides for corresponding separation of selection (both in terms of selectorates and of the selection form); there may be no appointment-dismissal congruence, etc.

111 See, for instance, more famously, Lijphart 1984: 177.

112 Treisman differentiates among two mechanisms acting in the fiscal behavior in the central-local dynamics: the "tax revenues decentralization" describes the situation in which the share of total tax revenues received by the subnational tiers is greater, whereas

(6) "personnel decentralization" (increase in the administrative and bureaucratic resources at the subnational tiers) (Treisman 2002: 6-12).

Paul Goodman cares to clear a series of theoretical and practical inconsistencies revolving around the notion of "decentralization":

> "Decentralization is not lack of order or planning, but a kind of coordination that relies on different motives from top-down direction, standard rules, and extrinsic rewards like salary and *status* to provide integration and cohesiveness. It is not 'anarchy'." (Goodman 2010/1971: 118; Goodman 1963: 3-27)

Furthermore, in order to meaningfully assess the extent of decentralization, Paul Hutchcroft employs ten control-and-check questions:

> "(1) Are local executives appointed by the center or elected by popular vote?"; (2) "Are there effective mechanisms for popular participation at the local level [...]?"; (3) "Are there municipal, provincial, state, and / or regional legislative bodies with substantial decision-making authority?"; (4) "[I]s there a concentration of socioeconomic and / or coercive power in local patrons and bosses [...]?"; (5) "Is there a national legislature with significant decision-making authority?"; (6) "If there are effective legislative bodies, do they function within a parliamentary or a presidential system?"; (7) "Are national legislators elected or appointed?"; (8) "To what extent does the electoral system provide for representation of local or regional interests in the national legislature?"; (9) "Are political parties organized along national or local / regional lines, and what is their level of internal cohesion?"; (10) "To what extent are administrative structures insulated from party patronage?" (Hutchcroft 2001: 34-36 [additions mine])

The range of questions are meant to discern between what Hutchcraft considers as the two fundaments of decentralization: (1) the decentralization of administration (i.e. at the territorial level), and (2) the centralization of politics: on a fourfold factor analysis, on a *continuum*, the scholar distinguishes among four cases: (a) a "relatively more centralized administration", with a "relatively more centralized politics"; (b) a "relatively more centralized administration", with a "relatively more decentralized politics"; (c) a "relatively more decentralized administration", with a "relatively more decentralized politics", and (d) a "relatively more decentralized administration", with a "relatively more centralized politics" (Hutchcroft 2001: 39).

Reviewing the theoretical subtleties of administration in a comparative and international vein, George M. Guess and Vache Gabrielyane affirm the termi-

---

"expenditure decentralization" is illustrative for the situation in which the share of total public expenditures from the subnational budgets is greater (Treisman 2002: 11-12). Even so, the legal framework concerning the fiscal policy between the center and the sub-national units poses additional difficulties, worthy of mention for the sake of proper conceptualization: the proportion of revenues may be established by law (fixed) or changeable, according to either the needs of each tier and municipality or to the discretion or arbitrariness of the central decision-makers; the subnational authorities may or may not have the prerogative and the ability to collect taxes independently, etc.

nological and definitional ambiguity gravitating around the concept and the reality of "decentralization":

> "There is considerable terminological debate over core terms of decentralization: principal-agent, delegation, devolution, and deconcentration. [...] Thus, the terms are often used interchangeably, with hair-splitting, nearly content-free distinctions that add to the confusion." (Guess and Gabrielyane 2007: 584)

For example, Hofman differentiates between "delegation" (i.e. "shifts of functions and accountability from central agencies to subnational units"), and "devolution" (i.e. "the shift of authority beyond central government chain of command to other levels of government subject to national guidelines") (Hofman 1994: 4). For Guess and Gabrielyane, "devolution" is

> "both the means or *process* by which the central government decentralizes authority, and also the most complete degree or *stage* in which autonomous local governments are empowered to raise revenues and operate services under broad national guidelines" (Guess and Gabrielyane 2007: 584 [italics in original]).

While studying basic services provision (water provision), George Mensah Laryea-Adjei describes the indicators used for pinpointing the three "features" of decentralization. Hence, the "political decentralization" is measureable through such indicators as: "involvement of consumers [citizens] in stages of service delivery", "involvement of civic associations in stages of service delivery". "Administrative decentralization" ("role distribution & partnerships") can be coded through: "responsibility for hiring, firing, and wages over staff", "clarity of responsibilities", "local responsibility for planning, O&M", "responsibility for regulatory framework", "responsibility for managing partnerships", "responsibilities devolved to partner", "capacity to manage partnerships", "co-financing arrangement". Finally, "fiscal decentralization" is operationalized through: "local expenditure on sector financed and earmarked by central transfers", "local expenditure on sector financed by central but controlled by district [municipality], "local investment on sector financed from local revenues", "share of revenue in sector raised and retained by district [municipality]" (Laryea-Adjei 2007: 57 [additions mine]). Following Cohen and Peterson (1997) and, famously, Rondinelli (1999), Laryea-Adjei identifies the "key elements of decentralization": (a) the "transfer of *authority* (that is *power*, by law) for (specified) public functions"; (b) the "transfer of *responsibility* (that is *roles* and *tasks*) for public functions"; (c) the "transfer of *resources*"; and (d) the "transfer [...] from a *higher level* of government to a *lower level* or from a level of government to a *quasi-independent government organization* or the *private sector*" (Laryea-Adjei 2007: 9 [additions mine]). Helmsing aptly isolates the essence of decentralization in "the enablement" of local governments (Helmsing 2000; see also Helmsing 2002: 317-341). The so-called "type-function framework" (TFF), put forward by the "Cheema-Nellis-Rondinelli-Silverman" School on decentralization theory, discusses decentralization in terms of "forms" and "types": while the "forms" are classifications on different basis of objectives (the result being "political", "market" under "privatization" and "deregulation", "fiscal", "spatial", and "administrative" decentralization), the "types" are the combinations of the forms (the result being "deconcentration", "delegation", and "devolution"). By the end of the day, decentralization is practicably analyzed under the banner of "multi-dimensionality of forms" the process actually embraces, or what Parker (1995) metaphorically and compellingly coined the "*soufflé* theory".

Most recently, Jean-Paul Faguet (2012) refers to "decentralization" from two dimensions, bearing in mind the example of Bolivia:

> "First, it [decentralization] encompasses reforms such as deconcentration, devolution, and delegation that in incentive terms are fundamentally different [...] Second, the word conceals great variation in the extent to which reform is effectively implemented across different countries" (Faguet 2012: 2 [additions mine]).

Similarly to Triesman, in a well-documented contribution on the evolution of the concept, Pollitt (2005: 371-397) presents a quite rich typology of decentralization, which contains, most notably, the distinctions between (a) "competitive" (i.e. authority parcelled out on the basis of competition) *versus* "non-competitive" decentralization (i.e. authority parcelled out on the basis of allocation); (b) "internal" (i.e. "authority parcelled out within an existing organization") *versus* "external" decentralization or "devolution" (i.e. "authority transferred to other [possibly new] organizations") (Pollitt 2005: 375 [additions mine]). Another, quite scholarly underexploited, species of decentralization is the "asymmetric decentralization" (see, for instance, Lele 2019, on the case of Indonesia), usually specific to multicultural states and triggered by differences in local development.

There is a constant concern within the literature regarding the new administrative developments, especially decentralization, and their impact on the outlook and orientations of the local / regional political elite. Such a concern has been focused primarily on Latin America, South Asia (see, for instance, among others: Bardhan 2002: 185-205; Beard, Miraftab, and Silver 2008; Burki, Perry, and Dillinger 1999; Escobar-Lemmon 2003: 683-697; Falletti 2005: 327-346; Garman, Haggard, and Willis 2001: 205-236; Smoke, Gómez, and Peterson 2006), and Africa (Cottingham 1970: 101-120), while the topic has been generally neglected for the developing democracies of East-Central Europe.

Dora Orlansky (2000: 196) discusses the impact of decentralization upon the power-sharing between the central and the local administrative layers and upon the extent of political power and responsibility local elites are expected to exert. Discussing a series of examples from Africa and South Asia, Devarajan, Khemani, and Shah (2009: 118-119) refer to the dangers of elite isolation with the increase in decentralized communities and to shifts in delivery of public services once with the process of decentralization. Quite interestingly,

270

Merilee S. Grindle (2007: 63-105) introduces the example of decentralization in Mexico, concluding that proper fiscal and administrative decentralization can result in high levels of political competition and satisfaction with the living in the town, both at the level of the local elites and the community.

It becomes apparent that local leadership modifies its outlook and prioritization strategy in the context of change of administrative organization leading to increased decentralization. Jonathan Rodden (2004: 481-500) presents the impact of different forms of decentralization upon the city management, but, most importantly, upon the degree of elite isolation and passive representation. Finally, opposing two main approaches in reference to the impact of decentralization policies – the "liberal-individualist" and "statist" approaches –, Aylin Topal (2012) describes forms of elite isolation after the proper implementation of decentralization policies and differences of agenda setting of local elites as response to increased decentralization. The fashion in which the elites' outlook, value orientation and strategy prioritization actually modify themselves is partially elaborated in this book, with a special focus on particular municipalities in six countries of East-Central Europe: Romania, Czech Republic, Poland, Hungary, Slovak Republic, and Bulgaria.

From an economist's standpoint, decentralization is seen as a method of better, most effectively and most efficiently (i.e. cost-effectively), respond to a certain constituency's preferences and needs in terms of service delivery. Oates coins this rationale as "the decentralization theorem" (Oates 1972: 35):

"[…] [S]tate and local governments, being closer to the people, will be more responsive to the particular preferences of their constituencies and will be able to find new and better ways to provide these [public] services." (Oates 1999: 1120 [additions mine])

More efficient service delivery will be juxtaposed, in the decentralization logic, to a more easily accountable government, situated closer to the citizens, at the local level. Moreover, fiscal decentralization, in particular, is conducive to economic growth locally (Canavire-Bacarreza, Martinez-Vazquez, Yedgenov 2020). Decentralization is perceived to favor a more coherent and performant mechanism of public procurement (Chiappinelli 2020). Following the same rationale, decentralization is prone to induce a higher quality of democratic practice[113] and, in administrative terms, to significantly reduce the

---

113 Empirical research in this sense has led to divergent results: a clear connection between higher degree of decentralization and better democratic practice (recte, citizen participation, governmental stability, high degree of institutionalization, electoral competitiveness, citizen satisfaction, etc.) (Huther and Shah 1998; Tvinnereim 2005) vs. no connection whatsoever between "democratic performance" (i.e. protection of minority rights, citizen participation, party competitiveness, etc.) and decentralization (See Foweraker and Landman 2002: 43-66).

levels of corruption[114] (due, primarily, to a less numerous bureaucratic *apparatus*). At the opposite pole, arguments and evidence are provided for quite an unusual hypothesis on the drawbacks of decentralization: Hal Wolman and Sharon McCormick sustain that the existence of strong local governments increases the overall public expenditure in the countries of the former "Eastern bloc", due primarily to the patron-client relations and to the establishment of local "barons" (Wolman and McCormick 1994: 249-266). A quite compelling argument, somehow reconciling the two previously-mentioned perspectives, is put forward by Frederick Kibon Changwony and Audrey S. Paterson, who link decentralization, corruption and accountability and highlight that decentralization as an effective obstacle against corruption can only work complementarily to a viable accounting mechanism (Changwony and Paterson 2019). Employing data from fifty-three states, Alfano, Baraldi, and Cantabene (2019) conclude that there is an "optimal" level of decentralization of 15% to 21% for actually putting in place mechanisms of combating corruption.

> "Like a *soufflé* that requires just the right combination of milk, eggs, and heat to rise, so a successful program of decentralization will need to include just the right combination of political, fiscal and institutional elements." (Parker 1995: 44)

It is Parker, then, who aptly differentiates among three types of decentralization, three "elements" to categorize this process: (1) "political decentralization", (2) "institutional decentralization" (i.e. the process during which formal governmental institutions are identified as proper for a new distribution of responsibilities, and a legal framework is found as suitable to define new power relations among different *loci* of government), and (3) "fiscal decentralization" (i.e. the process through which "an appropriate level of financial resources to cover the costs of public goods and services" is identified, by three main means: (a) "own or locally generated revenues", (b) "transfers from higher-level institutions", and (c) "resources from borrowing" (Parker 1995: 44). Traditionally, Montero and Samuels utilize the distinction among "administrative decentralization", "fiscal decentralization", and "political decentralization", with a particular focus on "decentralization policy types" (Montero and Samuels 2004: 3-34). According to the degree of authority devolved and the type of actors to which authority is transferred (*recte*, either central agencies, parastatal organizations, or subnational governments, Cheema et al. discriminate

---

114 Similarly, in what concerns the impact of increased decentralization on the levels of corruption, the empirical findings were puzzling if not contradictory: Huther and Shah 1998: 1-35; Gurgur and Shah 2002: 46-67; Fisman and Gatti 2002: 325-345; Arikan 2004: 175-195; Yerkes and Muasher 2018, sustained a positive correlation between the two variables, while Bardhan and Mookherjee 2000: 135-139 and Treisman 2007, pondered the above-mentioned enthusiastic outcomes by adding a series of control variables that significantly changed the high correlation coefficient. One, particularly compelling, reading on the increase in the corruption level with a high level of decentralization, is: Teets 2004, 50 p.

between "forms" of decentralization (which, in turn, can be: "political", "spatial", "market", and "administrative"), and "types" of decentralization (Cheema and Rondinelli 1983). Cohen and Peterson gather under the umbrella of "administrative decentralization" the three most typical forms of administrative rearrangement: "deconcentration" (i.e. "the least extensive type of decentralization where it is defined as the transfer of authority over specified decision-making, financial and management functions by administrative means to different levels under the jurisdictional authority of the central government"), "devolution" (i.e. the situation in which "authority is transferred by central governments to local-level governmental units holding corporate *status* granted under state legislation"), and "delegation" (i.e. "the transfer of government decision-making and administrative authority and / or responsibility for carefully defined tasks to institutions and organizations that are either under its indirect control or independent") (Cohen and Peterson 1996). The same logic is applicable to the decentralization scheme advanced by Prud'homme. Here, three types are distinguished: (a) "spatial decentralization" (i.e. "a process of diffusing urban population and activities away from large agglomerations"); (b) "market decentralization" (i.e. "a process of creating conditions in which goods and services are provided by market mechanism", another phrase for "economic liberalization"); (c) "administrative deconcentration" (i.e. "the transfer of responsibility for planning, management, and the raising and allocation of financial resources from the central government and its agencies to field units of government agencies, or subordinate units or levels of government") (Prud'homme 1994 [additions mine]). Consequently, Prud'homme's theoretical construction is quite similar to Cohen and Peterson's: "administrative decentralization" presents three cardinal types: "de-concentration" (i.e. "the redistribution of decision-making among different levels within the central government"); "delegation" (i.e. "the transfer of responsibilities from the central government to semi-autonomous organizations not whole controlled by the central government, but ultimately accountable to it"); and "devolution" (i.e. "the transfer of power from the central government to independent subnational governments") (Prud'homme 1994: 2). As a matter of fact, Rémy Prud'homme provides one of the most pragmatic definitions of decentralization: "a political strategy by ruling elites to retain most of their power to relinquishing some of it" (Prud'homme 1994)[115]. The same logic is replicated by Richard M. Bird and Francois Vaillancourt, for the two scholars develop on the three mechanisms captured under the banner of "decentralization": (a) "deconcentration" (i.e. "giving regional or local offices of the central government decision-making power previously held in the central offices in the capital"); (b) "delegation" (i.e. "making a sub-national government responsible for carrying out a function for which the central government retains responsibility");

---

115 Of course, most of Prud'homme's observations on decentralization are based on the experiences of the African states.

(c) "devolution" (i.e. "transferring responsibilities from the central government to sub-national governments") (Bird and Vaillancourt 2006). Under the generic label of "decentralization", Vito Tanzi discusses the topic under two principal categories: (a) "de-concentration" (i.e. "only a delegation of administrative control to lower levels (sub-national governments in the administrative hierarchy)"), and (b) "decentralization" (i.e. "genuine possession of independent decision-making power by decentralized units") (Tanzi 1996)[116]. One of the most prominent scholars of administrative organization and reform, James Manor preserves a theoretical scheme of threefold categorization rather of the processes taking place under the generic name of "decentralization": (1) "de-concentration" is "administrative decentralization" (i.e. "dispersal of agents of higher level of government into lower level arena"); (2) "fiscal decentralization" (i.e. "downward fiscal transfers to lower levels influencing over budgets and financial decisions"); (3) "devolution" is "democratic decentralization" (i.e. "the transfer of resources and power (and tasks) to lower level authorities which are largely or wholly independent of higher levels of government, and which are democratic in some way and to some degree") (Manor 1999). *Nota bene!*: the first two processes occurring in isolation or separately can result in a continued involvement of the central authorities in the governmental matters of the local constituencies, particularly in the case in which the latter lack specialized and qualified bureaucratic personnel and fiscal capacity to collect and to manage local budgets. While discussing this particular administrative dynamic in the sphere of healthcare, Mills et al. discriminates among (a) "deconcentration", (b) "delegation" or "functional decentralization", and (c) "devolution" (Mills et al. 1990). From the purely economist's perspective, Jerry M. Silverman presents five type of decentralization – "deconcentration", "delegation", "devolution", "top-down principal agency", and "bottom-up principal agency" –, proposing, at the same time, a sixth type: "hybrid decentralization" (Silverman 1992: 15). Cai and Treisman's intention is to illuminate on a more comprehensive taxonomy of decentralization; their differentiation includes: (1) "administrative decentralization" (i.e. "subnational agents are permitted by national authorities to make certain policy decisions, subject to review"); (2) "political decentralization" (i.e. (a) "subnational governments have the right to make certain policy decisions not subject to being overruled by higher levels", or (b) "subnational officials are chosen by local residents"); (3) "fiscal decentralization" (i.e. "various forms of fiscal allocation to subnational governments depending on a specific government") (Cai and Treisman 2006: 505-535). Finally, Aechyung Kim subscribes to the threefold taxonomy of: "administrative decentralization" (i.e. "funds are allocated to decentralized units that carry out their spending activities even if most taxes are raised centrally"), "fiscal decentralization" (i.e. "sub-national governments have decision-making power,

---

116 What exactly and specifically means "genuine" Tanzi does not care to explain in detail.

authorized by the constitution or legislation, to raise revenues (taxes) and to perform spending activities"), and "political decentralization" (i.e. "public officials (e.g. governor, mayor, council member) at sub-national governments are elected by secret ballots, and sub-national governments are given independent power for decision-making by constitutional or legislative authority") (Kim 2008). Probably one of the most comprehensive taxonomies of decentralization is presented by Mark Turner et al., who isolate six types, underpinned by two *criteria*: (1) the "nature of delegation" (i.e. (a) "within formal political structures", (b) "within public administrative or parastatal structures", or (c) "from state sector to private sector"), and (2) the "basis for delegation" (i.e. (a) "territorial", or (b) "functional"). Combining the two sets of *criteria*, six forms of decentralization result: (1) "devolution" (i.e. when delegation occurs within the formal political structures, territorially; e.g. political decentralization, democratic decentralization, local government, etc.); (2) "interest group representation" (i.e. when delegation happens within the formal political structures, as well, but functionally); (3) "deconcentration" (i.e. in which delegation is conducted within public administrative / parastatal structures, in a territorial manner; e.g. administrative decentralization, field administration, etc.); (4) "establishment of parastatals and *quangos*[117]" (i.e. in which delegation is done within public administrative or parastatal structures, in a functional manner); (5) "privatization of devolved functions" (i.e. where delegation develops from state sector to private sector, in a territorial fashion; e.g. deregulation, contracting out, voucher schemes, etc.); (6) "privatization of national functions" (i.e. where delegation develops from state sector to private sector, in a functional fashion; e.g. divestiture, deregulation, economic liberalization) (Turner, Hulme and McCourt 2015/1997: 206). The *First Global Report by the United Cities and Local Governments* uses a new typology: (a) "administrative" decentralization (i.e. "local authorities are accountable to higher authorities"), (b) "political"

---

117 See, for a detailed explanation of this process of "decentralization towards quasi-nongovernmental organizations" (Rondinelli and Nellis 1986: 3-23). In their turn, Rondinelli and Nellis isolate four types of decentralization: "deconcentration" (i.e. "shifting some authority or responsibility from centrally located offices and staff to [...] local administrative units outside of the national capital"), "delegation" (i.e. "the transfer of managerial responsibility for specifically defined functions to organizations outside the regular bureaucratic structure, though ultimate responsibility is retained by the central authority"), "devolution" (i.e. "the creation or strengthening of local units of government which can, to a large extent, operate outside of the direct control of the central authority"), "privatization" (i.e. "governments transferring some of their responsibilities to private organizations and/ or voluntary organizations") (Rondinelli and Nellis 1986: 6-10). Rondinelli's typology of decentralization categories has become sketchy in time: "deconcentration" (i.e. "the transfer of power to local administrative offices of the central government"), "delegation" (i.e. "the transfer of power to parastatals"), "devolution" (i.e. "the transfer of power to subnational political entities"), and "privatization" (i.e. "the transfer of power (and responsibility) to private entities") (Rondinelli 1990).

decentralization (i.e. "local authorities are theoretically independent of the state, invested with powers and elected"), (c) "budgetary" decentralization (i.e. "the transfer of resources necessary for the exercise of the transferred powers and responsibilities"), and (d) "market" decentralization or "divestment" (i.e. "a transfer of functions to the private sector (companies, NGOs,...), including planning and administration, previously held by public institutions") (United Cities and Local Governments & World Bank 2009: 310). This typology adds to what Cheema and Rondinelli define as "governance decentralization", i.e. "a new decentralization category", including "'economic decentralization' [...], 'market liberalization, deregulation, privatization of public enterprises and public-private partnerships'" (Cheema and Rondinelli 2007: 6). Quite importantly, the same *Global Report by the United Cities and Local Governments* warns about the difference between "decentralization" proper and "deconcentration":

> "Deconcentration is *the opposite of decentralization*, in that it governs the relations within an administrative hierarchy, whereas decentralization excludes any hierarchical relations between the state and local authorities." (United Cities and Local Governments & World Bank 2009: 314 [italics added]).

Following the completion of the process of decentralization, D. L. Craythorne contends, in each municipality enjoying the principle of "local autonomy", nine systems should properly function: (1) the social system (i.e. the communities living in the area of the municipality and their interlocking interactions); (2) "a system of government and representation"; (3) the "organizational, managerial, and operational systems" for service provision and service delivery; (4) the "systems of needs, related to individuals and groups of people"; (5) the system of planning for meeting the needs and grievances, according to a specific prioritization strategy; (6) the "allocative" system; (7) the delegative system; (8) "a diplomatic system", (9) "a leadership / co-ordinative system" (Craythorne 2006/1980: 120).

As a repercussion of the implementation of decentralization policies, the role, the prerogatives, and the attributions of the Municipal Councils and of the institution of the Mayor increase exponentially. Due to space limitations, this book will predominantly refer to the attributions of the Municipal / Local Councils, as they were envisaged by the institutional construct after 1989. The distribution and the amplitude of attributions at the local level, related to the central authority, should also be considered in the discussion regarding the typology of local government systems.

The problem of defining, operationalizing and measuring the concept of "decentralization" has constituted a perennial one in the sphere of administrative studies, primarily due to the difficulties in gathering *data* at the local level. The *de facto* degree of decentralization has been measured employing a series of complementary indicators: (1) the level of proclivity towards decentralization (Dun and Wetzel 2000: 242-250); (2) the share of subnational government to the public consumption or to the GDP level (IMF 2001); (3) other qualitative indicators, such as: government credibility, social capital (De Mello 2000), soft or hard budget constraints (Kornai 1979: 801-819; Kornai 1980; Kornai 1986: 3-30), levels of corruption, administrative capacity (Gargan 1981: 649-658), the magnitude of bureaucracy, etc.

The book assumes that the fashion in which the concept of "decentralization" is operationalized and instrumentalized in studies concerning the "local-central" relations has been frequently founded on a *de jure* perspective, taking into consideration the ways in which each East-Central European country has constructed the legal fundaments on which a process of decentralization has been undertaken. Surely, the pieces of legislation constitute important indicators for establishing a series of traits or different levels of decentralization to be subsequently identified and measured throughout the region. Nevertheless, the legislation in each case has presented and continues to present significant contingencies in actual implementation, driven primarily by the autonomous administration of local finances. The *de facto* degree of decentralization and its effective measurement represent a cumbersome topic for both political scientists and policy-drafters. Thusly, besides the pieces of legislation establishing the functioning of the mechanisms presupposed by the said administrative process, additional markers and indicators should be equally considered, in order to determine the manner and the extent in which the legal framework is put into practice, is implemented and developed in the field. In measuring fiscal decentralization in Eastern European countries, Slovenian scholar Aleksander Aristovnik (2012: 5-22) utilizes Vo's framework for the operationalization of fiscal decentralization, under the form of the "*FDI*" (the "fiscal decentralization index"), underpinned on the geometrical average of two major elements: (1) "the fiscal autonomy" ("*FA*": the ratio of subnational governments' own-sourced revenue to subnational governments' expenditure), and (2) "the fiscal importance of subnational governments" ("*FI*" (Vo 2009: 399-419): the ratio of subnational governments' expenditure to the total public sector expenditures of all levels of government within a country). Employing his own calculations of the FDI, Aristovnik concludes that: the least fiscally decentralized country (for the region under scrutiny here, Aristovnik's inquiry is broader in scope, encompassing Central Europe, South-East Europe, the Baltic states, Transcaucasia, and three former Soviet states[118]) is Slovakia (FDI ≈ 28); Bulgaria (FDI ≈ 34), Hungary (FDI ≈ 36), and Romania (FDI ≈ 38) follow, whereas the most fiscally decentralized countries are the Czech Republic (FDI ≈ 41), and Poland

---

118 The states on which Aristovnik's study on fiscal decentralization focuses are: Armenia, Belarus, Bulgaria, Croatia, the Czech Republic, Estonia, Hungary, Latvia, Lithuania, Macedonia, Moldova, Poland, Romania, Russia, Serbia, the Slovak Republic, Slovenia, Ukraine.

(FDI ≈ 50)[119]. One of the most comprehensive measurements of (fiscal) decentralization is developed by Woller and Phillips, who employ four indicators: (a) "the ratio of local government revenues to total government revenues", (b) the ratio of local government revenues minus grants-in-aid to total government revenues", (c) "the ratio of local government expenditures to total government expenditures", and (d) "the ratio of local government expenditures to total government expenditures minus defense and social security expenditures" (Woller and Phillips 1998: 139-148).

Probably the most commonly employed form of operationalizing the concept of "decentralization" is the one currently utilized by the World Bank and the IMF in the issuing of their annual reports. Along a series of domains of considerable interest at the local level (infrastructure, education, healthcare, public security, transportation, social services (including housing and unemployment relief), cultural and recreational activities, etc.), it evaluates the extent to which they are dealt with nationally, regionally and locally. This evaluation is constructed primarily based on pieces of legislation, bylaws, internal regulations of different administrative and executive bodies, as well as on some empirical endeavors undertaken by the World Bank and the IMF expertise. This book employed the World Bank / IMF averages indexes of subnational share of general government expenditure in the operationalization of "decentralization", by establishing thresholds thusly: (a) a significant level of administrative and fiscal decentralization describes the countries whose average subnational share of general government expenditure is higher than 50%; (b) a standard level of decentralization is specific for those countries with an average local and regional share of general government expenditure higher than 30%, but lower than 50%; and (c) a low level of decentralization characterizes the countries with a subnational share of general government expenditure lower than 30%.

---

119 This author's estimations based on Figure 1: "Average FDI in selected EECs and OECD countries", in Aristovnik 2012: 11.

	Public order & Safety	Education	Health	Social Security & Welfare	Housing & Communal Amenities	Recreation & Culture	Transporta-tion & Com-munication	Average
Bulgaria	2.17	59.53	44.11	8.30	68.95	26.69	12.19	31.70%
Czech Republic	17.20	17.22	5.98	8.03	68.47	61.89	46.53	32.18%
Hungary	6.86	46.99	44.83	11.99	74.10	43.97	27.64	36.62%
Poland	34.30	72.47	87.36	17.49	86.92	76.13	65.34	62.85%
Romania	4.80	9.23	0.36	2.97	83.01	34.74	17.55	21.80%
Slovakia	5.69	2.40	0.26	0.49	56.74	27.00	18.78	15.90%

(*Source*: International Monetary Fund, *Government Finance Statistics Yearbook* (Washington, DC: IMF, 2001). The *data* is selected only for the countries of East-Central Europe, former satellites of USSR.)

The significance of the level of decentralization is evident especially in the sphere of the priorities the six leadership groups displayed, but also in their interactions with other groups, the establishment and functioning of the networks of power at the local level and in the values embraced. In analyzing the six elite groups, a general pattern appears as dominant in the hierarchical prioritization each of the members of the Municipal Councils provided: when the level of administrative decentralization is higher, covering an increasingly important *palette* of local responsibilities, the local political elite appears more concerned with the problems of the community, becoming more open to efficient decision-making and problem-solving. In this sense, one of the most relevant indicators is the distribution of the spheres of priorities at the local level; the manner in which each local / municipal councilor positioned himself / herself to the four spheres of competence considered here was particularly instrumental: (1) spheres to which a special importance should be granted; (2) spheres in which considerable measures can be taken at the local level; (3) spheres in which effective measures had already been taken, and (4) spheres in which each of the local / municipal councilor exerted a personal influence. Due to a different level of decentralization, many councilors in Tecuci and in Targovishte felt impotent, as compared to their Polish, Czech and Slovakian counterparts, in taking effective and efficient measures in such important spheres as economic development, healthcare, education or public safety, probably four of the main domains the community founds its grievances on; the sphere in which the local political elites in Tecuci and Targovishte, organized in the form of the Local Council, considered themselves politically capable and able, having the political authority to operate beneficial changes, was the one referring to culture, sport, recreation and youth activities, surely an important domain, but definitely not the most pregnant, problematic one. It is on the background of both the benefits and the drawbacks of decentralization that the members of the Municipal Councils in Česká Lípa, Levice, Oleśnica, and Gyula coolly rethought the impact of this process and displayed reluctance, rather than complete acceptance, when assessing the advantages, in the long run, of the process of decentralization. Even so, the local political elites in Česká Lípa, Levice, Oleśnica, and partly Gyula acquired, due to a more consistent set of prerogatives in a diversity of domains, an increasingly responsible stance in respect to the level of political power one could actually exert at the local level to perform effective, efficient, meaningful measures and changes for the community. The sense of decisional impotence of the Local Councils in Tecuci and Targovishte was determined by the level of centralization and dependence towards the central, national elites, in the same fashion in which the Municipal Councils in Oleśnica, Česká Lípa, and Levice felt more responsible, more prepared, more capable to forge change and to decide for their towns. The distribution of domains in which each elite group perceived itself capable to operate was telling for the impact of decentralization on the shaping of priorities of the local political elite.

Decentralization presupposes a series of local government reforms, out of which Shah puts a special emphasis on three sets: the "responsive governance", the "responsible governance", and the "accountable governance" (Shah 2006: 15)[120]. The discussion about the difference among these three "principles" of local administrative and governmental reform is particularly significant, for it first clarifies the differences among the terms revolving around "responsibility" (which are oftentimes used interchangeably, and sometimes mistakably), and, secondly, it sheds some light on the level of prioritization of local political elites, in their communities, and the extent, in practice, of actual autonomous decision-making of these elites. Hence, "responsive governance" means essentially service delivery congruent to local needs and preferences; "responsible governance" means fiscal capacity and efficient use of financial and material resources; finally, "accountable governance" means effective scrutiny by the electorate over the elected. Focusing on municipal reform in Canada, Garcea and LeSage consider five types of local government reforms completing and defining the complex process of decentralization: "jurisdictional reforms", "functional reforms", "financial reforms", internal and managerial reforms, and structural reforms. The five reform "elements" describe rather series of key decisions to be taken in establishing the course of local autonomy (Garcea and LeSage, Jr. 2005: 3-22). Quite clearly, decentralization "implies a higher degree of accountability for politicians and administrators" (Dollery and Robotti 2008: 12), although constant pressures from within and from below and an inflamed level of accountability might produce constraints in coordination between the activity of civil servants and decision-making in the Municipal Council. The epitome of "fiscal federalism", the "benevolent local government", becomes, in this sense, far-fetched, for "maximizing total welfare" for the community is unrealistically for the region of East-Central Europe, where any *desideratum* of "welfare" is counterbalanced by poor fiscal capacity and weak financial revenues.

The form embraced by the relations between the center and the periphery (regional, provincial, local) is generated by the answer to the question: What should be the range of spheres in which the local authority can meaningfully imagine and implement policies and exercise changes compatible to the needs of the community? In answering this question, different types of local organization and distribution of powers were imagined (from centralization, vertical decentralization, horizontal decentralization, functional decentralization, territorial decentralization, to de-concentration and devolution, in the latter's

---

120 See, also, most importantly for this discussion, Shah and Shah 2006, in which the authors differentiate among ten models of local government: the Nordic, the Swiss, the French, the German, the British, the Indian, the Chinese, the Japanese, the North American, and the Australian models.

administrative or legislative variants[121]). According to the legal regulations framed by the Constitutional Act No. 294/1990 Col., the Act of the Czech National Council Nr. 367 / 1990 Col. on Municipalities, amended as 410 / 1992, and the Act of the Czech National Council Nr. 425 / 1990 Col. on District Offices, the Regulation of the Sphere of Their Activities (and the subsequent amendments to Acts of the Czech National Council Nr. 266 / 1991, Nr. 542 / 1991, Act Nr. 21 / 1992, Act Nr. 403 / 1992 and Act Nr. 254 / 1994) – for the Municipal Council of Česká Lípa –, by Law 215 / 2001 on Local Public Administration – for the Local Council of Tecuci –, by the Law of March 8, 1998 on Local Self-government – for the Municipal Council of Oleśnica –, by the Law on Local Self-government No. LXV of 1990 and the Cardinal Act on Local Government No. CLXXXIX of 21st of December 2011 – for the Municipal Council of Gyula –, by the Slovak National Council Act 369/1990, Law No. 221/1996 on the territorial and administrative subdivisions of the Slovak Republic – for the Municipal Council of Levice –, and by the Local Self-Government and Local Administration Act of 1991, the Municipal Budgets Act of 1998, and the Local Taxes and Fees Act of 1997 – for the Local Council of Targovishte –, it appears that the Czech and Polish cases present almost the entire range of decentralization and de-concentration features, while in the other four cases, attempts have been undertaken for larger, more comprehensive decentralization measures. In this sense, for instance, Law 215 / 2001 is the act to confine the five main principles on which the functioning of the local administration in Romania is founded: local autonomy, decentralization of public services, legality, the eligibility of the authorities of the local public administration and the citizens' consultation in local matters of special interest (Stoica 2003: 72, quoting art. 1, paragraph (1) of the Law 69/1991 of Public Local Administration). By "local administration", the text of the Law describes the context in which

> "the right and the effective capacity of the authorities of the local public administration [can] resolve and manage, in the name and in the interest of the local *collectivities* which they represent, the public matters, in the conditions prescribed by the law." (art. 3, paragraph (1) of the Law 215/2001 of the Local Public Administration [italics added])

Surely, one would wonder, reading the Law 215 / 2001, what are, in effect, the decisional limitations of the local elite since their communities enjoy, according to the law, the local autonomy and they function according to the principles of decentralization? Why was this local elite of Tecuci reluctant in implementing and taking responsibility for the changes needed by its community? Part of the answer lies in a "tradition" of servile local politics, totally dependent to the

---

121 The variety of forms that might be established between the center and its peripheries, i.e. between central authorities and local/ regional ones, is beautifully detailed in Stoica 2003: 63-66.

center, inherited from the defunct communist period, but also in the general manner in which the distribution of funds from the central authorities to the local administrations is done: undoubtedly politically influenced, the distribution of the budgetary funds towards the peripheral communities is still problematic.

Essentially, therefore, decentralization is a process touching primarily the repercussions of the decision-making, rather than the democratic representation facet. Moreover, the general study of local elites through the prism of the Municipal Councils revealed a paradoxical situation, in all of the six cases, even though in a dissimilar fashion. For the Romanian and the Bulgarian cases, it was paradoxical that, in the context of a highly personalized politics in which the focus constructed around individualizing political figure, monolithism was still preserved at the local level, even in the presence, within the membership of the Local Councils, of some high-profiled individuals, clearly dominating the community which they represented; the spirit of collegiality, of resonating and being empathic to the attitudes and views of their peers in the restrictive, exclusive elite group appeared properly conserved in the Local Councils of Tecuci and Targovishte. Although eager to colonize and monopolize all forms of power in their small communities – starting from the political and continuing with the economic and cultural ones (or, increasingly, *vice-versa*) –, the large majority of the local councilors in Tecuci and in Targovishte did retain and value the sentiment of team, even in the detriment of social sensitivity and care for the large community of the electorate. Conversely, in the Czech and the Slovak cases, the unity of the solidified group forming the Municipal Councils in Česká Lípa and Levice was less significant in the conception of those comprising the Councils, who were inclined towards a pragmatic approach towards their *status* as local political elites within their communities, in which, at least rhetorically and conceptually, the dedication towards the needs of the town and towards the developmental prospects and opportunities reigned supreme. Despite the diversity characterizing these groups – dominantly, in terms of socio-demographical features, of their political affiliation, of the interactions they established and entertained, of the values embraced (e.g. their diverse conceptions regarding the protectionist state, greater decentralization and democratic values) –, the members of the Municipal Councils in Česká Lípa, Levice, and Oleśnica cherished and guided their activity in accordance to a model that emphasized the political experience and will and the dedication to the town's improvement plans, devotion, respect for the community, desire to change, intelligence, vision, perspective and intuition for development – all of them predominantly oriented towards the towns they represented.

Additionally, the lack of significance of party politics at the local level, at the level of small-to-medium-sized towns in two of the cases studied here, Oleśnica (Poland) and Levice (Slovakia), is one of the most pertinent paths for further research. The departure from party politics and ideological loyalties could indicate a propensity towards a pragmatic approach on local politics and prioritization strategy, a focus on the community's needs. At the same time, the absence of interest in party politics denotes a low degree of electoral competitiveness – especially, in the context of extramural recruitment –, and an equally low level of party institutionalization. These deficits are prone to produce political dynamics aptly described by L. Buštíková:

> "A related characteristic is the formation of coalitions at local level which respect neither left-right oppositions within the political *spectrum* nor the guidelines of central party *apparatuses*, but instead match the inter-personal networks of a local social system." (Buštíková 1999)

Zdenka Vajdová adds on this *problématique*, with reference to the Czech case of local political elite (although, empirical evidence of this study shows at least a formal affiliation to party politics):

> "The rejection of party organization by local political elites can be interpreted as a willingness to compromise, but it also problematises the essence of a political system based on competition between parties aspiring to power, governance and decision-making." (Vajdova 2003: 151)

Indeed, Vajdová's observations are substantiated by the conclusions of this study on the pragmatic dominance of the "ideal portrait" of the local councilor in the cases of the Czech, Slovak, and, to some extent, Polish towns:

> "Local politicians understand their role as one of solving practical problems in which there is no room for politics. [...] [They] continued to view local politics as a technical-professional activity in which expertise should have the decisive say." (Vajdova 2003: 151 [additions mine])

The sense of unity of the group constituting the Municipal Council is not a priority and is yet to be forged. Surely, the question remains open concerning the need and the actual importance of creating a sense of group cohesion, a group solidity and unity, for the efficiency and effectiveness of the local elite in the leadership of their community. In other words, is it truly important for the local leadership to nurture and sustain a sentiment of group cohesion – more or less exclusionary and clearly conducive to a sense of distinctiveness and "elitism" – in order to demonstrate effectiveness in decision-making in the interest of their community?

Practical exercise: Explaining interactions and priorities of the local political elites by the two variables

Perceived correlations among dependent variables can also constitute paths for further interpretation of the results for the six cases, and consequently, for generalization. The local political elites' interactions and contacts, with an undeniable impact upon the recruitment process, present a remarkable importance in what concerns prioritization at the local level, as well: according to the hierarchical classification of interactions, done by each municipal councilor, one could construct valid arguments on the manner in which the local councilors presented their interests and coordinated their activities. Generally, the preference for certain groups denotes an interest from the part of the local elite towards a certain field of activity or set of interests; the quotidian interactions can thusly sketch the agenda of a local decision-maker to a very significant extent. The differences among the six cases claim some explanatory attempts. As already stated, this study proposes two major explanatory trajectories, but, in tentatively explaining the outlook of local political elites' interactions, the emphasis fell on one of them, namely the level of decentralization of the community represented by each elite group. The main working hypotheses regarding the relationship between the form and the nature of the local political elites' interactions and contacts, of the networks of power at the local level, on the one hand, and the level of decentralization regulated and practiced by the government, have been constructed as follows: H1: The local political elite is the more geographically isolated as the level of decentralization of the community is more significant. H2: The local political elite is the more "elitistically" isolated as the political culture of the elites of the *ancien régime* favored a larger gap between the governed and the government and as the character of the former regime's government is a monolithic, unitary one. In addition, some observations appear as evident and are worth highlighting. Firstly, a series of interactions and contacts which appear as essential for the consolidation of a democratic governance – even at the local level –, as are those with the trade-unions, with reform and civic groups, with local media, were seemingly fragile. From the comparative analysis of the results obtained following the administration of the questionnaire, a series of regularities corresponding to the six cases were distinguishable. In this sense, this study proposes a series of differentiations and taxonomies meant to systematize and synthesize the discrepancies among cases, but also to sketch a theoretical framework, a conceptual scheme for future generalizations concerning the contacts, interactions, and the networks of power at the level of the local political elites. Alongside the main independent variable of decentralization for explaining both the differences and the regularities among the six cases, this study utilizes also the variable of the "legacy of the *ancien régime*" ("political culture"): there are a series of traits in the attitudinal and behavioral models of the local political elites in East-Central Europe which can be identified as being transmitted, replicated, reproduced from "the political culture of the (former) regime" and from "the elite political culture" deposited during the half-a-century of state socialism. In this respect, the fashion in which the nodes are placed, and the paths, the connections which the nodes establish could be explained, outside the legislative-administrative framework (i.e. the effective level of decentralization specific to each of the six communities), also by the traits reproduced from the rather informal structure and the behavioral characteristics of the elite group governing previous to the communist breakdown. Regarding the variable of decentralization, one could notice a significant degree of isolation, particularly a geographical isolation, of the decentralized elites, their contacts and interactions with the elites at the other administrative-government tiers being considerably reduced as the *palette* of responsibilities extends at the local level. On the other hand, for the less decentralized administrative-government systems, the local political elites retained the links with the national and regional elites, links which were motivated especially by the lack of a legislative framework which might have turned the local decision-makers accountable in an exhaustive manner, and by the lack of financial, budgetary resources which might have conferred to the later the independence in decision-making. Concerning the variable of the "legacy of the former regime" ("political culture"), the differences among the six cases regarding the establishment and the preservation of local political elites' contacts and interactions, and the construction of the networks of power enfolded on the differentiation proposed by Kitschelt et al. (1999) among three major types of communist dictatorships (or types of state socialism): "national accommodative" (Poland and Hungary), "bureaucratic-authoritarian" / "welfare" (Czechoslovakia and East Germany) (Jarausch 1999: 47-69, esp. 59-60), and "patrimonial" / "modernizing-nationalizing" (Petrescu 2010: 48 and 404) (Romania and Bulgaria) (Kitschelt, Mansfeldova, Markowski, and Tóka 1999). Each of these species of communist dictatorships – further developed upon above – generated a sort of elite "political culture" and, consequently, three different sets of traits which can be considered as transmitted from the "political culture" of the political elites of the defunct regime. An example at hand is the characteristic of the monolithism of the political elites group, in the case of the former communist dictatorships of patrimonial vein, which generated, during contemporaneity, an "elitistically" isolated elite (even at the local level), an elite with an overemphasized sense of distinction (with respect to the population of the community this elite governs). See, in the case of the towns of Tecuci and Targovishte, a high degree of interactions within the elite group (19.48%, and 19.51%, respectively), an indicator quite specific for these two cases, translating a potentiated tendency of monolithism of the local political elite group, the absence of divergences of opinion within the group, avoidance of political conflict within the Local Council, and appreciation of collegiality among the members of the Council. But the tendency of the local elites of Tecuci and Targovishte to interact with other elites (at different administrative levels), more than any other cases, is primarily linked to the level of decentralization characterizing Romania and Bulgaria, where even party affiliation of local elites influences the distribution of central government funds to administrative-territorial units (see, for instance, Coman 2018, for a new perspective on this issue). In addition, the significance, within the structure of the network of power at the local level, of some groups could be partly explained by the specific type of "legacy" preserved from state socialism: the former "national-accommodative" dictatorships have granted, through their general dynamics, a unique place for the civic and reform groups, as well as to trade-unions, hence, generally, to those contesting groups towards the established power. The cases of Poland and Hungary (and, here and there, that of the Czech Republic), through the local elites in Oleśnica, Gyula, and Česká Lípa, showed a high importance given to the interactions with such groups, unencountered and unmatched in the cases of the former "patrimonial" dictatorships: 20.35% (for Gyula) and 21.05% (for Oleśnica) – for the former "national-accommodative" dictatorships –, and 23.23% (for Levice) and 25.39% (for Česká Lípa) – for the former "bureau-cratic-authoritarian" dictatorships –, regarding the weight of the local political elites' contacts with the civic and reform groups. On the other hand, the tendency towards patrimonialism and monolithism was translated, at the local level and within the process of democratic consolidation, through an accentuation of the links and the contacts of the political elite with the economic elite, the result being a juxtaposition and an intermingling of the two types of elites. Illustrative, in this sense, is the weight which the local councilors' interaction with the local entrepreneurship bore out of the total of local elites' interactions, for the case of the towns of Tecuci and Targovishte: 19.51% and 14.28%, respectively.

Actually, the stake of the construction of the networks of power and of identifying and analyzing the local political elites' contacts and interactions with other groups and institutions is to be found, not only in setting up the influences of various groups on the local political agenda, but also in the pressure on, and, afterwards, in the accountability of the local political elite in front of the governed community. Inquiring into the vast field of interest groups and their pressure on the formulation and implementation of public policies in American cities, Glenn Abney and Thomas P. Lauth differentiate between (1) "pluralistic" pattern of influencing the local agenda, and (2) "elitist" pattern of influence (Abney and Lauth 1986: 195); while the former presupposes local political elite's interactions with many potentially pressure-generating groups, the latter is effectuated within the local elite group, most casually, among the political elite and the economic one. The latter is favored by William Domhoff, as well, for in his multiple studies, he sees "major policy formation processes" as being dramatically and definitely marked by the "agenda-setting power of elites":

> "[W]hile pluralistic interest group competition does occur on specific issues, the general parameters of public discourse and public policy are set in advance and behind the scenes" (Domhoff 1978; see also Domhoff and Dye 1987),

by various elite groups. Consequently, the barycenter of those studies pursued from a relational perspective is represented precisely by the object of government, by the formulation of public policies, by getting the local political elites accountable. The intensity, the force of the (rather contesting) groups' pressures on the elite group, within the community, generates a certain impact level, a certain importance on the public policy agenda and on those decisions taken at the local level, of those key-areas (domains) of activity for which the groups had interacted, in a targeted way, with the political elite. Expectedly, hence, a higher level of local councilors' interactions with the ethnic or religious groups determined a high degree of valuing, by the elites themselves, of the importance of decisions in the sphere of interethnic or inter-confessional relations; the prioritization at the local level is maybe the most profoundly influenced dynamics of political decision-making by those pressures, interactions, contacts, and links initiated by different groups with the local political elite. Consequently, below, this study will attempt to test two theories underpinned by the analysis of the elites' interactions with other groups and by the power relations, namely: (1) the approach according to which the resultant of the networks of power and of interactions represent a certain scheme, strategy of policy prioritization at the local level, on key-areas; (2) the approach according to which a certain relational model determines a certain value pattern, whose impact on governance remains an unexplored soil, a "*terra incognita*" thus far. In the case of the latter, the sense of causality remains problematic, as well, for it is one of those aspects on which the conclusion of this book is far from being rushed: is the value charge of elite's personality that which generates the orientation and the frequency of its interactions, or the very intensity and nature of its relationships with other groups determine the elite's value orientation? More exactly, the frequent interaction with the civic and reform groups is expected to determine not only a high degree of elites' social integration, but also a higher degree of positivity of citizen participation as a democratic value. One can contend, also, that an increased and consistent frequency with the groups of local entrepreneurship (the business groups) can generate, among the political elite, a lower level of acceptability of economic equality as a value of democracy. For the six cases selected here, this study considered the policy prioritization at the local level on the basis of the registered answers, for the applied questionnaire on the members of the Local /

288

Municipal Councils, calculated as an average mean, to questions Q4 and Q6: "To which of the fields below do you consider a special attention should be given?", and "In which of the fields below do you consider efficient and beneficial measures had been already taken in your town during the last years?". On the other hand, with respect to the values embraced by the local political elites, this analysis isolates the following values: citizen participation, economic equality, the avoidance of political conflict. Regarding the local elites' prioritization strategies, function of the frequency of the interactions with other groups, a series of regularities could be observed, hence toning down the impact of the local political elites' contacts upon the setting-up of the working agenda. Firstly, a constant and more frequent interaction with the neighbours, with the supporters, with the civic and reform groups, could generate a more pragmatic view on the working agenda at the local level, and on the specific needs of the community. One can hypothesize that frequent links with these groups, not only inform the local elite on the major grievances of the town, but they also make them accountable in decision-making in those fields seen as problematic for any small administration (the so-called "hard domains", in which political decision presupposes significant and long-termed investments and changes: infrastructural improvements, public safety, economic development, healthcare, etc.). The links with the business groups present, again, a remarkable importance, for they can generate a prioritization in the direction of such domains as the economic development and infrastructural development. From the *data* collected following the administration of the questionnaire, one could observe a better delineated orientation of those political elites who established and maintained links with the above-mentioned groups towards the "hard" domains of the local agenda (it was the case of the town of Česká Lípa, but this tendency was present among the municipal councilors in Levice and Gyula). The interactions with the economic elites did not generate, as it has been initially hypothesized, a reorientation of the local political elites towards the sphere of economic development, for instance (the cases with the most frequent interactions with the local entrepreneurship, Tecuci and Targovishte, did no present high indices for the "economic development" domain); this inconsistency is partly explicable by the overlapping of the two types of local elites who could not thusly reconcile the private interest with the public one. At the opposite pole, the absence of consistent contacts with the ethnic groups in each of the six cases generated a corresponding impact on the measures at the local level, especially regarding the assessment of the importance policies in the sphere of minority rights and of the interethnic relations held at the local level. What is more, a large majority of the measures taken in this field sum up, at the local level, to cultural activities (ethnic festivals, fairs and conferences of the "intercultural dialogue", etc.), an aspect which divides the percentage weight of this domain on the local elite's agenda. Nevertheless, the exceptions were to be noted, in this respect, as well: Tecuci

(10.41%), and Targovishte (12.65%), two communities in which the weight and the frequency of interactions with the ethnic groups, placed around the value of 5%, were outperformed by the importance their pressure represented for the local political elite, and by their place on the working agenda. Otherwise, these exceptions, alongside the general manner in which the local leaders built the policy agenda of the community in the six cases, found their explanation in an exogenous variable (for example, the pressure played by the aspiration of an entire region to align itself to the exigencies of democracy and civil society, imposed by the belonging to the European Union, etc.), or an endogenous one (for example, the activity, previous to the mandate in the Council, of some local councilors in Oleśnica, in the sphere of social services), which could be different, in each case.

The scope of this contribution is contingent to the process of verifying the applicability, for the selected cases, of the influence bore by the consistency of the local elite's interactions with key-groups in the construction of the policy agenda. This applicability verified to a little extent, for the given situations, for the instruments which could evidence more clearly the way of translating the pressures originating out of the frequent interaction into importance on the public agenda are lacking from the analysis. In spite of the low applicability of this hypothesis for the situations scrutinized here, a series of inconsistencies should be remarked, which could provide an ampler image on the manner in which the government is effectuated at the local level: (1) the local political elite's interactions with the local economic elite were not of a contesting, opposing nature, especially in the communities with a "patrimonial" component (discussed above), a mark of a certain type of defunct communist regime; (2) the interactions with the neighbors, the supporters, and with the civic and reform groups were not, more often than not, of a contesting nature, but could generate pressures, especially in the case of a "populist"-typed elite, pressures which could have led to the increase in the importance of social security on the local agenda (as a matter of fact, the highest indices of importance were registered in this sphere); hence, following these interactions, one could presuppose that the political elite extracts citizens' grievances and socio-economic needs, not only electoral support; (3) in the arithmetic of the networks of power, the contacts with the groups with contesting potential had the purpose of re-conducting, of reorienting the trajectory of the local agenda, particularly in the sphere of "hard" domains, in which adopted policies have a special importance (see, in this respect, the fact that the members of the Municipal Councils under scrutiny here correctly identified the foreground significance of these domains: economic development, improvements in infrastructure, social services); (4) this type of identification of the key-domains for welfare at the community level was to be found, here and there, in counterpoint to the lack of a high frequency of the contacts with the political elite at the other levels of government – regional, but, most importantly, central one –, precisely because the

290

legislation in reference to decentralization, and the distribution of competences in each of the six states presuppose – surely, in different degrees – a series of indispensable dialogues for policy construction and decision-making in the above-mentioned domains; in other words, without the interactions between the local elite and the regional or the central one (at least, at a formal level) in such fields as improvements in infrastructure, for instance, a large number of measures are stuck in the implementation phase, in the shaw of distributing responsibilities and attributions. The absence of a frequent contact with the political elites placed at the other levels of government is symptomatic especially for the communities where the level of decentralization is more advanced, allowing for a greater discretion of the local elites in decision-making; even so, measures included in a national strategy in key-domains, for instance, require direct dialogue between the local and the central administrations. (5) Finally, education and healthcare recorded average weights (9 to 21%, for education; 4 to 12%, for healthcare), in the prioritization scheme at the local level, in the six cases, but it is hazardous to speculate what type of interactions determined such values for the two domains, except, probably, the same interactions with neighbors, civic groups, and, in those situations in which they played an important role within the community – trade unions.

With respect to the second approach (i.e. that according to which a certain relational model determines a certain value pattern of the political elite), one could hypothesize that the frequency and the intensity of some interactions and contacts could generate changes in the value orientation of the members of the political elite. This type of dependency of the political elites' value orientation was theorized by Robert Putnam (1976: 80), who differentiates, in this sense, among four types of "orientations" in the construction of elite attitudes, already discussed above: (a) "cognitive orientations", (b) "normative orientations", (c) "interpersonal orientations" (central for this analysis), and (d) "stylistic orientations". Two by two, the attitudinal indices are analyzed in an aggregate manner, as in "Aggregate Tables 1 and 2" in the Annexes. Following the administration of the questionnaire on the members of the Local / Municipal Councils in the six towns, the following distribution resulted: Tecuci, Targovishte, Oleśnica, Gyula – "populists", Česká Lípa, Levice – "democrats"; Tecuci, Targovishte – "statists-antiegalitarianists"; Oleśnica, Gyula, Česká Lípa, Levice – "statists-egalitarianists". How can these orientations be explained through the resultant relational model? A series of hypotheses or correspondences could be advanced:

IV. The local political elites who overlap on the local economic elites, or those who have frequent contact with the local entrepreneurship, develop a generally anti-egalitarianist attitude, appreciating dominantly the competition, the individual private initiative (it was the case of the local councilors in Tecuci and Targovishte);

V. Local political elites who maintain frequent and consistent interactions with the reform groups, the civic groups, with the ethnic and religious groups, with the trade unions (in those communities in which they are still vocal), are more prone to accept contestation, the opposition, and the political conflict, which they see as necessary to any democratic government, accepting – almost as an adjuvant – the citizen participation, as well (the "democratic" type, it was the case of the municipal councilors in Česká Lípa and Levice);

VI. Local political elites who place the interaction with the neighbors and the groups of supporters among the first most important links within the community they govern have the tendency of developing a "populist"-typed attitude, embracing citizen participation as a *sine qua non* principle, but avoiding those groups with contesting potential (out of these interactions, political conflict is inescapable), preferring the dialogue with the supporters to the detriment of opponents (it was the case of the majority of the elites under scrutiny: Tecuci, Targovishte, Gyula, Oleśnica, though each elite group, in its own respect, presented different motivations and diverse bases, both for encouraging citizen participation in the public business of the community, and for avoiding political conflict within the same community);

VII. The local political elites who establish frequent contacts with those groups with a social and socio-economic vocation (especially, trade unions, but the social reform groups, as well), as well as with neighbors (when their group is diverse, from a socio-economic standpoint), tend to develop, at least declaratively, rhetorically, an attitude favorable to a more equitable socio-economic arrangement, and to "social justice" (the cases of the elites in the Czech, the Polish, and the Slovak towns were telling);

VIII. Finally, expectedly, the local political elites who prioritize the relationships with the business group display a refractory attitude towards the interventionist state (predominantly, in the situations in which the two groups coalesce): the collected empirical observations showed, on the other hand, a positive attitude towards the "welfare state", probably as a result of another exogenous variable, that of the economic crisis, whose effects had been felt especially in the small-to-medium-sized towns in East-Central Europe, all throughout the time the empirical analysis was conducted (December 2010 – August 2015 period). Practically, all the six groups of local / municipal councilors were preponderantly "statists", a symptomatic aspect for the local political elite of the region, rather conservative from an economic standpoint, in spite of the equally profoundly statist recent past.

Of course, in the context of a relatively small number of cases scrutinized (a sampled population of $n \approx 120$ local / municipal councilors), and confronting an incontrollable number of exogenous variables, the impact of the relational model of the local political elites on (a) the prioritization strategies and of the working agenda, at the local level, and (b) the value orientations, remains only an exploratory, speculative endeavor, rather than a statistically-founded one.

The main intention of these two attempts was that of showing two dimensions of the outlook of the local political elites and the profile of the local government, upon which the specific of the local elites' interactions and contacts, and of the resulting networks of power, could have a significant impact and could constitute a valid explanation in interpreting the actions of local leadership. Otherwise, the distribution of the frequencies and of the consistency of the local political elites' interactions with other groups could explain the positioning of some local actors on a certain pace on the ladder of local government and administration. As this study puts forward only explanatory paths, the role of the relational model on the two above-mentioned fields still remains an unexplored research topic.

Limitations and contingencies of the research

As the first elitists had observed, political ranking and stratification is inherent in any type of society, during all historical periods, even in democratic societal arrangements. However, as James Bryce has rightly assessed, "[p]erhaps no form of government needs great leaders so much as democracy does." (Bryce 1985/1888: 432) The formula "great leaders" can be quite tricky and puzzling, since the classical Aristotelian perspective on "virtuous" men and morally fitted leaders was abandoned and is nowadays considered a supersaded method in leadership selection. In contemporary times, "great" is more and more synonymous with "competent", "specialized", "managerially efficient", "democratic". More locally focused research on leadership structures in democratic and democratizing societies can provide an insight on the contemporary meaning of the phrase "great leaders". Consulting social biographies and political pathways and interviewing members of the local elite can lead to a reassessment of the typical, experience-validated method of researching elites.

The author acknowledges the conspicuous limitations of his inquiry and, subsequently, the present study considers a series of errors and contingencies inherent to it. A significant proportion of such incongruences are of methodological nature, while other spring from the researcher's choices. The descriptive nature of the study was initially intended as the exhaustive scope of this study, though descriptive, exploratory, non-explanatory, quantitative approaches are prone to generally stir comprehensive criticism. While fully acknowledging the criticism, the study of the local political elites in Tecuci, Česká Lípa, Oleśnica, Gyula, Levice, and Targovishte remains a largely descriptive inquiry, especially due to the novelty of the topic: the endeavor constitutes a series of rather tentative results, to be further developed and accounted for subsequently.

While understanding the limitations of the "positional" approach in identifying and analyzing local elites, this study acknowledges that not any leadership construction can be coined, in an instant, as "elitist"[122]: a concession would have been to employ the word "class" instead of "elite" for positionally-determined leadership. Nonetheless, the overwhelming sociological bibliographical notes employed in this study utilize the phrase "political elite" for the group of individuals positionally, reputationally, or decisionally placed in a position of power, at a certain moment.

Skeptical positions in respect to the dominantly empirical method of researching elites were constantly raised. The limitations of the intended research – apart from the ones self-imposed by the researcher, motivated pri-

---

122 Indeed, this objection has been raised by the scholarly quite early in the 1970s. See, most illuminating, Shils 1982: 13-32.

marily by time and by the respondents' availability – are properly identified by statistician A. Cochrane under the form of two pertinent questions on the issue of elite interviewing:

> (1) "Is it possible to maintain an attitude of critical engagement? [...] Who has power within the research process?", and (2) "Is it really possible to identify and explore power through interviews, however carefully constructed they are? What about the dimensions of power that are inaccessible to the interviewers?" (Cochrane 1998: 2121-2132 [additions mine])

Therefore, often voiced criticisms refer to the overwhelmingly empirical and exploratory nature of the study, for it conspicuously lacks a hypothetical fundament to be verified during a deductive undertaking; to the very selection of the populations of the applied survey, upon which the large portion of the subsequent observations are based, for it has been put forward that the subjects of this study, i.e. the local / municipal councilors, are by no means the epitomes, the exponential figures compatible to the classical understanding of the concept of "elite". However, one should not overlook the very reality that the said concept is operationalized positionally, and that, generally, the notion of "elite" has been gradually deprived of its initial Aristotelian charge: "elite", in the realm of local politics, is not synonymous with "excellence" – while not actually becoming its antonym –, it ceased to denote a local aristocracy, earning some form of noble distinctiveness. At the local level – at least for the six cases selected –, what definitely lacks is the tradition of elitism, the groups of municipal councilors do not possess a historical consciousness of the leading caste. Consequently, the profiles of these individuals are thusly constructed as not to utilize the prominence of exceptional skillfulness, extraordinary prestige and unchallenging intelligence, but rather on the socio-demographical, descriptive, sociological aspects of these portraits. These local elites are usually part of the "new elite", in the course of professionalization and about to acquire their elite group consciousness and sense of distinctiveness. They are not elites because they excel (or are supposed to excel, in the public's eyes), but because they occupy a certain elected position at a certain moment.

A series of quite well-placed remarks – occasioned by the presentation of the first results of the intended study to large audiences formed of scholars of political science – have been raised concerning the relevance of the selected cases to the outlook of local elites for the countries under scrutiny. Generally, as Rodríguez-Teruel and Daloz (2018) have rightly pointed out, such forms of surveying and observing elites might pose significant representativity problems, alongside problems derived from the lack of control of the units of analysis. However, since the proposed inquiry does not seek generalization and its main purpose is by no means the extrapolation of final, overarching conclusions drawn from isolated and very specific case-studies, the sole contingency arouses in the construction of the threefold classification of the local leadership as outcome of the analysis of the profiles of the members of the six Local /

Municipal Councils; customarily, designing a model implies the usage of multiple results from a variety of cases, while not being isolated and circumscribed to conspicuous specificities and particularities. As a matter of fact, the focus of the study lies in the specificities of the six cases selected, their immediate relevance in view of future generalizations being only subsidiarily considered. The selection of the cases follows, nevertheless, a certain pattern determined by the accessibility of the populations under scrutiny and by the researcher's capacities and capabilities in respect to these populations.

Indeed, a secondary intention of the study is to account for the differences between the six groups of local political elites in East-Central Europe with the help of the concept of "elite political culture", applied at the local level and including both matters of "elite consciousness" and *ancien régime* heritage (particularly in the context in which the six groups selected belong to countries previously experiencing state socialism clearly in quite different variants). The results of such type of explanation through the prism of "elite political cultures" are rather limited and they remain contingent to the six Municipal Councils chosen for the study, with no generalization intended. While the book acknowledges the difficulties in operationalizing the collocation "elite political culture" properly and to actually pinpoint dimensions and developments clearly contingent to such a variable explaining differences and discrepancies between the six selected cases, the instrumentality of the concept appears, for the limited scopes of the book, conspicuous.

Alongside the descriptive character of the study lies another source of possible criticism: the volatility of such a descriptive inquiry on local elites, mainly and more specifically the problem of the inevitable anachronism, perishability of the selected population, inherent in this case. Such an issue is virtually unavoidable since the population of this inquiry is deemed to change every four or five years, making the entire approach, if not futile and insignificant, at least time-bound. But the study is constructed, in this sense, rather as a snapshot, not a *status-quo*, being a largely quantitative tool in every consideration about local political elites in East-Central Europe. Henceforth, the longitudinal inquiries on political elites in a certain administrative space do not represent the concern of this study, though such inquiries might be indeed useful for providing an account on the evolution of local elites in terms of social capital and personnel.

An attempted typology of local political elites in ECE

Based on the observations drawn from the six cases under scrutiny, regarding the local political elites' socio-demographical profile, the attitudes and orientations they display, their interactions with other groups, and their prioritization strategy at the community level, this book advances a tentative threefold typology, meant to isolate and to systematize the main differences between the cases. Consequently, the proposed taxonomy differentiates among: (1) "predominantly elitistic" local elites, (2) "democratic elitist" local elites, and (3) "predominantly democratic" local elites.

Thusly, the study proposes and favors the differentiation among three types of elites, underpinned on the specific content of elite political culture and on the set of attributions provided by a certain degree of decentralization:

- **"Predominantly elitistic"** (e.g. Tecuci and Targovishte), corresponding to a former "modernizing-nationalizing", "patrimonial" communist dictatorship, followed by "elite reproduction", and low levels of administrative decentralization and local autonomy, presently; characterized by a significant degree of "elite distinctiveness";
- **"Democratic elitist"** (e.g. Česká Lípa and Levice), corresponding to a defunct "bureaucratic-authoritarian", "welfare" communist dictatorship, followed by "elite circulation", and significant levels of decentralization and local autonomy, in the present;
- **"Predominantly democratic"** (e.g. Oleśnica and Gyula), corresponding to a former "national-accommodative" communist dictatorship, followed by "elite circulation", a tradition of administrative decentralization, and high levels of local autonomy, nowadays.

"Predominantly elitistic" (e.g. Tecuci and Targovishte) are those elites characterized by a significant degree of "elite distinctiveness", i.e. perceiving themselves, as a group or individually, as separate from the bulk of the town's population, as part of a special, superior caste of notables and local potentates, hence prone to favor the clear gap between the rulers and the ruled; enjoying considerable levels of prestige and reputation, this type of local elites display however a sense of reluctance in effectively dealing with the community's main problems, on the basis that power at the local level is insufficient to allow the leadership here to implement change. Therefore, it might be concluded that the "predominately elitist" local leadership corresponds to those communities presenting low degrees of decentralization and local autonomy. Additionally, the "predominantly elitistic" local elites are tightly linked to a "political" model, for their recruitment is almost exclusively intramural, all those comprising the local leadership being party members and benefiting from the otherwise indispensable support of the party, whose local branches are highly dependent of the central one. Interestingly, the "predominantly elitistic" groups are those that most closely approximate the Aristotelian *desideratum* in their construction, conception and self-perception: they tend to adhere to an "ethical" model of the ideal local councilor, at least declaratively cherishing moral attributes that would provide them with some sort of moral superiority as prime marks of distinctiveness in respect to their constituency, to the population of their community.

"Democratic elitist" (e.g. Česká Lípa and Levice) are those elites whose traits and profiles point to some form of *aurea mediocritas* between a sense of distinctiveness and the prestige they enjoy within the community, on the one hand, and the effective and meaningful dedication to their community's developmental plans, on the other hand; as such, though they form a "caste" of notables within the town and are hardly representative to the population of the establishments they lead, in socio-demographical terms, they can act decisively for the benefit of their town due to a considerable degree of local autonomy and decentralized prerogatives, responsibilities and attributions. The local councilors of the "democratic elitist" sort remain still dependent, to some extent, on the support of the political parties, but the local parties appear independent in respect to their central branch; occasionally, "democratic elitist" type corresponds to intramural recruitment of locally-established parties, splinters or other quite localized political movements and organizations, responding to extremely specific needs and demands or describing relatively strong political localism and allowing for factionalism and decentralized, territorialized "backbencher"-ism, or they are simply recruited in an extramural fashion, as independent. In addition, the "democratic elitist" groups overlap on a rather "pragmatic" or "technocratic" model of the local councilor, as the most cherished attributes of the leadership come to be the professionalism of the local leadership, its capacity in decision-making, policy designing and problem-solving.

"Predominantly democratic" (e.g. Oleśnica and Gyula) are those elites featuring a sense of identification with the masses, with the ordinary citizens of the community they happen to represent temporarily, a dominating "social sensitivity" that would determine their propensity towards social security and welfare strategies in local leadership; this type of local elites are juxtaposed to a tradition of decentralization and devolution mechanisms that permit them to identify and to implement policies responding to the needs of the town. The "predominantly democratic" type of local elites is probably the closest to the population it represents in terms of passive representation, for it may include persons of lower education, or people previously involved in directly advocating for the interests of some segments in the community (pupils, women, unemployed, workers, etc.). These local leaders are usually quite familiar to the problems their town confronts with, being especially concerned with social issues (e.g. unemployment, social benefits, housing, etc.). The methods of recruiting elites in this context differ, are highly inclusive, from clearly intramural methods to independent candidacy, but the actual specificity of these elites is the extramural fashion in which they are selected, as their political affiliation is futile if existent; the role of the party in the recruitment process, either local or central branches, is virtually insignificant. Consequently, the "predominantly democratic" local elites correspond to rather "pragmatic" and "moral" profiles, while the "political" model is virtually absent in their case.

Clearly, both the level of decentralization process undertaken in each of the six East-Central European countries (Romania, Czech Republic, Poland, Hungary, the Slovak Republic, and Bulgaria) and "the legacy" of the old communist regime have generated different outcomes in the local elites' profile, attitudes, prioritization, and interactions. More significant levels of administrative and fiscal decentralization indicate a more responsible, pragmatic local elite, though largely isolated to the central authorities and skeptical, cautious, regarding the edulcorated image of the benefits of decentralization. Conversely, a low level of decentralization is prone to determine an elite who is prepared to acknowledge political responsibility only for those "soft" spheres of policy-design and implementation at the local level; they seem impotent to act effectively locally in such domains as economic and infrastructural development, for instance. Yet, the impact of decentralization on the "impoverishment" of small-to-medium-sized towns – as are those studied here – remains an open question, worthy of proper and comprehensive consideration. Equally, the "elite political culture" generated by each of the three types of defunct communist regime puts a specific imprint on the profile and attitudes of the present local elite in ECE: a background of "modernizing nationalizing" communist dictatorship influences a high level of social mobility among the elites and high degree of monolithism, while a "national accommodative" legacy is conducive to relatively low levels of social mobility and a more favourable attitude to economic equality and gradual change.

As mentioned, the initial intent of the research was predominantly exploratory; with the gathering of the data, the differences pinpointed needed to be accounted for. The resort to two tentative explanations and an attempted typology of local leadership in ECE bears inherently both future research trajectories and limitations for the models proposed here. The envisaged study proposes a more encompassing approach, extended to the cases of other countries of former Sovietized Europe, employing the tentative typology proposed by the book, hence further testing its validity. The features, definitions and types of decentralization and the "legacy of the past" differ greatly from one instance to the other. It is particularly this diversity that entails differences in the local "elite (general) outlook", i.e. its attitudes, priorities, value orientations, interactions, profiles, degree of representativeness, patterns of recruitment, etc. Indeed, the contention this book advances refers precisely to the impacts of both the degree of decentralization and the "legacy of the former regime" upon the general portrait of the local political elite. Four such impacts are discussed here, namely the impacts of the level of decentralization and of the type of the "legacy of the past" on: (a) local elite's socio-demographical profile, (b) local elite's interactions, (c) local elite's attitudes towards key features of democracy and the state, and (d) local elite's strategy prioritization. Nevertheless, these differences in the local elite's "outlook" in East-Central Europe cannot and should not be traced back to the level of decentralization and the "legacy of the past" alone. Due to the limitations of this study, other, equally important, independent variables explaining the variations for the selected cases, are not considered (e.g. patterns of recruitment, the "system" variables, such as the characteristics of the political and the party systems, the tradition of "decentralization", etc.), variables which remain instrumental in accounting for the results. The book acknowledges also other significant limitations, such as: matters of representativeness and significance in the case selection (the actual limits of "the most similar systems" research design); the shortcomings in generalization and statistical analysis, due to the small number of units of analysis; the limits of comparison, due to the actual relevance of the selected cases, and those sprung from the employ of the questionnaire as the main method of *data* collection; the difficult operationalization of "decentralization" and of the "legacy of the past", of the "political culture", etc. While being aware of the important limitations, this endeavor might contribute significantly to the existing literature on the effects of decentralization and the "legacy of the past" on the portrait of the local leadership in East-Central Europe. During the last decades, the research in "elite studies" has faced a setback, while the interest in East-Central Europe has lowered significantly, following the NATO and EU accession (and the alleged end of democratic transition) of the countries in the region. Nonetheless, in the context of globalization, regionalization, and local autonomy, there is an increased focus on "local government" and "regional governance" research, concerned with the manner in which local actors (including local political elites) can provide for their community, outside the "traditional" three-layered administrative and political structure and in the absence of the dependency to the central, national authority (see, for instance, Tomaney 2019: 1-7; Havlík 2020; Peiró-Palomino, Picazo-Tadeo, and Rios 2020), or, conversely, concerned with the mechanisms and dynamics through which citizens become an equal partner to political elites in "local governance" (e.g. the recent studies on "market cities" v. "people cities"[123], though so far applicable to rather big cities) or in "sub-municipal governance" (see Hlepas, Kersting, Kuhlmann, Swianiewicz, and Teles 2018), and thus generally redefining the "polity" (especially, in the EU context; see Tatham and Mbaye 2018). Since research on political elites in the peculiar region of East-Central Europe should always be "inside looking out" (Best 1997: 8), hence profoundly acknow-

---

123 See, for the definition of "market cities" and "people cities", Oluf Emerson and Smiley 2018.

ledging the historical and cultural specificities of each state comprising the region, the variable of "the legacy of the *ancien régime*" is indispensable in the inquiry into the outlook of the local political elites in Eastern and Central Europe. Further research on other countries and regions undergoing processes of decentralization or democratization (e.g. Latin America, south-east Asia, India, etc.) might add a comparative note on the present endeavor.

References

Primary sources (legislation, party statutes, etc.)

Law 215/2001 on Local Public Administration (Romania).

The Statute of the Liberal-Democrat Party (*Partidul democrat-liberal*: PD-L) (Romania).

The Statute of the National Liberal Party (*Partidul Naţional Liberal*: PNL) (Romania).

The Statute of the Social-Democratic Party (*Partidul social democrat*: PSD) (Romania).

The Statute of the TOP 09 (*Tradice Odpovědnost Prosperita 09* – Tradition, Responsibility, Prosperity: TOP 09) (the Czech Republic) (http://en.top09.cz/documents/top-09-statutes/, last accessed: 02.03.2012).

The Statute of the Czech Social Democratic Party (*České strany sociálně demokratické*: ČSSD) (the Czech Republic).

The Statute of the Civil Democratic Party (*Občansko demokratické strany*: ODS) (the Czech Republic).

The Statute of the Communist Party of Bohemia and Moravia (*Komunistická strana Čech a Moravy*: KSČM) (the Czech Republic)

The Statute of the "Mayors for the Liberec Region" (*Starostové pro Liberecký Kraj: SLK*) (the Czech Republic)

The Statute of "Public Affairs" (*Věci veřejné*: VV) (the Czech Republic)

The Statute of "Sovereignty – Jana Bobošíková" Bloc (*SUVERENITA – blok Jany Bobošíkové*) (the Czech Republic)

The Statute of the Green Party (*Strana zelených*: SZ) (the Czech Republic)

The Statute of "Law and Justice" Party (*Prawo i Sprawiedliwość*: PiS) (Poland)

The Statute of the "Civic Platform" (*Platforma Obywatelska*: PO) (Poland)

The Statute of the "Palikot's Movement" (*Ruch Palikota*: RP) (Poland)

The Statute of the Democratic Left Alliance (*Sojusz Lewicy Demokratycznej*: SLD) (Poland)

The Statute of the Hungarian Civic Party (Fidesz – *Magyar Polgári Szövetség*) (Hungary)

The Statute of the Hungarian Socialist Party (*Magyar Szocialista Párt*: MSZP) (Hungary)

The Statute of the Movement for a Better Hungary (*Jobbik Magyarországért Mozgalom* – Jobbik) (Hungary)

The Statute of the Christian Democratic People's Party (*Kereszténydemokrata Néppárt*: KDNP) (Hungary)

The Statute of the Movement "Politics Can Be Different" (*Lehet Más A Politika*: LMP) (Hungary)

The Statute of the Municipal Council of Targovishte, http://www.targovishte.bg/
municipality/file/reshenia/2015/Sesia2Noemvri2015/PravilnikObS2015-
2019.pdf, last accessed: 14.02.2016 (Bulgaria)

The Statute of the Movement for Rights and Freedoms (*Dvizhenie za prava i svo-
bodi*: DPS) (Bulgaria)

The Statute of the Bulgarian Socialist Party (*Bulgarska sotsialisticheska partiya*:
BSP) (Bulgaria)

The Statute of the "Citizens for European Development of Bulgaria" (*Grazhdani
za evropeysko razvitie na Balgariya* – GERB) (Bulgaria)

The Statute of "Direction – Social Democracy" (*Smer – sociálna demokracia*:
Smer-SD) (Slovakia)

The Statute of the Christian Democratic Movement (*Krest'anskodemokratické
hnutie*: KDH) (Slovakia)

The Statute of "Most-Híd" (*az együttműködés pártja – strana spolupráce*: Most-
Híd) (Slovakia)

The Statute of the Slovak Democratic and Christian Union – Democratic Party
(*Slovenská demokratická a krest'anská únia – Demokratická strana*: SDKÚ-
DS) (Slovakia)

The Statute of "Freedom and Solidarity" (*Sloboda a Solidarita*: SaS) (Slovakia)

The Statute of the People's Party – Movement for a Democratic Slovakia (*L'udová
strana – Hnutie za demokratické Slovensko*: L'S-HZDS) (Slovakia)

The Statute of the Movement for Democracy (*Hnutie za demokraciu*: HZD) (Slovakia)

The Statute of the Green Party (*Strana zelených*: SZ) (Slovakia)

Constitutional Act No. 294/1990 Col. (the Czech Republic).

Act of the Czech National Council No. 367/1990 Col. on Municipalities, amended
as 410/1992.

Act of the Czech National Council No. 425/1990 Col. on District Offices, the Regulation of the Sphere of Their Activities; amendments to Acts of the Czech
National Council No. 266/1991, No. 542/1991, Act No. 21/1992, Act No.
403/1992, Act No. 152/1994 and Act No. 254/1994.

Law of March 8, 1998 on Local Self-government (Poland).

Law on Local Self-government No. LXV of 1990 (Hungary).

Cardinal Act on Local Government No. CLXXXIX of 21st of December 2011
(Hungary).

Slovak National Council Act 369/1990.

Law No. 221/1996 on the territorial and administrative subdivisions of the Slovak
Republic.

Local Self-Government and Local Administration Act of 1991, the Municipal
Budgets Act of 1998 (Bulgaria).

Local Taxes and Fees Act of 1997 (Bulgaria).

Council of Europe & Steering Committee on Local and Regional Authorities.
Structure and Operation of Local and Regional Democracy: Czech Republic.
2nd ed. Strasbourg (France): Council of Europe Publishing, 1998, and 2001.

Books

Abbink, Jon, and Tijo Salverda, eds. *The Anthropology of Elites: Power, Culture, and the Complexities of Distinction*. New York & Basingstoke, UK: Palgrave Macmillan, 2013.

Aberbach, Joel D., Robert D. Putnam, and Bert A. Rockman. *Bureaucrats and Politicians in Western Democracies*. Cambridge, MA: Harvard University Press, 1981.

Abney, Glenn, and Thomas P. Lauth. *The Politics of State and City Administration*. Albany, NY: State University of New York Press, 1986.

Aesop. *Fables*. Edited and Translated by Laura Gibbs. Oxford & New York: Oxford University Press, 2002.

Anderson, James E. *Public Policymaking*. Boston, MA: Houghton Mifflin Company, 1997.

Apostol Tofan, Dana. *Drept administrativ*. 2nd rev. ed. Bucureşti: C.H. Beck, 2008.

Aristotle. *Nicomachean Ethics*. Edited and Translated by Robert C. Bartlett and Susan D. Collins. Chicago & London: University of Chicago Press, 2011.

Bachrach, Peter. *The Theory of Democratic Elitism*. Boston, MA: Little Brown, 1967.

Bachrach, Peter, ed. *Political Elites in a Democracy*. New York: Atherton Press, 1971.

[Bachrach, Peter, ed. *Political Elites in a Democracy*. New Brunswick, NJ, & London: Aldine Transaction, 2010.]

Bachrach, Peter, and Morton S. Baratz. *Power and Poverty; Theory and Practice*. London & New York: Oxford University Press, 1970.

Bäck, Henry, Hubert Heinelt, and Annick Magnier, eds. *The European Mayor. Political Leaders in the Changing Context of Local Democracy*. Wiesbaden & Berlin (Germany): VS Verlag für Sozialwissenschaften, 2006.

Baldersheim, Harald, Michal Illner, Audun Jon Offerdal, Lawrence Rose, and Paweł Swianiewicz, eds. *Local Democracy and the Processes of Transformation in East-Central Europe*. Boulder, CO: Westview Press, 1996.

Baldersheim, Harald, Michal Illner, and Hellmut Wollmann, eds. *Local Democracy in Post-Communist Europe*. Urban Research International 2. Opladen: Leske + Budrich, 2003.

Beard, Victoria A., Faranak Miraftab, and Christopher Silver, eds. *Planning and Decentralization: Contested Spaces for Public Action in the Global South*. London & New York: Routledge, 2008.

Bennett, Robert John. *Territory and Administration in Europe*. London: Frances Pinter, 1989.

Bennett, Robert John, ed. *Local Government in the New Europe*. London & New York: Belhaven Press, 1993.

Bennett, Robert J., ed. *Local Government and Market Decentralization: Experiences in Industrialized, Developing, and Former Eastern Bloc Countries*. Tokyo (Japan): United Nations University Press, 1994.

Bentley, Arthur F. *The Process of Government: A Study of Social Pressures*. Chicago, IL: University of Chicago Press, 1908.

Berend, Iván T. *History Derailed. Central and Eastern Europe in the Long Nineteenth Century*. Berkeley, CA: University of California Press, 2003.

Best, Heinrich, and Ulrike Becker, eds. *Elites in Transition: Elite Research in Central and Eastern Europe*. Opladen: Leske und Budrich, 1997.

Best, Heinrich, and Maurizio Cotta, eds. *Parliamentary Representatives in Europe, 1848-2000: Legislative Recruitment and Careers in Eleven European Countries*. Oxford: Oxford University Press, 2000.

Best, Heinrich, and John Higley, eds. *Democratic Elitism: Comparative and Evolutionary Perspectives*. Leiden (The Netherlands) & New York: Brill, 2009.

Best, Heinrich, and John Higley, eds. *Democratic Elitism: New Theoretical and Comparative Perspectives*. Leiden (The Netherlands): Brill, 2010.

Bird, Richard M., Robert D. Ebel, and Christine I. Wallich. *Decentralization of the Socialist State: Intergovernmental Finance in Transition Economies* (World Bank Regional and Sectoral Studies). Washington, DC: The International Bank for Reconstruction and Development & The World Bank, 1995.

Bird, Richard M, and François Vaillancourt, eds. *Perspectives on Fiscal Federalism*. Washington, DC: World Bank Institute, 2006.

Bledsoe, Timothy. *Careers in City Politics: The Case for Urban Democracy*. Pittsburgh, PA: University of Pittsburgh Press, 1993.

Boissevain, Jeremy, and James Clyde Mitchell, eds. *Network Analysis: Studies in Human Interaction*. The Hague (the Netherlands): Mouton, 1973.

Bonilla, Frank. *The Failure of Elites*. Cambridge, MA: The MIT Press, 1970.

Bottomore, Tom. *Elites and Society*. New York: Routledge, 1993.

Boudon, Raymond, ed. *Traité de sociologie*. Paris: *Les Presses Universitaires de France* PUF, 1992.

[Boudon, Raymond, ed. *Tratat de sociologie*. Translated by Delia Vasiliu and Anca Ene. Bucharest: Humanitas, 1997.]

Bovaird, Tony A. G., Elke Löffler, and Salvador Parrado Díez, eds. *Developing Local Governance Networks in Europe*. Baden-Baden (Germany): Nomos Verlagsgesellschaft, 2002.

Browne, Stephen Howard. *Edmund Burke and the Discourse of Virtue*. Tuscaloosa, AL: University of Alabama Press, 1993.

Bryce, James. *American Commonwealth*. New York: Macmillan, 1888.

[Bryce, James. *American Commonwealth*. 3rd ed. New York: Macmillan, 1985.]

Brym, Robert. *Intellectuals and Politics*. London: George Allen & Unwin, 1980.

Bugajski, Janusz. *Political Parties of Eastern Europe: A Guide to Politics in Postcommunist Era*. Armonk, NY: M. E. Sharpe, 2002.

Burki, Shahid Javed, Guillermo E. Perry, and William R. Dillinger, eds. *Beyond the Center: Decentralizing the State*. Washington, DC: The World Bank, 1999.

Butler, David, Howard R. Penniman, and Austin Ranney. *Democracy at the Polls.* Washington DC: American Enterprise Institute, 1981.

Cars, Göran, Patsy Healey, Ali Madanipour, and Claudio De Magalhães, eds. *Urban Governance, Institutional Capacity and Social Milieux.* Aldershot, UK: Ashgate, 2002.

Caulfield, Janice, and Helge O. Larsen, eds. *Local Government at the Millenium.* Opladen: Leske + Budrich, 2002.

Chandler, J. A., ed. *Local Government in Liberal Democracies: An Introductory Survey.* London: Routledge, 1993.

Cheema, G. Shabbir, and Dennis A. Rondinelli. *Decentralization and Development.* Beverly Hills, CA: Sage Publications, 1983.

Cheema, G. Shabbir, and Dennis A. Rondinelli, eds. *Decentralizing Governance: Emerging Concepts and Practices.* Washington, DC: Brookings Institution Press, 2007.

Clingermayer, James C., and Richard C. Feiock. *Institutional Constraints and Policy Choice. An Exploration of Local Governance.* Albany, NY: State University of New York Press, 2001.

Cohen, John M., and Stephen B. Peterson. *Methodological Issues in the Analysis of Decentralization.* Cambridge, MA: Harvard Institute for International Development, 1996.

Cohen, John M., and Stephen B. Peterson. *Administrative Decentralization: A New Framework for Improved Governance, Accountability, and Performance.* Cambridge, MA: Harvard Institute for International Development, 1997.

Coleman Selden, Sally. *The Promise of Representative Bureaucracy: Diversity and Responsiveness in a Government Agency.* Armonk, NY, & London: M.E. Sharpe, 1997.

Copus, Colin. *Party Politics and Local Government.* Manchester, UK: Manchester University Press, 2004.

Coulson, Andrew, ed. *Local Government in Eastern Europe: Establishing Democracy at the Grassroots.* Cheltenham, UK: Edward Elgar, 1995.

Craythorne, Donald Leslie. *Municipal Administration: The Handbook.* 6th ed. Cape Town (South Africa): Juta & Co. Ltd, 2006. First published 1980.

Crewe, Ivor, ed. *British Political Sociology Yearbook, Vol. 1: Elites in Western Democracies.* London: Croom Helm, 1974.

Culic, Irina. *Câştigătorii. Elită politică şi democratizare în România, 1989-2000* [*The Winners. Political Elites and Democratization in Romania, 1989-2000*]. Cluj-Napoca: Limes, 2002.

Cusack, Thomas R. *A National Challenge at the Local Level: Citizens, Elites and Institutions in Reunified Germany.* Aldershot, UK, & Burlington, VT: Ashgate Publishing, 2003.

Czudnowski, Moshe M., ed. *Does Who Governs Matter? Elite Circulation in Contemporary Societies.* DeKalb, IL: Northern Illinois University Press, 1982.

Czudnowski, Moshe M., ed. *Political Elites and Social Change: Studies on Elite Roles and Attitudes.* DeKalb, IL: Northern Illinois University Press, 1983.

Dahl, Robert Alan. *Who Governs? Democracy and Power in an American City.* New Haven, CT, & London: Yale University Press, 1961.

Dahl, Robert A. *Poliarchy; Participation and opposition.* New Haven, CT: Yale University Press, 1971.

Dahl, Robert A. *Modern Political Analysis.* Englewood Cliffs, NJ: Prentice-Hall, 1984.

Denters, Bas, and Lawrence E. Rose, eds. *Comparing Local Governance: Trends and Developments. Government Beyond the Centre.* Basingstoke, UK, & New York: Palgrave Macmillan, 2005.

Dogan, Mattei, ed. *Pathways to Power: Selecting Rulers in Pluralist Democracies.* Boulder, CO: Westview, 1989.

Dogan, Mattei, ed. *Elite Configurations at the Apex of Power.* Leiden (The Netherlands) & Boston, MA: Brill, 2003.

Dogan, Mattei, and John Higley, eds. *Elites, Crises and the Origins of Regimes.* Lanham, MD: Rowman and Littlefield, 1998.

Dollery, Brian E., and Lorenzo Robotti, eds. *The Theory and Practice of Local Government Reform.* Glos, UK: Edward Elgar Publishing, 2008.

Domhoff, G. William. *Who Really Rules? New Haven and Community Power Reexamined.* New Brunswick, NJ: Transaction Publishers, 1978.

Domhoff, George William, and Thomas R. Dye, eds. *Power Elites and Organizations.* Newbury Park, CA: Sage Publications, 1987.

Dostál, Petr F., Michal Illner, Jan Kára, and Max Barlow, eds. *Changing Territorial Administration in Czechoslovakia: International Viewpoints.* Amsterdam (The Netherlands): University of Amsterdam, Charles University, and the Czechoslovak Academy of Sciences, 1992.

Dunleavy, Patrick. *Urban Political Analysis: The Politics of Collective Consumption.* London: Macmillan, 1980.

Dyrberg, Torben Bech. *The Circular Structure of Power: Politics, Identity, Community.* London & New York: Verso, 1997.

Eldersveld, Samuel. *Political Elites in Modern Societies. Empirical Research and Democratic Theory.* Ann Arbor, MI: The University of Michigan Press, 1989.

Elliot, Michael J. *The Role of Law in Central-Local Relations.* London: Social Science Research Council, 1981.

Elster, Jon, ed. *Retribution and Reparation in the Transition to Democracy.* Cambridge: Cambridge University Press, 2006.

Emerson, Michael Oluf, and Kevin T. Smiley. *Market Cities, People Cities: The Shape of Our Urban Future.* New York: New York University Press, 2018.

Engelstad, Fredrik, and Trygve Gulbrandsen, eds. *Comparative Studies of Social and Political Elites.* Vol. 23 of *Comparative Social Research.* Oxford, UK, & Amsterdam (The Netherlands): Elsevier Science, 2007.

Etzioni-Halevy, Eva, ed. *Classes and Elites in Democracy and Democratization: A Collection of Readings.* New York and London: Garland Publishing, 1997.

Eulau, Heinz, and Moshe M. Czudnowski, eds. *Elite Recruitment in Democratic Polities. Comparative Studies Across Nations.* New York: Sage Publications, John Wiley & Sons, 1976.

Eulau, Heinz, and Kenneth Prewitt. *Labyrinths of Democracy; adaptations, linkages, representation, and policies in urban politics.* Indianapolis, IN: Bobbs-Merrill, 1973.

Eyal, Gill, Eleanor Townsley, and Iván Szelényi. *Making Capitalism without Capitalists: The New Ruling Elite in Eastern Europe.* London: Verso Books, 1998.

Faguet, Jean-Paul. *Decentralization and Popular Democracy: Governance from Below in Bolivia.* Ann Arbor, MI: University of Michigan, 2012.

Fairbanks, Robert B., and Patricia Mooney-Melvin, eds. *Making Sense of the City. Local Government, Civic Culture, and Community Life in Urban America.* Columbus, OH: Ohio State University Press, 2001.

Falkenhausen, Friedrich F. Von. *Im Schatten Napoleons. Aus den Erinnerungen der Frau von Remuzat.* Leipzig: Koehler and Amelang, 1941.

Farkas, Gergei M., ed. *Essays on Elite Networks in Sweden.* Stockholm Studies in Sociology, n.s., no. 52. Stockholm (Sweden): Stockholm University Press, 2012.

Field, G. Lowell, and John Higley. *Elitism.* London: Routledge, 1980.

Frederickson, H. George, Gary A. Johnson, and Curtis H. Wood. *The Adapted City: Institutional Dynamics and Structural Change.* Armonk, NY: M.E. Sharpe, 2004.

Freeman, Linton C., Douglas R. White, and A. Kimball Romney, eds. *Research Methods in Social Network Analysis.* New Brunswick, NJ: Transaction Publishers, 1992.

Frège, Xaviér. *La decentralization.* Paris: Éditions La Découverte, 1986.

Gabriel, Oscar W., Vincent Hoffmann-Martinot, and Hank Savitch, eds. *Urban Democracy.* Opladen: Leske + Budrich, 2000.

Galaskiewicz, Joseph. *Exchange Networks and Community Politics.* Beverly Hills, CA: Sage Publications, 1979.

Gallagher, Michael, and Michael Marsh, eds. *Candidate Selection in Comparative Perspective: The Secret Garden of Politics.* London: Sage Publishers, 1988.

Gallina, Nicole. *Political Elites in East Central Europe. Paving the way for 'negative Europeanisation'?.* Leverkusen (Germany): BudrichUni Press, 2008.

Gamson, William Anthony. *Power and Discontent.* Homewood, IL: Dorsey Press, 1968.

Girvetz, Harry K., ed. *Democracy and Elitism.* New York: Scribner's, 1967.

Goldfarb, Jeffrey C. *Civility and Subversion: The Intellectual in Democratic Society.* Cambridge: Cambridge University Press, 1998.

Goodman, Paul. *People or Personnel.* New York: Random House, Inc., 1963.

Granovetter, Mark. *Getting a Job: A Study of Contacts and Careers.* Cambridge, MA: Harvard University Press, 1974.

Grindle, Merilee Serrill. *Going Local. Decentralization, Democratization and the Promise of Good Governance.* Princeton, NJ: Princeton University Press, 2007.

Grofman, Bernard, and Arend Lijphart, eds. *Electoral Laws and Their Political Consequences.* New York: Agathon Press Inc. / Algora Publishing, 2003.

Grzymała-Busse, Anna. *Rebuilding Leviathan: Party Competition and State Exploitation in Post-communist Democracies*. Cambridge & New York: Cambridge University Press, 2007.

Gurr, Ted Robert, and Desmond S. King. *The State and the City*. London & Chicago, IL: Macmillan & University of Chicago Press, 1987.

Hajdù, Zoltán, ed. *Regional Processes and Spatial Structures in Hungary in the 1990s*. Pécs: Hungarin Academy of Sciences, Center for Regional Studies, 1999.

Hamilton, Alexander, James Madison, and John Jay, Publius [pseud.]. *The Federalist [Papers] (with Letters of "Brutus")*. Edited by Terence Ball. Cambridge & New York: Cambridge University Press, 2003. First published 1788.

Hankiss, Elemér. *East European Alternatives*. Oxford: Clarendon Press & Oxford University Press, 1990.

Hanšpach, Daniel. *Political, Organizational and Policy Transformation at the Municipal Level: The case of Liberec*. Working Paper WP 97:1. Prague: Institute of Sociology of the Academy of Science of The Czech Republic, 1997.

Harary, Frank, Robert Zane Norman, and Dorwin Cartwright. *Structural Models: An Introduction to the Theory of Directed Graphs*. New York: J. Wiley & Sons, 1965.

Harasymiw, Bohdan. *Political Elite Recruitment in the Soviet Union*. New York: St. Martin Press, 1984.

Harváth, Tamás M., ed. *Decentralization: Experiments and Reforms*. Budapest (Hungary): Local Government and Public Service Reform Initiative, 2000.

[Harváth, Tamás M., ed. *Local Governments in Central and Eastern Europe*. London: Routledge, 2004.]

Haus, Michael, Hubert Heinelt, and Murray Stewart, eds. *Urban Governance and Democracy: Leadership and Community Involvement*. London: Routledge, 2005.

Hazan, Reuven Y., and Gideon Rahat. *Democracy within Parties. Candidate Selection Methods and Their Political Consequences*. Oxford & New York: Oxford University Press, 2010.

Healey, Patsy, Stuart Cameron, Simin Davoudi, Stephen Graham, and Ali Madanipour, eds. *Managing Cities: The New Urban Context*. Sussex, UK: John Wiley & Sons, 1995.

Helmsing, Bert. *Externalities, Learning and Governance. Perspectives on Local Economic Development*. Den Haag (The Netherlands): Institute of Social Studies – ISS, 2000.

Hesse, Jens Joachim, ed. *Local Government and Urban Affairs in International Perspective: Analyses of Twenty Western Industrialized Countries*. Baden-Baden (Germany): Nomos Verlagsgesellschaft, 1991.

Hesse, Jens Joachim, ed. *Administrative Transformation in Central and Eastern Europe*. Oxford & Cambridge: Blackwell Publishers, 1993.

Hesse, Jens Joachim, ed. *Rebuilding the State: Public Sector Reform in Central and Eastern Europe*. Baden-Baden (Germany): Nomos Verlagsgesellschaft, 1995.

Hesse, Jens Joachim, and Klaus Goetz. *Public Sector Reform in Central and Eastern Europe: The Case of the Czech and Slovak Federative Republic* (report). Oxford and Geneva: Nuffield College Oxford & Center for European Studies, July 1992.

Heywood, Andrew. *Politics*. London: Macmillan, 1997.

Higley, John. *Elite Theory and Analysis*. Lisbon (Portugal): *Estudos Politicos, Livros Horizontes*, 2009.

Higley, John, and Michael G. Burton. *Elite Foundations of Liberal Democracy*. Boulder, CO: Rowman & Littlefield, 2006.

Higley, John, and György Lengyel, eds. *Elites After State Socialism: Theories and Analysis*. Lanham, MD: Rowman & Littlefield, 2000.

Higley, John, Jan Pakulski, and Wlodzimierz Wesolowski, eds. *Postcommunist Elites and Democracy in Eastern Europe*. Basingstoke, UK: Macmillan, 1998.

Hlepas, Nikolaos-Komninos, Norbert Kersting, Sabine Kuhlmann, Paweł Swianiewicz, and Filipe Teles, eds. *Sub-Municipal Governance in Europe: Decentralization Beyond the Municipal Tier*. Basingstoke, UK: Palgrave Macmillan & International Institute of Administrative Sciences, 2018.

Hofman, Bert. *Decentralization and Financial Management. Background Note for Government Expenditure and Financial Management Course*. Washington, DC: World Bank, 1994.

Homans, George C. *The Human Group*. London & New York: Routledge & Kegan Paul, 1951.

Hook, Sidney. *The Hero in History*. New York: Cosimo Classics, 2008.

Hořák, Martin. *Governing the Post-Communist City: Institutions and Democratic Development in Prague*. Toronto (Canada): University of Toronto Press, 2007.

Hulst, Merlijn van. *Town Hall Tales: Culture as Storytelling in Local Government*. Delft (The Netherlands): Eburon Publishers, 2008.

Hunter, Floyd. *Community Power Structure. A Study of Decision Makers*. Chapel Hill, NC: University of North Carolina Press, 1953.

Hunter, Floyd, Ruth C. Schaffer, and Cecil G. Sheps. *Community Organization: Action and Inaction*. Chapel Hill, NC: University of North Carolina Press, 1956.

Iankova, Elena Atanassova. *Business, Government, and EU Accession: Strategic Partnership and Conflict*. Lanham, MD: Lexington Books, 2009.

Illner, Michal, and Bohumil Jungmann. *Výzkum městských národních výborů* [*The Investigation of Municipal Councils*]. Prague (Czech Republic): Institute for State Administration, 1988.

International Monetary Fund. *Government Finance Statistics Yearbook*. Washington, DC: IMF, 2001.

Jackson, Matthew O. *Social and Economic Networks*. Princeton, NJ: Princeton University Press, 2010.

Jacob, Betty, Krzysztof Ostrowski, and Henry Teune, eds. *Democracy and Local Governance: Ten Empirical Studies*. Honolulu, HI: Matsunaga Institute for Peace, 1993.

Jacob, Philip E., ed. *Values and Active Community*. New York: The Free Press, 1971.

Jarausch, Konrad Hugo, ed. *Dictatorship as Experience: Towards a Socio-Cultural History of the GDR*. Translated by Eve Duffy. New York: Berghahn Books, 1999.

John, Peter. *Local Government in Western Europe*. London & Thousand Oaks, CA: Sage Publications, 2001.

Jowitt, Kenneth. *The New World Disorder: The Leninist Extinction*. Berkeley, CA: University of California Press, 1992.

Judge, David, Gerry Stoker, and Harold Wolman, eds. *Theories of Urban Politics*. London & Thousand Oaks, CA: Sage Publications, 1995.

Keller, Suzanne. *Beyond the Ruling Class: Strategic Elites in Modern Society*. New York: Random House, 1963.

Kersting, Norbert, and Angelika Vetter, eds. *Reforming Local Government in Europe. Closing the Gap between Democracy and Efficiency*. Urban Research International 4. Opladen (the Netherlands): Leske + Budrich &, 2003.

Kimball, Jonathan D., ed. *The Transfer of Power: Decentralization in Central and Eastern Europe*. Budapest: Local Government and Public Service Reform Initiative, 1999.

King, Lawrence Peter, and Iván Szelényi. *Theories of the New Class: Intellectuals and Power*. Minneapolis, MN: University of Minnesota Press, 2004.

Kirchner, Emil Joseph, ed. *Decentralization and Transition in the Visegrad: Poland, Hungary, the Czech Republic and Slovakia*. Basingstoke, UK, & New York: Macmillan & St. Martin's Press, 1999.

Kitschelt, Herbert, Zdenka Mansfeldova, Radoslaw Markowski, and Gábor Tóka. *Post-Communist Party Systems: Competition, Representation, and Inter-Party Cooperation*. Cambridge: Cambridge University Press, 1999.

Konrád, György, and Iván Szelényi. *The Intellectuals on the Road to Class Power*. New York: Harcourt Brace Javanovich, 1979.

Kornai, János. *Economics of shortage*. Amsterdam (the Netherlands): North-Holland, 1980.

LaPalombara, Joseph, and Myron Weiner, eds. *Political Parties and Political Development*. Princeton, NJ: Princeton University Press, 1966.

Lasswell, Harold D., Daniel Lerner, and C. Easton Rothwell. *The Comparative Study of Elites: An Introduction and Bibliography*. Stanford, CA: Stanford University Press, 1952.

Laumann, Edward O., and Franz Urban Pappi. *Networks of Collective Action: A Perspective on Community Influence Systems*. New York: Academic Press, 1976.

LeDuc, Lawrence, Richard G. Niemi, and Pippa Norris, eds. *Comparing Democracies: Elections and Voting in Global Perspective*. London: Sage, 1996.

Leland, Suzanne M., and Kurt Thurmaier, eds. *Case Studies of City-County Consolidation: Reshaping the Local Government Landscape*. Armonk, NY: M.E. Sharpe, 2004.

Lengyel, György, Heinrich Best, Petr Hartos, John Higley, Pavel Machonin, Martin Nekola, and Milan Tucek. *Elites in Central-Eastern Europe*. Budapest (Hungary): Friedrich Ebert Foundation, 2007.

Lewin, Kurt. Field *Theory in the Social Sciences*. New York: Harper & Row, 1951.

Lijphart, Arend. *Democracies: Patterns of Majoritarian and Consensus Government in Twenty-one Countries*. New Haven, CT: Yale University Press, 1984.

Lijphart, Arend. *Patterns of Democracy: Government Forms and Performance in Thirty-six Countries*. New Haven, CT: Yale University Press, 1999.

Linz, Juan J., and Alfred C. Stepan. *Problems of Democratic Transition and Consolidation. Southern Europe, South America, and Post-Communist Europe*. Baltimore, MD, & London: The Johns Hopkins University Press, 1996.

Lipset, Seymour Martin, and Stein Rokan, eds. *Party Systems and Voter Alignments: Cross-National Perspectives*. New York: Free Press, 1967.

Loewenberg, Gerhord, Samuel C. Patterson, and Malcom E. Jewell, eds. *Handbook of Legislative Research*. Cambridge, MA, & London: Harvard University Press, 1985.

Loughlin, John, Frank Hendriks, and Anders Lidström, eds. *The Oxford Handbook of Local and Regional Democracy in Europe*. Oxford, UK: Oxford University Press, 2011.

Lukes, Steven. *Power: A Radical View*. London: Macmillan Education, 1974.

Lynd, Robert Staughton, and Helen Merrell Lynd. *Middletown: A Study in Contemporary American Culture*. New York: Harcourt, Brace and World, 1929.

Lynd, Robert Staughton, and Helen Merrell Lynd. *Middletown in Transition: A Study in Cultural Conflicts*. New York: Harcourt, Brace and World, 1937.

Machiavelli, Niccolo. *The Prince*. Edited by Quentin Skinner, and Russell Price. Cambridge Texts in the History of Political Thought. Cambridge & New York: Cambridge University Press, 1998. First published 1532.

MacLean, Ian, Alan Montefiore, and Peter Winch, eds. *The Political Responsibility of Intellectuals*. Cambridge: Cambridge University Press, 1990.

Malia, Martin E. *History's Locomotives: Revolutions and the Making of the Modern World*. New Haven, CT, & London: Yale University Press, 2006.

Manin, Bernard. *The Principles of Representative Government*. Cambridge & New York: Cambridge University Press, 1997.

Manor, James. *The Political Economy of Democratic Decentralization*. Washington, DC: World Bank, 1999.

Mansbridge, Jane J. *Beyond Adversary Democracy*. New York: Basic Books, 1980.

March, James G., and Johan P. Olsen. *Rediscovering Institutions. The Organizational Basis of Politics*. New York & London: The Free Press, 1989.

Marcou, Gérard, and Imre Verebélyi, eds. *New Trends in Local Government in Western and Eastern Europe*. Brussels (Belgium): International Institute of Administrative Sciences, 1993.

Marsden, Peter V., and Nan Lin, eds. *Social Structure and Network Analysis*. Beverly Hills, CA: Sage Publications, 1982.

Marvick, Dwaine, ed. *Political Decision-Makers*. New York: Free Press, 1961.

Mawhood, Philip D. *Local Government in the Third World*. London: Chichester-Wiley, 1983.

Mayo, Elton. *The Human Problems of an Industrial Civilization*. Cambridge, MA: Macmillan, 1933.

McFarland, Andrew S. *Power and Leadership in Pluralist Systems*. Stanford, CA: Stanford University Press, 1969.

Meisel, James. *The Myth of the Ruling Class*. Ann Arbor, MI: The University of Michigan Press, 1962.

Mensah Laryea-Adjei, George Quaye. *Decentralization plus pluralism for basic services provision: Water and sanitation in Ghana*. Delft (The Netherlands): Eburon Academic Publishers & Institute for Housing and Urban Development Studies (IHS), 2007.

Michels, Roberto. *Political Parties*. New York: Free Press, 1962.

Millar, James R., and Sharon L. Wolchik, eds. *The Social Legacy of Communism*. New York: Woodrow Wilson Center Press & Cambridge University Press, 1994.

Mills, Anne, J. Patrick Vaughan, Duane L. Smith, and Iraj Tabibzadeh, eds. *Health System Decentralization: Concepts, Issues, and Country Experiences*. Geneva (Switzerland): World Health Organization (WHO), 1990.

Mills, Charles Wright. *The Power Elite*. Paris: Maspero, 1969.

Montero, Alfred P., and David J. Samuels, eds. *Decentralization and Democracy in Latin America*. Notre Dame, IN: The University of Notre Dame Press, 2004.

Moore, Gwen, ed. *Studies of the Structure of National Elite Groups*. Greenwich, CT: JAI Press, 1985.

Moreno, Angel-Manuel, ed. *Local Government in the Member States of the European Union: A Comparative Legal Perspective*. Madrid (Spain): *Instituto Nacional de Administración Pública* / National Institute of Public Administration, Spain, 2012.

Moreno, Jacob Levy. *Who Shall Survive?: A New Approach to the Problem of Human Interrelations*. New York: Beacon Press, 1934.

Morriss, Peter. *Power: A Philosophical Analysis*. Manchester, UK: Manchester University Press, 1987.

Mosca, Gaetano. *The Ruling Class*. Translated by Hannah D. Kahn. New York & London: McGraw-Hill, 1939.

Mouffe, Chantal. *Deliberative Democracy or Agonistic Pluralism*. Vienna: Institute for Advanced Studies, 2000.

Mouritzen, Poul Erik, and James H. Svara. *Leadership at the Apex: Politicians and Administrators in Western Local Governments*. Pittsburgh, PA: University of Pittsburgh Press, 2002.

Moyser, George, and Margarett Wagstaffe, eds. *Research Methods for Elite Studies*. London: Unwin Hyman Ltd., 1987.

Nadel, Siegfried Frederick. *The Theory of Social Structure*. London: Cohen and West, 1957.

Nelson, Daniel N. *Democratic Centralism in Romania: A Study of Local Communist Politics*. Boulder, CO & New York: East European Monographs & Columbia University Press, 1980.

Newton, K. *Second City Politics*. Oxford: Clarendon Press, 1976.

O'Dwyer, Conor. *Runaway State-Building: Patronage Politics and Democratic Development*. Baltimore, MD: The Johns Hopkins University Press, 2006.

Oates, Wallace E. *Fiscal Federalism*. New York: Hartcourt, Brace, Javanovich, 1972.

Olsen, Marvin E., and Martin N. Marger, eds. *Power in Modern Societies*. Boulder, CO: Westview Press, 1992.

Page, Edward C. *Localism and Centrism in Europe. The Political and Legal Bases of Local Self-Government*. Oxford, UK, & New York: Oxford University Press, 1991.

Page, Edward C., and Michael J.F. Goldsmith, eds. *Central and Local Government Relations: A Comparative Analysis of Western European Unitary States*. Beverly Hills, CA, & London: Sage Publications, 1987.

Paige, Glenn. *The Scientific Study of Political Leadership*. London & New York: Free Press & Macmillan, 1977.

Panara, Carlo, and Michel Varney. *Local Government in Europe: The 'fourth level' in the EU multilayered system of governance*. London & New York: Routledge, 2013.

Pareto, Vilfredo. *The Mind and Society*. Translated by Arthur Livingstone. New York: Harcourt-Brace, 1936.

Pareto, Vilfredo. *Sociological Writings*. Edited by Samuel Edward Finer. Translated by Derek Mirfin. New York & London: F. A. Praeger Publishers & Pall Mall, 1966. First published 1916.

Parry, Geraint. *Political Elites*. Colchester, UK: ECPR & University of Essex, 2005. First published 1969 by George Allen & Unwin (London).

Paterson, Peter. *The Selectorate: The Case for Primary Elections in Britain*. London: Macgibbon and Kee, 1967.

Payne, James L., Olivier H. Woshinsky, Eric Veblen, William H. Coogan, and Gene E. Bigler. *The Motivation of Politicians*. Chicago, IL: Nelson-Hall Publishers, 1984.

Petrescu, Dragoş. *Explaining the Romanian Revolution of 1989: Culture, Structure, and Contingency*. Bucharest: Editura Enciclopedică, 2010.

Pierre, Jon, and Desmond S. King, eds. *Challenges to Local Government*. London: Sage, 1990.

Pitkin, Hanna Fenichel. *The Concept of Representation*. Berkley & Los Angeles, CA: University of California Press, 1967.

Polsby, Nelson W. *Community Power and Political Theory*. New Haven, CT: Yale University Press, 1963.

[Polsby, Nelson W. *Community Power and Political Theory*. 2nd ed. New Haven, CT, & London: Yale University Press, 1980.]

Popa, Eugen. *Organizarea şi funcţionarea administraţiei publice locale în România*. Arad: Servo-Sat, 1997.

Prakash, Gyan, and Kevin M. Kruse, eds. *The Spaces of the Modern City: Imaginaries, Politics, and Everyday Life*. Princeton, NJ: Princeton University Press, 2008.

Presthus, Robert Vance. *Elites in the Policy Process*. Cambridge and New York: Cambridge University Press, 1974.

Prewitt, Kenneth. *The Recruitment of Political Leaders: A Study of Citizen-Politicians*. Indianapolis, IN, & New York: Bobbs-Merrill, 1970.

Pridham, Geoffrey, and Paul G. Lewis, eds. *Stabilizing Fragile Democracies. Comparing New Party System in Southern and Eastern Europe*. London: Routledge, 1996.

Prud'homme, Rémy. *Regional Development Problems and Policies in Poland*. Paris: OECD, 1992.

Putnam, Robert D. *The Beliefs of Politicians. Ideology, Conflict, and Democracy in Britain and Italy*. New Haven, CT: Yale University Press, 1973.

Putnam, Robert D. *The Comparative Study of Political Elites*. Englewood Cliffs, NJ: Prentice-Hall, 1976.

Putnam, Robert D. *Making Democracy Work*. Princeton, NJ: Princeton University Press, 1993.

Quandt, William B. *The Comparative Study of Political Elites*. Beverly Hills, CA: Sage Professional Paper, 1970.

Regulski, Jerzy, Susanne Georg, Henrik Toft Jensen, and Barrie Needham, eds. *Decentralization and local government: a Danish-Polish comparative study in political systems*. Roskilde (Denmark) & Łódź (Poland) & New Brunswick, NJ: GEO-RUC / Roskilde University Press & Łódź University Press & Transaction Publishers, Inc., 1988.

Rhodes, Rod A.W., Paul 't Hart, and Mirko Noordegraaf, eds. *Observing Government Elites: Up Close and Personal*. Basingstoke, UK, & New York: Palgrave Macmillan, 2007.

Richardson, John G., ed. *Handbook of Theory and Research for the Sociology of Education*. New York: Greenwood Press, 1986.

Roth, Ralf, and Robert Beachy, eds. *Who Ran the Cities? City Elites and Urban Power Structures in Europe and North America, 1750-1940*. Aldershot, UK, & Burlington, VT: Ashgate Publishing, 2007.

Rothkopf, David. *Superclass. The Global Power Elite and the World They Are Making*. New York: Farrar, Strauss & Giroux, 2008.

Said, Edward W. *Representations of the Intellectual*. London: Vintage Books, 1994.

Saunders, Peter. *Urban Politics. A Sociological Interpretation*. London: Hutchinson & Co., 1983.

Schattschneider, Elmer Eric. *Party Government: American Government in Action*. New York: Holt, Rinehart & Winston, 1942.

Schiller, Theo, ed. *Local Direct Democracy in Europe*. Wiesbaden (Germany): VS Verlag für Sozialwissenschaften & Springer, 2011.

Schils, Edward. *The Intellectuals and the Powers and Other Essays*. Chicago, IL: University of Chicago Press, 1972.

Schumpeter, Joseph. *Capitalism, Socialism, and Democracy.* New York: Harper & Row, 1942.

Scott, John, ed. *Sociology of the Elites.* Aldershot, UK: Edward Elgar, 1990.

Seligman, Lester G. *Recruiting Political Elites.* New York: General Learning Press, 1971.

Šević, Željko, ed. *Local Politic Finance in Central and Eastern Europe.* Glos, UK, & Northampton, MA: Edward Elgar Publishing, 2008.

Shah, Anwar, ed. *Local Governance in Developing Countries.* Washington, DC: The World Bank, 2006.

Shah, Anwar, ed. *Local Governance in Industrial Countries.* Washington, DC: The World Bank, 2006.

Shipman, Alan, Bryan S. Turner, and June Edmunds. *The New Power Elite: Inequality, Politics and Greed.* London & New York: Anthem Press, 2018.

Shlapentokh, Vladimir, Christopher Vanderpool, and Boris Doktorov, eds. *The New Elite in Post-communist Eastern Europe.* College Station, TX: Texas A&M University Press, 1999.

Sills, David L., and Robert K. Merton, eds. *International Encyclopedia of the Social Sciences.* London & New York: Macmillan & Free Press, 1968.

Sloterdijk, Peter. *Dispretuirea maselor. Eseu asupra luptelor culturale în societatea modernă.* Translated by Aurel Codoban. Cluj-Napoca: Idea Design and Print, 2002.

Smith, Simon, ed. *Local Communities and Post-Communist Transformation: Czechoslovakia, the Czech Republic and Slovakia.* London & New York: Routledge Curzon, 2003.

Smoke, Paul J., Eduardo J. Gómez, and George E. Peterson, eds. *Decentralization in Asia and Latin America: Towards a Comparative Interdisciplinary Perspective.* Cheltenham Glos, UK, & Northampton, MA: Edward Elgar, 2006.

Soós, Gábor, Gábor Tóka, and Glen Wright, eds. *The State of Local Democracy in Central Europe.* Budapest: Local Government and Public Service Reform Initiative, 2002.

Soós, Gábor, and Violetta Zentai, eds. *Faces of Local Democracy: Comparative Papers from Central and Eastern Europe.* Budapest: Open Society Institute-LGI, 2005.

Staniszkis, Jadwiga. *The Dynamics of Breakthrough in Eastern Europe: The Polish Experience.* Berkeley, CA: University of California Press, 1991.

Steen, Anton. *Between Past and Future: Elites, Democracy and the State in Post-communist Countries. A Comparison of Estonia, Latvia and Lithuania.* Aldershot, UK: Ashgate, 1997.

Steen, Anton. *Political Elites and the New Russia: The Power Basis of Yeltsin's and Putin's Regimes.* London: Routledge-Curzon, 2003.

Ştefan, Laurenţiu. *Patterns of Political Elite Recruitment in Post-Communist Romania.* Bucharest: Ziua, 2004.

Stern, Alan Joel. *Local Political Elites and Economic Change: A Comparative Study of Four Italian Communities.* New Haven, CT: Yale University Press, 1971.

Stoica, Virgil. *Cine conduce Iasiul?*. Iaşi: Fundaţia Axis Publishing House, 2003.

Stoker, Gerry. *The Politics of Local Government*. London: Macmillan, 1991.

Suleiman, Ezra, and Henri Mendras, eds. *Le recrutement des élites en Europe*. Paris: Ed. La Découverte, 1997.

[Suleiman, Ezra, and Henri Mendras, eds. *Recrutarea elitelor în Europa*. Translated by Beatrice Stanciu. Timişoara: Amarcord, 2001.]

Svejnar, Jan, ed. *The Czech Republic and Economic Transition in Eastern Europe*. San Diego, CA: Academic Press, 1995.

Swianiewicz, Pawel, ed. *Public Perception of Local Governments*. Budapest: Local Government and Public Service Reform Initiative & Open Society Institute, 2001.

Szalai, Erzsébet. *Útelágazás. Hatalom és értelmiség az államszocializmus után* [*Cross-Roads. Power and the Intelligentsia after State Socialism*]. Budapest (Hungary): Pesti Szalon Könyvkiadó, 1994.

Szalai, Erzsébet. *The Hungarian Economic Elite After the Political Transition*. Budapest (Hungary) & Prague (the Czech Republic): Open Society Institute & Research Support Scheme, 1999.

Szücs, Stefan, and Lars Strömberg, eds. *Local Elites, Political Capital and Democratic Development. Governing Leaders in Seven European Countries*. Wiesbaden (Germany): VS Verlag für Sozialwissenschaften, 2006.

Topal, Aylin. *Boosting Competitiveness Through Decentralization. Subnational Comparison of Local Development in Mexico*. Farnham Surrey, UK, & Burlington, VT: Ashgate, 2012.

Turner, Mark, David Hulme, and Willy McCourt. *Governance, Management and Development: Making the State Work*. 2nd ed. London: Palgrave, 2015. First published 1997.

United Cities and Local Governments & World Bank. *Decentralization and Local Democracy in the World: First Global Report by the United Cities and Local Governments*. Washington, DC: United Cities and Local Governments & The World Bank, 2009.

Van Riper, Paul P. *History of the United States Civil Service*. New York: Harper & Row, 1958.

Venter, Annelise, and Gerrit van der Waldt, eds. *Municipal Management: Serving the People*. Cape Town (South Africa): JUTA & Company, 2007.

Verba, Sidney, and Norman H. Nie. *Participation in America: Political Democracy and Social Equality*. New York & Chicago, IL: Harper and Row & The University of Chicago Press, 1972.

Vetter, Angelika. *Local Politics a Resource for Democracy in Western Europe? Local Autonomy, Local Integrative Capacity, and Citizens' Attitudes towards Politics*. Translated by Antje Matthäus. Lanham, MD: Lexington Books, 2007.

Voicu, George. *Pluripartidismul. O teorie a democraţiei*. Bucharest: Editura All, 1998.

Waldt, Gerrit van der, ed. *Municipal Management: Serving the People*. Cape Town (South Africa): Juta & Company Ltd, 2007.

318

Warner, William Lloyd, and Paul Sanborn Lunt. *The Social Life of a Modern Community. Yankee City Series, Vol. I*. New Haven, CT: Yale University Press, 1941.

Warner, William Lloyd, and Paul Sanborn Lunt. *The Status System of a Modern Community. Yankee City Series, Vol. II*. New Haven, CT: Yale University Press, 1942.

Warner, William Lloyd, and Leo Strole. *The Social Systems of American Ethnic Groups. Yankee City Series, Vol. III*. New Haven, CT: Yale University Press, 1945.

Warner, William Lloyd, and Josiah Orne Low. *The Social System of a Modern Factory. Yankee City Series, Vol. IV*. New Haven, CT: Yale University Press, 1947.

Warner, William Lloyd. *The Living and the Dead: A Study in the Symbolic Life of Americans. Yankee City Series, Vol. V*. New Haven, CT: Yale University Press, 1959.

Warner, William Lloyd. *Yankee City*. New Haven, CT: Yale University Press, 1963.

Watson, Douglas J., and Wendy L. Hassett, eds. *Local Government Management. Current Issues and Best Practices*. ASPA Classics Volumes. Armonk, NY: M.E. Sharpe, 2003.

Weber, Max. *Economy and Society*. Edited by Guenther Roth, and Claus Wittich. Berkeley, CA: University of California Press, 1978. First published 1921.

Wesołowski, Włodzimierz. *Classes, Strata, and Power*. London: Routledge & Kegan Paul, 1977.

Whipple, Tim D., ed. *After the Velvet Revolution: Václav Havel and the New Leaders of Czechoslovakia Speak Out*. New York: Freedom House, 1991.

Wildawski, Aaron. *Speaking Truth to Power*. Boston MA: Little Brown, 1979.

Yerkes, Sarah, and Marwan Muasher. *Decentralization in Tunisia: Empowering Towns, Engaging People*. Washington, DC: Carnegie Endowment for International Peace, 2018.

Young, Ken, ed. *Essays on the Study of Urban Politics*. London: Croom Helm, 1975.

Book chapters

Akard, Patrick. "Social and Political Elites". In Vol. 4 of *Encyclopedia of Sociology*. 2nd ed., edited by Edgar F. Borgatta, and Rhonda J. V. Montgomery, 2622-2630. New York: Macmillan, 2000.

Bäck, Henry. "The institutional setting of local political leadership and community involvement". In *Urban Governance and Democracy: Leadership and Community Involvement*, edited by Michael Haus, Hubert Heinelt, and Murray Stewart, 65-101. London: Routledge, 2005.

Berend, Iván T. "The historical evolution of Eastern Europe as a region". In *Power, Purpose, and Collective Choice. Economic Strategy in Socialist States*, edited by Ellen Comisso, and Laura D'Andrea Tyson, 153-170. Ithaca, NY, & London: Cornell University Press, 1986.

Boissevain, Jeremy. "Networks". In *The Social Science Encyclopedia*, edited by Adam Kuper, and Jessica Kuper, 557-558. London: Routledge, 1989.

Brusis, Martin. "The Czech Republic". In *Changing Government Relations in Europe. From localism to intergovernmentalism*, edited by Michael J. Goldsmith, and Edwards C. Page, 30-46. Abingdon, Oxon, UK, & New York: Routledge & ECPR Studies in European Political Science, 2010.

Burton, Michael, Richard Gunther, and John Higley. "Introduction: Elite Transformations and Democratic Regimes". In *Elites and Democratic Consolidation in Latin America and Southern Europe*, edited by John Higley, and Richard Gunther, 1-37. Cambridge: Cambridge University Press, 1992.

Čapková, Soňa. "Slovakia: Local Government: Establishing Democracy at the Grassroots". In *The Oxford Handbook of Local and Regional Democracy in Europe*, edited by John Loughlin, Frank Hendriks, and Anders Lidström, 191-213. Oxford, UK: Oxford University Press, 2011.

Coman, Pena, Eugen Crai, Monica Rădulescu, and Gabriella Stănciulescu. "Local Government in Romania". In *Stabilization of Local Governments*, edited by Emilia Kandeva, 351-416. Budapest: OSI / LGI, 2001.

Czudnowski, Moshe M. "Political Recruitment". In Vol. II of *Micropolitical Theory of Handbook of Political Science*, edited by Fred I. Greenstein, and Nelson Polsby, 155-242. Reading, MA: Addison Wesley, 1975.

Czudnowski, Moshe M. "Aspiring and Established Politicians: The Structure of Value Systems and Role Profiles". In *Elite Recruitment in Democratic Polities: Comparative Studies across Nations*, edited by Heinz Eulau, and Moshe M. Czudnowski, 45-78. New York: John Wiley and Sons, 1976.

Dahl, Robert A. "A Critique of the Ruling Elite Model". In *C. Wright Mills and the Power Elite*, edited by William G. Domhoff, and Hoyt B. Ballard, 25-36. Boston, MA: Beacon Press, 1968.

Davey, Kenneth. "The Czech and Slovak Republics". In *Local Government in Eastern Europe: Establishing Democracy at the Grassroots*, edited by Andrew Coulson, 41-56. Cheltenham, UK: Edward Elgar, 1995.

Davey, Kenneth. "Local government in Hungary". In *Local Government in Eastern Europe: Establishing Democracy at the Grassroots*, edited by Andrew Coulson, 57-75. Cheltenham, UK: Edward Elgar, 1995.

Denters, Bas. "Local Governance". In *The SAGE Handbook of Governance*, edited by Mark Bevir, 313-329. London & Thousand Oaks, CA: Sage Publications, 2011.

Devarajan, Shantayanan, Stuti Khemani, and Shekhar Shah. "The politics of partial decentralization". In *Does Decentralization Enhance Service Delivery and Poverty Reduction?*, edited by Ahmad Ehtisham, and Giorgio Brosio, 102-121. Cheltenham Glos, UK, & Northampton, MA: Edward Elgar, 2009.

Dezső, Márta, Eszter Bodnár, and Bernadette Somody. "General Introduction, Chapter 3. State Territory (geographical data)". In *Constitutional Law in Hungary*, edited by Márta Dezső, 39-42. Alphen aan der Rijn (The Netherlands): Kluwer Law International, 2010.

Dezső, Márta, Eszter Bodnár, and Bernadette Somody. "General Introduction, Chapter 4. State Population (demographic data)", and "Chapter 3. Decentralized Authorities". In *Constitutional Law in Hungary*, edited by Márta Dezső, 43-44, and 219-220. Alphen aan der Rijn (The Netherlands): Kluwer Law International, 2010.

Dobre, Ana Maria. "Romania: From Historical Regions to Local Decentralization via the Unitary State". In *The Oxford Handbook of Local and Regional Democracy in Europe*, edited by John Loughlin, Frank Hendriks, and Anders Lidström, 271-297. Oxford, UK: Oxford University Press, 2011.

Dunn, Jonathan, and Deborah Wetzel. "Fiscal Decentralization in Former Socialist Economies: Progress and Prospects". In Vol. 92 of *Proceedings. Annual Conference on Taxation and Minutes of the Annual Meeting of the National Tax Association*, Atlanta, GA, Sunday 24th to Tuesday 26th October 1999, 242-250. Washington, DC: National Tax Association, 2000.

Etzioni, Eva. "Elites. Sociological Aspects". In Vol. 7 of *International Encyclopedia of the Social and Behavioral Sciences*, edited by Neil J. Smelser, and Paul B. Baltes, 4420-4424. Oxford & New York: Elsevier, 2001.

Eyerman, Ron. "Intellectuals and Progress: The Origins, Decline, and Revival of a Critical Group". In *Rethinking Progress: Movements, Forces and Ideas at the End of the 20th Century*, edited by Jeffrey C. Alexander, and Piotr Sztompka, 91-105. Winchester, MA: Unwin Hyman, 1990.

Foucault, Michel. "Governmentality". In *The Foucault Effect: Studies in Governmentality with Two Lectures by and an Interview with Michel Foucault*, edited by Graham Burchell, Colin Gordon, and Peter Miller, 87-104. Chicago, IL: University of Chicago Press, 1991.

Garcea, Joseph, and Edward C. LeSage, Jr. "Municipal Reform Agendas and Initiatives: Analytical Framework and Overview". In *Municipal Reform in Canada: Reconfiguration, Re-empowerment, and Rebalancing*, edited by Joseph Garcea, and Edward C. LeSage, Jr., 3-22. Don Mills (Ontario, Canada): Oxford University Press, 2005.

Guess, George M., and Vache Gabrielyan. "Comparative and International Administration". In *Handbook of Public Administration*. 3rd ed., edited by Jack Rabin, W. Bartley Hildreth, and Gerald J. Miller, 565-604. New York: Taylor and Francis, 2007.

Gurgur, Tugrul, and Anwar Shah. "Localization and Corruption: Panacea or Pandora's Box?". In *Managing Fiscal Decentralization*, edited by Ehtisham Ahmed, and Vito Tanzi, 46-67. London: Routledge, 2002.

Heinelt, Hubert, and Nikolaos-K. Hlepas. "Typologies of Local Government Systems". In *The European Mayor. Political Leaders in the Changing Context of Local Democracy*, edited by Henry Bäck, Hubert Heinelt, and Annick

Magnier, 21-42. Wiesbaden & Berlin (Germany): VS Verlag für Sozialwissenschaften, 2006.

Hesse, Jens Joachim, and Laurence J. Sharpe. "Local Government in International Perspective: Some Comparative Observations". In *Local Government and Urban Affairs in International Perspective: Analyses of Twenty Western Industrialized Countries*, edited by Jens Joachim Hesse, 603-621. Baden-Baden (Germany): Nomos Verlagsgesellschaft, 1991.

Higley, John. "Elites". In *Encyclopedia of Political Revolutions*, edited by Jack A. Goldstone, 153-155. Washington: Congressional Quarterly Press, 1998.

Illner, Michal. "Problems of Local Government in the Czech Republic (Past, Present and Future)". In *Events and Changes: The First Steps of Local Transition in East-Central Europe*, edited by Gaibor Péteri, 19-31. Local Democracy and Innovation Foundation Working Papers. Budapest (Hungary): Local Democracy and Innovation Foundation, 1991.

Illner, Michal. "The Czech Republic: Local Government in the Years After the Reform". In *The Oxford Handbook of Local and Regional Democracy in Europe*, edited by John Loughlin, Frank Hendriks, and Anders Lidström, 124-147. Oxford, UK: Oxford University Press, 2011.

Iluţ, Petru, and Irina Culic. „Analiza reţelelor sociale". In *Abordarea calitativă a socioumanului: concepte şi metode*, edited by Petru Iluţ, 113-133. Iaşi: Polirom, 1997.

Jowitt, Kenneth. "The Leninist Legacy". In *Revolutions of 1989*, edited by Vladimir Tismăneanu, 207-223. London & New York: Routledge, 1999.

Keller. Suzanne. "Elites". In Vol. 5 of *The International Encyclopedia of the Social Sciences*, edited by David L. Sills, 26-29. London: Macmillan, 1968.

Konrád, György, and Iván Szelényi. "Intellectuals and Domination in Post-Communist Societies". In *Social Theory for a Changing Society*, edited by Pierre Bourdieu, and James Samuel Coleman, 337-361. Boulder, CO: Westview, 1991.

Lacina, Karel, and Zdean Vajdova. "Local Government in the Czech Republic". In *Decentralization: Experiments and Reforms*, edited by Tamás M. Harváth, 255-295. Budapest (Hungary): Local Government and Public Service Reform Initiative, 2000.

Láštic, Erik. "Slovakia – restricted direct democracy in local politics". In *Local Direct Democracy in Europe*, edited by Theo Schiller, 237-244. Wiesbaden (Germany): VS Verlag für Sozialwissenschaften & Springer, 2011.

Lynch, Thomas Dexter, and Cynthia E. Lynch. "Democratic Morality: Back to the Future". In *Ethics and Integrity in Public Administration: Concepts and Cases*, edited by Raymond W. Cox III, 5-25. Armonk, NY: M.E. Sharpe, 2009.

Nemec, Juraj, Peter Bercik, and Peter Kuklis. "Local Government in Slovakia. Decentralization: Experiments and Reforms". In Volume 1 of *Decentralization: Experiments and Reforms. Local Governments in Central and Eastern Europe*, edited by Tamás M. Horváth, 297-342. Budapest: Local Government and Public Service Reform Initiative & Open Society Institute, 2000.

Nikolova, Pavlina. "Bulgaria: The Dawn of a New Era of Inclusive Subnational Democracy?". In *The Oxford Handbook of Local and Regional Democracy in Europe*, edited by John Loughlin, Frank Hendriks, and Anders Lidström, 257-270. Oxford, UK: Oxford University Press, 2011.

Norris, Pippa. "Legislative Recruitment". In *Comparing Democracies: Elections and Voting in Global Perspective*, edited by Lawrence LeDuc, Richard Niemi, and Pippa Norris, 184-216. Thousand Oaks, CA, & London: Sage Publications, 1996.

Norris, Pippa. "Introduction". In *Passages to Power: Legislative Recruitment in Advanced Democracies*, edited by Pippa Norris, 1-14. Cambridge: Cambridge University Press, 1997.

Orlansky, Dora. "Decentralization Politics and Policies". In *Critical Issues in Cross-national Public Administration: Privatization, Democratization, Decentralization*, edited by Stuart S. Nagel, 181-204. Westport, CT: Greenwood Publishing, 2000.

Perron, Catherine. "Local political elites' perceptions of the EU". In *The Road to the European Union: The Czech and Slovak Republics*, edited by Jacques Rupnik, and Jan Zielonka, 199-219. Manchester, UK: Manchester University Press, 2003.

Piasecki, Andrzej K. "Twenty years of Polish direct democracy at the local level". In *Local Direct Democracy in Europe*, edited by Theo Schiller, 126-137. Wiesbaden (Germany): VS Verlag für Sozialwissenschaften & Springer, 2011.

Pollitt, Christopher. "Decentralization: A central concept in contemporary public management". In *The Oxford Handbook of Public Management*, edited by Ewan Ferlie, Laurence E. Lynn, and Christopher Pollitt, 371-397. Oxford: Oxford University Press, 2005.

Przeworski, Adam. "Democracy and Economic Development". In *The Evolution of Political Knowledge: Democracy, Autonomy and Conflict in Comparative and International Politics*, edited by Edward D. Mansfield, and Richard Sisson, 300-324. Columbus, OH: Ohio State University Press, 2004.

Rodríguez-Teruel, Juan, and Jean-Pascal Daloz. "Surveying and Observing Political Elites". In *The Palgrave Handbook of Political Elites*, edited by Heinrich Best, and John Higley, 93-113. London: Palgrave Macmillan, 2018.

Rondinelli, Dennis A. "What is Decentralization". In *Decentralization Briefing Notes*, edited by Jennie Litvack, and Jessica Seddon, 2-5. Washington, DC: World Bank Institute Working Papers, 1999.

Rudebeck, Karin. "Administraţia locală în România". In *Democraţia în România*, edited by IDEA International, 154-155. Bucharest: Humanitas, 1997.

Schils, Edward. "The Political Class in the Age of Mass Society: Collectivistic Liberalism and Social Democracy". In *Does Who Governs Matter? Elite Circulation in Contemporary Societies*, edited by Moshe M. Czudnowski, 13-32. DeKalb, IL: Northern Illinois University Press, 1982.

Scott, John. "Modes of Power and the Re-conceptualization of Elites". In *Remembering Elites*, edited by Michael Savage, and Karel Williams, 27-43. Oxford: Blackwell, 2008.

Shah, Anwar, and Sana Shah. "The New Vision of Local Governance and the Evolving Roles of Local Governments". In *Local Governance in Developing Countries*, edited by Anwar Shah, 1-46. Washington, DC: The World Bank, 2006.

Shah, Anwar. "A Comparative Institutional Framework for Responsive, Responsible, and Accountable Local Governance". In *Local Governance in Industrial Countries*, edited by Anwar Shah, 1-39. Washington, DC: The World Bank, 2006.

Shore, Cris. "Introduction: Towards an Anthropology of Elites". In *Elite Cultures. Anthropological Perspectives*, edited by Cris Shore, and Stephen Nugent, 1-21. London & New York: Routledge, 2002.

Smith, Michael L. "The uneasy balance between participation and representation: local direct democracy in the Czech Republic". In *Local Direct Democracy in Europe*, edited by Theo Schiller, 33-53. Wiesbaden (Germany): VS Verlag für Sozialwissenschaften & Springer, 2011.

Soós, Gábor. "Hungary". In *Changing Government Relations in Europe. From localism to intergovernmentalism*, edited by Michael J. Goldsmith, and Edwards C. Page, 108-126. Abingdon, Oxon, UK, & New York: Routledge & ECPR Studies in European Political Science, 2010.

Soós, Gábor, and László Kákai. "Hungary: Remarkable Successes and Costly Failures: An Evaluation of Subnational Democracy". In *The Oxford Handbook of Local and Regional Democracy in Europe*, edited by John Loughlin, Frank Hendriks, and Anders Lidström, 163-190. Oxford, UK: Oxford University Press, 2011.

Stoica, Virgil. "Rețele politice locale". In *Instituții și mentalități: Carențe de mentalitate și înapoiere instituțională în România modernă*, edited by Adrian Paul Iliescu, 189-209. Bucharest: Ars Docendi, 2002.

Swianiewicz, Paweł. "Poland: Europeanization of Subnational Governments". In *The Oxford Handbook of Local and Regional Democracy in Europe*, edited by John Loughlin, Frank Hendriks, and Anders Lidström, 103-123. Oxford, UK: Oxford University Press, 2011.

Swianiewicz, Paweł, and Terry N. Clark. "The New Local Parties". In *Local Democracy and the Processes of Transformation in East-Central Europe*, edited by Harald Baldersheim, Michal Illner, Audun Offerdal, Lawrence Rose, and Pawel Swianiewicz, 141-159. Boulder, CO, & Oxford, UK: Westview Press, 1996.

Swianiewicz, Paweł, and Mikołaj Herbst. "Economies and Diseconomies of Scale in Polish Local Govenrments". In *Consolidation or Fragmentation? The Size of Local Governments in Central and Eastern Europe*, edited by Paweł Swianiewocz, 219-325. Budapest (Hungary): Open Society Institute, 2002.

Swianiewicz, Paweł, and Adam Mielczarek. "Parties and political culture in Central and Eastern European local governments". In *Faces of Local Democracy: Com-*

parative Papers from Central and Eastern Europe, edited by Gabor Soos, and Violetta Zentai, 13-78. Budapest: Open Society Institute, 2005.

Tanzi, Vito. "Fiscal Federalism and Decentralization: A Review of Some Efficiency and Macroeconomic Aspects". In *Annual Bank Conference on Development Economics 1995*, edited by Michael Bruno, and Boris Pleskovic, 295-315. Washington, DC: World Bank, 1996.

Taralezhkova, Iva. "Towards a law on local direct democracy in Bulgaria". In *Local Direct Democracy in Europe*, edited by Theo Schiller, 184-192. Wiesbaden (Germany): VS Verlag für Sozialwissenschaften & Springer, 2011.

Tomaney, John, "Regional Governance". In *The Wiley Blackwell Encyclopedia of Urban and Regional Studies*, edited by Anthony M. Orum, 1-7. New York: John Wiley & Sons, 2019.

Vajdová, Zdenka. "Local community transformation: The Czech Republic, 1990-2000". In *Local Communities and Post-Communist Transformation: Czechoslovakia, the Czech Republic and Slovakia*, edited by Simon Smith, 143-160. London & New York: Routledge Curzon, 2003.

Vidláková, Olga, and Pavel Zářecký. "Czechoslovakia: The Development of Public Administration". In *Territory and Administration in Europe*, edited by Robert John Bennett, 168-179. London & New York: Frances Pinter Publishers, 1989.

Vincze, Attila, and Márta Dezső. "Part V. Specific Problems, Chapter 2. Taxing and Spending Power, §2. Local Level". In *Constitutional Law in Hungary*, edited by Márta Dezső, 328-329. Alphen aan der Rijn (The Netherlands): Kluwer Law International, 2010.

Wasilewski, Jacek. "Three Elites of the Central East European Democratization". In *Transformative Paths in Central and Eastern Europe*, edited by Radoslaw Markowski, and Edmund Wnuk-Lipiński, 133-142. Warsaw (Poland): Fiedrich Ebert Stiftung – PAN ISP (Institute of Political Studies), 2001.

Wolman, Hal, and Sharon McCormick. "The effect of decentralization on local governments". In *Local Government and Market Decentralization: Experiences in Industrialized, Developing, and Former Eastern Bloc Countries*, edited by Robert J. Bennett, 249-266. Tokyo (Japan): United Nations University Press, 1994.

Articles

Adam, Frane and Matevž Tomšič. "Transition Elites: Catalysts of Social Innovation or Rent-Seekers (Reproduction/Circulation Thesis Reconsidered)". *Druzboslovne Razprave* XVI, nos. 32-33 (July-October 2000): 138-160.

Adam, Frane and Matevž Tomšič. "Elite (Re)configuration and Politico-Economic Performance in Post-Socialist Countries". *Europe-Asia Studies* 54, no. 3 (May 2002): 435-454.

Alexandru, Dana Georgeta, and Beata Guziejewska. "Administrative Capacity as a Contraint to Fiscal Decentralization. The Case of Romania and Poland".

Comparative Economic Research. Central and Eastern Europe 23, no. 1 (February 2020): 127-143.

Alfano, Maria Rosaria, Anna Laura Baraldi, and Claudia Cantabene. "The Effect of Fiscal Decentralization on Corruption: A Non-linear Hypothesis". *German Economic Review* 20, no. 1 (Febraury 2019): 105-128.

Amin, Ash. "An Institutionalist Perspective on Regional Economic Development". *International Journal of Urban and Regional Research* 23, no. 2 (June 1999): 365-378.

Arikan, Guzin Gulsun. "Fiscal Decentralization: A Remedy for Corruption?". *International Tax and Public Finance* 11, no. 2 (March 2004): 175-195.

Aristovnik, Aleksander. "Fiscal Decentralization in Eastern Europe: Trends and Selected Issues". *Transylvanian Review of Administrative Sciences* 37, no. E (October 2012): 5-22.

Armstrong, Hilary. "The Key Themes of Democratic Renewal". *Local Government Studies* 25, no. 4 (Winter 1999): 19-25.

Ashworth, Rachel, Colin Copus, and Andrew Coulson. "Local Democratic Renewal: An Introduction". *Local Government Studies* 30, no. 4 (Winter 2004): 459-466.

Ball, Terence. "Models of Power: Past and Present". *Journal of the History of the Behavioural Sciences* 11, no. 3 (July 1975): 211-222.

Bardhan, Pranab. "Decentralization of Governance and Development". *The Journal of Economic Perspectives* 16, no. 4 (Fall 2002): 185-205.

Bardhan, Pranab K., and Dilip Mookherjee. "Capture and Governance at the Local and National Levels". *American Economic Review* 90, no. 2 (May 2000): 135-139.

Bibó, István. "The elite and social sensitivity". *Review of Sociology of the Hungarian Sociological Association* 10, no. 2 (29th of November 2004): 103-114. First published 1942.

Bunce, Valerie. "Regional Differences in Democratization: The East Versus the South". *Post-Soviet Affairs* 14, no. 3 (July-September 1998): 187-211.

Burton, Michael G., and John Higley. "The Elite Variable in Democratic Transitions and Breakdowns". *American Sociological Review* 54, no. 1 (February 1989): 17-32.

Burton, Michael, and John Higley. "Types of Political Elites in Postcommunist Eastern Europe". *International Politics* 34, no. 2 (June 1997): 153-168.

Cai, Hongbin, and Daniel Treisman. "Did Government Decentralization Cause China's Economic Miracle?". *World Politics* 58, no. 4 (July 2006): 505-535.

Canavire-Bacarreza, Gustavo, Jorge Martinez-Vazquez, and Bauyrzhan Yedgenov. "Identifying and disentangling the impact of fiscal decentralization on economic growth". *World Development* 127 (March 2020), 104742.

Changwony, Frederick Kibon, and Audrey S. Paterson. "Accounting practice, fiscal decentralization and corruption". *The British Accounting Review* 51, no. 5 (Special Issue: "Accounting Control, Governance and Anti-Corruption Initiatives in Public Sector Organisations") (September 2019), 100834.

Chiappinelli, Olga. "Decentralization and Public Procurement Performance: New Evidence from Italy". *Economic Inquiry* 58, no. 2(April 2020): 856-880.

Christl, Michael, Monika Köppl-Turyna, and Dénes Kucsera. "Determinants of Public-Sector Efficiency: Decentralization and Fiscal Rules". *Kyklos: International Review of Social Sciences* 73, no. 2 (May 2020): 253-290.

Cochrane, A. "Illusions of Power: Interviewing Local Elites". *Environment and Planning A* 30, no. 12 (July 1998): 2121-2132.

Coman, Emanuel Emil. "Local elites, electoral reform and the distribution of central government funds: Evidence from Romania". *Electoral Studies* 53, no. 3 (June 2018): 1-10.

Coman, Emanuel Emil. "Local leaders and the distribution of central government funds: Evidence from 18 European democracies". *European Journal of Political Research* 59, no. 1 (February 2020): 206-225.

Cornwell, Christopher, and J. Edward Kellough. "Women and Minorities in Federal Government Agencies: Examining New Evidence from Panel Data". *Public Administration Review* 54, no. 3 (May – June 1994): 265-270.

Cottingham, Clement. "Political Consolidation and Centre-Local Relations in Senegal". *Canadian Journal of African Studies / Revue Canadienne des Études Africaines* 4, no. 1 (Special Issue: "Local-Central Politics") (Winter 1970): 101-120.

Dahl, Robert A. "A Critique of the Ruling Elite Model". *American Political Science Review* 52, no. 2 (June 1958): 463-469.

Doucouliagos, Hristos, and Mehmet Ali Ulubaşoğlu. "Democracy and Economic Growth: A Meta-analysis". *American Journal of Political Science* 52, No. 1 (January 2008): 61-83.

Dye, Thomas R., and James Renick. "Political Power and City Jobs: Determinants of Minority Employment". *Social Science Quarterly* 62, no. 3 (September 1981): 475-486.

Edinger, Lewis J., and Donald D. Searing. "Social Background in elite analysis: a methodological inquiry". *American Political Science Review* 61, no. 2 (June 1967): 428-445.

Eisinger, Peter K. "Black Employment in Municipal Jobs: The Impact of Black Political Power". *American Political Science Review* 76, no. 2 (June 1982): 380-392.

Elander, Ingemar. "Analysing Central-Local Government Relations in Different Systems: A Conceptual Framework and Some Empirical Illustrations". *Scandinavian Political Studies* 14, no. 1 (March 1991): 31-58.

Escobar-Lemmon, Maria. "Political Support for Decentralization: An Analysis of the Colombian and Venezuelan Legislatures". *American Journal of Political Science* 47, no. 4 (October 2003): 683-697.

Eyal, Gill. "Anti-politics and the Spirit of Capitalism: Dissidents, Monetarists, and the Czech Transition to Capitalism". *Theory and Society* 29, no. 1 (February 2000): 49-92.

Fábián, Katalin, and Jeffrey D. Straussman, "Post-communist transition of local government in Hungary: Managing emergency social aid". *Public Administration and Development* 14, no. 3 (January 1994): 271-80.

Falletti, Tulia. G. "A Sequential Theory of Decentralization: Latin American Cases in Comparative Perspective". *The American Political Science Review* 99, no. 3 (August 2005): 327-346.

Fish, Michael Steven. "The Determinants of Economic Reform in the Post-Communist World". *East European Politics and Societies* 12, no. 1 (Winter 1998): 31-78.

Fisman, Raymond, and Roberta Gatti. "Decentralization and Corruption: Evidence Across Countries". *Journal of Public Economics* 83, no. 3 (March 2002): 325-345.

Foweraker, Joe, and Todd Landman. "Constitutional Design and Democratic Performance". *Democratization* 9, no. 2 (Summer 2002): 43-66.

Gallas, Nesta M. "Representativeness: A New Merit Principle". *Public Personnel Management* 14, no. 1 (Spring 1985): 25-31.

Gargan, John J. "Consideration of Local Government Capacity". *Public Administration Review* 41, no. 6 (November/December 1981): 649-658.

Garman, Christopher, Stephan Haggard, and Eliza Willis. "Fiscal Decentralization: A Political Theory with Latin American Cases". *World Politics* 53, no. 2 (January 2001): 205-236.

Garnham. David. "Foreign Service Elitism and U.S. Foreign Affairs". *Public Administration Review* 35, no. 1 (January – February 1975): 44-51.

Gerring, John, Philip Bond, William T. Barndt and Carola Moreno. "Democracy and Economic Growth: A Historical Perspective". *World Politics* 57, no. 3 (April 2005): 323-364.

Gift, Thomas, and Carlos X. Lastra-Anadón. "How voters assess elite-educated politicians: A survey experiment". *Electoral Studies* 56, no. 6 (December 2018): 136-149.

Goldsmith, Michael. "Local Government". *Urban Studies* 29, nos. 3-4 (May 1992): 393-410.

Grødeland, Åse Berit. "'Red Mobs', 'Yuppies', 'Lamb Heads' and Others: Contacts, Informal Networks and Politics in the Czech Republic, Slovenia, Bulgaria and Romania". *Europe-Asia Studies* 59, no. 2 (March 2007): 217-252.

Guziejewska, Beata, and Katarzyna Walerysiak-Grzechowska. "A Local Government Revenues System under Macroeconomic Pressure – The Case of Poland". *Prague Economic Papers* 29, no. 1 (January 2020): 29-52.

Hanson, Stephen E. "The Leninist Legacy and Institutional Change". *Comparative Political Studies* 28, no. 2 (July 1995): 306-314.

Harding, Alan. "Urban Regimes and Growth Machines: Towards a Cross-national Research Agenda". *Urban Affairs Quarterly* 29, no. 3 (March 1994): 356-382.

Havlík, Vratislav. "Europeanization as the Reterritorialization of the State: Towards Conceptual Clarification". *Journal of Common Market Studies* 58, no. 5 (September 2020): forthcoming.

Heinz, John P., Edward O. Laumann, Robert H. Salisbury, and Robert L. Nelson. "Inner Circles or Hollow Cores? Elite Networks in National Policy Systems". *Journal of Politics* 52, no. 2 (May1990): 356-390.

Hellman, Joel S. "Winners Take All: The Politics of Partial Reform in Postcommunist Transitions". *World Politics* 50, no. 2 (January 1998): 203-234.

Helmsing, A. H. J. (Bert). "Decentralisation, Enablement, and Local Governance in Low-Income Countries". *Environment and Planning C: Politics and Space* 20, no. 3 (June 2002): 317-340.

Heo, Uk, and Alexander C. Tan. "Democracy and Economic Growth: A Causal Analysis". *Comparative Politics* 33, no. 4 (July 2001): 463-473.

Higley, John, Ursula Hoffmann-Lange, Charles Kadushin, and Gwen Moore. "Elite Integration in Stable Democracies: A Reconsideration". *European Sociological Review* 7, no. 1 (May 1991): 35-53.

Higley, John, and Jan Pakulski. "Revolution and Elite Transformation in Eastern Europe". *Australian Journal of Political Science* 27, no. 1 (March 1992): 104-119.

Higley, John, and Jan Pakulski. "Elites Transformation in Central and Eastern Europe". *Australian Journal of Political Science* 30, no. 3 (October 1995): 415-435.

Higley, John, Judith Kullberg, and Jan Pakulski. "The Persistence of Post-Communist Elites". *Journal of Democracy* 7, no. 2 (April 1996): 133-147.

Higley, John, and Jan Pakulski. "Elite and Leadership Change in Liberal Democracies". *Comparative Sociology* 6, nos. 1-2, (June 2007): 6-26.

Holmes, Stephen T. "The End of Decommunization". *East European Constitutional Review* 3, nos. 3-4 (Summer-Fall 1994): 33-36.

Hook, Sidney. "The Fetishism of Power". *The Nation* 148, no. 20 (May 13, 1939): 562-563.

Hindera, John J. "Representative Bureaucracy: Further Evidence of Active Representation in the EEOC District Offices". *Journal of Public Administration Research and Theory: J-PART* 3, no. 4 (October 1993): 415-429.

Hindera, John J. "Representative Bureaucracy: Imprimis Evidence of Active Representation in the EEOC District Offices". *Social Science Quarterly* 74, no. 1 (March 1993): 95-108.

Hutchcroft, Paul. D. "Centralization and Decentralization in Administration and Politics: Assessing Territorial Dimensions of Authority and Power". *Governance* 14, no. 1 (January 2001): 23-53.

Huther, Jeff, and Anwar Shah. "Applying a simple measure of good governance to the debate on fiscal decentralization". *Policy Research Working Papers*, no. WPS1894 (March 1998). Washington, DC: World Bank, 1998.

Illner, Michal. "The Territorial Dimension of Public Administration Reforms in East-Central Europe". *Polish Sociological Review* I, no. 117, 1997: 23-45.

Ishiyama, John T. "The Communist Successor Parties and Party Organizational Development in Post-Communist Politics". *Political Research Quarterly* 52, no. 1 (March 1999): 87-112.

Jackson, John E., and David C. King. "Public Goods, Private Interests, and Representation". *American Political Science Review* 83, no. 4 (December 1989): 1143-1164.

Jacob, Herbert. "Initial recruitment of elected officials in the United States – A model". *Journal of Politics* 24, no. 4 (November 1962): 703-716.

Karabel, Jerome. "Towards a Theory of Intellectuals and Politics". *Theory and Society* 25, no. 2 (April 1996): 205-233.

Kellough, J. Edward. "Federal Agencies and Affirmative Action for Blacks and Women". *Social Science Quarterly* 71, no. 1 (March 1990): 83-92.

Kellough, J. Edward. "Integration in the Public Workplace: Determinants of Minority and Female Employment in Federal Agencies". *Public Administration Review* 50, no. 5 (September / October 1990): 557-566.

Kellough, J. Edward, and Euel Elliot. "Demographic and Organizational Influences on Racial/Ethnic and Gender Integration in Federal Agencies". *Social Science Quarterly* 73, no. 1 (March 1992): 1-11.

Kim, Pan Suk. "Racial Integration in the American Federal Government: With Special Reference to Asian-Americans". *Review of Public Personnel Administration* 13, no. 1 (January 1993): 52-66.

Kim, Pan Suk, and Berhanu Mengistu. "Women and Minorities in the Workforce of Law-Enforcement Agencies". *American Review of Public Administration* 24, no. 2 (June 1994): 161-179.

Knoke, David. "Networks of Elite Structure and Decision Making". *Sociological Methods and Research* 22, no. 1 (August 1993): 23-45.

Kornai, János. "Resource-Constrained versus Demand-Constrained Systems". *Econometrica* 47, no. 4 (July 1979): 801-819.

Kornai, János. "The Soft Budget Constraint". *Kyklos* 39, no. 1 (February 1986): 3-30.

Lane, David. "Transition under Eltsin: The *Nomenklatura* and Political Elite Circulation". *Political Studies* 45, no. 5 (December 1997): 855-874.

Ledyaev, Valeri. "Urban Regimes in Small Russian Towns". *City and Community* 18, no. 3 (September 2019): 812-833.

Lele, Gabriel. "Asymmetric Decentralization and the Problem of Governance: The Case of Indonesia". *Asian Politics & Policy* 11, no. 4 (October 2019): 544-565.

León, Sandra. "Muddling up Political Systems? When Regionalization Blurs Democracy: Decentralization and Attribution of Responsibility". *Journal of Common Market Studies* 56, no. 3 (April 2018): 706-716.

Lewis, Gregory B., and David Nice. "Race, Sex, and Occupational Segregation in State and Local Governments". *American Review of Public Administration* 24, no. 4 (November 1994): 393-410.

Liddle, Joyce, John Gibney, Markku Sotarauta, and Andrew Beer. "Exploring Varieties of Leadership in Urban and Regional Development". *Regions Magazine* 302, no. 1 (January 2016): 12-13.

Lipset, Seymour Martin. "Some Social Requisites of Democracy: Economic Development and Political Legitimacy". *American Political Science Review* 53, no. 1 (March 1959): 69-105.

Long, Norton E. "The Local Community as an Ecology of Games". The *American Journal of Sociology* 64, no. 3 (November 1958): 251-261.

Majchierkiewicz, Tatiana. "Polish Regional Elite Career Paths and the Impact of a Multilevel System". *Politics in Central Europe* 16, no. 1 (April 2020): 283-307.

Mansbridge, Jane. "Rethinking Representation". *American Political Science Review* 97, no. 4 (November 2003): 515-528.

Mansbridge, Jane. "A 'Selection Model' of Political Representation". *Journal of Political Philosophy* 17, no. 4 (December 2009): 369-398.

Mansbridge, Jane. "Clarifying the Concept of Representation". *American Political Science Review* 105, no. 3 (August 2011): 621-630.

Martin, Bill, and Iván Szelényi. "Three Waves of New Class Theories". *Theory and Society* 17, no. 5 (September 1988): 645-667.

Martinsen, Kåre Dahl. "From Impotence to Omnipotence: The State and Economic Transition, 1989-1994". *Bohemia* 36, 1995: 330-361.

Meier, Kenneth John, and Lloyd G. Nigro. "Representative Bureaucracy and Policy Preferences: A Study in the Attitudes of Federal Executives". *Public Administration Review* 36, no. 4 (July – August 1976): 458-469.

Meier, Kenneth John, and Joseph Stewart, Jr. "The Impact of Representative Bureaucracies: Educational Systems and Public Policies". *American Review of Public Administration* 22, no. 3 (September 1992): 157-171.

Meier, Kenneth John. "Latinos and Representative Bureaucracy: Testing the Thompson and Henderson Hypotheses". *Journal of Public Administration Research and Theory: J-PART* 3, no. 4 (October 1993): 393-414.

Merelman, Richard M. "On the Neo-Elitist Critique of Community Power". *American Political Science Review* 62, no. 2 (June 1968): 451-460.

Merkaj, Elvina, Riccardo Lucchetti, and Fabio Fiorillo. "The role of local leaders in regional development funding: Evidence from an elite survey". *Journal of Regional Science* (Early View) (2020): 1-26.

Miller, Delbert C. "Industry and Community Power Structure. A Comparative Study of an American and an English City". *American Sociological Review* 23, no. 1 (February 1958): 9-15.

Miller, Delbert C. "Design Strategies for Comparative Inter Studies of Community Power". *Social Forces* 51, no. 3 (March 1973): 261-274.

Mladenka, Kenneth R. "Barriers to Hispanic Employment Success in 1,200 Cities". *Social Science Quarterly* 70, no. 2 (June 1989): 391-407.

Mladenka, Kenneth R. "Blacks and Hispanics in Urban Politics". *American Political Science Review* 83, no. 1 (March 1989): 165-191.

Mladenka, Kenneth R. "Public Employee Unions, Reformism, and Black Employment in 1,200 American Cities". *Urban Affairs Quarterly* 26, no. 4 (June 1991): 532-548.

331

Nelson, Daniel N. "Background Characteristics of Local Communist Elites: Change vs. Continuity in the Romanian Case". *Polity* 10, no. 3 (Spring 1978): 398-415.

Oates, Wallace E. "An Essay on Fiscal Federalism". *Journal of Economic Literature* 37, no. 3 (September 1999): 1120-1149.

Padgett, John F., and Christopher K. Ansell. "Robust Action and the Rise of the Medici, 1400-1434". *American Journal of Sociology* 98, no. 6 (May 1993): 1259-1319.

Payne, James L., and Oliver H. Woshinsky. "Incentives for Political Participation". *World Politics* 24, no. 4 (July 1972): 518-546.

Peiró-Palomino, Jesús, Andrés J. Picazo-Tadeo, and Vicente Rios. "Well-being in European regions: Does government quality matter?". *Papers in Regional Science* 99, no. 3 (June 2020): 555-582.

Peterson, Paul E. "Forms of Representation: Participation of the Poor in the Community Action Program". *The American Political Science Review* 64, no. 2 (June 1970): 491-507.

Polsby, Nelson W. "How to Study Community Power: The Pluralist Alternative". *Journal of Politics* 22, no. 3 (August 1960): 474-484.

Pop, Ana Monica, "A Brief Analysis of the Public Institutions Budget: Theoretical and Practical Approaches". *Studia Universitatis Babeş Bolyai – Negotia* 63, no. 4 (December 2018): 69-93.

Prewitt, Kenneth. "Political Socialization and Leadership Selection". *The Annals of the American Academy of Political and Social Science* 361 (September 1965): 96-111.

Prud'homme, Rémy. "The Dangers of Decentralization". *The World Bank Research Observer* 10, no. 2 (August 1995): 201-220.

Putnam, Robert D. "Elite Transformation in Advanced Industrial Societies: An Empirical Assessment of the Theory of Technocracy". *Comparative Political Studies* 10, no. 3 (October 1977): 383-412.

Riccucci, Norma M. "Female and Minority Employment in City Government. The Role of Unions". *Policy Studies Journal* 15, no. 1 (September 1986): 3-15.

Rice, Erick M. "Public Administration in Post-Socialist Eastern Europe". *Public Administration Review* 52, no. 2 (March-April 1992): 116-124.

Rodden, Jonathan. "Comparative Federalism and Decentralization: On Meaning and Measurement". *Comparative Politics* 36, no. 4 (July 2004): 481-500.

Rondinelli, Dennis A., and John R. NELLIS. "Assessing Decentralization Policies in Decelopping Countries: The Case for Cautious Optimism". *Development Policy Review* 4, no. 1 (March 1986): 3-23.

Rondinelli, Dennis A. "Decentralization, Territorial Power and the State: A Critical Response". *Development and Change* 21, no. 3 (July 1990): 491-500.

Rosenbloom, David H., and Jeannette G. Featherstonhaugh. "Passive and Active Representation in the Federal Service: A Comparison of Blacks and Whites". *Social Science Quarterly* 57, no. 4 (March 1977): 873-882.

Rosenbloom, David H., and Douglas Kinnard. "Bureaucratic Representation and Bureaucrats' Behavior: An Exploratory Analysis". *Midwest Review of Public Administration* 11, no. 1 (March 1977): 35-60.

Saltzstein, Grace Hall. "Female Mayors and Women in Municipal Jobs". *American Journal of Political Science* 30, no. 1 (February 1986): 140-164.

Seleny, Anna. "Old Political Rationalities and New Democracies: Compromise and Confrontation in Hungary and Poland". *World Politics* 51, no. 4 (July 1999): 484-519.

Seligman, Lester G. "The Study of Political Leadership". *American Political Science Review* 44, no. 4 (December 1950): 904-915.

Seligman, Lester G. "Elite Recruitment and Political Development". *Journal of Politics* 26, no. 3 (August 1964): 612-626.

Serritzlew, Søren. "Shaping local councillor preferences: party politics, committee structure and social background". *Scandinavian Political Studies* 26, no. 4 (December 2003): 327-348.

Shabad, Goldie, and Kazimierz M. Slomczynski. "The Emergence of Career Politicians in Post-Communist Democracies: Poland and the Czech Republic". *Legislative Studies Quarterly* 27, no. 3 (August 2002): 333-359.

Šiklová, Jiřina. "The 'Gray Zone' and the Future of Dissent in Czechoslovakia". *Social Research* 57, no. 2 (Summer 1990): 347-363.

Stein, Lana. "A Representative Protection Service: Concept, Demand, Reality". *Review of Public Personnel Administration* 5, no. 3 (Summer 1985): 78-89.

Stein, Lana. "Representative Local Government: Minorities in the Municipal Work Force". *Journal of Politics* 48, no. 3 (August 1986): 694-713.

Stein, Lana. "Privatization, Work-Force Cutbacks, and African-American Municipal Employment". *American Review of Public Administration* 24, no. 2 (June 1994): 181-191.

Stoilova, Desislava. "Financial Decentralization in Bulgaria: Which are the most important achievements of the transition period and how to move forward?". *Analele Științifice ale Universității „Alexandru Ioan Cuza" din Iași, Seria Științe Economice* LVI, 2009: 166-177.

Szelényi, Iván, and Szonja Szelényi. "Circulation or Reproduction of Elites during the Postcommunist Transformation of Eastern Europe: Introduction". *Theory and Society* 24, no. 5 (Special Issue on Circulation vs. Reproduction of Elites during the Postcommunist Transformation of Eastern Europe) (October 1995): 615-638.

Tatham, Michaël, and Heather A. D. Mbaye. "Regionalization and the Transformation of Policies, Politics, and Polities in Europe". *Journal of Common Market Studies* 56, no. 3 (April 2018): 656-671.

Thompson, Frank J. "Civil Servants and the Deprived: Socio-Political and Occupational Explanations of Attitudes Toward Minority Hiring". *American Journal of Political Science* 22, no. 2 (May 1978): 325-347.

Toole, James. "The Historical Foundations of Party Politics in Post-Communist East-Central Europe". *Europe-Asia Studies* 59, no. 4 (June 2007): 541-566.

Treisman, Daniel. "What Have We Learned About the Causes of Corruption from Ten Years of Cross-National Empirical Research?". *Annual Review of Political Science* 10 (June 2007): 211-244.

Van Waarden, Frans. "Dimensions and types of policy networks". *European Journal of Political Research* 21, nos. 1-2 (February1992): 29-52.

Vo, Duc Hong. "Fiscal Decentralization in Vietnam: Lessons from Selected Asian Nations". *Journal of the Asia Pacific Economy* 14, no. 4 (September 2009): 399-419.

Weissberg, Robert. "Collective vs. Dyadic Representation in Congress". *American Political Science Review* 72, no. 2 (June 1978): 535-547.

Welch, Susan, Albert K. Karnig, and Richard A. Eribes. "Changes in Hispanic Local Public Employment in the Southwest". *Western Political Quarterly* 36, no. 4 (December 1983): 660-673.

Werning Rivera, Sharon. "Elites in Post-Communist Russia: A Changing of the Guard?". *Europe-Asia Studies* 52, no. 3 (May 2000): 413-432.

Wesołowski, Wlodzimierz. "The Role of Political Elites in Transition from Communism to Democracy. The Case of Poland". *Sisyphus Social Studies* VIII, no. 2, 1992: 77-100.

Wise, Lois Recascino. "Social Equity in Civil Service Systems". *Public Administration Review* 50, no. 5 (September / Octoer 1990): 567-575.

Wolfinger, Raymond E. "Nondecisions and the Study of Local Politics". *American Political Science Review* 65, no. 4 (December 1971): 1063-1080.

Woller, Gary M., and Kerk Phillips. "Fiscal Decentralization and LDC Economic Growth: An Empirical Investigation". *Journal of Development Studies* 34, no. 4 (April 1998): 139-148.

Wollmann, Hellmut. "Urban leadership in German local politics: the rise, role and performance of the directly elected (chief executive) mayor". *International Journal of Urban and Regional Research* 28, no. 1 (March 2004): 150-165.

Wollmann, Hellmut. "Local Government Reforms in Great Britain, Sweden, Germany and France: Between multi-function and single-purpose organizations". *Local Government Studies* 30, no. 4 (Winter 2004): 639-665.

Woods, Michael J. "Rethinking Elites: Networks, Space, and Local Politics". in *Environment and Planning A* 30, no. 12 (April 1998): 2101-2119.

Wyatt, Madeleine, and Jo Silvester. "Do voters get it right? A test of the ascription-actuality trait theory of leadership with political elites". *The Leadership Quarterly* 29, no. 5 (October 2018): 609-621.

Zartman, Ira William. "The Study of Elite Circulation. Who's on First and What's He Doing There?". *Comparative Politics* 6, no. 3 (April 1974): 465-488.

Zárecky, Pavel. "Vývoj reformy veřejné správy v České republice po roce 1989" ["The Development of Public Administration Reform in the Czech Republic after 1989"]. *Státní správa a samospráva* 96, no. 12 (1996): 20-24.

Theses and conference papers, Working papers

Bozóki, András. "From New Class Theory to Elite Research. Research on Political Elites in East Central Europe". Paper presented for the ECPR Conference on Political Science Research in East-Central Europe, at the Robert Schuman Center for Advanced Study and European University Institute, Florence, Italy, November 9, 2001.

Bozóki, András. "The Making of Reform: Elite Dilemmas and Political Options". Paper presented for the 4th ed. of ECPR Conference on Political Science Research in East-Central Europe, at the Robert Schuman Center for Advanced Study and European University Institute, Pisa, Italy, September 6-9, 2007.

Buštíková, Lenka. "Známosti osobností lokální politiky" ["Acquaintances of Local Political Leaders"]. *Sociologický ústav AV ČR* Working Papers s. 3, no. 99. Prague: *Sociologický ústav er*, 1999.

De Mello, Luiz. "Can Fiscal Decentralization Strengthen Social Capital?". IMF Working Paper No. 129. Washington, DC: IMF, 2000.

Helmsing, A. H. J. (Bert). "Decentralisation, Enablement, and Local Governance in Low-Income Countries." Inaugural Professorial Address at the Faculty of Geographical Sciences, University of Utrecht (The Netherlands), April 27, 2000.

Hindera, John J. "Representative Bureaucracy: Are Active and Passive Representation Linked?". PhD diss., University of Houston, 1990.

Kim, Aehyung. "Decentralization and the Provision of Public Services: Framework and Implementation". World Bank Policy Research Working Papers, no. WPS 4503 (January 2008). Washington, DC: The World Bank, 2008.

Kolosi, Tomaś, and Ákos Róna-Tás. "The First Shall Be Last? The Social Consequences of the Transition from Socialism". Paper presented at the Meeting of the ISA Research Committee on Social Stratification, Trento, Italy, Spring 1992. Unpublished manuscript at the CEU Library, 1992.

Malíková, Ludmila. "Formation of politico-administrative relations on local level in Slovakia". Paper presented at the 11th NISPAcee Annual Conference, Bucharest, Romania, April 10-12, 2003, 1-8. Available on the United Nations Online Network in Public Administration and Finance, 2000, at: http://unpan1.un.org/intradoc/groups/public/documents/nispacee/unpan009025.pdf, last accessed: 12.02.2016.

Mansbridge, Jane. "The Many Faces of Representation". Politics Research Group Working Papers. Cambridge, MA: Harvard University & John F. Kennedy School of Government, 1998.

Menocal, Alina Rocha. "Analyzing the Relationship between Democracy and Development: Defining Basic Concepts and Assessing Key Linkages". Paper prepared for the Wilton Park Conference on Democracy and Development, West Sussex, UK, October 23-25, 2007, 1-17.

Oliveira, João do Carmo, and Jorge Martinez-Vazquez. "Czech Republic: Intergovernmental Fiscal Relations in the Transition". Europe and Central Asia

Poverty Reduction and Economic Management Series World Bank Technical Paper no. 517. Washington, DC: The International Bank for Reconstruction and Development / The World Bank, 2001.

Parker, Andrew N. "Decentralization: The Way Forward for Rural Development". World Bank Policy Research Working Papers, no. 1475 (June 1995). Washington, DC: World Bank, 1995.

Prud'homme, Rémy. "On the Dangers of Decentralization". World Bank Policy Research Working Papers, no. WPS 1252 (February 1994). Washington, DC: World Bank, Infrastructure and Urban Development Department, 1994.

Silverman, Jerry M. "Public Sector Decentralization: Economic Policy and Sector Investment Programs". World Bank Technical Paper no. 188. Washington, DC: World Bank, 1992.

Stoilova, Desislava. "Local Government Reforms in Bulgaria: Recent Developments and Key Challenges". Paper presented at the 16th NISPAcee Annual Conference on Public Policy and Administration: Challenges and Synergies, Working Group on Local Government, Bratislava, Slovak Republic, May 15-17, 2008, 1-10, at http://unpan1.un.org/intradoc/groups/public/documents/nispacee/unpan045241.pdf, last accessed: 12.02.2016.

Treisman, Daniel, "Defining and Measuring Decentralization: A Global Perspective". UCLA manuscript. Los Angeles, CA: Department of Political Science, University of California at Los Angeles, 2002, 1-38, www.sscnet.ucla.edu/polisci/faculty/treisman/Papers/defin.pdf.

Teets, Jessica. "The Origins of Corruption in Developing and Transitional Countries: Institutional Decentralization and Social Norms". Paper presented at the Annual Meeting of the Western Political Science Association, Portland, OR, March 11, 2004.

Tvinnereim, Endre Meyer. "Democracy in Europe's Regions: Party Competition, Government Accountability, and Citizen Satisfaction". PhD diss., Harvard University, Department of Government, May 2005.

A Typology of Local Political Elites in East-Central Europe

Type of local political elite	Level of decentralization	Type of local government system	The "legacy" of the ancien régime	Degree of (geographical) isolation
"Predominantly elitistic"	Low	(1) vertical power relations[1]: (1.a) "mixed"[2]; (1.b) "Southern" hybrid[3]: (1.c) the "clientelistic/ patronage model" ("support")[4], the "market-enabling model"[5], (1.d) the "Central-East European type"[6]. (2) horizontal power relations: (2.a) accentuated "dualistic"[7]; (2.b) "consociational", (2.c) the "semi-presidentialism" ("dualism" + "consociationalism", with majoritarian traces)[8]	"Patrimonial", "modernizing-nationalizing" communism	Significant, still low at elite level
"Democratic elitist"	Standard	(1) vertical power relations: (1.a) "fused"; (1.b) "Northern"-styled; (1.c) "the "economic-development model" ("partnership"), the "market-enabling model"; (1.d) the "Central-East European type". (2) horizontal power relations: (2.a) moderate-to-weak "dualistic"; (2.b) "majoritarian"; (2.c) hybrid "presidentialism" ("dualism" + "majoritarianism"), with "parliamentarian" tendencies.	"Bureaucratic-authoritarian", "welfare" communism	High, including at elite level
"Predominantly democratic"	Significant	(1) vertical power relations: (1.a) "dual"; (1.b) "Northern"-styled; (1.c) the "welfare-state model" ("social empathy/ sensitivity"), the "market-enabling model"; (1.d) the "Central-East European type". (2) horizontal power relations: (2.a) accentuated "dualistic"; (2.b) "consociational", (2.c) the "semi-presidentialism" ("dualism" + "consociationalism", with majoritarian traces).	"National-accommodative"	High

Type of local political elite	Strategy prioritization	Patterns of recruitment	Attitudes towards decentralization	Attitudes towards democracy	Quality-based portrait	Level of "elite distinctiveness" and representativeness
"Predominantly elitistic"	Culture, social services, public improvements + low political responsibility	Intramural selection; the dominance of national / regional selectorates	Unrestrained enthusiasm	"statist-anti-egalitarianists"; "populists"	"ethical" + "political" models	High, but standard level of passive representativeness
"Democratic elitist"	Social services, culture, public safety + high level of political responsibility	Intramural selection; the autonomy of local selectorates; localized political movements, mergers, splinters	General approval, but realistic (reserved) stance	"statists-egalitarianists"; "democrats"	"ethical" + "pragmatic" models	Pondered by high level of dedication to the community; very low passive representativeness
"Predominantly democratic"	Public improvements, culture, education, social services + high political responsibility	Extramural selection	Cautious enthusiasm	"statists-egalitarianists"; "populists"	"pragmatic" model	Low, with significantly low passive representativeness, pondered by "social sensitivity"

1 One might raise the criticism that fitting the three East-Central European cases of decentralization into the existing, Western-typed typologies is a rather procrustean task, since such cases are rather "hybrid", "catch-all", "catch-all" ones (see, for instance, Swianiewicz & Mielczarek 2005: 13–78). However, the present attempt is founded on the need for particularizing the three cases and tentatively pinpointing the discrepancies between them. 2 Bennett 1989; Bennett 1993: 28–47. 3 Page & Goldsmith 1987; John 2001. 4 Goldsmith 1992: 393–410. 5 Heinelt & Hlepas 2006: 21–42. 6 Hesse & Sharpe 1991: 603–621. 7 Wollmann 2004: 150–165; Wollmann 2004: 639–665. 8 Bäck 2005: 65–101.

John Trent • Laura Schnurr

A United Nations Renaissance

What the UN is, and what it could be

2018 • 166 pp. • Pb. • 19,90 € (D) • 20,50 € (A)
ISBN 978-3-8474-0711-9 • eISBN 978-3-8474-0860-4

This short introduction to the United Nations analyzes the organization as it is today, and how it can be transformed to respond to its critics. Combining essential information about its history and workings with practical proposals of how it can be strengthened, Trent and Schnurr examine what needs to be done, and also how we can actually move toward the required reforms. This book is written for a new generation of change-makers – a generation seeking better institutions that reflect the realities of the 21st century and that can act collectively in the interest of all.

From the Contents:
Evolving International Organizations: the UN Past and Present • Peace and Security: Fixing the Security Council • Social and Economic Development • Promoting and Protecting Human Rights • Workable Global Institutions: How to Get from Here to There?

The Authors:
Prof. John Trent, Fellow of the Centre on Governance at the University of Ottawa, Canada, formerly professor and chair of the University's Department of Political Science and Secretary General of the International Political Science Association for more than a decade
Laura Schnurr, MA, works on social innovation with the J.W. McConnell Foundation, completed an MA in Global Studies at the University of Freiburg, and runs a social enterprise operating in Canada and Uganda

www.shop.budrich.de

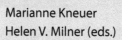

Marianne Kneuer
Helen V. Milner (eds.)

Political Science and Digitalization – Global Perspectives

2019 • 290 pp. • Hardcover • 60,00 € (D) • US$85.00, GBP 53.00
ISBN 978-3-8474-2332-4 • eISBN 978-3-8474-1488-9

Digitalization is not only a new research subject for political science, but a transformative force for the discipline in terms of teaching and learning as well as research methods and publishing. This volume provides the first account of the influence of digitalization on the discipline of political science including contributions from 20 different countries. It presents a regional stocktaking of the challenges and opportunities of digitalization in most world regions.

Marianne Kneuer is Professor for Political Science and Director of the Institute of Social Sciences and Co-founder of the Center for digital Change at the University of Hildesheim, Germany.

Helen V. Milner is B.C. Forbes Professor of Politics and International Affairs at Princeton University as well as Director of the Niehaus Center for Globalization and Governance at Princeton's Woodrow Wilson School, USA.

www.barbara-budrich.net

Pamela M. Barnes | Ian G. Barnes

Maria Marczewska-Rytko (ed.)

The Politics of Nucelar Energy in the European Union

Framing the Discourse: Actors, Positions and Dynamics

Handbook of Direct Democracy in Central and Eastern Europe after 1989

For the foreseeable future the overall use of nuclear electricity in the European Union is unlikely to change significantly despite the controversies surrounding its use amongst the EU's nation states. The author questions the role that nuclear electricity plays in meeting the challenges of providing secure, competitive and sustainable energy to support the development of the low carbon economy in the EU.

Since the collapse of the Soviet Union the political history of Central and Eastern Europe has been mainly the story of arise, consolidation, transformation and struggles of new democratic regimes and societies. This handbook offers an instructive approach to that history focusing on the relevance of practices and institutions of direct democracy.

2018 · 292 pp. · Pb.
58,00 € (D) · 59,70 € (A)
ISBN 978-3-8474-0687-7
eISBN 978-3-8474-0831-4

2018 · 351 pp. · Pb.
64,90 € (D) · 66,80 € (A)
ISBN 978-3-8474-2122-1
eISBN 978-3-8474-1110-9

www.barbara-budrich.net

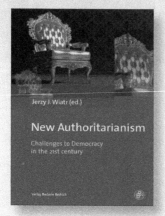